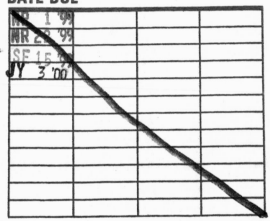

THE

American Heritage

Series

UNDER THE GENERAL EDITORSHIP OF

LEONARD W. LEVY AND ALFRED YOUNG

Democracy, Liberty, and Property

The State Constitutional Conventions

of the 1820's

EDITED BY

MERRILL D. PETERSON

THE BOBBS-MERRILL COMPANY, INC.
INDIANAPOLIS · NEW YORK

FOREWORD

In the springtime of American federalism, the history of American democracy was state-centered. Under the constitutional system as it then existed the states had virtually exclusive jurisdiction over almost all matters of concern to the average citizen. Nowadays presidential action, congressional legislation, and Supreme Court decisions bring within the ambit of the national government such subjects as jobs, school construction, maternity benefits, criminal justice, monopolies, dependent children, race relations, hours of labor, legislative apportionment, church-state relationships, juvenile delinquency, medical care for the aged, and other vital matters once the business of the states only. Before the Civil War the states dominated the federal system. Basic institutions such as schools and churches; basic freedoms such as the right to vote, to worship freely, to hold office, or speak one's mind; basic conditions of life, such as the status of labor, business, women, children, or minority groups—all were state controlled.

State government and state policy were pretty much a reflection of state constitutional systems, and the state constitutions, in turn, were the product of state constitutional conventions. The phrase "constitutional convention" ordinarily brings to mind the Philadelphia Convention of 1787, which framed the United States Constitution. That convention, however, had its antecedents in the states during the Revolution, and there have been over two hundred conventions in the United States since that time. The constitutional convention as an institution of government ranks with judicial review, federalism, and written constitutions as one of America's most original and important political inventions. The idea of having a special convention to frame a body of supreme and fundamental law that defined the government, its powers and limitations, was novel at the time of the Revolution. A patriot-orator could declare that by a constitutional convention the people "convened in a state of nature" and "reduced to practice the wonderful theory" of the social compact and natural rights. Madison exultantly cried, "Nothing has excited more admiration in the world than the manner in which free governments have been established in America; for it was the first instance, from the creation of the world . . . that free inhabitants have been seen deliberating on a form of government and selecting such of their citizens as possessed their confidence, to determine upon and give effect to it."

The wonder is that the first constitutions of the original states lasted at all, considering their unprecedented nature and the fact that they were framed during wartime. It is all the more remarkable, then, that many survived without revision for half a century. By the 1820's, time had brought transforming changes in society and new political ideas that demanded expression in fundamental law. New conventions that would liberalize the existing constitutional system were held in which statesmen of a new generation, the Websters and Van Burens, joined by the surviving giants of a dying age, engaged in great debates on the sources and ends of government. They confronted each other on the most controversial issues—whether there should be property qualifications on the right to vote, a more equitable apportionment of representation in the legislature, an established church, increased governmental services, and a government more directly responsible to the people. The issues varied from state to state, but everywhere they were sharply contested and the debates were the most profound since the conventions that ratified the Constitution of the United States.

James Bryce wrote that the state constitutions and their successive amendments are so full of interest because they "are a mine of instruction for the natural history of democratic communities." In this collection, Merrill D. Peterson shows that the proceedings of the state conventions are of even greater interest and value. He has focused on the three greatest conventions of the middle period, those of Massachusetts, New York, and Virginia, the leading states of their respective sections. For each of the three states Professor Peterson has provided a separate analytical introduction and a generous selection of the debates on the most enduringly interesting issues, those related to the title of this book, *Democracy, Liberty, and Property*. Students of constitutional and political history will find these debates, hitherto available only in rare editions, "a mine of instruction."

This book is one of a series the aim of which is to provide the essential primary sources of the American experience, especially of American thought. The series when completed will constitute a documentary library of American history, filling a need long felt among scholars, students, libraries and general readers for authoritative collections of original materials. Some volumes will illuminate the thought of significant individuals, such as James Madison or Louis D. Brandeis; some will deal with movements, such as those of the Antifederalists or the Populists; others will be organized around special themes, as this volume is.

Many volumes will take up the large number of subjects traditionally studied in American history for which surprisingly there are no documentary anthologies; others will pioneer in introducing new subjects of increasing importance to scholars and to the contemporary world. The series aspires to maintain the high standards demanded of contemporary editing, providing authentic texts, intelligently and unobtrusively edited. It will also have the distinction of presenting pieces of

substantial length which give the full character and flavor of
the original, rather than the usual butchered snippet. The
series will be the most comprehensive and authoritative of
its kind.

LEONARD W. LEVY
ALFRED YOUNG

CONTENTS

I

THE MASSACHUSETTS CONVENTION OF 1820–1821

II

THE NEW YORK CONVENTION OF 1821

III

THE VIRGINIA CONVENTION OF 1829-1830

GENERAL INTRODUCTION

The constitutional convention has been called "America's basic institution." It developed in the actual process of state-making during the American Revolution. When the people of the thirteen colonies declared their independence, they had not only to prove their claim on the battlefield but also to reestablish the foundations of political authority. The fundamental principle was stated in the Declaration of Independence: "That governments are instituted among men, deriving their just powers from the consent of the governed." But how could the people, thrown into the figurative state of nature by the dissolution of old bonds and allegiance, reduce the principle to practice? History furnished no models; and political philosophers, though they had speculated on the sovereignty of the people, had not descended to the lowly realm of political means and institutional contrivance to implement their theory.

The Revolutionary Americans discovered the answer to the riddle in the constitutional convention. A product not of abstract theory but of developing practice, of essentially *ad hoc* experimentation under the trying conditions of the Revolutionary War, the first state constitutions were at best imperfect realizations of the principle of popular consent in the making of government. In 1780, however, the Massachusetts constitution produced a model from which the theory of *constituent sovereignty* could be formulated. It contained three main elements. First, the people, through their elected delegates, "represent" their sovereignty in a convention called to constitute a government. Second, the constitution thus framed is ratified by the people and given effect by their majority. Third, the people retain the right to revise, and presumably to abolish, the constitution by the ongoing exercise of their sovereignty.

It was scarcely to be expected that the first state constitutions would endure beyond the age that produced them. The age was a time of peril; American society was in its infancy; self-government was a daring experiment; and democracy had not been born. "In truth," Thomas Jefferson later observed,

the abuses of monarchy had so much filled all the space of political contemplation, that we imagined everything republican which was not monarchy. We had not yet penetrated to the mother principle, that "governments are republican only in proportion as they embody the will of their people, and execute it."

The movement for the reform of the original state constitutions got underway after 1800, but the principal impetus developed in the years following the Peace of Ghent. Problems of war and foreign relations receded from view, and the people turned inward to catch up with nearly a half-century's growth and to fix the direction of further advance. The mere process of growth made manifest the errors and defects of the Revolutionary state constitutions. Where they obstructed progress or blocked the aspirations of newly ascendant groups in the community, there were demands for constitutional reform; and backed by the force of Revolutionary ideas of freedom and equality, these demands became irrepressible. The expanding American West opened new political vistas. Six new states—Indiana, Illinois, Mississippi, Alabama, Missouri, and Maine—entered the Union between 1816 and 1821. Their constitutions, while in most respects imitative of Eastern models, registered important democratic gains, particularly in the provision for universal white manhood suffrage. Of the original states, only Maryland had taken this step.

All the states felt the pressure for democratization, and slowly, haltingly, responded to it. Democracy was the political talisman of the new age—the age that had its symbol in Andrew Jackson, elevated to the Presidency in 1829. "There was a kind of democratic fanaticism in the air," wrote a prominent historian of several decades ago. "A kind of metaphysical entity called the People (spelled with a capital) was set up for men to worship. Its voice was the voice of God; and, like the king, it could do no wrong." But many Americans challenged the wisdom or the legitimacy of this voice. From conviction or habit or interest—or all together—they were attached to established institutions and profoundly distrustful of this brazen pretender King Numbers. The confrontation between conservatives and democratic reformers—the old order and the new— occurred in many areas of public life; but nowhere more meaningfully than in the state constitutional conventions of the time. Conventions were the visible embodiments of the people's sovereignty. They were unsurpassed arenas of ideological encounter and potent instruments of reform.

The three state conventions that are the subject of this volume—Massachusetts in 1820-1821, New York in 1821, and Virginia in 1829-1830—were the most interesting, in some respects the most important, of the age. No others are likely to prove so instructive to the student of American history. The three states were leaders of their respective sections—New England, Middle Atlantic, and Southern. Each stood for something greater than itself; each convention registered the tone, the problems, the conflicts of a traditional center of American society and thought; and each was bound to have an influence in neighboring states. The three states had a history in common, of course; they faced some of the same challenges of reform; and the main lines of controversy in these conventions converged on two sets of political assumptions, one basically conservative, the other basically democratic. But beyond this it is difficult to generalize. Each state, each convention, was a phenomenon unto itself and must be understood in terms of its own peculiar history. In Massachusetts the issue of religious liberty was of paramount importance. In New York the most troublesome problems were those of institutional structure, especially in the executive and judicial branches of government. And in Virginia the underlying issue was equality of representation between the two great divisions of the state.

But whatever the particular issues, the fundamental problem of each convention was to work out some sort of balance between three primary values—democracy, liberty, and property. Thus the theme of this volume. *Democracy* meant several things: first, the right of the people to establish or reform the constitution; second, the equality of rights—suffrage, representation, access to public office—under the constitution; and third, the continuing responsibility of the government to the majority opinion of the community. Reformers advocated the expansion of democracy, some to moderate, others to radical, lengths, while conservatives sought to retard and curb it by traditional or new-model restraints on popular power. Both were advocates of *liberty.* As associated with democracy, however, the concept premised equality of rights and majority rule. It consisted not only in individual free exercise of "natural rights," reinforced by constitutional guarantees, but also in the power of the people to govern with as little hindrance as possible; and reformers generally relied on the good sense of the people to keep individual freedom and popular sovereignty compatible. Conservatives feared the consequences of this marriage. The egalitarian and majoritarian conception of liberty threatened, in their opinion, the paramount rights, privileges, and interests upon which the order and well-being of the community depended. In order to secure the greatest aggregate liberty, they believed the state must deny the claims of some citizens, throw a mantle of protection around certain minorities, and maintain a discriminatory balance between the competing interests of the community. *Property*, according to the conservatives, was the principal value requiring protection from a democratic majority. Property being of different kinds and unequally distributed in society, these disparities should be reflected in the constitution of political power. Property and power must go together, conservatives said; otherwise, property will purchase power or power will ravage property. Reformers were equally solicitous of property—it was a necessary ingredient of "life, liberty and the pursuit of happiness"—but they felt it had nothing to fear from democracy in the United States, where property was, in fact, widely distributed and every man had an interest in its security. The idea of a fundamental antagonism between property and numbers belonged to the Old World, they said; it had no correspondence to American realities. Here a uniformly democratic government, one that reinforced the public will, was in perfect accord with the principles of liberty and property and made unnecessary those contrivances of balance and restraint that were the product of another age and continent.

Because these convention debates pitched on perennial problems of American government, they have an enduring import and a high degree of theoretical interest. But they are political, not academic, debates; one must not expect to find in them the coherence and consistency of cloistered philosophy. And although they speak, often with great cogency, to our time, they cannot be detached from their place in the stream of history, which was at the point of deepest disturbance between the faintly aristocratic republican order of the nation's classic age and the new democracy of the nineteenth century.

MERRILL D. PETERSON

UNIVERSITY OF VIRGINIA

July 1964

SELECTED BIBLIOGRAPHY

General

DE GRAZIA, ALFRED. *Public and Republic: Political Representation in America.* New York: Knopf, 1951.

DOUGLASS, ELISHA P. *Rebels and Democrats: The Struggle for Equal Rights and Majority Rule During the American Revolution.* Chapel Hill: University of North Carolina Press, 1955.

HARTZ, LOUIS. *The Liberal Tradition in America.* New York: Harcourt, Brace & World, 1955. Also, New York: Harvest Books (Harcourt, Brace & World), paperback.

MERRIAM, CHARLES E. *A History of American Political Theories.* New York: Macmillan, 1920.

MIMS, EDWIN, JR. *The Majority of the People.* New York: Modern Age, 1941.

SWISHER, CARL BRENT. *American Constitutional Development.* Boston: Houghton Mifflin, 1954.

TOCQUEVILLE, DE, ALEXIS. *Democracy in America.* Trans. Phillips Bradley. 2 vols. New York: Knopf, 1944. Also, New York: Schocken Books, paperback.

TURNER, FREDERICK JACKSON. *Rise of the New West: 1819–1829.*

Gloucester: Peter Smith, 1959. Also, New York: Collier Books, paperback.

WILLIAMSON, CHILTON. *American Suffrage from Property to Democracy: 1760–1860.* Princeton: Princeton University Press, 1960.

WRIGHT, BENJAMIN F., JR. *American Interpretations of Natural Law: A Study in the History of Political Thought.* New York: Russell and Russell, 1962.

Massachusetts

BIRDSALL, RICHARD D. *Berkshire County: A Cultural History.* New Haven: Yale University Press, 1959.

GREENE, EVARTS B. *Religion and the State: The Making and Testing of an American Tradition.* New York: New York University Press, 1941. Also, Ithaca: Cornell Paperbacks.

HANDLIN, OSCAR and MARY F. *Commonwealth: A Study of the Role of Government in the American Economy, Massachusetts, 1774–1861.* Cambridge: Harvard University Press, 1947.

Journal of Debates and Proceedings in the Convention of Delegates, Chosen to Revise the Constitution of Massachusetts. Boston: Boston Daily Advertiser, 1853.

MEYER, JACOB C. *Church and State in Massachusetts from 1740 to 1833.* Cleveland: Western Reserve University Press, 1930.

ROBINSON, WILLIAM A. *Jeffersonian Democracy in New England.* New Haven: Yale University Press, 1916.

TAYLOR, ROBERT J. *Massachusetts, Colony to Commonwealth: Documents on the Formation of Its Constitution, 1775–1780.* Chapel Hill: University of North Carolina Press, 1961. Also, by same publisher, in paperback.

New York

ALEXANDER, DEALVA STANWOOD. *A Political History of the State of New York.* Vol. I. New York: Holt, 1906.

Fox, Dixon Ryan. *The Decline of Aristocracy in the Politics of New York.* New York, 1919.

Hammond, Jabez D. *The History of Political Parties in the State of New York. . . .* 2 vols. Fourth Edition. Syracuse: Hall, Mills, 1852.

Horton, John Theodore. *James Kent: A Study in Conservatism, 1763–1847.* New York: Appleton-Century, 1939.

Lincoln, Charles Z. *The Constitutional History of New York.* Vol. I. Rochester: Lawyers Publishing, 1906.

Litwack, Leon. *North of Slavery: The Negro in the Free States, 1790–1860.* Chicago: University of Chicago Press, 1960.

Reports of the Proceedings and Debates of the Convention of 1821, Assembled for the Purpose of Amending the Constitution of the State of New York. Albany: E. & E. Hosford, 1821.

Street, Alfred B. *The Council of Revision of the State of New York.* Albany, 1859.

Virginia

Ambler, Charles H. *Sectionalism in Virginia from 1776 to 1860.* Chicago: University of Chicago Press, 1910.

Chandler, J. A. C. *History of Suffrage in Virginia.* Baltimore: Johns Hopkins University Press, 1901.

———. *Representation in Virginia.* Baltimore: Johns Hopkins University Press, 1896.

Green, Fletcher M. *Constitutional Development in the South Atlantic States, 1776–1860.* Chapel Hill: University of North Carolina Press, 1930.

Grigsby, Hugh Blair. *The Virginia Convention of 1829-30.* Richmond: Virginia Historical Society, 1855.

Journal, Acts and Proceedings, of a General Convention of the Commonwealth of Virginia, Assembled at Richmond. . . . Richmond: T. Ritchie, 1829.

Peterson, Merrill D. *The Jefferson Image in the American*

Mind. New York: Oxford University Press, 1960. Also, New York: Galaxy Books (Oxford University Press), paperback.

PLEASANTS, HUGH B. "Sketches of the Virginia Convention of 1829–30," *The Southern Literary Messenger* (Richmond), XVII (1851), 147–154, 297–304.

POLE, JOHN R. "Representation and Suffrage in Virginia," *Journal of Southern History* (Lexington, Kentucky), XXIV (1958), 16–50.

Proceedings and Debates of the Virginia State Convention of 1829–30. Richmond: Ritchie & Cook, 1830.

SYDNOR, CHARLES. *The Development of Southern Sectionalism, 1819–1843*. Baton Rouge: Louisiana State University Press, 1853.

EDITOR'S NOTE

The published texts of the debates of the three conventions are of uneven quality. That of the Virginia convention is unquestionably the fullest and the best. Thomas Ritchie, editor of the *Richmond Enquirer,* employed Arthur Stansbury to report the debates. Because Stansbury was both skilled in shorthand and experienced in legislative proceedings, as a recorder of Congressional debates, he was able to offer a superb stenographic transcription of everything said and done in the convention. The Massachusetts volume, the least satisfactory of the three, was composed from the day-to-day reports published in the *Boston Daily Advertiser.* Reprinted in 1853, this edition is used here. Two newspaper editors compiled the New York volume with the object of preserving in more regular and durable form than the fugitive columns of public journals a full and accurate record of the convention proceedings. They were assisted by a stenographer.

The selections from the texts have been reprinted literally. In the effort to provide a rounded view of each convention within the scope of this volume, it has been necessary to abridge most of the selections from the debates. Where one paragraph or more has been deleted from a speech, ellipses appear at both the beginning and end of the part deleted. Editorial insertions in the text are bracketed. The editor's footnotes are clearly designated by the use of "[Ed.]."

The editor has provided a general introduction and historical introductions to each of the conventions, chronologies, headnotes to speeches or issues, a number of analytical tables, and a selective bibliography.

Democracy, Liberty, and Property

The State Constitutional Conventions

of the 1820's

I

THE MASSACHUSETTS CONVENTION
OF 1820–1821

INTRODUCTION

The Massachusetts constitution of 1780, the last of the Revolutionary constitutions, was the first to embody the full-blown theory of constituent sovereignty. It had been framed in special convention and ratified by the people in town meetings. In this and in its provisions for an elective chief magistrate, a broadly representative legislature, and an independent judiciary, it avoided some of the paramount errors of the early constitutions. John Adams was its principal architect; and as the consumate expression of his political science, the constitution, together with its declaration of rights, represented a masterful adaptation of Massachusetts political custom and habit to Revolutionary theory, as well as an ingenious blending of "aristocratic" and "monarchical" elements into the republican fabric according to the canons of "balanced" government. In this character particularly, the constitution was the pride of the conservative men who led the Federalist Party and guided the affairs of the commonwealth through most of its history.

But the very features of the constitution they most admired were, of course, viewed as anachronisms by men who espoused a government uniformly free and republican. The latter had voiced their opposition to key provisions of the constitution in the course of its ratification. Although they were never entirely reconciled to the frame of government, it tended to vindicate itself in its working; and

3

when the opportunity came for revision in 1795, as provided by the constitution, they let it pass. Perhaps they realized that in the political complexion of the state at that time no satisfactory reform was possible. The minority of dissenters identified their cause with the rising Republican Party. It was sometimes in power after 1800, but it lacked the strength to reform the constitution. Caught up in the heated dissension between the parties, the issue of reform could not be resolved. Only when political tempers cooled in "the era of good feelings," shriveling the Federalist ranks and making Republicanism respectable, even in Massachusetts, was a constitutional convention decided upon.

The separation of the District of Maine and its admission to statehood furnished the suitable occasion. The change in Maine's status called for revision of the system of representation, a subject entangled in other difficulties as well, and this problem, together with a mounting crisis in the religious life of the commonwealth, caused the legislature to place the question of a convention before the electorate in August 1820. The issue was little discussed publicly. Massachusetts then had a population of more than half a million, and the overwhelming majority of adult males could presumably qualify for the franchise. But, in practice, voting was the exception rather than the rule; on the convention issue, only 18,349 citizens cast their votes—a smaller return than usual in state elections. They favored the convention nearly 2 to 1. In October the towns elected delegates, 490 in all, in accordance with the scale of representation for the lower house of the legislature.

Massachusetts was at that time divided into fourteen counties. *Suffolk* (46 delegates), the wealthiest of the counties, was virtually coterminous with the burgeoning city of Boston. *Essex* (68 delegates) stood to the north, once a Federalist stronghold—the home ground of the notorious Essex Junto[1]—and still dominated by the merchants and shipmasters of Salem, Newburyport, Marblehead, and Glou-

---

[1] The name commonly applied to a group of Federalist extremists, some but not all of them Essex County men, who were associated with New England disunionism during the administrations of Jefferson and Madison.

cester. Just west of Boston and bordering Essex to the north lay *Middlesex* (60 delegates), primarily a farming area though, as in Essex, several of its peaceful towns were absorbing the first shocks of the industrial revolution. South of Boston and circling Cape Cod to Provincetown lay the counties of *Norfolk* (34 delegates), *Plymouth* (35), *Bristol* (40), and *Barnstable* (17), an old settled area, equally varied in its economic and its religious character, much of it poor and cut off from the main stream of the state's development. The offshore islands *Nantucket* (6 delegates), and Martha's Vineyard, called *Dukes* (2), had never recovered from the blow struck by the Revolution to the fishing and whaling industries. The county lines of *Worcester* (70 delegates) bounded the large east-central portion of the state, agricultural, of course, and, on the whole, conservative in politics. In the rich Connecticut River valley lay the counties of *Hampshire* (25 delegates), *Hampden* (29), and *Franklin* (26), dominated by the towns of Northampton and Springfield. The valley had a reputation for orthodoxy in politics as in religion, despite Shays's Rebellion; but it also prided itself on its independence, and the "river gods" had long been at odds with Boston, State Street, and Harvard College. The county of *Berkshire* (32 delegates) embraced the entire western hill country. Here, if anywhere, was the center of radical discontent in Massachusetts. Yet it is risky, as the proceedings of the convention prove, to pin a political label on any of the counties or the larger geographical divisions of the state. In all of them were friends of liberal reform. They had no common program and formed no solid bloc in the convention. It was, nevertheless, true that most of the reform leadership and following came from the outlying areas, while the conservatives centered in Boston and the Essex-Middlesex-Norfolk perimeter.

On November 15 the delegates crowded the representatives' chamber of the State House in Boston, and the convention was called to order. The new generation paid its respects to the old by choosing the venerable John Adams president. He declined. ("Old time has shaken me by the hand, and paralyzed it," he remarked in a letter to Thomas Jefferson.) Whereupon the convention chose Isaac Parker,

chief justice of the Massachusetts supreme court, and on the following day ceremoniously conducted Adams to a permanent seat at the
right hand of the president. The convention speedily organized itself.
The constitution was divided into ten parts, each part assigned to a
select committee to consider changes and report to the convention,
these reports to be individually discussed and passed upon in committee of the whole, and the convention finally deciding upon the
changes proposed. Some delegates questioned this procedure. Once
the constitution had been dissected by ten separate committees, who
could put it together again? "It is like sending mechanics into the
woods in different directions to hew down trees and fit them for a
building."[2] They wished, rather, to attack the constitution as a unit.
In so numerous a body such a plan might have been disastrous. The
chosen line of procedure proved its efficiency; New York adopted it
the next year. Expertly controlled by adept parliamentarians, most
of them of conservative stripe, the convention was a model of deliberative conduct by a body of nearly five hundred men.

Counting all the men who wished fundamental changes in the constitution, the reform ranks undoubtedly numbered a majority of the
convention. In James T. Austin, Henry Dearborn, Levi Lincoln,
Henry Halsey Childs—Republicans to the man and sons of the
first Jeffersonians in the Bay State—they had strong leaders. But
the reformers were divided among themselves, disorganized, out-
maneuvered, and outclassed by a small but powerful cadre of conservatives. Daniel Webster, just then coming into prominence as a
statesman, and Supreme Court Justice Joseph Story were their brilliant champions, ably supported by such Federalist stalwarts as
Leverett Saltonstall, Josiah Quincy, and Samuel Hoar. Revering the
historic frame of government and united in their determination to
save it from the assaults of "radicalism," their strategy was a defensive
one—their tactics conciliatory on minor points, obstinate on major
principles. It succeeded magnificently. Story summarized the result
with a measure of self-congratulation:

---

[2] Joseph B. Varnum, a delegate from Middlesex County.

I firmly believe that those who ultimately prevailed in the Convention, were always in a minority in number, but with a vast preponderance of talent and virtue and principle. It was no small thing to prevent sad mischiefs to the Constitution. The struggle on our part was not for victory, but for the preservation of our best institutions.

What were these "best institutions" saved from destruction? First, the pecuniary qualification for the franchise; second, town representation in the house; third, the independence of the judiciary; fourth, the propertied basis of the senate; fifth, government support of religious worship. Four and five were the most seriously threatened. And the long-festering issue of state-supported religion gave more difficulty than any other.

The ruling order had not forgotten that Massachusetts began as a Holy Commonwealth. The faith of the Puritan founders had degenerated, of course, dissenting sects had sprung up and flourished, and Revolutionary ideas had upset the historic commitment to an established church; but in the face of these difficulties the state had endeavored to maintain its religious character and to enforce a corporate piety upon the entire community. Freedom of religious conscience was not denied in Massachusetts; indeed, it was expressly guaranteed by the second article of the declaration of rights. But it was rendered incomplete, and in the eyes of many dissenters nugatory, by other provisions of the constitution of 1780. Elected officials, senators, and representatives must declare their belief in the Christian religion. Ministers of Congregational churches in and around Cambridge held appointment as overseers of Harvard University, an institution sanctioned and supported by the state, yet dominated by this old, established clergy. Although the constitution did not formally establish the Congregational as the state church, it was the principal beneficiary of an ingenious compromise worked out by the framers to meet two sharply conflicting demands—religious freedom for the individual and public support of Christian worship for the peace and good order of the community. Embodied in the third article of the declaration of rights, the compromise required the several towns and parishes to make provision for public worship and instruction by Protestant ministers, provided, however, that "all monies paid by the subject to the support of public worship, and of the public teachers aforesaid, shall, if he require it, be uniformly applied to the support of the public teacher or teachers of his own religious sect or denomination. . . ." What this amounted to was the establishment of Protestant Christianity, though not without preference as to sect, because it operated within the historic framework of the Congregational system. Parish and town boundaries were usually coterminous, thus enabling church and town to act as one. The statute enacted in 1786 to implement the third article by authorizing the parishes, as bodies corporate, to assess polls and property for the support of religion confirmed, in effect, the locally established Congregational religion. Dissenters, to be sure, could file certificates with the local authorities declaring that they worshipped outside the fold and requesting that their tax money be transferred to their own ministers. But not only was this an awkward business; it was also an avowal of religious inequality, an admission of the right of government to interfere in affairs of religion, and an affront to the private conscience.

The third article, hotly contested from the start, threw the state into religious turmoil at intervals for forty years. The Baptists spearheaded the opposition, but increasingly other dissenting sects, which multiplied and grew until they represented a formidable challenge to the standing Congregational order, lent their support. They called for a dissolution of the state's connections with religion and the introduction of a "voluntary system" of religious life. Every other state of the Union came to this solution before 1820. The crusading Baptist preacher Elder John Leland, who returned to his native state after laboring many years in Virginia, championed the Jeffersonian way for Massachusetts. Religion in Virginia and most other states was entirely free of official sanction or support, Leland said, "yet they are not sunk with earthquakes or destroyed with fire and brimstone." Christian faith, as well as republican principle, demanded the Jeffersonian solution: "According to our best judgments, *we* cannot pay legal taxes for religious services, descending even to the grade of a chaplain for the legislature. It is disrobing Christianity of her virgin beauty—turning the churches of Christ into creatures of state—and metamorphosing gospel ambassadors to state pensioners."

Not surprisingly, the religious issue became involved in party politics. In opposing the Federalists, the Republicans appealed to the dissenting sects and necessarily opposed the clerical establishment, which was violently anti-Jeffersonian. The government passed briefly into Republican hands in 1807, and under Governor James Sullivan they endeavored to enact a reform bill. It failed. But the Massachusetts system was rapidly being undermined by dissenter resistance, variant practices in the towns, litigation and court decisions, and, finally, by divisions within the Congregational church itself. In 1811 the legislature passed the Religious Freedom Act, which exempted unincorporated religious societies from the payment of the parish taxes, thereby placing the dissenters on an equality with the Congregationalists in respect to supporting their own ministers. The law ended the annual scramble of the sects, often succeeded by long drawn-out lawsuits, for their shares of parish tax money. Staunch defenders of the third article assailed the law, saying it opened the door to evasion, and they foresaw a flight from the parishes in order to escape payment of religious taxes.

By 1820 the inherent contradictions in the Massachusetts experiment were tearing it apart. To these difficulties were now added those produced by a deep cleavage in the orthodox church. Unitarianism had grown up within that church. Adherents of this milder, rationalistic faith wished ministers of their own persuasion, and so intradenominational disputes between Unitarians and Trinitarians rocked the church already besieged by the host of dissenters. As their following increased in the eastern towns, though still a minority of the faithful in most instances, they seized upon the parish system and by polling majorities in town meetings took over scores of churches, forcing the orthodox to form new societies on a voluntary basis. Thus victimized by the unified town and parish system, many Congregationalists turned against it and lost interest in state-supported religion. The dissenters won some wholly unexpected allies.

Culminating two decades of bitter controversy, the courts upheld the Unitarian claims in the case of the Dedham church in December 1820, just as the third article came before the convention in Boston.

The select committee on the declaration of rights recommended several concessions to American opinion and practice, while at the same time preserving the fundamental principle of the third article. Its coverage was extended to Catholics and unincorporated religious societies. The provision empowering the legislature to enjoin attendance at religious worship was stricken. This far the convention agreed to go. In acting on other parts of the constitution, the delegates eliminated the religious test for officeholders and opened the board of overseers of Harvard to ministers of all denominations. However, the convention balked at the recommendation to give constitutional status to the act of 1811 relieving sworn communicants of dissenting sects from the payment of parish taxes. The reformers, of course, wished to go all the way to the voluntary system; a few, very few, would have liked to strike the third article in entirety. They were repeatedly beaten down. The crucial vote came on January 6, 1820, on the substitute resolution, earlier defeated in committee of the whole, sponsored by Henry H. Childs of Pittsfield. After acknowledging the dependence of civil government upon the piety and morality fostered by the public worship of God, the resolution declared that this end is best achieved by leaving every man free to worship as he pleases and therefore that every society of Christians should be equal in the eyes of the law and empowered to support itself. The resolution fell on a record vote of 136 to 246. Only two counties, Bristol and Berkshire, where denominational democracy and religious liberalism were most advanced, gave majorities for the Childs's substitute (see Table 1.2). The conservatives then beat back an eleventh hour move to graft the 1811 statute on the constitution. Perhaps the most important change in the third article grew out of the Unitarian controversy. This permitted a Congregationalist of one persuasion to have his tax money appropriated to a minister or society of the same persuasion within the denominational fold; in short, a Trinitarian need not support a Unitarian minister. Although Hoar and others,

Unitarians for the most part, viewed this clause as a death blow to the establishment, simple justice required it as long as the fiction of one orthodox church persisted in Massachusetts.

Next to religion the most troublesome problem for the delegates was that of representation in the legislature. Suffrage, although considered, was a minor issue. Few men otherwise qualified were excluded from the franchise by the constitutional requirement of a freehold worth £60 or productive of an annual income of £3, roughly translated as $200, or $10 (in American currency of 1820). Even this limitation was loosely enforced. Actual practice, if not the law, approximated universal male suffrage. Reformers were more concerned with the expediency than the justice of the requirement. A resolution to abolish it passed by a substantial margin, only then to be reversed when conservatives like Josiah Quincy held up the specter of a propertyless rabble multiplying in the new factory-towns and assailing the liberties and estates of the commonwealth. The convention quickly settled on an amendment extending the suffrage to men qualified by age and residence who also paid any tax to the state or county. This tax-paying qualification merely brought the constitution abreast of prevailing practice.

In accordance with the theory of balanced government and wishing to secure property against the masses, the framers of the Revolutionary constitution had based representation in the house on numbers, in the senate on property, or, to be strictly accurate, on the proportion of taxes paid by the senatorial districts. The select committee on this subject recommended no change. The delegates, in committee of the whole, signified their agreement. Then Henry Dearborn, in a long, impassioned speech—barely summarized in the *Journal of Debates*—attacked this "aristocratical principle" of property representation in the senate and offered a resolution to base that body on population by districts. Amazingly, the delegates adopted it without debate. When it was pointed out that the resolution was inconsistent with the rest of the report on the legislature branch, the delegates voted to reconsider. For the first time in the convention, the conservatives brought out their big guns against this "subversion of fundamental principle." John Adams rose in defense of the property basis of the senate, recalling the doctrines of his elaborate *Defense of the American Constitutions* in 1787. The long speeches of Webster and Story made deep impressions and may, indeed, by sheer power of argument, have reversed the convention's decision on this question. As Story pointed out, the actual difference between property and numbers was not great, and it was likely to diminish because of the rapid growth of population in the eastern cities, particularly Boston, which paid the largest share of taxes and were, therefore, favored in senatorial representation. Nevertheless, whether viewed in the light of principle or of power, the system was undemocratic. Western delegates could readily demonstrate that while it assigned six senators to Suffolk, it gave the three valley counties, twice as populous, only four. Suffolk and Essex together held one-third of the representation in the senate. The interest of a majority of the delegates clearly supported a senate based upon population, but the majority withered under the conservative counterfire. When the Dearborn resolution came to a vote in the committee of the whole on December 15, it was rejected 164 to 247. It met the same fate later in the convention.

The question of the senate was inseparable from the question of representation in the house. A meaningful balance required that the two chambers of the legislature be based upon different principles that had some logical relationship. If under the revised constitution representatives were to be paid out of the state treasury for the first time—and most delegates agreed they should be—this was further reason for basing the senate on taxes. Moreover, men had generally assumed, quite correctly, that the composition of the house in Massachusetts gave a preponderant representation to the small towns at the expense of the large; and since the report of the legislative committee looked to a continuation of this system, though on a reduced scale, it seemed unjust to expect the large towns to give up their superior position in the senate. The organization of the legislative branch in the constitution of 1780 embodied a compromise as well as a balance, and not only between property and numbers but also between the large eastern towns and the hundreds of hinterland villages. What the former had gained in the senate had to a considerable extent been offset by the latter's gain in the house. Everyone in the convention recognized the reciprocity. Dearborn confessed, after the initial acceptance of his resolution on the senate, that he had no idea of making it popular and at the same time leaving representation in the house on a town basis. The other part of his plan, only now introduced, was to apportion representatives according to population in new electoral districts of about 13,000 inhabitants. The plan was thoroughly democratic; even Story conceded its justice. Moreover, it had the merit of skirting the critical problem of a vastly overpopulated house of representatives—five hundred members under the existing system of town representation. This was one of the problems that had brought the convention into being. It had to be solved.

Three solutions were offered. Dearborn's, of course, simply abandoned the historic representation of the towns, deeply embedded along with the parish and the town meeting in Massachusetts tradition. And this was enough to sink the plan regardless of other considerations. The Worcester leader Levi Lincoln proposed a kind of federal system in reverse—corporate town representation in the house, the whole amounting to 334 members, and a popular senate. By mixing separate principles in the composition of the bicameral legislature, the plan allegedly met the old Whig criterion of balanced government. But the house remained too numerous and the representation grossly unequal. According to the analysis of William Prescott, 169 small towns, less than one-third the entire population, would choose a majority of the house. "Thus the liberties of the majority would be put in subjection to the minority in violation of the principle of every free government." Obviously something was amiss when a Boston Federalist could appeal to majority rule and equal rights against a Jeffersonian outlander! Lincoln's plan was buried in the committee of the whole, and he did not later attempt to resurrect it. The convention, by a substantial majority, gave its support to the plan of the legislative committee. Corporate towns of 1,200 inhabitants were to elect one representative, those of 3,600, two, and so on. Over one-half the towns of the state were thus deprived of annual representation; they were permitted, however, to send a delegate every other year or to join with neighboring towns similarly situated to meet the minimum population required. The new system would result in a house not exceeding 275 members. A majority of the delegates of only two counties, Plymouth and Bristol, voted against the revised plan (see Table 1.2).

Of the other issues in the convention, the one touching the independence of the judiciary stirred the most controversy. Story was a fanatic on this point; and as chairman of the judiciary committee, he reported an amendment requiring a two-thirds vote of both chambers, instead of the simple majority of the 1780 constitution, before the executive could remove a judge. The measure failed to pass. But Story gained some small additional protection for judges and single-handedly defeated a motion, reported to the convention from the great committee, empowering the legislature to reduce the salaries of judges. (Unfortunately, his speech on this question, together with the debate, which he described as the most brilliant of the convention, have not been preserved.) As in other states, the common provision of the early constitutions for an executive council to advise or act in concert with the governor gave trouble in Massachusetts. Here, however, since the governor was elective and the council had little authority, the question raised no fundamental issue of executive power and responsibility. The problem was that nine of the councillors (the tenth being the lieutenant governor) were elected from the senate on the joint ballot of the two chambers. This upset the senate; often the senators elected to this fifth wheel of the government declined to serve; and a council adhering to a party opposed to the governor caused disharmony in the executive branch. Reformers wished either to abolish the council or to make it elective of the people. It was retained, however, with a reduced complement of councillors to be elected by both chambers from the people at large. Before finishing its work, the convention wisely added a provision for popular amendment of the constitution, thereby postponing to a far distant day any repetition of their ordeal.

The convention adjourned *sine die* on January 9, 1821. Since its task was to revise the old constitution, not to frame a new one, the mode of presenting the amendments to the people for ratification was a difficult question. Webster saw the problem clearly, and midway in their proceedings the delegates adopted his resolution for grouping the amendments in distinct articles, so arranged "that, upon the adoption or rejection of any one or more of them, the other parts of the constitution may remain complete, and consistent with each other." Applying this method, the convention proposed fourteen articles of amendment, which were explained in an "Address to the People." In accordance with the act calling it into being, the convention directed that these articles be presented for ratification in town meetings by men qualified to vote for representatives in the legislature.

On April 9 the towns voted, the selectmen of each forwarding the returns to an examining committee appointed by the convention. The people approved nine of the articles, including the extension of the franchise, abolition of the test oath, the amendment article, and a stiff ban on plural officeholding. They disapproved of those articles, 1, 2, 5, 9, and 10, that the convention had labored hardest and longest to perfect (see Document 10). Article 1 embodied the revision of the third article; 2 altered the political year and provided for one, instead of two, annual sessions of the legislature; 5 was the article on representation, both house and senate, including the changes in the executive council; 9 contained new safeguards for the judiciary; and 10 confirmed the charter and the historic rights and privileges of Harvard University, except to open its board to clergy of any denomination. This article, in fact, was rejected by the largest majority of all—only Suffolk County favored it—suggesting that the democratic prejudice against Harvard, or perhaps against private corporations generally, ran wide and deep. The representation article also lost by a large majority. An analysis of the vote gives no clue to the reason. Essex returned the largest margin against it; two of the valley counties narrowly approved it.

With respect to the article on religion, however, it seems clear that the nearly 2 to 1 rejection was founded not on opposition to the minor changes proposed but on opposition to its retention in any substantial form. The article encountered strongest opposition in Bristol and Berkshire, whose delegates in the convention had supported the reform minority. Those from Bristol voted 2 to 1 for the Childs substitute, while their constituents voted 17 to 1 against the amended article. The three eastern-most counties returned modest majorities in favor, while the counties from Worcester westward voted 2½ to 1 against it. In all probability the convention's revision pleased neither side, or any side, in the religious disputes of the commonwealth.

The Massachusetts experiment in state-supported religion deteriorated rapidly during the next decade. A legal system of public worship could not be maintained in a community characterized by a mulitiplicity of sects and, partly for that reason, by a profound regard for religious liberty. Bowing to the inevitable in 1833, the legislature sent to the people an amendment of the third article, basically the same as Childs had proposed a dozen years before. It was ratified by a majority of 10 to 1. In time, too, the people reformed the political year, altered the system of representation in the house, and placed the senate on a popular base.

The amendment article thus proved to be the most important reform introduced into the Massachusetts constitution in 1821. Democracy expressed itself more effectively through the slower and more cautious amendment process than through the convention medium. At first glance the vote on ratification of the fourteen articles might suggest that the populace was even more conservative than the convention. On closer inspection, however, it is apparent that the people approved the articles that came up to the democratic standard and disapproved those that did not. In general, then, the popular vote expressed a democratic judgment on the work of the convention. Marshaled and controlled by a conservative elite, the convention was a highly successful rearguard action against the advance of democracy. The speeches of Webster and Story, in particular, gave intellectual form and content to the conservative resistance everywhere.

Significantly, the *North American Review,* the Boston quarterly and citadel of New England letters, devoted an article to these speeches, which at once became famous and which remain even today the most memorable features of the convention. But the resistance could not endure. As democratic leadership matured and acquired effective political organization, the electorate gradually reformed the historic constitution that was so little disturbed by the convention of 1820–1821.

1820

June 16   A statute provides for a referendum on the question of a convention to revise the constitution and for the election of delegates if a majority of the voters approve.

August 21   In town meetings the people endorse a convention; the vote is 11,756 to 6,593.

October 16   The convention delegates are elected in town meetings.

November 15   The convention opens in Boston.

November 24   The delegates commence debate in committee of the whole on the reports submitted by the select committees.

1821

January 1   The convention begins consideration of amendments reported by the committee of the whole.

January 2   The convention approves, 245 to 147, the revised plan—the eighth resolution of the legislative committee—for the apportionment of representatives.

January 6   The convention rejects, 136 to 246, Childs's substitute amendment for the third and fourth articles of the bill of rights.

January 8   The convention takes up the report of the committee appointed to reduce the approved amendments to form.

January 9   The convention gives final approval to fourteen amendments and to an "Address to the People" and adjourns *sine die*.

April 9   Nine of the fourteen amendments are ratified by the people in town meetings.

1. The Test Oath

*The question of religion in its connections with civil government
was first discussed in the convention on December 4. At issue was
the test oath—a declaration of belief in the Christian religion—required of all elective officials. The select committee on this chapter of
the constitution called for abolition of the oath. Daniel Webster, the
chairman, opened the debate with a justification of the change on
grounds of expediency rather than of right. The thirty-eight-year-old
Webster, though a native of Massachusetts, had not yet embarked on
his distinguished political career in that state. He had moved to
Boston to practice law in 1816, having served for several years in
Washington as a New Hampshire Congressman. He apparently held
no firm convictions on the question before the convention.*

*The speakers who followed him did, however. James Prince, of
Boston, condemned the test oath on the principles of religious liberty.
Joseph Tuckerman, a Unitarian minister who later became famous
for his ministry to the poor of Boston, held that a Christian people
had a right to demand Christian rulers. James T. Austin, a prominent
Boston attorney, Republican, and legislator, concisely and cogently
defended the resolution.*

Mr. Webster. It is obvious that the principal alteration, proposed by the first resolution, is the omission of the declaration of
belief in the Christian religion, as a qualification for office, in
the cases of the governor, lieutenant governor, counsellors and
members of the Legislature. I shall content myself on this occasion with stating, shortly and generally, the sentiments of the
select committee as I understand them on the subject of this
resolution. Two questions naturally present themselves. In the
first place; have the people a right, if in their judgment the
security of their government and its due administration demand

---

From *Journal of Debates and Proceedings in the Convention of Delegates, Chosen to Revise the Constitution of Massachusetts* (Boston, 1853),
pp. 160–167, 169–171, 173–174.

it, to require a declaration of belief in the Christian religion as a qualification or condition of office? On this question, a majority of the committee held a decided opinion. They thought the people had such a right. By the fundamental principle of popular and elective governments, all office is in the free gift of the people. They may grant, or they may withhold it at pleasure; and if it be for them, and them only, to decide whether they will grant office, it is for them to decide, also, on what terms, and with what conditions, they will grant it. Nothing is more unfounded than the notion that any man has a *right* to an office. This must depend on the choice of others, and consequently upon the opinions of others, in relation to his fitness and qualification for office. No man can be said to have a *right* to that, which others may withhold from him, at pleasure. There are certain rights, no doubt, which the whole people—or the government as representing the whole people—owe to each individual, in return for that obedience, and personal service, and proportionate contributions to the public burdens which each individual owes to the government. These rights are stated with sufficient accuracy in the tenth article of the bill of rights in this constitution: "Each individual in society has a right to be protected by it, in the enjoyment of his life, liberty, and property, according to the standing laws." Here is no right of *office* enumerated; no right of governing others, or of bearing rule in the State. All bestowment of office remaining in the discretion of the people, they have, of course, a right to regulate it, by any rules which they may deem expedient. Hence the people, by their constitution, prescribe certain qualifications for office, respecting age, property, residence, &c. But if office, merely as such, were a *right*, which each individual under the social compact was entitled to *claim*, all these qualifications would be indefensible. The acknowledged rights are not subject, and ought not to be subject to any such limitation. The right of being protected in life, liberty, and estate, is due to all, and cannot be justly denied to any, whatever be their age, property, or residence in the State. These qualifications, then, can only be made requisite as qualifications for office, on the ground that *office* is not what any man can demand as matter of right, but rests in the confidence and good will of those who are to bestow it. In short, it seems to me too plain to be questioned, that the right of office is a matter of discretion, and option, and can never be *claimed* by any man, on the ground of obligation. . . . However clear the right be, (and I can hardly suppose any gentleman will dispute it) the *expediency* of retaining the declaration is a more difficult question. It is said not to be necessary, because in this Commonwealth, ninety-nine out of every hundred of the inhabitants profess to believe in the Christian religion. It is sufficiently certain, therefore, that persons of this description, and none others, will ordinarily be chosen to places of public trust. There is as much security, it is said, on this subject, as the necessity of the case requires. And as there is a sort of opprobrium—a marking out for observation and censorious remark, a single individual, or a very few individuals, who may not be able to make the declaration, it is an act, if not of injustice, yet of unkindness, and of unnecessary rigor to call on such individuals to make the declaration. There is, also, another class of objections which has been stated. It has been said that there are many very devout and serious persons—persons who esteem the Christian religion to be above all price—to whom, nevertheless, the terms of this declaration seem somewhat too strong and intense. They seem, to these persons, to require the declaration of that *faith* which is deemed essential to personal salvation; and therefore not at all fit to be adopted by those who profess a belief in christianity, merely in a more popular and general sense. It certainly appears to me that this is a mistaken interpretation of the terms; that they imply only a general assent to the truth of the Christian revelation, and, at most, to the supernatural occurrences which establish its authenticity. There may, however, and there appears to be, *conscience* in this objection; and all conscience ought to be respected. I was not aware, before I attended the discussions in the committee, of the extent to which this objection prevailed. . . . For my own part, finding this declaration in the constitution, and hearing of no practical evil resulting from it, I should have been willing to retain it; unless considerable objection had been expressed to it. If others were satisfied with it, I should be. I do not consider it, however, essential to retain it, as there is another part of the constitution which recognizes in the fullest manner the benefits which civil society derives from those Christian institutions which cherish piety, morality and religion. I am conscious, that we should not strike out of the constitution all recognition of the Christian religion. I am desirous, in so solemn a transaction as the establishment of a constitution, that we should keep in it an expression of our respect and attachment to christianity;—not, indeed, to any of its peculiar forms, but to its general principles.

Mr. PRINCE. . . .There are, said Mr. P., two distinct rights belonging to man—UNALIENABLE and NATURAL—among those of the first class are the rights of conscience in all matters of religion. Now I hold that religion is a matter exclusively between God and the individual; and "the manner of discharging it, can be directed only by reason or conviction; and thus, I repeat it, this right is in its nature an *unalienable right,* because it *depends on the evidence* as it strikes his mind; and consequently the RESULT is *what is his duty towards his Creator.*" And therefore, as man owes supreme allegiance to God, as the Creator, and as the undivided governor of the universe, he cannot absolve himself, nor can others absolve him from this supreme allegiance; and hence, on entering into a social compact, the rights he gives up, and the powers he delegates must be tributary to, and in subordination to this high and first allegiance—and among the first enumeration of rights and duties in the present constitution of the Commonwealth, this principle is recognized: "It is the duty and the right of all men (says the constitution) to worship the Supreme Being, the great Creator and preserver of the universe, and NONE shall be molested or restrained for worshipping God in *the manner* and season most agreeable to the dictates of his own conscience, *nor* for his religious professions or sentiments." This is reasonable, wise and just. In forming or revising the social compact, let us then take heed, that we do not insert or retain any principle, which by *possible construction* may interfere with, or abridge such sacred, such inestimable rights by an inquiry into opinions for which man is only accountable to his God. Social duties are between man and man. Religious duties are between God and the individual. While we are solicitous to "render unto Caesar the things that are Caesar's"—take heed, I beseech you, that "you leave unto God, the things that are God's." Nor will the argument hold good that because during the forty years the test has been engrafted into and been in force under the present constitution, no extensive evils have presented themselves, and therefore it is inexpedient to expunge it from the constitution, lest it might be construed as an indirect abandonment of the cause of christianity. On revising the constitution, every unnecessary point, *even the most trivial,* ought to be stricken out, and every possible evil guarded against. The American revolution fully recognizes this principle;—it was not the pressure of evils actually existing which induced the patriots of the revolution to resist the encroachments of Great Britain, but it was a dread of the consequences which they believed would result from submitting to the doctrines advanced by the mother country—hence, I repeat it, it is not from the multiplicity of cases which have occurred, whereby men of sterling integrity, pure morals and great strength of intellect *may* have been precluded from participating either in the advantages of office, or assisting in the public councils, but it is that by continuing this principle in the constitution *you may* preclude them. . . . I submit then the following positions, first, admitting the right, (which, however, I do not) of the citizens when forming a social compact to prescribe such terms as a majority may deem expedient and proper, yet I hold it to be unjust to introduce a principle into the compact which, while it provides that the individual shall afford his personal aid, and risk his life for the common defence and yield up all his property (if need be) for the maintenance of the government and its laws, yet virtually precludes him from participating in any of the advantages resulting from offices, or from any share in the administration of the government, because he differs on a subject with which society has but a doubtful right to interfere; although in point of morality and strength of intellect he shines as "a star of the first magnitude." Secondly—I hold that this act of injustice toward the individual is neither politic nor expedient; first, because as before observed, it may deprive society of talent and moral excellence, which should always be secured and cherished as one of the best means of preserving the prosperity of the Commonwealth; and secondly, while it may thus exclude men possessing such useful and amiable qualification, yet it is no effectual safeguard whereby to keep out ambitious, unprincipled men from office, or a seat in the public councils. And, I moreover hold, that the cause of christianity doth not require such a qualification to support it. This religion is founded on a rock and supported by a power which humanity cannot affect—it does not want the secular arm to defend it—its divine origin, and its own intrinsic merit, ever have been, and ever will be, its firmest support. What have the powers of the world to do with such a religion? Experience has demonstrated that when left to the umpire of reason and of argument, it has triumphed the most brilliantly over the attacks of infidelity. Inquisitions, test acts and fanaticism, with their gibbets—their racks—and their faggots, may produce martyrs and hypocrites, but such writers as Watson[1] and Paley

---

[1] Probably Richard Watson (1737–1816), English divine, philosopher, and philanthropist; and William Paley (1743–1805), English theologian [Ed.].

have displayed its true character by arguments, which have put infidelity in the entire back ground. And may I not add from experience that in those countries where there are religious tests, they have not been productive of any advantage; even in that nation from whom many of us derived our origin, and where, in addition to a test act, the most solemn of the Christian ordinances are obliged to be adhered to as an additional qualification for office—-there is either an almost total evasion, or the compliance is often made under circumstances which, while it gives pain to many a serious Christian, excites mirth in the breast of every infidel. I also believe the qualifications of candidates ought to be confided to the electors, who generally take them from the neighborhood, and will therefore be the best judges of their moral and mental powers, and should it unfortunately happen that an unfit citizen has been introduced into office—the electors, so long as virtue, patriotism and christianity predominate, will avail themselves of the frequency of elections to obtain a remedy by a change of character; and that the evil will be much sooner remedied than if it is left to be done through the crucible of a test act. I moreover think, that while the scriptures seem to reprobate the presumption of demanding, and the fallacy of trusting, to mere professions of faith, they plainly point to the policy of preferring a trust in moral worth and excellence. . . . In making the aforegoing observations, I hope it will not be considered as in any manner intending to weaken the cause of christianity or of aiding the cause of infidelity. I make them because I verily believe, in forming or revising the social compact, we ought wholly to exclude every principle which by possible construction may interfere with the consciences of men, thereby leaving them and their religious opinions *where alone they* ought to be left, *"to Him who searcheth the heart and knows our inmost thoughts."*[2] Whether the individual has or has not formed a correct religious opinion is nothing to us, as civilians.

---

[2] I Chronicles 28:9; Romans 8:27 [Ed.].

"For modes of faith, let graceless zealots fight,
His can't be wrong whose life is in the right."[3]

Indeed, sir, I think that so far from injuring of the Christian cause, I am aiding it—when doubting men are left to the freedom of their own wills, they will be the more apt to listen to the arguments in support of christianity than when shackled by test acts, or any other interference of the civil government. . . . Believing then sir, as I verily do, that to retain any religious test, however liberal, is neither required for the safety of religion, nor for the safety of the Commonwealth; that it is unjust in principle—fallacious as to the effect to be produced—pernicious in its consequences—and an unwarrantable assumption of the unalienable rights of a citizen, and also that it is repugnant to one of the most essential moral precepts of christianity which inculcates, "that whatsoever I would that men should do unto me, *this* I ought to do unto them"; I hope the principle to which I have alluded will be left out of the constitution, now that we are called to revise it. . . .

. . . Mr. TUCKERMAN of Chelsea observed that he supposed the question now before the committee to be, whether the religious test in the constitution of 1780, shall be retained, or whether the resolutions now proposed by the select committee shall be adopted. He observed that, at the hazard of being accused of bigotry, and narrowness of mind, he must take the ground of defence of the constitution on this subject, as it now stands. He said that, in reflecting upon the test, he had not anticipated the suggestion of any doubt concerning the *right*, should this Convention have the disposition, to retain it. The constitution declares every man to be eligible to all the high offices of the State, on the condition of certain prescribed qualifications. Yet if there was any probability that any people of color would be elected to fill either of these offices, he presumed that no doubt would be felt, either as to the right, or

---

[3] Alexander Pope, *Essay on Man*, Part III, Lines 305–306 [Ed.].

the propriety, of their exclusion. There would, without doubt, be a provision in the constitution for their exclusion; or, it would be required, that these offices should be holden only by the white inhabitants of the Commonwealth. And if, as is without doubt a fact, ninety-nine out of a hundred of the people of this Commonwealth are in their faith Christians, it seems to be as unquestionable as any one of the rights of a people, to require that their rulers shall, in their faith, be Christians. . . . He would say no more on the subject of *the right*. He thought that, on no good ground, it could be contested. The great questions then on the subject regard the *expediency* of abolishing the existing test, and the *propriety* of the substitution proposed in the resolution. On the question of giving up the test, he remarked, that an argument for its abolition was, that the State would thus obtain, in its high and important offices, the talents of a few men, who do not believe the Christian religion. He replied, that during forty years in which this test has stood in our constitution, we have never wanted men, in sufficient abundance, for all the offices in which it is required. And that no apprehension can be felt, whether we shall continue to have candidates enough, who will not shrink from the test, for every department of government which they can be called to fill. The test is so very broad, that it excludes no one of all the denominations of Christians. He remarked, that we should be exposed to much confusion and error on this subject, if we should consider the test now required, as having any relation to the very objectionable tests which have sometimes been required. The test established by the English constitution, for example, required a belief of the thirty-nine articles of the church of England. He would resist, with all the energy of the small powers that he possessed, any definition in the constitution, of what christianity is, as a faith to be required of those who may be elected to office; and had he not heard the suggestion of the honorable chairman of the select committee, that there were gentlemen in that committee

who thought that a solemn declaration of belief of the Christian
religion could be made by those only, who were assured also
of an eternal interest in the promises of our religion, he should
have thought that every man, who had been convinced by
evidence of the truth of this religion, and who felt the divine
authority of its doctrines and precepts, would conscientiously
have made this declaration. He respected the opinions of
gentlemen, who gave this construction to the language of the
test; though he could not think the language to be fairly susceptible of this import. As he understood the declaration, it
implied only that belief, which is a security to the people, that
their rulers receive the great fundamental principles, which
are the best security of good laws, and of a good administration
of government. He said that, in his view, the most beautiful
feature of those parts of our present constitution, which concern religion, is, that it recognizes christianity as the religion
of the State, in the great principles in which its various sects
agree; leaving unnoticed those in which they differ. Any man
therefore, he thought, who believes that christianity is a divine
revelation, can make the declaration now required, and comprehend in that declaration, all that it is intended to embrace.

On the question of the *propriety* of abolishing the test, he
said, his objections were still more solemn. Either the religion
of Jesus Christ is from God or it is not. Either we are accountable to God for all our means and opportunities of advancing
the interests of this religion, or we are not. If our religion be
from God, and if it be our duty, by all means which are consistent with its spirit, to promote its progress, it is a question
on which we ought to pause, whether we shall open the door
of office indiscriminately to those who believe, and to those
who reject, this revelation of God's will. We all know the
descending influence of example. If men should be elevated
to high and responsible stations, who are enemies of christianity, may we not look with some apprehension to the consequences? Sir, if this test had not been established in 1780, I am

not certain that I should now have been disposed to advocate it; I might have felt a sufficient security in the election of Christian magistrates without it. But it has now become associated with the sentiments, and habits, and feelings of forty years; and if you now remove it, you declare to the people, and they will not misunderstand the declaration,—that you do not deem it to be of importance that our magistrates should be Christians. Changes which affect long established associations should be made very cautiously. The gentleman from Boston cites to us the words of our Lord, *render to Caesar the things that are Caesar's;* I hope that we shall feel the importance of the precept. But my New Testament does not add, "leave to God the things that are God's." I am told to RENDER *to God the things that are God's.* And, sir, we owe it to God, to Christ, and to our own souls, to do what we may for the extension and security of our faith as Christians; and to give our influence, whatever it may be, to the election of magistrates, who will make laws, and administer justice, in the spirit of christianity. On these grounds I am opposed to the resolutions of the committee; and wish that the test, from which no inconvenience has yet been experienced, may be retained in the constitution. . . .

. . . Mr. AUSTIN. . . .He did not agree with the chairman of the select committee who reported the resolution, that we had a right to demand this qualification. On the contrary he held that we had no right to demand it—that every one who contributes to the expenses of government and bears his share of the public burthens, has a right to be a candidate for popular favor. This was the general rule. He admitted there were exceptions. We have the right to demand the qualifications of age, property and residence, because they are necessary to insure the proper performance of the duties of the office. But this qualification related to opinions which do not bear upon the duties of government and are not connected with the public safety. This was the distinction—if we pass this line there is no place to stop. No one would say that a belief in christianity was indispensable in legislators. If the laws would not be well made—if the government could not be carried on—if society would be in danger without a declaration of belief in the doctrines of christianity, then this would be within the exceptions to the general rule. But it is argued that although it is not necessary for the preservation of civil society, it is necessary to show our respect for the institutions of christianity. The first is a legitimate purpose, the other an unlawful one. If it was agreed that it was proper that all those who held public offices should believe in the Christian religion, he was willing to say that he held in little respect the judgment of any one who in the present enlightened state of society, and with the present means of information, should not be satisfied with the evidences of christianity, and still less the integrity of any one who should disbelieve without examination. But this was merely his opinion as an individual. And who should judge the people—it is their right—let them judge—give them means of information. But place him who believes, and him who sneers at religion, side by side as candidates for office, and let the people decide between them. They may be trusted to decide correctly. This is the theory of our government. He proceeded to the question of expediency. Has the test a good tendency? The test was relied upon as a security, and the people have sometimes been imposed upon, because they supposed that the government would look to the object. But the test was evaded, and the laws brought into contempt. The Christian religion needs not oaths and tests to protect it any more than it does force. Its empire will be maintained and extended by neither the one nor the other, but the only aid which can be given to secure its triumph, is the diffusion of knowledge. It was argued that the test being a part of the present constitution, it ought not to be taken out. By taking it from the constitution we no more violate the principles adopted by the framers of this instrument, than they violated principles previously established.

In 1631, it was ordained that no one should be a freeman, and have the right of voting, who was not a church member. This he contended was the true theory if we would have a religious test. We should go to the source—stand at the ballot box, and as each individual came with his vote in his left hand, require him to hold up his right, and swear to his belief in the Christian religion. This was the system of our ancestors, but it was afterwards abolished, and in 1651 they adopted a stricter rule of exclusion. They required that the voter should not only be a member of the church, but should believe in the Christian religion, as it was proclaimed by the orthodox writers of the day. At the time the constitution was adopted, by a belief in the Christian religion was meant an adherence to the orthodox church of the day. This interpretation would exclude very many whom at the present day gentlemen would not exclude. By taking out this provision of the constitution, we adopt the spirit of those who framed that instrument. It was not very discreditable to them, if, after forty years' experience of the test, it should be found inapplicable to our present condition, and he did not think that in rejecting it we should show any disrespect to them or to religion itself. We only say it is unnecessary to mix the affairs of church and state. . . .

2. The Third Article

Not until December 20 was the report of the committee on the bill of rights taken up in committee of the whole. Debate immediately centered on the aggravating third article. After the delegates endorsed the recommendation to strike the antiquated provision empowering the legislature to enjoin attendance at religious worship, Leverett Saltonstall moved that except for two further amendments of a minor nature the third article be left undisturbed. The Salem attorney and

legislator with an old Massachusetts name was a prominent member
of the small eastern conservative group that dominated the conven-
tion. So too was Samuel Hoar, Jr., of Concord, who spoke in favor of
Saltonstall's motion. Enoch Mudge, a delegate from the incipient
industrial center of Lynn, in Essex County, then explained why he
opposed the motion.

The next day the motion was passed over in favor of Childs's reso-
lution, which would more clearly test the opinion of the convention
on the basic issue. Henry Halsey Childs came from the Berkshire
town of Pittsfield, long a center of religious liberalism and Republi-
canism. A physician by profession, he also served in the legislature
from 1816 to 1827. The debate lasted two days. Many delegates
spoke for the substitute. The remarks of a dissenting minister from
Beverly, N. W. Williams, were particularly pointed. Saltonstall de-
livered the longest and most forthright speech against the motion.
Soon after he finished, the question was called, the motion defeated.

Mr. SALTONSTALL moved to amend the report by striking out
the third and fourth resolutions, and substituting a resolution
declaring that it is not expedient to make any further amendment to the third article of the declaration of rights than to
substitute the word "Christian" for "Protestant," and also to
provide that real estate shall be taxed for the support of public
worship in the town, parish or precinct in which it shall be
situated.

Mr. HOAR of Concord said it appeared to him, that the
amendment proposed by the gentleman from Salem, must necessarily bring the whole subject of the third article into discussion. If it should be adopted, it would show that the committee
were in favor of the article as it now stands, in preference to the
substitution proposed by the select committee, or by the gentleman from Chester [Mr. Phelps], or from Pittsfield [Mr. Childs],
and to any other which may be offered. He was desirous that

From *Journal,* pp. 352–359, 381–382, 385–390.

the present amendment might be adopted. He was on the select committee, but did not vote with the majority in reporting these resolutions. If they were wrong, therefore, he was not responsible for their defects, and if right, he was entitled to no part of the credit. He considered the alteration proposed by the report of the committee to be in substance pernicious. It was going to change one of the fundamental principles of our government. If there was in our constitution one principle more than another on which the public happiness and welfare depended, and which was entitled to greater favor, he thought it was this; and it was here peculiarly proper to call on gentlemen for an application of the rule so often brought forward, that before any principle in the constitution was changed, it ought to be shown clearly and decisively that experience had proved it capable of producing an ill effect on the community. If this was acknowledged to be an important and an operative principle and not a dead letter, and if the effect produced by it was not a bad one, but the contrary, it ought to be retained. He was unwilling to destroy the effect of this principle. We had had experience of its beneficial operation, not for forty years only, but for more than a century; and he would not exchange this experience for any theory however wise in appearance. Theory might deceive, but experience could not. And if any experience was useful, that of the particular community for which the constitution was intended, was to be preferred. Although other countries may have been able to do without this principle, it by no means followed that it would do no good here. He knew that a distinguished individual in Great Britain had professed his ability to make constitutions and laws for all latitudes, and all habits and manners that could be named; he should however give more credit to our own experience. If gentlemen who wish a change should show the operation of the third article to be prejudicial to this country, he should cheerfully vote with them; otherwise he should think it ought to be retained. He said it had been judicially determined that

by the law of 1811, real estate, belonging to non-resident proprietors of a different sect or denomination, cannot be taxed
for the support of public worship in the town where it is situated. This report proposes to extend to all Christians, the rights
which were peculiar to persons of a different denomination
from Congregationalists. It gives power to a Congregationalist,
for any reason, to change his religious instructor, and prevents
his being taxed in any place except where he attends public
worship; the consequence will be, that all lands of non-resident
proprietors will be exempted from taxation for the support of
religious worship in any place. Was not this a great evil? He
could name towns in which one third part of the land was
owned by citizens of different towns, and was assessed for the
support of public worship in the towns where it was situated.
Deduct this portion of the taxes, and in many towns it would
in a great degree derange their system of supporting public
worship. It might be supposed that this evil would be remedied
on account of tenants being liable to be taxed. But there were
a great many towns to which he referred, where the lands
were not occupied by tenants, but used by the non-resident
owners merely as pastures for cattle. Another inconvenience
and injustice would arise from adopting the report that these
lands would escape all taxation, as the assessors in the towns
where the owners lived would not know of lands so situated,
or would be ignorant of their value. For this reason alone, the
report ought not to be accepted, and it was incumbent on those
in favor of it, to show something equivalent to the derange-
ment to the system of taxation. But although this inequality
would be created by the report, yet this was but the dust of
the balance, compared with the rest of the consequences. . . .
Mr. H. spoke of the detriment which would happen to that
class of society who depend for their religious instruction on
public worship. He spoke only as a citizen and not as a divine.
He considered religious instruction, in a political point of view,
to be as necessary as literary instruction. It might be said that

religion would be supported voluntarily. He wished for better evidence of the fact than he had had; and if true now, it might not be hereafter. Much had been said about inalienable rights; he asked if this meant that society could not do what was most for its good? If a man could not give up any rights for his greatest benefit? No interference with the rights of conscience was intended or felt from the first article. To say that the Legislature shall not regulate anything relating to religion, was to say that they shall not encourage any virtues or punish any vices or crimes. If we could trust to anything in history, it was to this, that our prosperity, and what most distinguishes Massachusetts, is owing to our provision for the support of religion and morality. He considered these a great support of civil society. He believed the only alternative was, to support it by religion and morality, or by a standing army. The proposition of the gentleman from Salem, was only to leave the constitution where it was before. It was not to repeal the law of 1811, which he considered as a bad law, but only to leave the Legislature the power, if necessary, instead of tying up their hands for all future time. He compared the provision for religious worship to that for town schools: those who have no children pay as great a tax as if they had; and if any person, having children, is not satisfied with the schoolmaster appointed by the town, he takes away his children, but never thinks of withholding his money from the support of the town schools; and yet the principle is the same; it is in fact a stronger case; for a man may withdraw to any religious society, and pay his money where he pleases, only he must pay somewhere. . . .

Mr. MUDGE was opposed to the adoption of the amendment of the gentleman from Salem [Mr. Saltonstall], because it would tend to introduce great confusion and evil. It proposed to give power to societies to tax real estate. Persons of all denominations have made that provision for the support of public worship which they think necessary. They do not wish to incur the trouble and expense of assessing taxes, that they may draw them out for the support of religious worship which they have already provided for in other modes. The arguments which the gentleman who had last spoke had used were precisely those which he would have used, to show that the provisions of the constitution ought not to be retained. He could show in every part of the Commonwealth instances in which great injustice and oppression had been suffered by individuals; he could point to an individual on the floor who had had his property taken from him to the amount of 300 dollars for the support of public worship in a form which he did not approve. But who shall be entitled to the right of taxing the whole property of the Commonwealth? In the town to which he belonged there were five distinct religious societies. Which of them should have the right to impose this tax? Some of the denominations of Christians were conscientiously opposed to the right of imposing any tax for the support of religion. The right therefore of taxing would operate unequally. The Episcopalians, the Baptists, the Friends, had never exercised the right. None he believed but the Congregational denomination had exercised the right. It was therefore granting to them an exclusive right. It had been contended that it was necessary for the support of religion. He did not agree that it was necessary. He contended that it was not. He found that all religious communities, besides supporting their own religious teachers, contributed large sums to the extension of the knowledge of Christianity to other countries. It was not necessary for securing the maintenance of the ministry, and it had a tendency to produce strife and contention. Persons were taxed in societies, who were accustomed to attend religious worship in other societies, and this produced jealousy, strife, ill feelings towards each other. The ministers in many instances do not wish it. They had rather labor with their own hands for their support, than that the stock and property of their flock should be taken and sold for their maintenance. He wished to strike from the constitution a provision that was not necessary for the support of religion, and which tended to produce strife and jealousy. It would reduce all the religious communities to a level, and would introduce a spirit of harmony and emulation for the support of religion, and he believed in a short time the amount of voluntary contribution for religious purposes, would be greater than can now be raised by the hand of power. If we would attend to the subject in its operation on religion, we should find it would have a good effect, to remove all restrictions, which operate to give exclusive privileges to a particular denomination. He wished to have the constitution so amended that there should be no inconsistency in it, and that each religious community should be entitled to equal privileges. . . .

. . . Mr. CHILDS stated as a general principle, that the right of every individual to worship God in a manner agreeable to the dictates of his own conscience, was one which no government could interfere with. Whenever government had undertaken to exercise an authority in this respect, it was an usurpation, and when this usurpation had been submitted to, the worship rendered was not sincere. In our own government, unless it could be demonstrated that it was necessary to the support of government, and clearly for the interest of the community, it could not be fairly exercised. He would call the attention of the committee to the argument of the gentleman from Boston. He would not admit that he or any other gentleman who would support the report of the select committee felt a greater interest in the support of religious institutions than gentlemen who would advocate the resolution which he had proposed. The gentleman had said that the committee were unanimously of opinion that the support of institutions for religious instruction and worship were essential to the happiness of the people and the good order of society, and therefore ought to be supported by legislative provision. He, Mr. C., would draw a different conclusion from the same premises. He argued that because religious instruction and worship were essential to the happiness of the people and good order and preservation of government, they ought to be left to the free support of every individual, according to the dictates of conscience. He contended that this was the only mode in which religious worship could be properly supported, and the mode in which in practice under the constitution it had been actually supported. The principles of the third article in the declaration of rights had been abandoned in practice, and the resolution before the committee did not deviate from what had been the practice for many years in the Commonwealth—what had been recognized by the Legislature—and from the general sentiment of the people. He believed there was no state where there was so much refinement—so much instruction, and so great a regard for religion as were to be found in this Commonwealth. He was willing to go as far as any gentleman in this eulogy of the character of the people in all parts of the State. But he would not admit that this character was to be attributed to the inefficient and inoperative recognition of a principle in the constitution. It was to be attributed to the general support of common schools—they were the *primum mobile* of improvement in the Commonwealth. He appealed to the example of the town of Boston where this principle of the constitution had no effect, and yet there was nowhere to be found a higher degree of improvement. The example of Rhode Island had been appealed to as a case to show the necessity of some constitutional provision for the support of religion. But Mr. C. said that the low state of morals and improvement in that state could not be attributed to the want of a compulsatory provision for the support of religion, but to their want of common schools. In Providence, where schools were encouraged, as much attention was paid to the support of religion as in Boston. This amounted to a demonstration that the effect was to be attributed to the general diffusion of education by common schools, and not to any provision for the support of religion. The example of New York, he said, had been appealed to, but there was there the same want of schools as in Rhode

Island. It was proposed to substitute the word Christian for protestant. He called on gentlemen to define Christian. Clergymen differed on the subject. What would be called christianity by one, would be called infidelity by another. Who knows what will be the state of things some years hence. The time was rapidly approaching when men professing to be Christians will be so opposed that if this part of the constitution is retained, the Commonwealth will be in a state of greater dissension from theological differences than they have ever been from political controversies. The resolution proposed by the select committee, declares the principle thus—the Legislature shall have power to compel the people to support religious teachers; but if gentlemen would examine it in its details, they would find that it would accord in practice with the principle in the resolution proposed by him as a substitute. In this construction his opinion was supported by the argument of the gentleman from Concord yesterday. That gentleman was consistent in his views, and for adopting a consistent course. Mr. C. said he would rather adopt the consistent principle of that gentleman, than the contradictory one of the committee. The proposition supported by him was explicit, and it would be known what was to be depended on. The principle maintained by the committee with the qualifications with which we had accompanied it, would keep the State in constant quarrels and collisions. He repeated that rather than take the report of the committee, he would take the proposition advocated by the gentleman from Concord. Our forefathers had been repeatedly brought forward as affording an illustrious example. He presumed, however, that their example was not to be adopted in everything, and contended that this was a domination of the same kind, and only differing in degree from that which every body at the present day disapproved. He would state how far, in his opinion, government has a right to interfere in matters of religion. So far as the laws can take cognizance of offences committed against good morals, government has a right to interfere; but the principle which leads us to worship God, is beyond the control of government. The gentleman from Concord had said, that if we abandon the means of supporting religious instruction, we should be obliged to resort to a standing army to enforce obedience to the laws. He, Mr. C., would reverse the proposition. Establish the principle that government has a right to compel the support of public worship, and a standing army will be necessary to carry it into effect. . . .

. . . Mr. WILLIAMS of Beverly said, that some gentlemen seemed to suppose, that all who were in favor of the present proposition, were in favor of removing all religion from the State. He wished to remove this impression. He considered that religion was of great consequence to the Commonwealth, and that the government should protect all persons in the enjoyment of their religious rights and privileges. He was opposed to the present provision in the constitution. He understood that the third article allows a tax which favored one religious denomination, and he understood that the report of the select committee had the same object. He thought the terms of the constitution were not so explicit and intelligible as some gentlemen had asserted. He admitted the premises in the third article, but not the conclusion. He considered that liberty of action and of opinion was given by the constitution to only one religious denomination, that of Congregationalists. He denied that the operation of the constitution had been equal, as the gentleman from Concord had asserted; but he said some persons had been obliged to pay, where they had received no benefit. Sometimes the taxes of minor children were paid to the support of public worship where the father attended, and where they did not. He understood it had been said that persons might go from one society to another at their pleasure. He denied the fact. He mentioned that in one town there was a society, comprising almost all the inhabitants, and that afterwards a society of Congregationalists grew up there, and taxes paid to the treasurer were applied to the support of this worship in consequence of the provisions of the constitution. He thought this was unequal. He agreed that contracts between the teachers and societies ought to be enforced; although some gentlemen thought otherwise. He did not apprehend, if the present proposition were adopted, that the Sabbath would be neglected, that public schools and other benevolent institutions would go down; for we had experience to the contrary. He objected that it was impossible to enforce the present provisions. He thought it unfair to say that religion did not take care of itself originally, because it was protected by its author; for its author had no power to protect it; except so far as miracles went—our Saviour derived no aid from the civil arm. He said that under the word *Protestant,* which applies to a great many varieties of religion, the government had established one particular denomination. He denied the propriety of mixing civil and religious institutions. When in the dark ages, from which we ought not to take example, the amalgamation of these two distinct things was made, it was done for improper purposes, and was attended with mischief. The people had no right to establish any religion, whether Protestant or Catholic, or any other. He hoped the substance, at least, of the proposition of the gentleman from Pittsfield would be adopted. . . .

. . . Mr. SALTONSTALL said he rose with unusual embarrassment, because the subject had been so ably discussed, and still more, because of its intrinsic importance; he thought it more important than any that had been considered. It is a trifling question comparatively, how the council shall be chosen, or whether there be any council; whether the senate be founded on valuation or population, or how the house of representatives is modified—we shall have a Legislature so constructed as to insure a free government—but strike out the constitutional provision for the support of public worship, and who can tell the consequences? As was said by the able gentleman from Boston, (Mr. BLAKE) we have heretofore been inspecting the superstructure—we are now examining the foundation, and he doubted not the result of the examination would be that the foundation would be found laid firm and deep, and capable of sustaining a superstructure that may rear its lofty head to the skies. Two questions arise—first as to the right of government, and second, whether there is anything in the subject—religion —which should prevent or restrict this right. There is no subject upon which such inadequate views are entertained as the duty, and of course the right, of government. A stranger acquainted with this subject, would be surprised at some of our debates upon the rights of the people in framing a government. They have a right to adopt such measures as will promote the happiness of the people and the good order and preservation of civil society. Whatever tends to promote these great objects, it is the duty of government to cherish and support, because these are the objects for which government is instituted. The design of government is not merely the security of life against those who would attack it, and property against those who would plunder it, but to improve the character and condition of those who are subject to it. Mr. S. enlarged upon this point. Is it true then, that the happiness of a people and the good order and preservation of civil government, do essentially depend upon piety, religion and morality? All seem to admit this, and yet their tendency to promote these great objects has not been sufficiently considered. The Christian religion is the great bond of civil society. It teaches us that we are all children of one beneficent Parent, who constantly watches over us for good, who notices all our actions, and will hereafter reward or punish us, as they have been good or evil. It teaches us that God is everywhere present, that he knows our most secret thoughts, that he sees us where no human eye can, and will call us to account when human laws cannot reach us. What an immense effect would the single doctrine of *accountability* have on the conduct, if properly realized. Our religion also contains the most comprehensive as well as minute **directions** for our conduct towards each other, declared under the most tremendous sanctions—all our hopes of happiness, all our fears of suffering; directions, which in proportion as they are obeyed, supersede the necessity of human laws. But this is not all—

> *"How small, of all the ills that men endure,*
> *That part which laws or kings can make or cure."*[4]

It is on the observance of duties of imperfect obligation, which human laws cannot reach, but which are the great care of religion, that our happiness essentially depends. Can the regulations of society make us kind and affectionate and faithful in the relations we bear in life? Religion extends to the heart—human laws concern actions alone. Religion cleanses the fountain that it may send forth pure streams to refresh society. Christianity also furnishes a model of the character she would form. Moreover, it reveals to us the perfections of Jehovah, the great object of worship and source of all good, and commands us to be "perfect as he is perfect." Who then can doubt that the happiness of a people and the good order and preservation of civil government do essentially depend upon such a system of "piety, religion and morality." These are principles in which all agree—the essential principles of *piety, religion* and *morality*. The constitution then asserts that these cannot be generally diffused, but by the institution of public worship and instruction. Mr. S. enforced this. It then follows as a necessary inference, that to promote these great objects, the people have a right to invest the Legislature with the power, &c. (as in the constitution). And why not this as a *civil institution*, as well as any other means for the same end? It provides a most beautiful and liberal system; making it the duty of towns and parishes

---

[4] Oliver Goldsmith, *The Traveller*, Lines 426–427.

> How small, of all that human hearts endure,
> That part which laws or kings can cause or cure!

[Ed.]

to make this provision, but consistently with perfect religious freedom. No denomination is established. The election is given expressly to each society, and of course to the majority of each. There is no more hardship than in being obliged to contribute towards the support of a minister than any other teacher. You may have no children to send to school, or may dislike his opinions, or his mode of instruction, or may be willing to contribute to the same object in some other way—but the tax you must pay. The right of society in both cases rests on the same foundation—the right to tax for the common good; and the reason is the same, the common benefit received, as members of society. Objections have been made to the abstract right of government, and to the particular provisions of the constitution. It is strange how much sensitiveness there is on this subject. No one hesitates to confer on government the power of inflicting any punishment, even death itself, for any crime; but the moment you would attempt by the influence of religion to destroy sin in embryo, an alarm is excited! Mr. S. then answered the objections made against granting the Legislature any power on the subject of religion,—as, that "religion is under the protection of the Almighty, who will take care of his church"; that "his kingdom is not of this world." His kingdom is not of this world in the highest sense, because our final reward will be in another; but in a most important sense it is, because it would make us good members of society—would prepare us for a better state by making us good in all the relations of life. We are told that the *kingdoms of this world* will become the kingdoms of our Lord. May not governments coöperate in this glorious design? (Mr. S. noticed other objections, which we have not room to insert.) We are told that the constitution grants exclusive favors to one denomination. Will gentlemen read the constitution? No language can be plainer. It is most explicitly declared that "every denomination shall be equally under the protection of the law." It is elevated far above all partial considerations—it regards all in the equal

favor as all agreeing in the same essential principles, and leading to the same great object, the Father of all. If one parish
alone, in some places where there are several societies, have
the right of taxing non-resident lands, &c. it is because they
have been left in the possession of this right. When a part of
a parish (referred to Lynn) became Methodists, they separated, and petitioned for an incorporation with certain powers,
which were granted, have they any right to complain? And so
of the other societies, and the little remnant is left with the
obligation to support public worship, and would you deprive
them of their ancient rights? Would you punish them for
adhering to the religion of their fathers? There is nothing
exclusive in this—it would be the same, should the majority of
a parish be of any denomination. This principle is not confined
to parishes; it is the same as to towns. When a part is separated,
the remainder has all the rights of the town not expressly
granted to the new corporation.

It is said also to be inoperative. It is indeed too inoperative,
and ought to be made more effectual; but this objection does
not well come from those who complain of it as *exclusive* and
oppressive. Some little cases of individual hardship have been
stated, and some law suits have grown out of it, in which however those who complain, claim always to have obtained a
remedy. What general law is there, or what part of the constitution against which such objections may not be made? They
prove nothing against a great principle. But it is said some do
not go to meeting, and shall they pay for what they receive no
benefit? They do receive a benefit in the greater security of
everything dear to them. One objection was not to be expected
—"that ministers were now too independent!" The great objection that meets us at every turn is that "religion will take care
of itself." Where has this experiment been tried? Not in Europe.
I know not where except in Asia Minor; and where are now
the "seven churches"? Those golden candlesticks have long
since been removed. We are referred to the support of **dis-**

senters in England, and of the various denominations here, but does it appear that this support would have been given, except religion had been established in England, and provided for in our constitution? In this country the fearful experiment is still in process, whether religion will take care of itself, and as far as tried, it has not been successful. Mr. S. then referred to several states, where, except in large cities, very few settled clergymen of education are to be found. As to the unequal operation of this article in Boston, &c., by its own terms it does not operate on any place where voluntary provision is made. Its indirect influence does much everywhere. Mr. S. made objections to the report of the select committee, and showed in what manner he thought the resolution under consideration would produce the same effect as expunging the third article. Is it then expedient to abolish this provision? It is for the advocates of the change to prove this beyond all question. Show the evil it has produced. Point to the oppression it has caused. Whose rights of conscience have been violated? Go not back a century for cause of persecution—point them out under the constitution. If a few cases of individual hardship have happened in the course of forty years, cannot the same thing be said of every part of the constitution? And is it wonderful, under a system extending through the Commonwealth and operating on so many thousands? Mr. S. then argued that there had been no oppression, no general complaint—referred to the small vote for a Convention as proof that no great evil was pressing on the community. But from the clamor that has since been raised, one would suppose we had been groaning under an inquisition! It is strange how men are carried away by sounds. What excesses have been committed under the name of "liberty," what excitement may be produced in a perfectly free country by the cry of "Priestcraft"—"Law-religion," and "Toleration!" This subject is closely interwoven with our history. We ought not to make a constitution on abstract principles merely. What arrangement it is expedient to make here, is a very different question from what it might be in some other states, where a similar provision has never existed. The support of religion has always been a great care of our government. Massachusetts is a religious Commonwealth. But for the devotion of our fathers to religion, the spot where we are assembled, might still have been a wilderness. It was this that inspired them with courage to brave the dangers of the ocean, and land on these shores. Their first care was the support of public worship. How soon did they lay the foundation of our venerable University,[5] and *"Christo et Ecclesiae"* was it dedicated! As the settlements extended, the little colonies of families always took with them a minister, as the pastor of the flock, and one of the first houses erected was always a place of worship. To provide religious instruction was always an important part of the municipal concerns of each town, and the same laws were made on the subject of schools and public worship. Through the whole period of our history, religion and education had gone hand in hand, and united in forming the character of the people. The temples of worship and instruction have been side by side. Our religious establishments are part of our system of education, schools of a higher order, to furnish instruction in "piety, religion and morality." How great and good must have been the influence of such institutions. To gather together in the house of God, and there be reminded of their common relation to our Father and to each other; to listen to the sublime doctrines and moral precepts of christianity—what a great though silent influence must it have had— "it falls like the gentle rain from heaven"—"it distills like the early dew." Mr. S. then described the manner in which the State had been divided into parishes, each with its pastor, &c.; the salutatary effect produced on the character of the people, and the cause of learning and civil liberty. Mr. S. thought the adoption of the resolution would end in the destruction of

---

[5] Harvard [Ed.].

very many religious societies, not immediately; the good influence of our institutions may prevent that. Our temples of
worship will decay and fall around us. Those beautiful spires
that now ornament our towns and villages will fall to the
ground. The effect on the character of the clergy will be pernicious; the inducements to enter into the profession will be
lessened, and there will be no permanency in contracts with
ministers. The dissolution of so many religious corporations
will be an act of great violence. We have heard much of the
corporate rights of towns—we must not touch them, even if
necessary to correct the greatest evil under the constitution,
the numerous house of representatives—no, corporate rights
and privileges are sacred things. And are not the rights of
parishes quite as ancient and sacred and much more important?
If any evils, correct them—but why destroy several hundred
corporations? Allusions have been made to the errors of our
ancestors. Time, which tends to the abuse of all human institutions, has improved ours. The bigotry and persecution are
gone—nothing remains but the good influence. Never was there
a denomination of Christians less sectarian, and proselyting,
and persecuting, than the prevailing denomination in Massachusetts have been under this constitution. I say it with confidence. Some have strange fears of an establishment! But what
is to be established? How is it to be brought about? Will the
government undertake the work? Have the church accumulated treasures for this purpose? Have we a body of aspiring
ecclesiastics aiming at this object? But how can an establishment be made under a constitution which declares that "no
subordination of one sect to another shall ever be established
by law," except the broad establishment of christianity. And
this without interfering with the rights of conscience of any
man. The question may now be, whether a great moral revolution shall take place in the Commonwealth. If this article is
struck out, what a shock will it give to the moral sentiments
and feelings of thousands,—the pious, the moral part of the

community, who feel that we have no right to deprive them of what was designed for the good of posterity as well as our own. I stand as in the presence of our ancestors; they conjure us not to destroy what they planted with so much care, and under the influence of which we have so long flourished; but to transmit to posterity what is only a *trust-estate* in us. I stand as in the presence of posterity, calling upon us not rashly to abolish what was intended for their good—their entailed estate, their precious inheritance. Let us not in one hour destroy the venerable work of two centuries! Above all, on this day, the anniversary of the landing of the Pilgrims—when two centuries have rolled away, and we by means of their principles and their institutions have grown up and become a great nation—let us not reject the great principles of our prosperity—let us not overthrow all that was dear to them. This will be a poor tribute to their memory, a poor expression of our gratitude. No—let us bring a better offering—let us cherish those principles and institutions, and transmit them to our children and to children's children to the latest posterity. This will be the most durable monument to the memory—the best memorial of the character of our forefathers. . . .

3. The "Poll Parish"

After the Childs substitute failed a second time, in convention, and the select committee's revision of the third article passed to a second reading on January 7, 1821, delegates sought alternate and more modest means of liberalization. Samuel P. P. Fay of Cambridge proposed to extend to Congregationalists and Unitarians the privileges of choosing the ministers to whom their tax money should be paid. As matters then stood a "poll parish," that is, a parish of the Congregational denomination but organized apart from the town or "terri-

torial parish," required a special act of legislation. Fay's resolution, by placing Congregationalists and Unitarians on the same footing as other denominations, struck at the parish system and the historic inviolability of ministerial contracts. It was vigorously opposed. The speeches of Samuel Hoar and Levi Lincoln in committee of the whole exhibit the two sides of this question.

Mr. HOAR was sorry that any gentleman had thought it necessary to bring this proposition before the Convention at this late period. It had been twice substantially before the House, and had been negatived when there were more than a hundred more members present than were now here. But as it had been thought fit to bring up the question, it was necessary to consider what would be its operation. It was a short and plain proposition, and at first view seemed very fair, but it would be found on examination that its effect would be to annul every parish in the Commonwealth. It puts an end to all acts of the Legislature, dividing the Commonwealth into convenient districts for the support of public worship. For what reason was this to be done? It was desirable to some persons to have the power of leaving their parish minister and going to another. This, no doubt, was sometimes a very convenient and pleasant thing, but there were two sides to the question. A parish forms a contract with a minister—an individual votes in making the contract, but the next year changes his mind, and wishes to be liberated. He is only to say he has changed his mind and he is liberated. Would this be borne in any other case? Suppose there was a banking institution in which the individual proprietors were responsible for its engagements, and an individual should withdraw from it and avoid his responsibility? It would be considered a breach of good faith. This provision authorizes every member of a parish, which has a contract with a minister, to go where he pleases, and no tax can **after-**

wards be assessed upon him for fulfilling the contract—this gives a new inducement to another to go—and the corporation may be left without corporators. The minister may sue and get execution against the corporation, but he can get no fruit of his execution—and there is no way in which his contract can be enforced. If all do not leave the parish—suppose only one half leave, those who remain will be compelled to pay a double tax, or to violate their contract. It was said that this might be the effect of the present law. This did not diminish the force of the objection. The law may be modified so as to prevent these consequences, but if the principle is incorporated into the constitution, it cannot be. It was said that these evil consequences had not resulted from the law. One reason why the consequences of the law had not been felt was, that it was not generally understood. It was generally supposed that to entitle one to leave a parish and withdraw his taxes, he must become a member of a society of a different denomination. But the law had recently received a different construction, which was no doubt correct. It was true that under the law a person who becomes of a different denomination, has a right to withdraw, but this was understood, and the contracts have been made subject to this condition. This provision might be liable to abuses and frauds, but it did not follow that there might not be benefit in the restriction. There were instances in which pretended changes of opinion to avoid taxation, had not availed. He stated an instance of a man who left a Congregational parish, joined a Baptist society and was immersed—and who, on being asked if he had washed away his sins, replied that he had washed away his taxes, which was his principal concern. This declaration being proved, he was still holden to the payment of his taxes in the Congregational parish in which he resided. The resolution, if adopted, would change the condition of all ministerial contracts. Whether it would annul contracts made by bond, he did [not] know, but there might be doubts. It disables a parish from forming a contract which shall be binding upon both parties. Suppose a minister is settled in the usual solemn form to-day, this amendment points out the mode in which any member of the parish may avoid the obligation entered into. It may be all fair in relation to future contracts, but it is not in relation to those now existing. He asked if gentlemen were prepared to adopt such a principle in the constitution. It was of infinite importance, and threatened the most pernicious consequences. There was no adequate reason for the change in the trifling inconvenience that had been felt. . . .

. . . Mr. LINCOLN said that originally every parish was of one sect and entertained a uniformity of sentiment. But now there was a great difference of sentiment in almost every town. In some towns there are persons who are obliged to play the hypocrite and associate with a society they do not agree with, or contribute to the support of doctrines they do not believe. What was the condition of almost every parish in the western part of the Commonwealth? Every person was born with the obligation of supporting religious instruction of a certain kind, for the dissemination of doctrines which many did not believe. He had the happiness to belong to an Unitarian society, where he could worship in a manner consistent with his views of the doctrines of Christianity. But what would be the condition of a man belonging to such a society, who, by what he conceives to be the operation of irresistible grace, is brought to believe in the trinity, and all the doctrines connected with it, and that his former opinions were erroneous? Shall he be bound to adhere to his society, or to contribute to the support of a teacher who according to his new views preaches what is without a particle of religion in it, and inculcates doctrines abhorrent to his conscience? It is only an act of justice to permit him to withdraw. As to its violating the obligation of contracts between the parish and the minister, it is done by the provision of the constitution already, and there is no mode of preventing it. If all are required to pay for the support of public worship in some society, it is all that can be done towards gaining the purposes of government. The differences between persons of the same denomination are many of them more essential than those which distinguish the different denominations. The latter are principally matter of form—the other may be a difference in fundamental doctrines. The learned gentleman proceeded to state the practice that was begun as early as 1807 by the Legislature, of incorporating poll parishes, and the operation and effect of the practice which he contended had been favorable in promoting attendance on public worship and the growth of piety and religion. . . .

4. Tax Exemption

Simple fact—the ineradicable split in the orthodox church—recommended the Fay resolution, and it passed. The delegates then took up the resolution of the Reverend Thomas Baldwin to exempt members of dissenting sects from the payment of taxes, thus raising the statute of 1811 to constitutional status. A similar resolution had been earlier rejected after lengthy debate. It represented the final effort of the dissenters to obtain a "second best" settlement. Samuel P. P. Fay was not a religious liberal. He voted against the Childs resolution, and his own was intended to help the Congregationalists. Baldwin, on the other hand, for several decades the minister of Boston's Second Baptist Church, spoke for the dissenting interest. Several delegates addressed themselves to different aspects of the question, and the debate was concluded by a leading conservative and a leading liberal, Joseph Story and Levi Lincoln, who agreed on opposing the motion, though they had divided on the Childs resolution. The motion failed.

From *Journal*, pp. 583–590.

Mr. BALDWIN said that some amendments to the third article of the declaration of rights, had been agreed upon by the Convention, but the most obnoxious part, perhaps, remained unrepealed. The most potent objection which had been urged against incorporating this resolution into the constitution, was, that the provision was liable to abuses. Particular instances had been mentioned, which, upon examination of the facts, would be found to have been misrepresented. He was sorry that such representations should be given, because they prejudice the minds of gentlemen, unjustly, against the merits of the resolution. The principle of the resolution was contained in the fourth resolution of the select committee on the declaration of rights. The whole thing claimed was, that the money of the members of a society of any denomination, should not be paid, so as to oblige them to draw it out of other hands. It was as contrary to the tenets of the Baptists, to levy compulsory taxes, as it was to those of the Friends to do military duty. The gentleman from Littleton had said, that seventy societies applied to the Legislature some years since, to be incorporated, only one of which was a Congregational society. The gentleman mistook the object of these applications. It was to get rid of paying taxes to other societies; not to obtain authority to tax their own members. He pitied that clergyman who depended on the compulsory taxation of his society to ensure him a subsistence. The exemption in this resolution lasted only so long as the person continued a member of the religious society to which he united himself.

Mr. WILDE of Newburyport. . . . What was the amount of this resolution? that any man may join any society, and on producing his certificate of having joined it, may be exempted from taxation for the support of public worship in every other society. Any man may join any society, or any number of men may form a society, by which any man may be exempted from all taxation for the support of public worship in the town where he resides. The consequence will be that all who want to get rid of paying taxes will join a society. It is not necessary to support public worship—there is no need of a public teacher —the society may be in this town or in any other. A religious exemption society will be formed—exempt not only from taxation, but from all religious duties. A society may consist of one hundred thousand persons from all parts of the Commonwealth, and all the members residing in their respective towns. If this was not totally expunging the third article, it was worse; because by putting this resolution into the constitution, the Legislaure would be deprived of the power to correct such abuses. . . .

Mr. SIBLEY of Sutton hoped the resolution would prevail. As experience was the best master, he would mention that it was twenty-five years since they had had any parish tax for the support of public worship. While taxes were assessed, the society continually diminished till it had almost come to nothing; but they adopted the method of taxing pews, and now the society flourished. No person was compelled to attend public worship or contribute to its support, but every person who had any claims to respectability contributed voluntarily. He did not like to hear so much said about the superior goodness of the seaports compared with the country towns. He was a Congregationalist, but he was in favor of the present resolution.

Mr. DUTTON. . . . This was the fourth attempt that had been made to do away the force and effect of the great principle in the bill of rights. This principle, a large majority had determined to maintain; and they were now called upon, again, to surrender it in the spirit of conciliation. Many moving appeals had been made to the candor and liberality of the majority; but he would ask gentlemen to consider what was the true meaning of this language. In his apprehension it was nothing short of this—give us all we ask and we shall be satisfied— yield the principle which you have sustained in every form, and which you deem vital to the best welfare of the State, and we shall be content; surrender, at this last trial, all that you have resolved to hold, and we shall give up the contest. Let it be remembered that the majority have acted on the defensive; that they have been compelled to defend their principles, assailed as they have been in every form that ingenuity could suggest, and with a perseverance which he should think praiseworthy if he thought the object so. But upon this subject it was in vain to attempt to disguise or conceal the truth. There was an irreconcilable difference of opinion; and whenever the reverend gentleman and his friends were satisfied, he was sure *he* should not be. The conciliation so much recommended, demanded everything and gave nothing; and before he could become a party to it, he must know upon what terms it was to be had. The gentleman who introduced these resolutions has frankly avowed his opinion that religion ought not to be supported except by voluntary contribution; the majority have determined, after a long and repeated discussion, that it is not only the unquestioned right of the State, but its solemn duty to compel men by law to maintain the public worship of God in all cases where it is not done voluntarily. Upon this subject there can be no compromise, no conciliation. The reverend gentleman had urged, that because a man was obliged to pay his taxes where he lived, though he might carry them where he attended public worship, it made one denomination of Christians subordinate to another. If this was ever true, the resolution passed this morning placed Congregationalists on the same footing; but in truth it never came within the meaning of the clause referred to in the constitution. The amendment which has passed recognizes the existence of unincorporated societies. He had voted for this, but he could go no farther. They now stood on the same ground with incorporated societies, were subject to the same duties, and equally under the control of the Legislature. But these resolutions now propose to engraft into the constitution the second section of the law of 1811. He was wholly opposed to this, not because he was opposed to the law, but because he was opposed to making it a part of the constitution. The whole difference, in his opinion, lay between having these provisions in a law, and having them in a constitution. So long as they remained a law, they were subject to revision and modification. . . .

Mr. STORY opposed the proposition. . . . The Convention had determined by a large majority that it was fit and proper that the Legislature should be invested with authority to require that towns, parishes and religious societies shall make provision for the institution of the public worship of God, and the support of religious teachers in all cases where it is not done voluntarily—they had placed the rights and duties of unincorporated societies on the same footing with those that are incorporated—they had extended the right of withdrawing from a territorial parish so as to permit a person to go from one society to another of the same denomination and pay his taxes there. In adopting these indulgences they had given the greatest latitude consistent with the preservation of the general principle. So far he was not only willing, but anxious to go. But they must stop somewhere. The proposition now offered, if adopted in the constitution, would really and vitally destroy the main principle which had been established. They would establish the principle in form, but would provide the means by which its object might be completely and silently done away. They had made already such provision that the right of equality of denominations could not be sacrificed, but if they engrafted this proposition into the constitution, it would take away the power of the Legislature to compel the support of public worship in any part of the Commonwealth. Its tendency would be by taking the subject out of the sphere of legislation, to put it out of the reach of law. He had no objection to its remaining as a law, and there was no probability that it would be repealed unless it was abused. If it was in the constitution, the Legislature, the courts and juries would be bound by their oaths to sanction even the abuses that might be committed under it. Should it be repealed, the great principles of it are already adopted in the amendments agreed to—that unincorporated societies shall be put on the footing of those that are incorporated, and that every person shall be free to go to what society he pleases, and have his taxes paid to the support of religious instruction there.

Mr. LINCOLN of Worcester said that what the ultra liberals and the ultra royalists in religion had acquiesced in, seemed to be a point at which we ought to stop. If this proposition were made originally, before any other propositions had been accepted, it would have been entitled to a more favorable hearing; but the Convention had adopted a principle that was repugnant to it. He had forewarned certain gentlemen that they were yielding more than they intended; but they acted for themselves, and he acted consistently in holding them to their concessions. The Congregationalists were not contending for superior privileges, but while they were willing on the one hand to extend to other denominations an equality of rights and immunities, they were not willing on the other to be bound in fetters, as they would be by this resolution. For what was the third resolution of the committee on the declaration of rights which had been adopted by the Convention? That resolution makes it imperative on the Legislature to compel Congregational societies to support public worship. While by this the gentlemen compel Congregationalists to support public worship, why should they call upon Congregationalists to free them from any compulsion? If the third resolution was a part of their proceedings which it was too late to alter, it was improper to call upon Congregationalists alone to support public teachers. All he contended for was equal rights. He stood there as a Congregationalist to resist being put under subordination. But if the proposition of the gentleman from Boston [Rev. Baldwin] should be adopted, there would be subordination. And of whom? Of the Congregationalists; if you compel them to pay for the support of religion and exonerate every other denomination of Christians. Let the gentleman from Boston, he said, consider that by the third resolution it is provided that every society, incorporated or unincorporated, shall support public worship. And what was the resolution passed in the morning? That every citizen shall appropriate his contributions to whatever society he pleases. He asked if by these provisions all classes of Christians were not on the same footing. If then you provide that a Congregationalist shall support religion and compel him to support a teacher of his denomination, it was altogether unequal to pass this resolution for giving an exemption to others. In this way, he contended, gentlemen *did* make a subordination. He was willing to go as far in liberality as any man, but there was a point, where he must pause; and instead of putting all other denominations in subordination to Congregationalists, he could not consent to put Congregationalists in subordination to every other denomination. . . .

5. The Suffrage

The principal debate on the suffrage came on December 11 on a motion to reconsider the vote in committee of the whole to abolish all pecuniary qualification for the franchise. The issue is developed in the brief speeches of the Reverend Edmund Foster of Littleton and Warren Dutton, George Blake, Josiah Quincy, and James T. Austin —all of Boston. Some reformers assailed the existing suffrage requirement as "aristocratical," but neither reformers nor conservatives put much stock in this objection and approached the question largely as one of expediency. Even Quincy, who was remembered as a Federalist champion in the Jeffersonian years and who was now embarking on a career in state politics, based his defense of the qualification on prospective rather than present dangers. The motion to reconsider passed on December 12 on the casting vote of the president. Blake, who had the responsibility of steering the revision of the third article through the convention, now backed away from the universal suffrage he had earlier advocated and proposed a taxpaying qualification. It was promptly approved and became one of the fourteen recommended amendments.

The resolution offered by Mr. KEYES, on Saturday, and referred to this committee, proposing to abolish all pecuniary qualification in electors of officers under this government, was taken up by the committee.

Mr. NICHOLS of South Reading moved that the committee should rise. Negatived.

Mr. PARKER of Charlestown moved to pass over the resolution, on account of the absence of the mover. Negatived.

The question was then taken on the resolution, and decided in the affirmative, 185 to 157.

Mr. ALVORD of Greenfield moved a reconsideration of the last vote.

Mr. FOSTER of Littleton said he was not present when the vote was taken, but he should have voted in the affirmative. He would not question the right to require such a qualification, but he had been for several years convinced that it was inexpedient and mischievous. Either a greater amount of property should be required, or none at all. Great difficulties were occasioned by this requisition at every election, and continual questions asked of this sort—what property have you? have you the tools of any trade? Yes. What else? A pair of steers my father gave me. And if this was not enough, then, he said, a note, which is never intended to be paid, makes up the balance. Men in this Commonwealth become freemen when they arrive at twenty-one years of age; and why oblige them to buy their freedom? They perform militia duty—they pay a tax for all they possess, that is, their polls. Nothing, he said, of so little consequence in itself, was so ardently desired, as an alteration in this part of the constitution. Men who have no property are put in the situation of the slaves of Virginia; they ought to be saved from the degrading feelings.

Mr. BOND of Boston said the reverend gentleman was mistaken on one point. The resolution did not confine the right of voting to those who paid a poll tax; but paupers also were embraced by it.

Mr. FOSTER said he did not mean to allow them the privilege of voting.

Mr. DUTTON said he was in favor of reconsideration. He had voted against the resolution, which, it is now understood by those who supported it, ought to be modified so as to exclude paupers. Although the resolution as it passed, was without limitation, still he was willing to consider it, as modified in the manner suggested. It introduced a new principle into the constitution. It was universal suffrage. There were two ways of considering it. 1st. As a matter of right. 2d. As a matter of expediency. As to the right, he inquired why paupers were excluded at all, if it was a common right; and if it was not, then there was the same right in the community to exclude every man, who was not worth two hundred dollars, as there was to exclude paupers, or persons under twenty-one years. In truth there was no question of right; it was wholly a question of expediency. He thought it expedient to retain the qualification in the constitution. It was in the nature of a privilege, and as such, it was connected with many virtues, which conduced to the good order of society. It was a distinction to be sought for; it was the reward of good conduct. It encouraged industry, economy and prudence; it elevated the standard of all our civil institutions, and gave dignity and importance to those who chose, and those who were chosen. It acted as a stimulus to exertion to acquire what it was a distinction to possess. He maintained that in this country, where the means of subsistence were so abundant, and the demand for labor so great, every

man of sound body could acquire the necessary qualification.
If he failed to do this, it must be, ordinarily, because he was
indolent or vicious. In many of the states a qualification of freehold was required. He thought that a wise provision; and if
any alteration was to be made, he should be in favor of placing
it there, rather than upon personal property. As it was, he
thought it valuable as a moral means, as part of that moral
force so essential to the support of any free government. He
would not diminish that, for in the same proportion it should
be, from any cause diminished, would the foundations of the
republic be weakened. He also considered it as unreasonable,
that a man who had no property should act indirectly upon the
property of others. If gentlemen would look to the statute book,
to the business of the Legislature, or to the courts of law, how
much of all that was done, would be found to relate to the
rights of property. It lay at the foundation of the social state,
it was the spring of all action and all employment. It was
therefore, he apprehended, wholly inequitable in its nature,
that men without a dollar should, in any way, determine the
rights of property, or have any concern in its appropriation.
He also contended, that the principle of the resolution was
anti-republican. It greatly increased the number of voters, and
those of a character most liable to be improperly influenced
or corrupted. It enlarged the field of action to every popular
favorite, and enabled him to combine greater numbers. The
time might come, when he would be able to command, as truly
as ever a general commanded an army, sufficient numbers to
affect or control the government itself. In that case, the form
of a republican constitution might remain, but its life and
spirit would have fled. The government would be essentially
a democracy, and between that and a despotism there would
be but one step. Such would be the tendency of the principle,
and so far as it operated, it would change the structure of the
constitution. The qualification which is required, was intended
as a security for property. He considered it as a barrier, which

ought not to be removed, and could not be, without danger
to the State. . . .

. . . Mr. BLAKE was in favor of reconsideration, because he
thought the subject had not been fairly examined. He was not
satisfied that the right of universal suffrage ought to be exercised, but many weighty reasons could be urged in favor of it,
some of which he would state. He did not consider it as changing a fundamental principle of the constitution, if he did, he
should oppose it. He said that the constitutions of most of the
states in the Union required no pecuniary qualification; those
of South Carolina and Virginia, which require a freehold, were
exceptions, and he did not mean to speak of the states newly
admitted. The example of other states, however, was not of
much weight, as we ought to be an example to ourselves. Life
was as dear to a poor man as to a rich man; so was liberty.
Every subject therefore, involving only life or liberty, could
be acted upon, with as good authority, by the poor as by the
rich. As to property, the case was different. But our constitution involves all three, and the question is, how the power in
relation to them shall be parcelled out. Our constitution has
made the senate the guardian of property. The senate is the
rich man's citadel. There, and there alone, the rich man should
look for his security. Every man who pays his tax—and he did
not know why not paupers, as they were liable to military duty,
ought to possess the privilege of voting. To deprive a man of
this privilege till he acquires property, was an encroachment
on the fundamental principles of our constitution. The constitutions of most of the other states give the right of voting to
every man who pays his taxes; not mentioning anything about
paupers. He said the requisition of property was in this town,
for a long time, a dead letter, until the Legislature, a few years
since, made some wise provisions concerning elections. . . .

. . . Mr. QUINCY said, that the proposition before the committee had been considered by those in favor, as well as those
against it, as one for universal suffrage; but that it was not such

a proposition. Universal suffrage is suffrage without qualification. Suppose the proposition adopted—still you have not universal suffrage. The qualification of age, and of sex, remains.
Women are excluded—minors are excluded. The real nature
of the proposition is the exclusion of pecuniary qualification.
This remark is material, because the only principle alleged in
favor of the exclusion of pecuniary qualification is just as strong
in favor of the exclusion of every other qualification. Other
gentlemen had alleged reasons in favor of the proposition from
considerations of inconvenience and of expediency. But the
only gentleman who had alleged in its favor a principle, as the
foundation of a right, was his colleague (Mr. BLAKE). His principle was this. "Life is precious. Liberty is precious. Both more
precious than property. Every man, whose life and liberty is
made liable to the laws, ought therefore to have a voice, in the
choice of his legislators." Grant this argument to be just. Is it
not equally applicable to women and to minors? Are they not
liable to the laws? Ought they not then to have a voice in the
choice? The denial of this right to them shows, that the principle is not just. Society may make a part of its members obnoxious to laws, and yet deny them the right of suffrage,
without any injustice.

Again—it has been said that pecuniary qualification was
contrary to the spirit of our constitution. Those who took this
ground had not favored the Convention with their definition of
the spirit of our constitution, though it was very plain from the
course of their arguments that what they understood by it, was
a spirit of universal or unlimited liberty. Now, this is not the
spirit of our constitution; which is a spirit of limited liberty; of
reciprocal control. Reduced to the form of a definition, this is
the meaning of the term, spirit of our constitution—*The will
of the people, expressed through an organization by balanced
power.* Every man, therefore, who would compare any given
provision, with the spirit of our constitution, ought not to recur
to principles of abstract liberty, but to principles of balanced

liberty. With respect to those checks and balances, which according to the form of our constitution, constitute the character of Massachusetts liberty, those gentlemen take a very narrow view of the subject who deem that they exist only in the separation of the powers of government into the legislative, judicial and executive; or in the division of the legislative power among three branches. Every limitation of the exercise of any right or power, under the constitution, makes a part of that balance, which will be disturbed by its removal. The provision of a pecuniary qualification is of this nature. It is one of the checks in our constitution. How it operates, whom it affects, whom it benefits, are worthy of consideration. In the course of the argument in the Convention, it has been considered as a check, in favor of the rich, and against the poor. Now the fact is, that it is directly the reverse. If we should suppose the rich, acting as a class, this is the first provision, which they ought to expunge. And on the other hand, it is the last, with which the poor ought to consent to part. In its true character, this provision is in favor of the poor, and against the pauper;—that is to say, in favor of those who have something, but very little; against those who have nothing at all. Suppose all qualifications of property taken away, who gains by it? The poor man, who has just property enough to be qualified to vote? Or the rich, whose property is a great surplus? The rich man's individual vote is, indeed, countervailed by it, as well as the poor man's. But the great difference is this, that the poor man has thus lost his political all; he has no power of indemnifying himself. Whereas the rich, by the influence resulting from his property over the class of paupers, has a power of indemnifying himself a hundred fold. The theory of our constitution is, that extreme poverty—that is, pauperism—is inconsistent with independence. It therefore assumes a qualification of a very low amount, which, according to its theory, is the lowest consistent with independence. Undoubtedly it excludes some, of a different character of mind. But this number is very few; and from the small amount of property required, is, in individual cases, soon compensated.

At the present day, the provision was probably worth very little. In the present results of our elections, it would not make one hair white or black. But prospectively, it was of great consequence. In this point of view he put it to the consideration of the landholders, and yeomanry of the country. The principle was peculiarly important to them. Everything indicates that the destinies of the country will eventuate in the establishment of a great manufacturing interest in the Commonwealth. There is nothing in the condition of our country, to prevent manufacturers from being absolutely dependent upon their employers, here as they are everywhere else. The whole body of every manufacturing establishment, therefore, are dead votes, counted by the head, by their employer. Let the gentlemen from the country consider, how it may affect their rights, liberties and properties, if in every county of the Commonwealth there should arise, as in time there probably will, one, two, or three manufacturing establishments, each sending, as the case may be, from one to eight hundred votes to the polls depending on the will of one employer, one great capitalist. In such a case would they deem such a provision as this of no consequence? At present it is of little importance. Prospectively of very great. As to the inconvenience resulting from the present provision, this was amply balanced by its effect as a moral means, and as an incentive to industry. . . .

. . . Mr. Austin of Boston said that gentlemen, who were unwilling to change the principles of the constitution, instead of striking out this qualification ought to increase the sum, on account of the change in the value of money; he thought, however, that it would be impossible for them to effect this, and experience had shown the impolicy of requiring the present qualification. He would not contend against the right of requiring it, though there were strong arguments on that side, but he considered it inexpedient. The provision could not be carried into effect; it was the cause of perjury and immorality—it did not prevent a fraudulent man from voting, who owed more than he was worth, but debarred an honest poor man who paid his debts—and it tended to throw suspicion of unfairness on the municipal authority. He asked, what will you do with your laboring men? They have no freehold—no property to the amount of two hundred dollars, but they support their families reputably with their daily earnings. What will you do with your sailors? Men who labor hard, and scatter with inconsiderateness the product of their toil, and who depend on the earnings of the next voyage. What will you do with your young men, who have spent all their money in acquiring an education? Must they buy their right to vote? Must they depend on their friends or parents to purchase it for them? Must they wait till they have turned their intelligence into stock? Shall all these classes of citizens be deprived of the rights of freemen for want of property? Regard for country, he said, did not depend upon property, but upon institutions, laws, habits and associations. This qualification was said to encourage industry;—it was better to depend on the principle of character and independence which a man feels in exercising the privilege of a freeman. If taking away this qualification would weaken the moral force in the community, as had been urged, he should be for retaining it; but that force depends on education, and the diffusion of intelligence. One gentleman (Mr. QUINCY) had looked forward to our becoming a great manufacturing people. God forbid. If it should happen, however, it was not to be expected, that this modicum of property required would exclude the laborers in manufactories from voting. It was better to let them vote—they would otherwise become the Lazaroni of the country. By refusing this right to them, you array them against the laws; but give them the rights of citizens—mix them with the good part of society, and you disarm them. . . .

6. The Basis of Representation

*After disposing of the suffrage question, the committee of the whole
proceeded to take up Henry Dearborn's resolution to change the
basis of representation in the senate from property to persons. Dearborn spoke at length, but the* Journal *preserves only a brief abstract
of his speech. The resolution passed. The convention voted to reconsider, and Dearborn explained his plan for a democratically based
representation encompassing both chambers of the legislature. Levi
Lincoln then introduced his plan, which he expounded on the floor
the next day, December 13. Dearborn and Lincoln, the foremost
democratic leaders in the convention, were both sons of Massachusetts Jeffersonians who had served in Jefferson's cabinet. Dearborn,
who represented Roxbury in Norfolk County, succeeded his father
as Collector of the Port of Boston in 1812 and remained in that post
until 1829. Lincoln, from Worcester, was a lawyer and, at intervals,
an influential member of the legislature. He was later governor of
the state for a solid decade, from 1825 to 1834. The speeches of
Saltonstall and John Adams—his longest in the convention—briefly
state the views of the two conservatives.*

Mr. DEARBORN. . . .He did not know whence the principle, by
which the senate is apportioned by the present constitution,
was derived. It was not to be found in the organization of any
of the republics, ancient or modern. It did not exist in Greece,
Rome, Venice or Genoa. It was found in the British House of
Lords. The members of that house support the rights of the
aristocracy, and are their own representatives. In the United
States there is but one class of people. They are all freemen and
have equal rights. The principle of a representation of property
in our constitution was not derived from the neighboring
states. New Hampshire was the only state whose constitution
contained a similar provision. If the principle was a good one,

From Journal, pp. 257–258, 265–266, 274–276, 277–279.

it was remarkable that it had not been adopted in any other state. The only reason he had ever heard of to justify the principle was, that the taxes are paid in proportion to property, and that the principle of apportionment was designed for the protection of property. But this protection was not necessary. Property secures respect whenever it is not abused, and the influence of those who possess it is sufficient for its protection. He apprehended nothing at present from the representation of wealth. But the time might come when the accumulation of property within twenty miles of the capital would be sufficient to control the senate. At present the county of Berkshire, of about equal population with Suffolk, would have but a third part of the representation, and the man of large property in the former county would have but a third part of the influence through the senate which was enjoyed by a man of the same property in the latter county. This was not just, equitable nor proper. He appealed to the magnanimity of the rich to yield to the poor their equal proportion of rights. The principle might be adopted now, but the people would be dissatisfied with it, they would constantly protest against it, and it would be at some time or other necessarily yielded to their importunity. . . .

. . . Mr. LINCOLN. . . . The question now under consideration was on what principle should the representation in the senate be founded? He agreed in the sentiment that a free government must be founded on a system of checks and balances—and it was on this principle that he supported the resolution offered by the gentleman from Roxbury. But he did not admit that to obtain this check it was necessary to assume the principle of a representation of property in either branch. It was attained by adopting a different mode of representation for the two branches as well as a different principle. The object of a check was equally attained by adopting different qualifications for electors, or different periods of election. If it was shown by argument, by experience, or by arithmetical calculation that any principle was unequal, that ought to be abandoned, and another adopted not susceptible of the objection. He should proceed to show the inequality and unjust operation of the old principle, and then endeavor to show that the effect contemplated from checks may be secured by another principle not liable to these objections. If it should be shown that representation according to valuation was not just, and that the object could be attained by letting the whole people vote for one branch, and freeholders only for the other—by choosing one for two years and the other for one, or in any other mode which is not unequal—this principle should be abandoned. He admitted that if senators were to be chosen from certain districts, and representatives from the same, and for the same period, according to the plan of the gentleman from Roxbury, there would be no check. But it was not so with the plan which he had proposed. He had proposed that the representatives in the other branch should be chosen by towns—and the system would then be analogous to that of the Congress of the United States, reversing the terms only, one representing the corporations of towns and the other the population. Was the principle of representation in the senate equal and just? Our government is one of the people, not a government of property. Representation is founded on the interests of the people. It is because they have rights that they have assumed the power of self government. Property is incompetent to sustain a free government. Intelligence alone can uphold any free government. In a government of freemen property is valuable only as the people are intelligent. Were it not for a government of the people, the people would be without property. But it is contended that this system is justified by another principle. Representation and taxation have been described as twin brothers. But this principle has not been fully understood. It does not follow that there shall be an unequal representation, that taxation may be represented. It is only necessary that all who are taxed should be represented, and not that they should be represented in proportion to their tax. Boston would be represented if it had

but a single member. This was the principle which was contended for in the revolution, and that revolution would never
have been effected if we had had a single representative in the
British parliament. Secure the right of representation; but in
the regulation of that right, you may restrict it to any proportion whatever. Whether you are represented by one or forty-
five, it is utterly in vain to complain that you have no representation. But any other distribution of representation than
according to population, is unequal and unjust. He alluded to
the case mentioned yesterday by the gentleman from Roxbury
of one senator for the county of Suffolk for every 7,500 inhabitants, while there was in the county of Berkshire but one for
every 20,000, which he pronounced to be an instance of most
gross and cruel inequality. He stated the case of an individual
lately deceased whose property of 1,300,000 dollars alone,
would have as much influence in the senate as 1300 independent farmers with a property of 1000 dollars each. This principle
conferred upon a dangerous part of the community an undue
and unwarrantable share in the representation. A man of
1,300,000 dollars property surrounded by 1299 others of no
property, confers on them an influence equal to the same number of independent men worth 1000 each. He contended that
if it was a sound principle that property should confer the
right of representation, it ought not to be restricted, and Suffolk should have eight senators. Imposing the restriction was
admitting that the principle was false and unjust. Taking
population as the basis, no inequality would result. He protested against any misapprehension of his feelings and motives
—he had no disposition to excite jealousies, nor to prevent the
exercise of rights—if they were founded upon principle. He
professed a great respect for the people of the metropolis—but
he protested against their borrowing, through the respect entertained for the town, any influence that was not secured to
every other part of the people. . . .

    . . . Mr. Saltonstall of Salem observed that this Convention exhibited a singular and most interesting scene. A free people by their delegates assembled to deliberate upon the constitution under which they have so long lived, inquiring into its operations, and whether there is any evil that requires amendment. It is a subject of gratitude that while the nations of the old world are obliged to submit to reforms, dictated by standing armies, we are witnessing this quiet scene. But there is also much cause of anxiety. A short time since we were all happy under the present constitution. There was no symptom of uneasiness, no project for a convention. Our government secured to us all the objects for which civil society was instituted. The separation of a part of the Commonwealth, rendered it expedient to propose to the people the question of a convention, and it was adopted by a very small vote,—a fact which shows conclusively that no evil was pressing on the people; that no grievance loudly demanded a remedy. But now, amidst constant professions of veneration for the instrument, every part of it is attacked, and we are called on to defend the elementary principles of government. First, we abolish one session of the Legislature, which has existed for two centuries; we then dispense with the necessity of a declaration which has existed from the beginning; we disown that the people ever enjoyed their rights in the election of counsellors. And now the foundation of a great branch of the government is attacked, as unjust and aristocratic. Is the constitution to be thrown by as an old-fashioned piece of furniture, that answered well enough in its day, but is now fit only to be stowed away in the lumber room with the portraits of our ancestors? Let us rather meet the objections, listen to the arguments, correct the evil, if one is shown to exist, and the constitution will come out of the fiery furnace unhurt, still more precious for the trial it has endured. Mr. S. then observed that he had not expected a serious attempt would be made to change the basis of the senate; that it had not been a cause of dissatisfaction; that nothing had been written or said against it until the separation of Maine; that there was occasionally some difficulty as to the fractions, and some irritation in the formation of districts, but no serious disaffection; and he believed no objection was ever made to it in the Legislature, as unjust or unequal. He had thought also that the constitution was endeared to the people from the circumstances under which it was made,—in the midst of war; our independence not yet secure; while our armies were yet in the field. At such a time the convention met, and deliberately discussed the great principles of government, and framed the present system of government. There were circumstances also calculated especially to endear this part of the constitution to us. When the convention assembled, a majority were opposed to two branches; they thought the people needed no check: like the gentleman from Worcester [Mr. Lincoln], they thought the people were capable of self-government. Its analogy to the old council had also a tendency to render it odious; it also savored a little of aristocracy, and the leaders of that day had been irritated under the influence of the old government; yet they listened to the sages who were with them, and adopted the principle. The present basis of the senate is perfectly defensible in theory. Some check on the popular branch is necessary; this is admitted by all. Mr. S. then referred to history,—the English parliament,—to the national assembly, &c., to show its necessity. There are times when popular ferments are excited, that would destroy everything fair and valuable in society, if unchecked. Mr. S. then remarked on the different systems proposed. That by Mr. DEARBORN would be no check. Both branches will be chosen by the same people in the same districts. Both would be subject to the same influence; be under the same control; and the senate would have no more operation as a check, than the same men in the other branch. Another proposition is the novel, the fanciful, the fallacious one by the gentleman from Worcester, which would have the senate the popular branch, to be checked by the house! A popular branch of thirty-six to be checked by three hundred and fifty!

But what is to check the house? That will be the popular branch, emanating from the people, warmed with all their passions. What are these corporate rights? There is nothing tangible in them, which can form a check. Mr. S. then went on to show that there was no analogy between this plan and the constitution of the United States, as had been argued by Mr. LINCOLN. He thought the people would never adopt a system of checks, by making different tenures to office, or different qualifications to voters. What then remains but to preserve the present basis; to cling to that which has been so wise in theory, and so salutary in practice? It is an admirable provision,—the representation of a great interest, and yet not dangerous to any other. It is the result of a new modification which will give a spirit of independence to the senate, and make them indeed a check—not to thwart the other branch, but to watch, to cause deliberation. Property should be represented, because it is the greatest object of civil society; it is not mere inert matter, but a living principle, which keeps the great machine of society in motion. It is the universal stimulus. The principle of the senate is not unequal in its operation, but the same everywhere, in all places; not for Suffolk or Essex— Essex has nothing to gain, but may lose much, by this arrangement. It is not for the rich, but for the security of all men and all interests, as it will make an effectual check for the preservation of every right. If in theory this is wise, how much more valuable is it after forty years' experience. Experiment is worth everything upon this subject. We should be unwilling to touch what is made venerable by age. We should cautiously advance any theory of our own, against a system that has been in operation half a century. The situation of Massachusetts is a proud one. She has braved the storm which has overwhelmed so many old governments. They that laughed us to scorn are now looking to us with admiration, and studying our systems. . . .

. . . Mr. LINCOLN rose to explain. He thought it disengenuous in gentlemen, to allude to a proposition which he had made, without any connection with any other. This question should depend on its own merits, and the Convention may reject or adopt the proposition which he had presented. He did not contend that it was just and equal in itself, but in connection with the representation in the senate, on the basis of valuation, it would form an effectual, and the only effectual check.

Mr. LOCKE proceeded to compare the three systems of representation which had been proposed, and to argue in favor of the adoption of that reported by the committee. He said he understood, that some gentlemen approved of the plan proposed by the gentleman from Roxbury, for the senate, and that they thought it fair to couple it with the house of representatives, proposed in the system of the select committee. To him it appeared manifestly unjust to take this part of the system, without at the same time adopting the part relating to the senate. He observed, that some went on the principle, that the senate was founded on the basis of property. This was not true. The basis was taxation. The wealthy districts were allowed a greater proportion of representation in the senate, not with a view to the protection of property, but because they were made to contribute so much to the support of the public burdens. He concluded by giving his testimony to the fairness and liberality of the members of the committee from the large towns, and their readiness to yield everything that could be demanded in the spirit of fair and equal compromise.

Mr. ADAMS of Quincy. I rise, with fear and trembling, to say a few words on this question. It is now forty years since I have intermingled in debate in any public assembly. My memory and strength of utterance fail me, so that it is utterly impossible for me to discuss the subject on the broad ground, on which gentlemen, who have spoken before me, have considered it. The constitution declares, that all men are born free and equal. But how are they born free and equal? Has the child of a North American Indian, when born, the same right which his father has, to his father's bow and arrows? No—no man pretends that all are born with equal property, but with equal rights to acquire property. The great object is to render property secure. Without the security of property, neither arts, nor manufactures, nor commerce, nor literature, nor science can exist. It is the foundation upon which civilization rests. There would be no security for life and liberty even, if property were not secure. Society is a compact with every individual, that each may enjoy his right for the common good. In the state of nature the Indian has no defence for his little hut, or his venison, or anything that he acquires, but his own strength. Society furnishes the strength of the whole community, for the protection of the property of each individual. . . .

. . . The report of the select committee is a compromise, a mutual concession of various parts. The large towns have made quite as great concessions as any part of the country. Suffolk is to have but six senators; in proportion to its property it would have more. The eloquent gentleman from Roxbury [Mr. Dearborn], has alluded, with propriety, to the ancient republics of Athens and Rome. My memory is too defective to go into details, but I appeal to his fresher reading, whether in Athens there were not infinitely greater advantages given to property, than among us. Aristides ruined the constitution of Solon, by destroying the balance between property and numbers, and, in consequence, a torrent of popular commotion broke in and desolated the republic. Let us come to Rome; property was infinitely more regarded than here, and it was only while the balance was maintained, that the liberties of the people were preserved. Let us look at the subject in another point of view. How many persons are there, even in this country, who have no property? Some think there are more without it, than with it. If so, and it were left to mere numbers, those who have no property would vote us out of our houses. In France, at the time of the revolution, those who were without property, were in the proportion of fifty to one. It was by destroying the balance, that the revolution was produced. The French revolution furnished an experiment, perfect and complete in all its stages and branches, of the utility and excellence of universal suffrage. The revolutionary government began with the higher orders of society, as they were called, viz., dukes and peers, archbishops and cardinals, the greatest proprietors of land in the whole kingdom. Unfortunately, the first order, although very patriotic and sincere, adopted an opinion that the sovereign power should be in one assembly. They were soon succeeded and supplanted—banished and guillotined, by a second order, and these in their turn by a third, and these by a fourth, till the government got into the hands of peasants and stage-players, and from them descended to jacobins, and from them to sans-culottes. . . . And thus it has happened in all ages and countries in the world, where such principles have been adopted, and a similar course pursued. All writers agree, that there are twenty persons in Great Britain, who have no property, to one that has. If the radicals should succeed in obtaining universal suffrage, they will overturn the whole kingdom, and turn those who have property out of their houses. The people in England, in favor of universal suffrage, are ruining themselves. Our ancestors have made a pecuniary qualification necessary for office, and necessary for electors; and all the wise men of the world have agreed in the same thing. . . .

7. Joseph Story on Representation

Justice Story and Daniel Webster delivered the most memorable speeches in the convention. Both occurred on the representation question, Story's on December 14, Webster's the following day, and both defended the taxation basis of the senate in particular. They are interesting from the standpoint of political theory. The idiom and doctrine are conservative, even faintly European. Story's speech,

*more than Webster's, exhibits that calm, dispassionate, and delib-
erative appeal to men's reason that had, in his opinion, "so powerful
and wholesome an effect" upon the delegates. Story's work in the
convention added significantly to his already considerable reputation.
For the past decade he had been a justice of the United States Supreme Court, to which he had been appointed by President Madison,
and in that time he had shrugged off the Jeffersonian Republicanism
of his youth. Only forty-one years of age in 1820, his remarkable
career as a justice and legal scholar still lay ahead of him. Unlike
Webster, Story was no orator. He prepared his speech, read it, and
furnished a copy to the reporter of the debates.*

. . . It is necessary for us for a moment to look at what is the
true state of the question now before us. The proposition of
my friend from Roxbury [Mr. Dearborn], is to make population the basis for apportioning the senate, and this proposition
is to be followed up,—as the gentleman, with the candor and
frankness which has always marked his character, has inti-
mated—with another, to apportion the house of representatives
in the same manner. The plan is certainly entitled to the praise
of consistency and uniformity. It does not assume in one house
a principle which it deserts in another. Those who contend on
the other hand, for the basis of valuation, propose nothing new,
but stand upon the letter and spirit of the present constitution.

Here then there is no attempt to introduce a new principle
in favor of wealth into the constitution. There is no attempt to
discriminate between the poor and the rich. There is no attempt to raise the pecuniary qualifications of the electors or
elected—to give to the rich man two votes and to the poor man
but one. The qualifications are to remain as before, and the
rich and the poor, and the high and the low are to meet at the
polls upon the same level of equality. And yet much has been
introduced into the debate about the rights of the rich and the

From *Journal*, pp. 284–295.

poor, and the oppression of the one by the elevation of the other. This distinction between the rich and poor, I must be permitted to say, is an odious distinction, and not founded in the merits of the case before us. I agree that the poor man is not to be deprived of his rights any more than the rich man, nor have I as yet heard of any proposition to that effect; and if it should come, I should feel myself bound to resist it. The poor man ought to be protected in his rights, not merely of life and liberty, but of his scanty and hard earnings. I do not deny that the poor man may possess as much patriotism as the rich; but it is unjust to suppose that he necessarily possesses more. Patriotism and poverty do not necessarily march hand in hand; nor is wealth that monster which some imaginations have depicted, with a heart of adamant and a sceptre of iron, surrounded with scorpions stinging every one within its reach, and planting its feet of oppression upon the needy and the dependent. Such a representation is not just with reference to our country. There is no class of very rich men in this happy land, whose wealth is fenced in by hereditary titles, by entails, and by permanent elevation to the highest offices. Here there is a gradation of property from the highest to the lowest, and all feel an equal interest in its preservation. If, upon the principle of valuation, the rich man in a district, which pays a high tax, votes for a larger number of senators, the poor man in the same district enjoys the same distinction. There is not then a conflict, but a harmony of interests between them; nor under the present constitution has any discontent or grievance been seriously felt from this source.

When I look around and consider the blessings which property bestows, I cannot persuade myself that gentlemen are serious in their views, that it does not deserve our utmost protection. I do not here speak of your opulent and munificent citizens, whose wealth has spread itself into a thousand channels of charity and public benevolence. I speak not of those who rear temples to the service of the most high God. I speak not of those who build your hospitals, where want, and misery, and sickness, the lame, the halt and the blind, the afflicted in body and in spirit, may find a refuge from their evils, and the voice of solace and consolation, administering food and medicine and kindness. I speak not of those, who build asylums for the insane, for the ruins of noble minds, for the broken hearted and the melancholy, for those whom Providence has afflicted with the greatest of calamities, the loss of reason, and too often the loss of happiness—within whose walls the screams of the maniac may die away in peace, and the sighs of the wretched be soothed into tranquillity. I speak not of these, not because they are not worthy of all praise; but because I would dwell rather on those general blessings, which prosperity diffuses through the whole mass of the community. Who is there that has not a friend or relative in distress, looking up to him for assistance? Who is there that is not called upon to administer to the sick and the suffering, to those who are in the depth of poverty and distress, to those of his own household, or to the stranger beside the gate? The circle of kindness commences with the humblest, and extends wider and wider as we rise to the highest in society, each person administering in his own way to the wants of those around him. It is thus that property becomes the source of comforts of every kind, and dispenses its blessings in every form. In this way it conduces to the public good by promoting private happiness; and every man from the humblest, possessing property, to the highest in the State, contributes his proportion to the general mass of comfort. The man without any property may desire to do the same; but he is necessarily shut out from this most interesting charity. It is in this view that I consider property as the source of all the comforts and advantages we enjoy, and every man, from him who possesses but a single dollar up to him who possesses the greatest fortune, is equally interested in its security and its preservation. Government indeed stands on a combination of interests and circumstances. It must always be a question of the highest moment, how the property-holding part of the community may be sustained against the inroads of poverty and vice. Poverty leads to temptation, and temptation often leads to vice, and vice to military despotism. The rights of man are never heard in a despot's palace. The very rich man, whose estate consists in personal property, may escape from such evils by flying for refuge to some foreign land. But the hardy yeoman, the owner of a few acres of the soil, and supported by it, cannot leave his home without becoming a wanderer on the face of the earth. In the preservation of property and virtue, he has, therefore, the deepest and most permanent interest.

Gentlemen have argued as if personal rights only were the proper objects of government. But what, I would ask, is life worth, if a man cannot eat in security the bread earned by his own industry? If he is not permitted to transmit to his children the little inheritance which his affection has destined for their use? What enables us to diffuse education among all the classes of society, but property? Are not our public schools, the distinguishing blessing of our land, sustained by its patronage? I will say no more about the rich and the poor. There is no parallel to be run between them, founded on permanent constitutional distinctions. The rich help the poor, and the poor in turn administer to the rich. In our country, the highest man is not *above* the people; the humblest is not *below* the people. If the rich may be said to have additional protection, they have not additional power. Nor does wealth here form a permanent distinction of families. Those who are wealthy today pass to the tomb, and their children divide their estates. Property thus is divided quite as fast as it accumulates. No family can, without its own exertions, stand erect for a long time under our statute of descents and distributions, the only true and legitimate agrarian law. It silently and quietly dissolves the mass heaped up by the toil and diligence of a long life of enterprise and industry. Property is continually changing like the waves of the sea. One wave rises and is soon swallowed up in the vast abyss and seen no more. Another rises, and having reached its destined limits, falls gently away, and is succeeded by yet another, which, in its turn, breaks and dies away silently on the shore. The richest man among us may be brought down to the humblest level; and the child with scarcely clothes to cover his nakedness, may rise to the highest office in our government. And the poor man, while he rocks his infant on his knees, may justly indulge the consolation, that if he possess talents and virtue, there is no office beyond the reach of his honorable ambition. It is a mistaken theory, that government is founded for one object only. It is organized for the protection of life, liberty and property, and all the comforts of society— to enable us to indulge in our domestic affections, and quietly to enjoy our homes and our firesides. . . .

. . . It has been also suggested, that great property, of itself, gives great influence, and that it is unnecessary that the constitution should secure to it more. I have already stated what I conceive to be the true answer; that a representation in the senate founded on valuation, is not a representation of property in the abstract. It gives no greater power in any district to the rich than to the poor. The poor voters in Suffolk may, if they please, elect six senators into the senate; and so throughout the Commonwealth, the senators of every other district may, in like manner, be chosen by the same class of voters. The basis of valuation was undoubtedly adopted by the framers of our constitution, with reference to a just system of checks and balances, and the principles of rational liberty. Representation and taxation was the doctrine of those days—a doctrine for which our fathers fought and bled, in the battles of the revolution. Upon the basis of valuation, property is not directly represented; but property in the aggregate, combined with personal rights—where the greatest burthen of taxation falls, there the largest representation is apportioned; but still the choice depends upon the will of the majority of voters, and not upon that of the wealthier class within the district. There is a peculiar beauty in our system of taxation and equalizing the public burthens. Our governor, counsellors, senators, judges, and other public officers are paid out of the public treasury,—our representatives by their respective towns. The former are officers for the benefit of the whole Commonwealth; but the right of sending representatives is a privilege granted to corporations, and, as the more immediate agents of such corporations, they are paid by them. The travel however of the representatives is paid out of the public treasury, with the view that no unjust advantage should arise to any part of the Commonwealth from its greater proximity to the capital. Thus the principle of equalizing burthens is exemplified. But even if it were true that the representation in the senate were founded on property, I would respectfully ask gentlemen, if its natural influence would be weakened or destroyed by assuming the basis of population. I presume not. It would still be left to exert that influence over friends and dependents in the same manner that it now does; so that the change would not in the slightest degree aid the asserted object, I mean the suppression of the supposed predominating authority of wealth.

Gentlemen have argued, as though it was universally conceded as a political axiom, that population is in all cases and under all circumstances the safest and best basis of representation. I beg leave to doubt the proposition. Cases may be easily supposed, in which, from the peculiar state of society, such a basis would be universally deemed unsafe and injurious. Take a state where the population is such as that of Manchester in England, (and some states in our Union have not so large a population) where there are five or ten thousand wealthy persons, and ninety or one hundred thousand of artizans reduced to a state of vice and poverty and wretchedness, which leave them exposed to the most dangerous political excitements. I speak of them, not as I know, but as the language of British statesmen and parliamentary proceedings exhibit them. Who would found a representation on such a population, unless he intended all property should be a booty to be divided among plunderers? A different state of things exists in our happy Commonwealth, and no such dangers will here arise from assuming population as the basis of representation. But still the doctrine, in the latitude now contended for, is not well founded. What should be the basis on which representation should be founded, is not an abstract theoretical question, but depends upon the habits, manners, character and institutions of the people, who are to be represented. It is a question of political policy, which every nation must decide for itself, with reference to its own wants and circumstances. . . .

. . . To the plan of the gentleman from Roxbury [Mr. Dearborn] two objections existed. The first was, that it destroyed the system of checks and balances in the government, a system which has been approved by the wisdom of ages. The value of this system has been forcibly illustrated by the gentleman from Boston [Mr. Prescott], in the extract which he read from the remarks of Mr. Jefferson on the constitution of Virginia.[6] I will not therefore dwell on this objection. The next objection is that it destroys all county lines and distinctions, and breaks all habits and associations connected with them. They might thus be broken up, but it was by tearing asunder some of the strongest bonds of society. The people of each county are drawn together by their necessary attendance upon the county courts, and by their county interests and associations. There is a common feeling diffused among the mass of the population, which extends to, but never passes the boundary of each

---

[6] In his *Notes on the State of Virginia,* Jefferson said of the Virginia constitution: "The senate by its constitution is too homogeneous with the house of delegates. Being chosen by the same electors, at the same time, and out of the same subjects, the choice falls of course on men of the same description. The purpose of establishing different houses of legislation is to introduce the influence of different interests or different principles" [Ed.].

county; and thus these communities become minor states. These are valuable associations, and I am not prepared to say that they ought to be given up altogether. The system of the gentleman from Roxbury, however, not only obliterates them, but at the same time is supposed to affect the interests and corporate representation of the towns—a representation which, with all its inconveniences, possesses intrinsic value. It appears to me that the system of the select committee, combining valuation as the basis of the senate with corporate representation of the towns as the basis of the house, has, both as a system of checks and balances, and convenient and practical distribution of powers, some advantages over that now under discussion. . . .

. . . After all, what will be the effect of changing the basis of the senate from valuation to that of population? It will take three senators from Suffolk, give two more senators to the old county of Hampshire, leaving Berkshire and Plymouth to struggle for one more, and Norfolk and Bristol to contend for another, the disposition of which may be doubtful. All the rest of the Commonwealth will remain precisely in the same situation, whether we adopt the one basis or the other. Yet even this change will not produce any serious practical result, if we look forward twenty years. Suffolk has increased within the last ten years, ten thousand in the number of its inhabitants, that is to say, one quarter part of its population; a much greater ratio of increase than the rest of the State. Population will probably from the like causes continue to increase on the seaboard, or at least in the capital, from its great attractions, in a ratio quite as great beyond that of the interior. So that in a short time the difference of the two systems will be greatly diminished, and perhaps finally the inland counties will gain more by the restriction of the districts to six senators than they will now gain by the basis of population. In fifty years Suffolk upon this basis may entitle itself not to six only, but to eight.

Now I would beg gentlemen to consider, if in this view of

the subject a change in the basis of the senate can be useful? The constitution has gone through a trial of forty years in times of great difficulty and danger. It has passed through the embarrassments of the revolutionary war, through the troubles and discontents of 1787 and 1788, through collisions of parties unexampled in our history for violence and zeal, through a second war marked with no ordinary scenes of division and danger, and it has come out of these trials pure and bright and spotless. No practical inconvenience has been felt or attempted to be pointed out by any gentleman in the present system, during this long period. Is it then wise, or just, or politic to exchange the results of our own experience for any theory, however plausible, that stands opposed to that experience, for a theory that *possibly* may do as well?

A few words as to the proposition of the gentleman from Worcester [Mr. Lincoln] for representation in the house. It seems to me—I hope the gentleman will pardon the expression—inconsistent not only with his own doctrine as to the basis of population, but inconsistent with the reasoning, by which he endeavored to sustain that doctrine. The gentleman considers population as the only just basis of representation in the senate. Why then, I ask, is it not as just as the basis for the house? Here the gentleman deserts his favorite principle, and insists on representation of towns as corporations. He alleges that in this way the system of checks and balances, (which the gentleman approves) is supported. But it seems to me that it has not any merit as a check; for the aggregate population of the county will express generally the same voice as the aggregate representatives of the towns. The gentleman has said that the poor man in Berkshire votes only for two senators, while the poor man in Suffolk votes for six. Is there not the same objection against the system of representation now existing as to the house, and against that proposed by the gentleman himself? A voter in Chelsea now votes for but one representative, while his neighbor, a voter in Charlestown, votes for six.

Upon the gentleman's own plan there would be a like inequality. He presses us also in reference to his plan of representation in the house, with the argument, that it is not unequal because we are represented, if we have a single representative; and he says he distinguishes between the right to send one and to send many representatives. The former is vital to a free government —the latter not. One representative in the British Parliament would have probably prevented the American revolution. Be it so. But if the doctrine be sound, does it not plainly apply as well to the senate as the house? If it be not unequal or unjust in the house, how can it be so in the senate? Is not Berkshire with its two senators, and Barnstable with its one senator, and Worcester with its four senators, upon this principle just as fully represented in the senate as Suffolk with its six senators? The argument of the gentleman may therefore be thrown back upon himself. . . .

. . . I beg however for a moment to ask the attention of the committee to the gross inequalities of the plan of the gentleman from Worcester respecting the house of representatives. There are 298 towns in the State, each of which is to send one representative. And upon this plan the whole number of representatives will be 334. There are but 24 towns, which would be entitled to send more than one representative. These 24 towns with a population of 146,000 would send 58 representatives, or only one upon an average for every 2526 inhabitants, while the remaining 274 towns with a population of 313,000 would send 274 representatives, or one for every 1144 inhabitants. I lay not the *venue* here or there in the Commonwealth, in the county of Worcester or the county of Essex; but such would be the result throughout the whole Commonwealth taken in the aggregate of its population. Salem would send one representative for every 3130 inhabitants and Boston one for every 4200 inhabitants, while every town but the 24 largest would send one for every 1144 inhabitants! What then becomes of the favorite doctrine of the basis of population? I would ask the gentleman in his own emphatic language, is not this system unjust, unequal and cruel? If it be equal, it is so by some political arithmetic, which I have never learned and am incapable of comprehending.

A few words upon the plan of the select committee, and I have done. Sir, I am not entitled to any of the merit, if there be any, in that plan. My own was to preserve the present basis of the senate, not because I placed any peculiar stress on the basis of valuation; but because I deemed it all-important to retain some element that might maintain a salutary check between the two houses. My own plan for the house of representatives was representation founded on the basis of population in districts, according to the system proposed by the gentleman from Northampton [Mr. Lyman]. Finding that this plan was not acceptable to a majority of the committee I acquiesced in the plan reported by it. I have learned that we must not, in questions of government, stand upon abstract principles; but must content ourselves with practicable good. I do not pretend to think, nor do any of its advocates think, that the system of the select committee is perfect; but it will cure some defects in our present system which are of great and increasing importance. I have always viewed the representation in the house under the present constitution, as a most serious evil, and alarming to the future peace and happiness of the State. My dread has never been of the senate, but of that multitudinous assembly, which has been seen within these walls, and may again be seen if times of political excitement should occur. The more numerous the body the greater the danger from its movements in times, when it cannot or will not deliberate. I came here therefore willing and ready to make sacrifices to accomplish an essential *reduction* in that body. It was the only subject relative to the constitution on which I have always had a decided and earnest opinion. It was my fortune for some years to have a seat in our house of representatives; and for a short time to preside over its sittings, at a

period when it was most numerous, and under the most powerful excitements. I am sorry to say it, but such is my opinion, that
in no proper sense could it be called a deliberative assembly.
From the excess of numbers deliberation became almost impossible; and but for the good sense and discretion of those who
usually led in the debates, it would have been impracticable to
have transacted business with anything like accuracy or safety.
That serious public mischiefs did not arise from the necessary
hurry and difficulty of the legislative business is to be accounted for only from the mutual forbearance and kindness,
of those who enjoyed the confidence of the respective parties.
If the State should go on in its population we might hereafter
have 800 or 900 representatives according to the present system; and in times of public discontent, all the barriers of legislation may be broken down and the government itself be
subverted. I wish most deeply and earnestly to preserve to my
native State a *deliberative* legislature, where the sound judgment, and discretion, and sagacity of its best citizens may be
felt and heard and understood at all times and under all circumstances. I should feel the liberties of the State secure, if
this point were once fairly gained. I would yield up the little
privileges of my own town and of any others, that our children
may enjoy civil, religious and political liberty, as perfectly, nay
more perfectly than their fathers. With these views I am ready
to support the report of the select committee—not in part, but
as a whole—as a system—and if part is to be rejected I do not
feel myself bound to sustain the rest. Indeed upon no other
ground than a great diminution of the house of representatives
can I ever consent to pay the members out of the public treasury. For this is now the only efficient check against an overwhelming representation. By the plan of the select committee
the small towns are great gainers—a sacrifice is made by the
large towns and by them only. They will bear a heavier portion
of the pay of the representatives, and they will have a less
proportionate representation than they now possess. And what

do they gain in return? I may say nothing. All that is gained is public gain, a really deliberative legislature, and a representation in the senate, which is in fact a popular representation, emanating from and returning to the people, but so constructed that it operates as a useful check upon undue legislation and as a security to property.

I hope that this system will be adopted by a large majority, because it can scarcely otherwise receive the approbation of the people—I do not know that it is even desirable that the people should, nay, I might go further, and say that the people ought not to adopt any amendment which comes recommended by a bare majority of this Convention. If we are so little agreed among ourselves, as to what will be for the future public good, we had much better live under the present constitution, which has all our experience in its favor. Is any gentleman bold enough to hazard the assertion, that any new measure we may adopt can be more successful? I beg gentlemen to consider too what will be the effect if the amendments we now propose should be rejected by the people, having passed by a scanty majority. We shall then revert to the old constitution—and new parties, embittered by new feuds, or elated by victory, will be formed in the State and distinguished as constitutionalists and anti-constitutionalists; and thus new discontents and struggles for a new convention will agitate the Commonwealth. The revival of party animosities in any shape, is mostly to be deprecated. Who does not recollect with regret the violence with which party spirit in times past raged in this State, breaking asunder the ties of friendship and consanguinity? I was myself called upon to take an active part in the public scenes of those days. I do not regret the course which my judgment then led me to adopt; but I never can recollect, without the most profound melancholy, how often I have been compelled to meet, I will not say the *evil* but *averted* eyes, and the hostile opposition of men with whom, under other circumstances, I should have rejoiced to have met in the warmth of friendship.

If new parties are to arise, new animosities will grow up, and stimulate new resentments. To the aged in this Convention, who now bow down under the weight of years, this can, of course, be of but little consequence—for they must soon pass into the tranquillity of the tomb;—to those of middle life it will not be of great importance, for they are far on their way to their final repose; they have little to hope of future eminence, and are fast approaching the period when the things of this world will fade away. But we have youth, who are just springing into life—we have children whom we love—and families, in whose welfare we feel the deepest interest. In the name of heaven, let us not leave to them the bitter inheritance of our contentions. Let us not transmit to them enmities which may sadden the whole of their lives. Let us not—like him of old, blind and smitten of his strength—in our anger seize upon the pillars of the constitution, that we and our enemies may perish in their downfall. I would rather approach the altar of the constitution and pay my devotions there, and if our liberties must be destroyed, I, for one, would be ready to perish there in defending them. . . .

8. Daniel Webster on Representation

Webster came into the convention crowned with the laurels of several triumphs at the bar of the United States Supreme Court. As already noted, he was a practicing lawyer in Boston and had not before served the state in any public capacity. "He was before known as a lawyer," Story said of his friend, "but he has now secured the title of an eminent and enlightened statesman. It was a glorious field for him, and he has had an ample harvest. He always led the van, and was most skilful and instantaneous in attack and retreat." Several days after his speech on the elective basis of the senate, Webster delivered one of his greatest orations, "The First Settlement of New England," at Plymouth in commemoration of the two-hundredth anniversary of the Pilgrims' landing. The oration elaborated the dominant idea of his earlier speech in the convention. In an entry in his journal for the year 1820, Ralph Waldo Emerson recorded this description of the orator: "Webster has a long head, very large black eyes, bushy eyebrows, a commanding expression—and his hair is coal-black, and coarse as a crow's nest. His voice is sepulchral—there is not the least variety or the least harmony of tone—it commands, it fills, it echoes, but is harsh and dissonant."

. . . In my opinion, sir, there are two questions before the committee; the first is, shall the legislative department be constructed with any other *check*, than such as arises simply from dividing the members of this department into two houses? The second is, if such other and further check ought to exist, *in what manner* shall it be created?

If the two houses are to be chosen in the manner proposed by the resolutions of the member from Roxbury [Mr. Dearborn], there is obviously no other check or control than a division into separate chambers. The members of both houses are to be chosen at the same time, by the same electors, in the same districts, and for the same term of office. They will of course all be actuated by the same feelings and interests. Whatever motives may at the moment exist, to elect particular members of one house, will operate equally on the choice of members of the other. There is so little of real utility in this mode that, if nothing more be done, it would be more expedient to choose all the members of the Legislature, without distinction, simply as members of the Legislature, and to make the division into two houses, either by lot, or otherwise, after these members, thus chosen, should have come up to the Capital.

I understand the reason of *checks* and *balances*, in the legis-

From *Journal*, pp. 305–315, 317–321.

lative power, to arise from the truth that, in representative governments, that department is the leading and predominating power; and if its will may be, at any time, suddenly and hastily expressed, there is great danger that it may overthrow all other powers. Legislative bodies naturally feel strong, because they are numerous, and because they consider themselves as the immediate representatives of the people. They depend on public opinion to sustain their measures, and they undoubtedly possess great means of influencing public opinion. With all the guards which can be raised by constitutional provisions, we are not likely to be too well secured against cases of improper, or hasty, or intemperate legislation. It may be observed, also, that the executive power, so uniformly the object of jealousy to republics, has become, in the states of this Union, deprived of the greatest part, both of its importance and its splendor, by the establishment of the general government. While the states possessed the power of making war and peace, and maintained military forces by their own authority, the power of the state executives was very considerable, and respectable. It might then even be an object, in some cases, of a just and warrantable jealousy. But a great change has been wrought. The care of foreign relations, the maintenance of armies and navies, and their command and control, have devolved on another government. Even the power of appointment, so exclusively, one would think, an executive power, is, in very many of the states, held or controlled by the legislature; that department either making the principal appointments, itself, or else surrounding the chief executive magistrate with a council of its own election, possessing a negative upon his nominations.

Nor has it been found easy, nor in all cases possible, to preserve the judicial department from the progress of legislative encroachment. Indeed, in some of the states all judges are appointed by the legislature; in others, although appointed by the executive, they are removable at the pleasure of the legislature. In all, the provision for their maintenance is necessarily to be made by the legislature. As if Montesquieu had never demonstrated the necessity of separating the departments of government; as if Mr. Adams had not done the same thing, with equal ability, and more clearness, in his defence of the American Constitution; as if the sentiments of Mr. Hamilton and Mr. Madison were already forgotten; we see, all around us, a tendency to extend the legislative power over the proper sphere of the other departments. And as the legislature, from the very nature of things, is the most powerful department, it becomes necessary to provide, in the mode of forming it, some check which shall ensure deliberation and caution in its measures. If all legislative power rested in one house, it is very problematical, whether any proper independence could be given, either to the executive or the judiciary. Experience does not speak encouragingly on that point. If we look through the several constitutions of the states, we shall perceive that generally the departments are most distinct and independent, where the legislature is composed of two houses, with equal authority, and mutual checks. If all legislative power be in one popular body, all other power, sooner or later, will be there also.

I wish now, sir, to correct a most important mistake, in the manner in which this question has been stated. It has been said, that we propose to give to property, merely as such, a control over the people numerically considered. But this I take not to be at all the true nature of the proposition. The senate is not to be a check on the *people*, but on the *house of representatives*. It is the case of an authority, given to *one* agent, to check or control the acts of *another*. The people, having conferred on the house of representatives, powers which are great, and, from their nature, liable to abuse, require for their own security another house, which shall possess an effectual negative on the first. This does not limit the power of the people; but only the authority of their agents. It is not a restraint on their rights, but a restraint on that power which they have delegated. It limits the authority of agents, in making laws to bind their principles. And if it be wise to give one agent the power of checking or controlling another, it is equally wise, most manifestly, that there should be some difference of character, sentiment, feeling, or origin, in that agent, who is to possess this control. Otherwise, it is not at all probable that the control will ever be exercised. To require the consent of two agents to the validity of an act, and yet to appoint agents so similar, in all respects, as to create a moral certainty that what one does the other will do also, would be inconsistent and nugatory. There can be no effectual control without some difference of origin, or character, or interest, or feeling, or sentiment. And the great question, in this country, has been, where to find, or how to create this difference, in governments entirely elective and popular? Various modes have been attempted, in various states. In some, a difference of qualification has been required, in the persons to be elected. This obviously produces little or no effect. All property qualification, even the highest, is so low as to produce no exclusion, to any extent, in any of the states. A difference of age, in the persons elected, is sometimes required; but this is found to be equally unimportant. It has not happened, either, that any consideration of the relative rank of the members of the two houses has had much effect on the character of their constituent members. Both in the state governments, and in the United States government, we daily see persons elected into the house of representatives who have been members of the senate. Public opinion does not attach so much weight and importance to the distinction, as to lead individuals greatly to regard it. In some of the states, a different sort of qualification in the electors is required, for the two houses; and this is probably the most proper and efficient check. But such has not been the provision in this Commonwealth, and there are strong objections to introducing it. In other cases, again, there is a double election for senators; electors being first chosen, who elect senators. Such is the constitution of Maryland; in which the senators are elected, for five years, by electors, appointed in equal numbers by the counties; a mode of election not unlike that of choosing representatives in Parliament for the boroughs of Scotland. In this State the qualification of the voters is the same, and there is no essential difference in that of the persons chosen. But, in apportioning the senate to the different districts of the State, the present constitution assigns to each district, a number proportioned to its public taxes. Whether this be the best mode of producing a difference in the construction of the two houses, is not now the question; but the question is, whether this be better than no mode.

The gentleman from Roxbury [Mr. Dearborn] called for authority on this subject. He asked what writer of reputation had approved the principle for which we contend. I should hope, sir, that even if this call could not be answered, it would not necessarily follow that the principle should be expunged. Governments are instituted for practical benefit, not for subjects of speculative reasoning merely. The best authority for the support of a particular principle or provision in government, is experience; and, of all experience, our own, if it have been long enough to give the principle a fair trial, should be most decisive. This provision has existed for forty years; and while so many gentlemen contend that it is wrong in theory, no one has shown that it has been either injurious or inconvenient in practice. No one pretends that it has caused a bad law to be enacted or a good one to be rejected. To call on us, then, to strike out this provision, because we should be able to find no authority for it in any book on government, would seem to be like requiring a mechanic to abandon the use of an implement, which had always answered all the purposes designed by it, because he could find no model of it in the patent office.

But, sir, I take the *principle* to be well established by writers of the greatest authority. In the first place, those who have treated of natural law have maintained, as a principle of that law, that, as far as the object of society is the protection of something in which the members possess unequal shares, it is just that the weight of each person in the common councils, should bear a relation and proportion to his interest. Such is the sentiment of Grotius, and he refers, in support of it, to several institutions among the ancient states.

Those authors, who have written more particularly on the subject of political institutions, have, many of them, maintained similar sentiments. Not, indeed, that every man's power should be in exact proportion to his property, but that, in a general sense, and in a general form, property, as such, should have its weight and influence in political arrangement. Montesquieu speaks, with approbation, of the early Roman regulation, made by Servius Tullius,[7] by which the people were distributed into classes according to their property, and the public burdens apportioned to each individual, according to the degree of power which he possessed in the government. By which regulation, he observes, some bore with the greatness of their tax, because of their proportionable participation in power and credit; others consoled themselves for the smallness of their power and credit, by the smallness of their tax. One of the most ingenious of political writers is Mr. Harrington,[8] an author not now read so much as he deserves. It is his leading object, in his "Oceana," to prove, that power *naturally* and *necessarily* follows property. He maintains that a government, founded on property, is legitimately founded; and that a government founded on the disregard of property is founded in injustice, and can only be maintained by military force. "If one man," says he, "be sole landlord, like the grand seignior,

---

[7] Sixth king of Rome (578–535 B.C.), reputedly a liberal constitutional monarch [Ed.].

[8] James Harrington (1611–1677), author of *Oceana* (1656), a republican political utopia [Ed.].

his empire is absolute. If a few possess the land, this makes
the gothic or feudal constitution. If the *whole* people be landlords, then is it a Commonwealth." "It is strange," says
Mr. Pope,[9] in one of his recorded conversations, "that Harrington should be the first man to find out so evident and
demonstrable a truth, as that of property being the true basis
and *measure* of power." In truth he was not the first: the idea
is as old as political science itself. It may be found in Aristotle,
Lord Bacon, Sir Walter Raleigh, and other writers. Harrington
seems, however, to be the first writer who has illustrated and
expanded the principle, and given to it the effect and prominence which justly belong to it. To this sentiment, sir, I entirely agree. It seems to me to be plain, that, in the absence
of military force, political power naturally and necessarily goes
into the hands which hold the property. In my judgment,
therefore, a republican form of government rests not more on
political constitutions than on those laws which regulate the
descent and transmission of property. Governments like ours
could not have been maintained, where property was holden
according to the principles of the feudal system; nor, on the
other hand, could the feudal constitution possibly exist with
us. Our New England ancestors brought hither no great capi-
tals from Europe; and if they had, there was nothing productive
in which they could have been invested. They left behind
them the whole feudal system of the other continent. They
broke away at once from that system of military service, established in the dark ages, and which continues, down even to the
present time, more or less to affect the condition of property
all over Europe. They came to a new country. There were, as
yet, no lands yielding rent, and no tenants rendering service.
The whole soil was unreclaimed from barbarism. They were,
themselves, either from their original condition, or from the
necessity of their common interest, nearly on a general level

---

[9] Alexander Pope (1688–1744), English poet and satirist [Ed.].

in respect to property. Their situation demanded a parcelling out and division of the lands; and it may be fairly said, that this necessary act *fixed the future frame and form of their government.* The character of their political institutions was determined by the fundamental laws respecting property. The laws rendered estates divisible among sons and daughters. The right of primogeniture, at first limited and curtailed, was afterwards abolished. The property was all freehold. The entailment of estates, long trusts, and the other processes for fettering and tying up inheritances, were not applicable to the condition of society, and seldom made use of. On the contrary, alienation of the land was every way facilitated, even to the subjecting of it to every species of debt. The establishment of public registries, and the simplicity of our forms of conveyance, have greatly facilitated the change of real estate from one proprietor to another. The consequence of all these causes has been, a great subdivision of the soil, and a great equality of condition; the true basis, most certainly, of a popular government. "If the people," says Harrington, "hold three parts in four of the territory, it is plain there can neither be any single person nor nobility able to dispute the government with them; in this case, therefore, *except force be interposed,* they govern themselves." . . .

. . . The true principle of a free and popular government would seem to be, so to construct it as to give to all, or at least to a very great majority, an interest in its preservation; to found it, as other things are founded, on men's interest. The stability of government requires that those who desire its continuance should be more powerful than those who desire its dissolution. This power, of course, is not always to be measured by mere numbers. Education, wealth, talents, are all parts and elements of the general aggregate of power. But numbers, nevertheless, constitute ordinarily, the most important consideration, unless indeed there be a *military force* in the hands of the few, by which they can control the many. In this country,

we have actual existing systems of government, in the protection of which it would seem a great majority, both in numbers and in other means of power and influence, must see their
interest. But this state of things is not brought about merely
by written political constitutions, or the mere manner of organizing the government; but also by the laws which regulate the
descent and transmission of property. The freest government,
if it could exist, would not be long acceptable, if the tendency
of the laws were to create a rapid accumulation of property
in few hands, and to render the great mass of the population
dependent and penniless. In such a case the popular power
must break in upon the rights of property, or else the influence
of property must limit and control the exercise of popular
power. Universal suffrage, for example, could not long exist in
a community where there was great inequality of property.
The holders of estates would be obliged in such case, either
in some way to restrain the right of suffrage, or else such right
of suffrage would ere long divide the property. In the nature
of things, those who have not property, and see their neighbors possess much more than they think them to need, cannot
be favorable to laws made for the protection of property. When
this class becomes numerous, it grows clamorous. It looks on
property as its prey and plunder, and is naturally ready, at all
times, for violence and revolution.

It would seem, then, to be the part of political wisdom to
found government on property; and to establish such distribution of property, by the laws which regulate its transmission
and alienation, as to interest the great majority of society in
the protection of the government. This is, I imagine, the true
theory and the actual practice of our republican institutions.
With property divided, as we have it, no other government than
that of a republic could be maintained, even were we foolish
enough to desire it. There is reason, therefore, to expect a long
continuance of our systems. Party and passion, doubtless, may
prevail at times, and much temporary mischief be done. Even

modes and forms may be changed, and perhaps for the worse. But a great revolution in regard to property must take place, before our governments can be moved from their republican basis, unless they be violently struck off by military power. The people possess the property, more emphatically than it could ever be said of the people of any other country, and they can have no interest to overturn a government which protects that property by equal laws.

If the nature of our institutions be to found government on property, and that it should look to those who hold property for its protection, it is entirely just that property should have its due weight and consideration in political arrangements. Life and personal liberty are, no doubt, to be protected by law; but property is also to be protected by law, and is the fund out of which the means for protecting life and liberty are usually furnished. We have no experience that teaches us, that any other rights are safe, where property is not safe. Confiscation and plunder are generally, in revolutionary commotions, not far before banishment, imprisonment and death. It would be monstrous to give even the name of government, to any association, in which the rights of property should not be competently secured. The disastrous revolutions which the world has witnessed; those political thunder-storms and earth-quakes which have overthrown the pillars of society from their very deepest foundations, have been revolutions *against property*. Since the honorable member from Quincy (President [John] ADAMS) has alluded, on this occasion, to the history of the ancient states, it would be presumption, in me, to dwell upon it. It may be truly said, however, I think, that Rome herself is an example of the mischievous influence of the popular power, when disconnected with property, and in a corrupt age. It is true, the arm of Caesar prostrated her liberty; but Caesar found his support within her very walls. Those who were profligate, and necessitous, and factious, and desperate, and capable, therefore, of being influenced by bribes and largesses, which were distributed with the utmost prodigality, outnumbered and outvoted, in the tribes and centuries, the substantial, sober, prudent and faithful citizens. Property was in the hands of one description of men, and power in those of another; and the balance of the constitution was destroyed. Let it never be forgotten that it was the popular magistrates, elevated to office where the bad outnumbered the good, where those who had no stake in the Commonwealth, by clamor, and noise, and numbers, drowned the voice of those who had, that laid the neck of Rome at the foot of her conqueror. When Caesar, manifesting a disposition to march his army into Italy, approached that little stream, which has become so memorable from its association with his character and conduct, a decree was proposed in the senate, declaring him a public enemy, if he did not disband his troops. To this decree the popular tribunes, the sworn protectors of the people, interposed their negative; and thus opened the high road of Italy, and the gates of Rome herself, to the approach of her conqueror. . . .

. . . I will now proceed to ask, sir, whether we have not seen, and whether we do not at this moment see, the advantage and benefit of giving security to property by this and all other reasonable and just provisions? The constitution has stood, on its present basis, forty years. Let me ask, what state has been more distinguished for wise and wholesome legislation? I speak, sir, without the partiality of a native, and also without intending the compliment of a stranger; and I ask, what example have we had of better legislation? No violent measures, affecting property, have been attempted. Stop-laws, suspension laws, tender laws, all the tribe of those arbitrary and tyrannical interferences between creditor and debtor which, wheresoever practised, generally end in the ruin of both, are strangers to our statute book. An upright and intelligent judiciary has come in aid of wholesome legislation; and general security for public and private rights has been the result. I do not say that this is peculiar, I do not say that others have not done as well.

It is enough, that in these respects we shall be satisfied that we are not behind our neighbors. No doubt, sir, there are benefits of every kind, and of great value, in possessing a character of government, both in legislative and judicial administration, which secures well the rights of property; and we should find it so, by unfortunate experience, should that character be lost. There are millions of personal property now in this Commonwealth, which are easily transferable, and would be instantly transferred elsewhere, if any doubt existed of its entire security. I do not know how much of this stability of government and of the general respect for it, may be fairly imputed to this particular mode of organizing the senate. It has, no doubt, had some effect. It has shown a respect for the rights of property, and may have operated on opinion, as well as upon measures. Now to strike out and obliterate it, as it seems to me, would be in a high degree unwise and improper.

As to the *right* of apportioning senators upon this principle, I do not understand how there can be a question about it. All government is a modification of general principles and general truths, with a view to practical utility. Personal liberty, for instance, is a clear right, and is to be provided for; but it is not a clearer right than the right of property, though it may be more important. It is therefore entitled to protection. But property is also to be protected; and when it is remembered how great a portion of the people of this State possess property, I cannot understand how its protection or its influence is hostile to their rights and privileges. . . .

. . . It is necessary here, sir, to consider the manner of electing representatives in this Commonwealth as heretofore practised, the necessity which exists of reducing the present number of representatives, and the propositions which have been submitted for that purpose. Representation by towns or townships, (as they might have been originally more properly called) is peculiar to New England. It has existed, however, since the first settlement of the country. These local districts are so small,

and of such unequal population, that if every town is to have
one representative, and larger towns as many more as their
population, compared with the smallest town, would numerically entitle them to, a very numerous body must be the
consequence, in any large state. Five hundred members, I
understand, may now be constitutionally elected to the house
of representatives; the very statement of which number shows
the necessity of reduction. I agree, sir, that this is a very difficult subject. Here are three hundred towns, all possessing the
right of representation; and representation by towns, is an
ancient habit of the people. For one, I am disposed to preserve
this mode, so far as may be practicable. There is always an
advantage in making the revisions which circumstances may
render necessary, in a manner which does no violence to
ancient habits and established rules. I prefer, therefore, a
representation by towns, even though it should necessarily be
somewhat numerous, to a division of the State into new districts, the parts of which might have little natural connection
or little actual intercourse with one another. But I ground my
opinion in this respect on fitness and expediency, and the
sentiments of the people; not on absolute right. The town corporations, simply as such, cannot be said to have any *right* to
representation; except so far as the constitution creates such
right. And this I apprehend to be the fallacy of the argument
of the hon. member from Worcester [Mr. Lincoln]. He con-
tends, that the smallest town has a *right* to its representative.
This is true; but the largest town (Boston) has a *right* also to
fifty. These rights are precisely equal. They stand on the same
ground, that is, on the provisions of the existing constitution.
The hon. member thinks it quite just to reduce the right of the
large town from fifty to ten, and yet that there is no power to
affect the right of the small town; either by uniting it with
another small town, for the choice of a representative, or otherwise. But I do not assent to that opinion. If it be right to take
away half, or three fourths of the representation of the large

towns, it cannot be right to leave that of the small towns undiminished. The report of the committee proposes that these small towns shall elect a member every other year, half of them sending one year, and half the next; or else that two small towns shall unite and send one member every year. There is something apparently irregular and anomalous in sending a member every other year; yet, perhaps, it is no great departure from former habits; because these small towns being, by the present constitution, compelled to pay their own members, have not, ordinarily, sent them oftener, on the average, than once in two years.

The honorable member from Worcester founds his argument on the *right* of town corporations, as such, to be represented in the Legislature. If he only means that right which the constitution at present secures, his observation is true, while the constitution remains unaltered. But if he intend to say that such right exists, *prior* to the constitution, and independent of it, I ask whence it is derived? Representation of the PEOPLE has heretofore been by towns, because such a mode has been thought convenient. Still it has been the representation of the people. It is no *corporate right* to partake in the sovereign power and form a part of the Legislature. To establish this right, as a corporate right, the gentleman has enumerated the *duties* of the town corporation; such as the maintenance of public worship, public schools, and public highways; and insists that the performance of these duties gives the town a right to a representative in the Legislature. But I would ask, sir, what possible ground there is for this argument? The burden of these duties falls not on any corporate funds belonging to the towns, but on the people, under assessments made on them individually, in their town meetings. As distinct from their individual *inhabitants*, the towns have no interest in these affairs. These duties are imposed by general laws; they are to be performed by the people, and if the people are represented in the making of these laws, the object is answered, whether they should be represented in one mode or another. But, further, sir; are these municipal duties rendered to the State, or are they not rather performed by the people of the towns for their own benefit? The general treasury derives no supplies from all these contributions. If the towns maintain religious instruction, it is for the benefit of their own inhabitants. If they support schools, it is for the education of the children of their inhabitants; and if they maintain roads and bridges, it is also for their own convenience. And therefore, sir, although I repeat that for reasons of expediency, I am in favor of maintaining town representation, as far as it can be done with a proper regard to equality of representation, I entirely disagree to the notion, that every town has a *right,* which an alteration of the constitution cannot divest, if the general good require such alteration, to have a representative in the Legislature. The honorable member has declared that we are about to *disfranchise* corporations, and destroy chartered rights. He pronounces this system of representation an outrage, and declares that we are forging *chains and fetters* for the people of Massachusetts. "Chains and fetters!" This Convention of delegates, chosen by the people, within this month, and going back to the people, divested of all power within another month, yet occupying their span of time here, in forging chains and fetters for themselves and their constituents! "Chains and fetters!" A popular assembly of four hundred men, by combining to fabricate these manacles for the people, and nobody, but the honorable member from Worcester, with sagacity enough to detect the horrible conspiracy, or honesty enough to disclose it! "Chains and fetters!" An assembly most variously composed; men of all professions, and all parties; of different ages, habits and associations—all freely and recently chosen by their towns and districts; yet this assembly, in one short month, contriving to fetter and enslave itself and its constituents! Sir, there are some things too extravagant for the ornament and decoration of oratory; some things too excessive, even for the fictions of poetry; and I am persuaded that a little reflection would satisfy the honorable member, that when he speaks of this assembly as committing outrages on the rights of the people, and as forging chains and fetters for their subjugation, he does as great injustice to his own character as a correct and manly debater, as he does to the motives and the intelligence of this body.

I do not doubt, sir, that some inequality exists in the mode of representatives proposed by the committee. A precise and exact equality is not attainable, in any mode. Look to the gentleman's own proposition. By that, Essex, with twenty thousand inhabitants more than Worcester, would have twenty representatives less. Suffolk, which according to numbers would be entitled to twenty, would have, if I mistake not, eight or nine only. Whatever else, sir, this proposition may be a specimen of, it is hardly a specimen of equality. As to the house of representatives, my view of the subject is this. Under the present constitution the towns have all a right to send representatives to the Legislature, in a certain fixed proportion to their numbers. It has been found, that the full exercise of this right fills the house of representatives with too numerous a body. What then is to be done? Why, sir, the delegates of the towns are here assembled, to agree, mutually, on some reasonable mode of reduction. Now, sir, it is not for one party to stand sternly on its right, and demand all the concession from another. As to right, all are equal. The right which *Hull* possesses to send one, is the same as the right of *Boston* to send fifty. Mutual concession and accommodation, therefore, can alone accomplish the purpose of our meeting. If Boston consents, instead of fifty, to send but twelve or fifteen, the small towns must consent, either to be united in the choice of their representatives with other small towns, or to send a representative less frequently than every year; or to have an option to do one or the other of these, hereafter, as shall be found most convenient. This is what the report of the committee proposes, and, as far as we have yet learned, a great majority of the delegates from small towns approve the plan. I am willing, therefore, to vote for this part of the report of the committee; thinking it as just and fair a representation, and as much reduced in point of numbers, as can be reasonably hoped for, without giving up entirely the system of representation by towns. It is to be considered also, that according to the report of the committee, the pay of the members is to be out of the public treasury. Every body must see how this will operate on the large towns. Boston, for example, with its twelve or fourteen members, will pay for fifty. Be it so; it is incident to its property, and not at all an injustice, if proper weight be given to that property, and proper provision be made for its security. . . .

9. "Address to the People"

When the convention finally approved of the fourteen amendments it also adopted an "Address to the People" that had been drafted by a committee especially appointed for the purpose. The document, only parts of which are given below, helps to reveal the spirit of the convention as well as to explain and justify in summary form the amendments proposed to the people.

FELLOW-CITIZENS,

It was provided in the constitution, established in the year one thousand seven hundred and eighty, that revision might be had, after an experiment of fifteen years. When these years had elapsed, the people declared that they were satisfied; and

From *Journal*, pp. 622–632.

that they desired no change. The same satisfaction was manifested during the next twenty-five years, and would probably have still continued, if the separation of Maine from Massachusetts had not made it proper to take the opinion of the people on the expediency of calling a *Convention*.

It appeared that not one *fourth part* of the qualified voters in the State saw fit to express any opinion; and that of the eighteen thousand three hundred and forty-nine votes given in, six thousand five hundred and ninety-three were *against* a revision.

We have inferred from these facts, that you did not desire any important and fundamental changes in your frame of government; and this consideration has had its just influence on our deliberations, in revising every part of the constitution, which we were required to do, by the words of the law, under which we are assembled.

We have kept in view that the will of the majority can alone determine what the powers of government shall be, and also the manner in which these powers shall be exercised; and that it is, consequently, your *exclusive* right to decide, whether all, or any of the amendments, which we think expedient, shall be adopted or rejected.

In the performance of our duty, we have been mindful of the character of MASSACHUSETTS; and, that the profit of *experience* is justly valued, and that the precious right of self-government is well understood in this community. Perfect unanimity is not to be expected in a numerous assembly. Whatever difference of opinion may have occurred as to expediency, there has been no difference as to the ultimate object, viz., the public security and welfare. If we have not all agreed in every measure which we recommend, we are satisfied, that natural, and honest difference of opinion, must ever prevent, in a like numerous meeting, greater accordance than has prevailed among us.

Every proposed change or amendment has been patiently

and fairly examined, and has been decided upon with the utmost care and solicitude to do right.

We have the fullest confidence that you will take these things into view, when you perform the serious duty of deciding, for yourselves, and for successive generations, on the result of our efforts.

In framing a constitution, or revising one, for an extensive Commonwealth, in which various interests are comprised, nothing more can be hoped for, than to establish general rules, adapted to secure the greatest good for the whole society. The revised constitution, which we now respectfully submit to you, can only be considered as one general law, composed of connected and dependent parts. If any one part, considered by itself, seem not to be the best that could be, its merit and the justice of its claim to approbation can be known only by its connection in the system to which it appertains.

With these remarks we beg leave to state the amendments which we have agreed on, and our reasons for having done so.

The Declaration of Rights.

It is known to us, that the eminent men who framed the constitution under which we have lived bestowed on the only article of the declaration of rights, which has occasioned much discussion among us, the greatest attention. They appear to have considered religion in a twofold view; first, as directory to every rational being, in the duties which he owes to the Creator of the universe; but leaving to every one to decide for himself, on the manner in which he shall render his homage, avow his dependence, express his gratitude, and acknowledge his accountability; and, secondly, as a social duty, prescribing rules to men in their intercourse with each other as members of the same family. They held social worship to be most intimately connected with social welfare. They believed moral excellence to be no less the effect of example, and of habit, than of precept. They seem to have been convinced, that in proportion as the members of civil society are impressed with reverence for the social rules contained in revealed religion, will they be faithful in performing those obligations on which political happiness depends. Upon such principles they rested those provisions which require an habitual observance of the Sabbath, and the support of public teachers in the sacred offices of that day. In all these sentiments we do most heartily concur.

But we have thought it necessary to propose some changes in the third article.

The public sentiment on that part of the article which invests the Legislature with authority to enjoin attendance on public worship, has long been definitely expressed, and is well understood; and we, therefore, propose that so much of this article as relates to this subject, should be annulled.

We are also of opinion that members of all religious societies ought to have the right and privilege to join, and worship with, any other society of the same denomination; as they now have the right to join themselves to any society, of a different denomination from that with which they have worshipped;— furthermore, that the power and duty of the Legislature to require provision to be made for the institution of public worship, and for the support and maintenance of public teachers, should extend, and be applied as well to societies which are unincorporated, as to those which are incorporated.

We recommend also, a provision, that all taxes assessed for the support of public worship, upon real estate of any nonresident proprietor, shall be applied towards the support of public worship in the town, precinct, or parish, by which such taxes are assessed; unless such proprietor shall be resident within the Commonwealth, and shall be of a different denomination of Christians from that of the town, precinct, or parish, by which such taxes are assessed.

We propose further to amend the declaration of rights, so as to provide, that persons on trial for crimes may be heard by themselves *and* counsel, instead of themselves *or* counsel, as the article now stands.

We propose another amendment, that no person shall suffer imprisonment, or other ignominious punishment, on official information; nor unless on indictment by grand jury; except in cases expressly provided for by law. This amendment takes from public prosecutors the common law right to arraign, of their own authority, any citizen for misdemeanors, or crimes, without the intervention of a grand jury representing the people of each county. . . .

ELECTORS.

. . . We are satisfied that the qualifications as now required in *electors,* produce some inconveniences, and are liable to some abuses. After a patient investigation of this subject, we have concluded that a residence of *twelve months* within the State, and of *six months* in a town, or district, next preceding an election, and payment of a state or county tax, in the Commonwealth, constitute a uniform and intelligible rule, as to the right of voting; and we propose the adoption of this rule, in all elections of State officers, and the abolition of all other qualifications now required.

We believe that the change, which we recommend in this respect, will relieve *selectmen* from much perplexity, and will enable them easily to distinguish between those who have a right to vote, and those who have not.

THE SENATE.

After the most careful and faithful examination of the principles of government, we have not found it expedient to change the basis on which the *senate* was placed, by the constitution which we have revised. It is an admitted principle, that the legislative power should be given to *two distinct assemblies,* each having an absolute negative on the other.

In considering this subject, we have distinguished between THE PEOPLE, of whom we are ourselves a part, and those who may be chosen *to legislate*. It is the *people* who are to be secured, in their rights and privileges, by a constitution, and not their *public servants*. This object can only be effected by a clear and permanent limitation of the power which is to be exercised.

The PEOPLE may impart whatsoever power they see fit. Their security consists in doing this in such manner, that the trust which they create may not be abused, nor the public welfare betrayed. It is therefore wise to provide for frequent elections; and to require certain qualifications in the elected; and the concurrence of different legislative branches on all public laws; and so to constitute those branches, as that no act shall obtain their joint approbation, which is not intended to promote the common welfare.

All free governments of modern times have found it indispensable, not only to have two distinct legislative branches, but to place them on such different foundations as to preclude, as much as possible, all such dangerous sympathy and union, as may govern and direct the will of a single assembly.

If the number of inhabitants be the rule by which the members of the two branches are to be apportioned, and all are to be chosen at the same time, and by the same electors, we think that the safety which the constitution is intended to effect, may not, always, be obtained. If an election should take place when very strong and general excitements are felt, (and from such, no human society can be always exempt) there would be little to choose between placing legislators so elected in the same, or in two different assemblies.

We repeat that the people's agents ought ever to be distinguished, in settling a frame of government, from the people themselves; and that no more should be hazarded on the manner in which power may be used, than necessarily must be, to give power enough to do that which should be done.

The mode in which the two branches should be constituted, to secure the check which we consider to be so highly important, is the only point, as to the senate, which has been much discussed among us.

In some of the states in our national confederacy, elections for two or more years have been adopted, as a security for the independence and fidelity of senators. In others of them, a senator must have a large landed estate; in others, such an estate is a required qualification in electors; and in some, a landed estate is required, both in the elector and the senator.

The basis adopted in the constitution of this State is, that senators shall be apportioned, throughout the State, according to the amount of public taxes paid in districts of the State. That is, that the liability to be taxed, shall be accompanied by the right to be represented. We have not heard that this principle has been complained of by the people; nor do we believe it is justly exceptionable, in itself; on the contrary, the experience of forty years entitles it to the most entire respect and confidence. We have not thought it expedient, nor do we believe that you expected of us, to make any fundamental change in this department. We have done no more than to make the necessary provisions as to districts, and to fix the number of senators. We recommend that the number should be thirty-six; this number can be more conveniently distributed than any other throughout the State. A smaller number is not sufficient to perform the duty required of the senate; nor should the power of negativing the will of the house of representatives, be confided to a smaller number.

The House of Representatives.

We have found great difficulty in amending the representative system in a satisfactory manner. We have all agreed, that whether the representatives are few, or many, representation should be according to population, in this branch. It was the general opinion, that the number should be reduced; that town representation should be preserved; that payment should be made from the State treasury. Such mode of payment has been repeatedly voted in the house, and on one occasion it obtained the concurrence of the senate. There is reason to believe that it will become the established mode of payment. But if it be so, and the present system of representation continues, the expense must soon become an insupportable burthen. A house composed of one hundred or one hundred and fifty members, may be fully sufficient for all purposes of legislation; but so great a reduction could not be made without dividing the State into districts, and consequently giving up representation by towns.

We endeavored in the system which we submit to you— 1. To reduce the number; 2. To preserve the privileges of town representation; 3. To provide for payment out of the State treasury; 4. To insure a general and constant attendance of the members throughout the session.

To accomplish these objects, we recommend that twelve hundred inhabitants should have one representative, and that twenty-four hundred be the mean increasing number for every additional representative.

But as nearly one half of the towns in the State contain on an average about eight hundred inhabitants, we propose that these towns should each choose a representative every other year, and that they should be divided, by the Legislature, into two classes for this purpose; one or the other of which classes will choose every year.

To show the application of this system; about seventy-four representatives will come every year, from the classed towns, which will be one representative for every 1632 inhabitants in all the classed towns; from those towns containing between twelve hundred and twenty-four hundred, will come one representative for every 1650 inhabitants; from those towns containing more than thirty-six hundred inhabitants will come one representative for every 2400 inhabitants. These calculations, (necessarily taken from the census of the year 1810) are not precisely accurate; but they are sufficiently so to show the effect of the system.

It is apparent that towns having between twelve hundred and thirty-six hundred inhabitants, can send but one representative; and that there will be large fractions in some of these towns. Perfect equality is not attainable under any system. There are fewer inequalities in the proposed system, than in any which we have been able to form, if the four objects which we have mentioned are to be provided for; and we believe that the progress of population will constantly diminish those inequalities which may now exist.

We propose that in those years in which the valuation is settled, every town shall be represented.

By the proposed system the number of representatives will be about two hundred and sixty. We have thought it proper to offer to you further provisions, intended to prevent an increase, in the number of representatives, over two hundred and seventy-five, in any future time. This may easily be done, by empowering the Legislature to augment the ratio, after successive enumerations of the inhabitants. There was very little difference of opinion among us on the expediency of providing, that no town shall be hereafter incorporated with the right of sending a representative, unless it contain twenty-four hundred inhabitants.

If you are not willing to district the Commonwealth to elect members of the house; if you are not willing to continue the present mode of numerous representation, with the liability to the enormous expense which would accrue from paying out of the public treasury, some such system as we propose must be resorted to. We will not say that this is the best that could be; but we may justly say, that we have spared no exertion to form, and to present to you, the best which we could devise. . . .

THE JUDICIARY.

. . . In the judicial department, we think two amendments are expedient.

An independent judiciary is a fundamental principle of a free government. We cannot so well express our sentiments on this important subject, as by referring to the twenty-ninth article of the declaration of rights.

It is there said, "It is the right of every citizen to be tried by judges as free, impartial, and independent, as the lot of humanity will admit": and therefore, "that judges should hold their offices as long as they behave themselves well."

The judges have not such tenure of office, unless the constitution be understood to mean, that they are not liable to removal, until they have had an opportunity to show that the alleged causes for removal are unfounded, or insufficient. The Legislature, in removing a judge, exercises not only a discretionary, but a judicial power. Judgment cannot justly be given, in any case affecting any interest, even of the humblest citizen, unless the cause has been first stated, and it has been permitted to him to show, what he considers to be the truth of his case.

It cannot, then, be consistent with the plainest principles of justice, that the public functions of a citizen, and perhaps his reputation, may be taken from him, without any other notice from those who may exercise such power, than that they have exercised it, and that his relation to the public has ceased.

In whatever estimation we may hold the rights and interests of any individual who sustains a high judicial office, it is rather the public right and interest, which move us to propose the subjoined amendment.

The people can have no dearer interest in anything pertaining to government, than in the interpretation of the laws, and in the administration of justice, affecting life, liberty, property, and character. The constitution, with the explanatory amendment which we propose, secures to the people the unquestionable right of removing the unfit, the unworthy, and the corrupt; while it secures to them the no less valuable right of preserving to themselves, the able, the upright, and the independent magistrate.

We propose, therefore, so to amend the constitution as to require that no judicial officer shall be removed from office, until the alleged causes of removal are stated on the records of the Legislature; nor until the individual, thereby affected, shall have had an opportunity to be heard.

In the second article of the third chapter it is provided, that each branch of the Legislature, as well as the governor and council, shall have authority to require the opinion of the judges, on important questions of law, and upon solemn occasions. We think this provision ought not to be a part of the constitution; because, *First,* each department ought to act on its own responsibility. *Second.* Judges may be called on to give opinions on subjects, which may afterwards be drawn into judicial examination before them, by contending parties. *Third.* No opinion ought to be formed and expressed, by any judicial officer, affecting the interest of any citizen, but upon full hearing, according to law. *Fourth.* If the question proposed should be of a public nature, it will be likely to partake of a political character; and it highly concerns the people that judicial officers should not be involved in political or party discussions.

We, therefore, recommend that this second article should be annulled. . . .

HARVARD UNIVERSITY.

. . . We have thought it proper to inquire into the present state of this ancient and respectable institution, and have done this by the agency of a fully competent committee. We have made this inquiry, because this seminary has experienced the patronage of government from its earliest foundation; and was justly held to be worthy of appropriate constitutional provisions, by our predecessors. It appears that the powers conferred on Harvard University have always been exercised, and that the duties required of it have always been performed, with a sincere and ardent desire to promote the diffusion of useful knowledge; and to establish and preserve an honorable reputation in literature and morals in this community.

We have, however, thought it proper, with the consent and approbation of the corporation and overseers of the University, to propose to you, that the constitution should be so amended as to make ministers of the gospel, of any denomination, eligible to the office of overseers. . . .

PROVISION FOR FUTURE AMENDMENTS.

. . . It may be necessary, that specific amendments of the constitution should hereafter be made. The preparatory measures in assembling a Convention, and the necessary expense of such an assembly, are obstacles of some magnitude, to obtaining amendments through such means; we propose that whenever two thirds of the house of representatives, and a majority of the senate in two successive Legislatures, shall determine that any specific amendment of the constitution is expedient, such proposed amendment shall be submitted to the people; and if accepted by the people, the constitution shall be amended accordingly. We believe that the constitution will be sufficiently guarded from inexpedient alterations, while all those which are found to be necessary, will be duly considered and may be obtained with comparatively small expense. . . .

TABLE 1.1

The Massachusetts Counties in Relation to Legislative Representation

COUNTY	POPULATION, 1810	TAXES PAID*	NO. OF REPS. ON THE BASIS OF POPULATION†	NO. OF REPS. ON THE REVISED BASIS	APPORTIONMENT OF SENATORS†† PRESENT	REVISED
Suffolk	34,381	$21,023	19	14	6	6
Essex	72,888	18,421	39	32	6	6
Middlesex	52,789	11,344	28	33	5	4
Norfolk	36,245	6,692	20	18	2	3
Plymouth	35,169	5,931	19	18	3	2
Bristol	37,168	5,975	20	18	3	2
Barnstable	22,211	2,428	12	12 }	2	2
Dukes	3,290	476	2	2 }		
Nantucket	6,807	2,188	4	3		
Worcester	64,910	12,749	35	41	5	5
Hampshire	23,545	4,021	13	14 }	4	4
Hampden	24,423	3,915	14	15 }		
Franklin	28,307	4,031	15	16		
Berkshire	35,907	5,323	20	21	2	2
Totals	472,040	$104,517	260	257	38	36

* Estimated for 1820

† On 1810 census figures

†† Excluding the four seats that had belonged to counties in the District of Maine

TABLE 1.2

The Division of the Vote by Counties on Two Questions in the Massachusetts Convention

A. *Vote on the revised plan (the eighth resolution of the legislative committee) for the apportionment of representatives in the lower house, January 2, 1821.*

County	Yea	Nay
Suffolk	31	14
Essex	22	22
Middlesex	38	19
Norfolk	20	7
Plymouth	13	18
Bristol	7	18
Barnstable	9	4
Dukes & Nantucket	1	0
Worcester	35	22
Hampshire	14	5
Hampden	17	5
Franklin	20	3
Berkshire	15	8
Unaccounted for	3	2
Totals	245	147

B. *Vote on Childs's substitute amendment for the third and fourth articles of the declaration of rights, January 6, 1821.*

County	Yea	Nay
Suffolk	5	37
Essex	18	36
Middlesex	12	42
Norfolk	13	17
Plymouth	10	17
Bristol	17	7
Barnstable	3	9
Dukes & Nantucket	1	0
Worcester	24	32
Hampshire	1	14
Hampden	9	9
Franklin	5	15
Berkshire	17	9
Unaccounted for	1	2
Totals	136	246

DOCUMENT 10

Statement of the Votes For and Against the Articles of Amendment, in the Several Counties.

COUNTIES.	1.		2.		3.		4.		5.		6.		7.	
	YES.	NO.	YES.	NO.	YES.	NO.	YES.	NO.	YES.	NO.	YES.	NO.	YES.	NO.
Suffolk, - -	1786	908	1529	1158	258	108	2473	213	1659	1026	2562	121	1842	852
Essex, - -	1429	2138	1333	2284	1823	1562	1653	1720	491	3096	2245	1290	1388	2013
Middlesex,	1996	1877	1875	2055	2668	876	1520	2023	1481	2414	3030	723	1842	1583
Plymouth,	597	1645	617	1620	751	1100	432	1548	189	2198	962	899	502	1379
Bristol, - -	115	2015	387	1703	433	1530	168	1861	53	2147	429	1399	253	1595
Barnstable,	321	160	424	62	413	38	352	102	344	145	435	7	300	125
Dukes and Nantucket, -	153	68	151	44	75	14	169	23	140	43	171	15	149	39
Norfolk, -	920	1337	881	1379	1314	902	844	1402	786	1513	1209	1015	918	1260
Worcester,	1419	4094	2025	3600	2968	2214	2271	2748	1919	3442	3067	2065	2525	2323
Hampshire,	595	1297	1264	635	1280	553	1193	607	960	901	1052	755	1169	561
Hampden,	410	1036	756	705	769	551	649	661	259	1144	637	763	758	563
Franklin, -	657	1313	1299	675	1297	539	1177	595	938	932	1300	448	1170	526
Berkshire,	667	1659	1623	808	1578	720	1467	803	685	1728	1603	650	1358	698
Total, -	11,065	19,547	14,164	16,728	17,949	10,707	14,368	14,306	9,904	20,729	18,702	10,150	14,174	13,517

From *Journal*, pp. 633–634.

COUNTIES.	8.		9.		10.		11.		12.		13.		14.	
	YES.	NO.	YES.	NO.	YES.	NO.	YES.	NO.	YES.	NO.	YES.	NO.	YES.	NO.
Suffolk, - -	2445	241	1789	907	1433	1252	2528	140	2464	211	2585	95	2489	205
Essex, - - -	2342	1155	1172	2107	800	2660	1806	1549	1465	1852	1922	1415	1472	2062
Middlesex,	3455	465	1616	1542	1117	2346	2611	632	1953	1178	2592	597	2492	886
Plymouth,	1709	319	451	1247	274	1567	925	623	588	941	1039	514	780	892
Bristol, - -	735	1119	200	1638	133	1730	557	1264	369	1404	530	1197	674	1318
Barnstable,	438	2	336	50	207	211	374	4	285	25	387	2	363	54
Dukes and Nan-tucket, -	155	16	90	76	87	88	128	32	136	25	145	18	155	17
Norfolk, -	1727	543	890	1278	584	1651	1268	910	1081	1114	1371	803	857	1376
Worcester,	3895	1242	2310	2393	1472	3389	2807	1964	2252	2283	2811	1805	3106	1834
Hampshire,	1377	423	1106	600	386	1334	1038	566	571	1077	1035	542	1097	615
Hampden,	1128	240	454	848	422	905	812	436	540	640	779	436	834	399
Franklin, -	1430	318	1072	597	769	938	1156	509	918	735	1195	452	899	798
Berkshire,	189	361	985	1145	336	2057	1542	615	1160	995	1657	537	1107	1205
Total, -	22,726	6,444	12,471	14,518	8,020	20,123	17,552	9,244	13,782	12,480	18,048	8,412	16,325	11,661

RECAPITULATION.

		YEAS.	NAYS.	MAJORITY.
1.	Bill of Rights,	11,065	19,547	8,482 negative.
2.	Political Year,	14,164	16,728	2,564 negative.
3.	Governor's Negative,	17,949	10,707	7,242 affirmative.
4.	City Government,	14,368	14,306	62 affirmative.
5.	Senate and House,	9,904	20,729	10,825 negative.
6.	Qualification of Voters,	18,702	10,150	8,552 affirmative.
7.	Notaries, &c.,	14,174	13,577	657 affirmative.
8.	Militia Voters,	22,726	6,444	16,282 affirmative.
9.	Removal of Judges,	12,471	14,518	2,047 negative.
10.	Harvard College,	8,020	20,123	12,103 negative.
11.	Oath of Allegiance,	17,552	9,244	8,308 affirmative.
12.	Repeal of Test,	13,782	12,480	1,302 affirmative.
13.	Incompatibilities,	18,048	8,412	9,636 affirmative.
14.	Mode of Amendments,	16,325	11,661	4,664 affirmative.

II

THE NEW YORK CONVENTION

OF 1821

INTRODUCTION

In the first half-century of independence New York developed more rapidly than any of her sister states. When the Revolutionary constitution of 1777 was framed, two-thirds of the state's inhabitants lived on both sides of the Hudson River between Albany and New York City; by 1820 two-thirds of the people lived on lands farther west and north—the old Iroquois lands—reaching to the Great Lakes and the St. Lawrence River. With a population of one million four hundred thousand, four times the number in 1790, New York was the fastest growing, wealthiest, and most populous of the states. The city of New York, which had grown at the same rate, was already a "melting pot" and such a center of commercial, financial, and manufacturing enterprise that men were calling it the future London of America. To connect this metropolis with the vast agricultural interior, the state had embarked upon the most ambitious project of internal improvement yet undertaken in the United States, the Erie Canal.

This amazing progress produced havoc in the state government and made its defects painfully evident. The defects were inseparable from the constitution of 1777. Considering the condition of the state in 1777—hemmed in by the Indians in the west, occupied by the British in the south, everywhere harassed by Tories—it was perhaps remarkable that the Revolutionary convention, from its refuge in

125

Kingston, succeeded in framing any kind of constitution at all. The instrument adopted, though it contained liberal features, as in the provision for religious freedom and a bold experiment in ballot voting, reflected the conservative opinions of its framers, of whom the most important was John Jay. The constitution maintained the freehold franchise but lowered the qualification somewhat. Renters of tenements worth forty shillings annually, freeholders worth £20, and freemen—merchants, artisans, and the like—of the cities of Albany and New York made up the electorate for the assembly (house) of the state legislature. Only freeholders worth £100 voted for members of the senate and for governor. Representation in the two chambers was apportioned according to the number of electors of each found in the counties, for the assembly; and in the four great districts —Southern, Middle, Eastern, and Western—for the senate. An elected official for the term of three years and uninhibited in day-to-day operations by an executive council, the New York governor had greater power than most state executives. He was, of course, commander-in-chief of the military forces, and the convention sought to give him the necessary strength to wage the infant state's war for survival.

But in their effort to combat anarchy and defeat, the framers also wished to avoid the risk of falling back into monarchy. Two institutions of their devising were destined to cheapen the executive office and bring contempt upon every branch of the government. The first of these institutions, the Council of Revision, associated the governor with the chancellor—the state's judicial head with exclusive jurisdiction in cases of equity—and the judges of the supreme court in the exercise of a negative on the legislature. The council reviewed legislative bills and vetoed those it deemed "improper" on constitutional or other grounds. It therefore united two functions, judicial review and executive veto, which most states separated. Whatever its intent, whether to restrain the governor or to reinforce the check on the legislature, the Council of Revision placed the judiciary in the crossfire between the other two branches of the government and plunged the judges deep into politics. The arrangement flouted the principle of separation of powers and in time furnished seemingly irrefutable evidence of its wisdom. Even more damaging was the Council of Appointment, surely one of the worst political contrivances ever invented. Annually, at each session of the legislature, the assembly elected one senator from each district to sit with the governor, who presided and held the casting vote, for the purpose of filling all the offices not otherwise provided for. These were always numerous, and in an expanding state they multiplied like rabbits. In 1821 fifteen thousand offices, civil and military, were at the disposal of the Council of Appointment. Politics in New York, always tempestuous, degenerated into a scramble for offices and spoils. Of course, the ascendant party or coalition in the assembly controlled the council; and if the governor adhered to another allegiance, the political warfare became deadly earnest.

As long as the state was divided between two reasonably coherent parties contending for different principles and policies, the defects of the constitution were patiently borne. From the first, the constitution framed by conservatives fell into the hands of reputed democrats led by George Clinton. During his imposing reign of twenty-one years no effort was made to refashion the constitution in the image of democracy. His Republican followers continued, with brief interruptions and in the face of relentless Federalist opposition, to dominate the state during the Jeffersonian years. It was at this time that DeWitt Clinton, the old governor's nephew, aided by Ambrose Spencer, later a judge and then chief justice of the state supreme court, used the machinery of the Council of Appointment to entrench the spoils system in New York politics. A constitutional convention met in 1801; its powers were severely limited, however, and it did nothing more than confirm the authority of the Council of Revision and revise the number of senators and representatives. With the collapse of parties following the War of 1812, discipline and responsibility in affairs of state lost their precarious hold. Several competing factions intrigued and bargained for control of the government. In 1817 the old master at this game, DeWitt Clinton, rode into the governorship on his great project for the Erie Canal. He and his followers, though nominally Republican, were opposed by a strong and growing Republican faction, the Bucktails, led by young Martin Van Buren. Clinton drew to him the main body of Federalists, who held the balance of power between the Republican foes. Van Buren also wooed the old Federalists. In 1820 he successfully backed Rufus King for a second term as United States Senator and made an *ad hoc* alliance with a group of anti-Clintonian Federalists, the so-called high-mindeds, with the object of electing Daniel P. Tompkins, then Vice-President of the United States, governor of New York. Clinton won the contest, but the Bucktails took control of the legislature in the winter session of 1820–1821 and, of course, named their adherents to the Council of Appointment, which swept from office such prominent Federalist Clintonians as Stephen Van Rensselaer. At the same time, the Bucktails scored an impressive victory in the Republican caucus, dropping the incumbent United States Senator Nathan Sanford in favor of Van Buren. Finally, as part of this spirited campaign against the Clintonians, the Bucktails forced upon the unwilling governor and Council of Revision legislation calling for reform of the state constitution.

Constitutional reform was thus a stratagem of political warfare. The Bucktails cleverly seized upon a movement that had the force of democratic opinion behind it in order to rout the Clintonians and complete their triumph. As it happened, adroit political opportunism coincided with the compelling needs of the state for reform. The collisions and conflicts of parties had made the defects of the constitution intolerable. The Council of Appointment was a disgrace, a political guillotine that could make today's executioners tomorrow's victims. The judiciary, although one of the most distinguished in the United States, was controlled by a few deeply conservative judges who were also immersed in politics. The highly centralized government of the Revolutionary constitution would not do for the great, expanding, disparate society New York had become. As a result of the growth of New York City and the regions upstate, there was actually less democracy at the ballot box in 1820 than there had been several decades before. By contrast, the neighboring states of

Massachusetts and Connecticut, both recently reformed, were pure democracies.

These problems pointed up the need for a constitutional convention. The Bucktails accurately calculated the force behind the demand and brought it to fulfillment. A convention bill was introduced in the assembly in 1818. Distrusting its auspices, Clinton and his followers blocked it. Democratic Bucktails stepped up their agitation in the towns and countryside. The following year Clinton agreed to a convention limited to a revision of the appointive power. The Bucktails refused. When they gained control of the legislature in 1820, they passed a bill for an unrestricted convention. Now the Council of Revision imposed its negative, hoping to delay the inevitable until the political complexion of the legislature changed, but holding, with meticulous concern for the theory of constituent sovereignty, that the people, not the legislature, must call for a convention. The majority party complied and in March 1821 passed a new bill, reluctantly accepted by the Clintonians, providing for a convention upon approval of the electorate. For this referendum the electorate was to include not only freeholders but taxpayers, militiamen, and men who worked on the public roads. The vote on the convention question was, therefore, the most democratic in New York's history.

The people favored the convention by a majority of better than 3 to 1. In the Western District the margin was 10 to 1. Although somewhat lacking in geographical or political coherence, each of the state's four districts had a vaguely definable character. The Southern District embraced New York County—Manhattan—the surrounding boroughs, Long Island, one county lying west of the Hudson River—Rockland—and three—Westchester, Putnam, and Dutchess —on the eastern side between the river and the Connecticut line. This district furnished the smallest majority for the convention. It was, of course, the oldest part of the state, and, except for New York City, it had in earlier times been a Federalist stronghold. The Middle District embraced Albany and adjoining Columbia County—the main center of Federalist influence—and the country west of the

Hudson extending to the Delaware River and a little beyond, where Republicanism prevailed. The Eastern District ran from the counties at the eastern terminus of the projected Erie Canal northward through the Adirondack Mountains to Lake Champlain on the east and the St. Lawrence River on the northern frontier. Much of this was new, sparsely settled country—one county, Hamilton, numbered but thirteen hundred inhabitants. It was decidedly favorable to reform. The great panhandle of the state, lying on either side of the canal route between Lake Ontario and the Pennsylvania line, made up the Western District. Here were dozens of small towns with names—Utica, Rome, Syracuse, Cicero—suggestive of Roman ideals and ambitions. Many of the settlers were Yankees, from Connecticut mainly, unaccustomed to Yorker ways. Thousands of these upright, independent farmers lacked the franchise; they demanded it, together with greater autonomy in local affairs and a decentralized judicial system. Unlike some of the other coastal states with expanding western districts, Virginia, for example, equality of representation was not a problem in New York. The Erie Canal would spread its riches from Buffalo to Manhattan. No peculiar interests of the older areas demanded protection from growing western influence in state affairs. The entire state united in support of western development.

A total of 126 delegates were elected to the convention on the basis of representation in the assembly. A majority were farmers; the next largest occupational group consisted of lawyers; and there was a smattering of merchants, artisans, and physicians. Just over half were native-born Yorkers; thirty-six had come from Connecticut. All but a score of the delegates can be classified as reformers. Though they came in greater numbers from New York's new lands, they did not form a sectional bloc. On the contrary, the proceedings of the convention tended to bear out the absence of serious sectional discord in New York (see Table 2.1). Since parties were in a fluid, not to say chaotic state, the delegates cannot be classified on this basis. The convention was a Bucktail affair, but no more than in Massachusetts was it a contest between organized parties with coherent programs. Convention politics simply continued the factional strife, the incessant bargaining and maneuver and race for the spoils, that had character-ized New York politics for years. As the game was played out, how-ever, the delegates classified themselves into three fairly uniform opinion groups—conservative, radical, and moderate.

On the basis of roll-call votes on several key issues (see Table 2.2), nineteen of the delegates were conservatives. They opposed any tampering with the judicial establishment, sought to maintain a free-hold suffrage at least for senatorial electors, preferred to retain the triennial election of the governor, and so on. They monopolized the delegations of two counties, Columbia and Albany, each with four delegates. Their leaders were Chancellor James Kent, Chief Justice Ambrose Spencer, and his associates on the supreme-court bench, William W. Van Ness and Jonas Platt. Radicals smeared them with Federalist opprobrium and assailed their witness to the charge that a judicial aristocracy ruled in the government of New York. Several of their friends must have agreed with Rufus King's opinion that their participation in the convention mortally impaired their reputations and the cause they represented. Also in the conservative group were Elisha Williams and Jacob R. Van Rensselaer, leaders of the old anti-Jeffersonian Columbia Junto of the Jeffersonian years; Peter Jay, heir of John Jay; and the one-time Massachusetts Republican Ezekial Bacon.

The radical group consisted of twenty-five delegates. Van Buren referred to them as "Mad-caps . . . old democrats, who think nothing wise that is not violent and flatter themselves that they merit Knight-hood by assailing every thing that is memorable in old institutions." They advocated universal white manhood suffrage, annual election of the governor, abolition of the court of chancery, and overturn of the entire judicial establishment. Most of them were farmers, not lawyers; just under half were New England born; and ten came from the Western District. Chief of this group was General Erastus Root, the Republican leader of Delaware County, whose politics seemed to come straight from the Levellers of Cromwell's England. It was afterward said there were three parties in the convention—Federal-ists, Republicans, and Erastus Root. Quick, slashing, aggressive beyond any other man in the convention, Root was the scourge of the conservatives and the despair of the moderates. In this leadership he was ably assisted by Peter R. Livingston of Dutchess and Samuel Young of Saratoga County.

The overwhelming majority of the delegates—Clintonians, Bucktails, Tammanyites, high-mindeds, and others—represented the interests of moderate reform. If this mixed assemblage can be characterized in terms of any single individual, that individual was Martin Van Buren. He opposed the Federalist diehards on the right and the democratic radicals on the left. He wished to satisfy the public appetite for reform without endangering the interests of property, the judicial establishment, and the centralized control of the state's political machinery. His approach to all questions was pragmatic rather than doctrinaire. He was shrewd, charming, temperate, conciliatory—the very image of bland reasonableness—and had it not been for his influence the radicals would probably have carried everything before them. Van Buren's senatorial colleague, Rufus King, who was politically beholden to the Bucktail leader, exerted the same moderating influence on his conservative friends.

The delegates convened in the capitol at Albany on August 28, promptly elected Vice-President Tompkins to preside, and copied the procedure earlier employed in Massachusetts for discharging the business of the convention. The constitution was parceled out to ten committees, each of seven members appointed by the president. A veteran Republican leader, respected even by his enemies, Tompkins sought far-reaching reform and frequently sided with the radicals. He appointed radicals to chair two of the committees, moderates, eight. The committee on the Council of Revision, headed by James Tallmadge, was the first to report. Nearly everyone agreed on the committee's recommendation to abolish the council, but the radicals opposed the adoption, in place of the recommendation, of an executive veto subject to reversal by two-thirds of both chambers of the legislature—the provision of the federal Constitution and a growing number of states. They likened the executive check to monarchy.

They arraigned the high-handed conduct of the Council of Revision for its obstruction of measures for the prosecution of the War of 1812 and the rearrangement of senatorial districts, and so on. Viewing the legislature as the embodiment of the popular will, the radicals demanded the ascendancy of the legislative majority in the government. The moderates replied with a defense of balanced government, while the conservatives warned against "ambitious demagogues," "bold and rude reformers," in the legislative branch and, though making no case for saving the odious council, felt called upon to defend its conduct. A bitter partisan debate ensued on the role of the supreme judiciary and the merits of a body that everyone, including the judges, wished to abolish. After a four-day debate the radicals failed to win their point—a majority instead of a two-thirds vote to override the governor's veto—and the committee resolution was adopted.

The radicals voiced the fear of many delegates that in the reforms contemplated for the executive department, particularly with regard to the appointive power, the governor would indeed become a king. They took away the governor's power to prorogue the legislature and the customary privilege of annually addressing the legislature in person—an alleged "relic of monarchy." They assailed the governor's pardoning power. The committee recommended a two-year term for the governor. The radicals responded with the old Whig axiom: "Where annual elections end, tyranny begins." In this, as in other matters, they were influenced by New England laws and traditions, especially those of Connecticut, which in its constitution of 1818 held the governor accountable to the people every year. The conservatives wished to continue the triennium; it was necessary, they said, both to the stability of the government and to the execution of great plans of internal improvement. Striking a balance between accountability and efficiency, the majority approved the two-year term. At a later stage of the convention, Root tried twice to upset this decision but failed.

The delegates waited apprehensively for the report of the committee on the appointing power. Van Buren was its chairman, an ominous sign, and many expected, as he later recalled, "that an effort was to be made to preserve the Council of Appointment in a form perhaps changed but of unabated efficiency." But the committee called for the elimination of the council. Not a good word could have been said for it, and it was quickly buried under a unanimous vote. The convention now had to create an entirely new system of appointment. The committee recommended that some local officers be popularly elected, that others receive their appointment from local bodies, that still others, together with high executive and judicial officers, be appointed by the legislature or by the governor with the advice and consent of the senate. The principal difficulty arose on the mode of appointing the justices of the peace. These local magistrates—more than twenty-five hundred of them—had extensive civil and criminal jurisdiction and, with the constables, pettifoggers, and others hanging upon them, constituted a mighty political engine. "Indeed," King said, "so important is this magistracy and its associates in this state . . . that he who would control and dispose of their appointments, would possess greater political influence, than were he able to dispose of all the other offices throughout the state." A bare majority of the committee, over Van Buren's opposition, recommended their election by the people of the towns. And now a strange ideological reversal occurred. The conservatives backed the committee plan, becoming the champions of local democracy, while the democrats condemned popular election of the justices as "the height of aristocracy." Power, not principle, was at stake in this contest. Federalists and their political heirs controlled most of the towns of the state; they would, therefore, benefit from town elections. The county governments, on the other hand, were generally Republican. Much was said, especially by the conservatives, of the importance of decentralizing the machinery of appointment in order to break the force of party and faction in the state. The Bucktail majority was hard put to deny the cogency of the argument or, in view of their democratic professions, the merits of popular election.

Van Buren's plan was cunningly designed to achieve a measure of local control and at the same time keep the machinery of appointment centralized in reliable hands. Under his plan, rejected in the committee of seven but then offered to the convention, two county bodies, the boards of supervisors and the county-court judges, would submit separate lists of nominees from which the governor would appoint the justices. The conservatives denounced it as a blatant party measure. It was rejected by a narrow margin, as also was the resolution calling for popular election. Other plans met with even less favor. Finally, a large majority approved the modification of Van Buren's plan introduced by the high-minder John Duer, which overcame the objection of centralism by giving the power of appointment as well as nomination to the county bodies. Except for the office of sheriff, where Root and popular election prevailed, and officers of the government of New York City, the redistribution of the appointive power was accomplished with little trouble once decision was reached on the justices of the peace.

In the reform of the elective franchise, the delegates marched to the door of universal suffrage but declined to enter. Under the dual electorate established by the constitution of 1777, perhaps 75 per cent of the adult males qualified as electors of the house and about 40 per cent of governor and senators. The suffrage was undemocratic and unrealistic. The state was passing from an economy based largely on landed enterprise to one containing great commercial and manufacturing interests. In some areas, certainly, the suffrage was more restrictive in 1821 than at the time of its adoption in 1777. This was especially true of New York City with its workers of little or no property and merchants who, however prosperous, might not possess the requisite real property. Moreover, in the burgeoning new lands north and west of Albany, farmers acquired their lands under long-term contracts that withheld title until payment was completed. Much of the sentiment for suffrage reform came from these western farmers who, despite their equity in land and their improvements on the land, could not qualify as freeholders. The question of what constituted a freehold received different interpretations from place to place, and many complained of fraudulent voting and fagot voting[1] by the tenants of great landlords.

The report of the suffrage committee recommended an extension of the franchise derived from the law calling the convention. White male citizens, qualified by age and residence, who had paid any tax or worked on a public road or served in the militia would be permitted to vote for *all* elective officers. This was too close to universal suffrage to suit the majority of delegates. The conservatives realized the inevitability of moderate reform and were prepared to concede it, but they fought to save "the old freehold anchor" in one branch of the legislature, the senate. Chief Justice Spencer moved that senatorial electors possess in law or equity, thus taking care of the so-called equitable freeholders in the west, $250 interest in land or tenements. Fearing that the "free and independent lords of the soil" would be submerged by the new monied classes, old Federalists quoted Jefferson as if he were scripture, denounced cities and manufactures, and hymned the praises of sturdy yeomen. The democrats replied that their fears were imaginary, that "character does not spring out of the ground," that the state is an association of persons, not a partnership founded on property. Spencer's motion failed, 19 to 100, only the conservatives voting for it.

So the rule of suffrage would be the same for all officers of government, but should it be as extensive as the committee asked? Many moderates thought not. They opposed this "cheapening," as Van Buren described it, of a precious privilege. They advocated a small taxpaying qualification. When the great committee became hopelessly entangled in competing motions, Ogden Edwards got the entire subject committed to a special committee of thirteen. Its report eliminated militia service as a qualification and curtailed, but did not eliminate, enfranchisement by way of work on the roads—a sore point with the New York delegates whose constituents had no high-

---

[1] A term applied to the control that landlords exercised over the votes of their tenants.

ways to work. At Root's instigation the militia clause was restored. Renewed efforts to restrict the franchise failed; the report passed, as amended, 74 to 38 and subsequently became Article II of the new constitution.

An interesting provision of that article, thus far passed over, read as follows:

> But no man of colour, unless he shall have been for three years [the residence qualification for whites was one year] a citizen of this state, and for one year preceding any election, shall be seized and possessed of a freehold estate of the value of two hundred and fifty dollars, over and above all debts and incumbrances charged thereon; and shall have been actually rated, and paid a tax thereon, shall be entitled to vote at such election.

Ironically, a democratic convention virtually disfranchised a whole class of citizens—the thirty thousand free Negroes of New York. Heretofore they had voted on equal terms with the whites; now they were required to possess that very property the delegates had held to be no fit test for the white man. The absurdity, the shamefulness of this act did not escape the scorn of the convention's conservative members.

When the report of the suffrage committee first came before the delegates, Peter Jay, an abolitionist like his father, moved to strike the word "white" from its resolution for a broad suffrage. Some of the fiercest democrats in the convention defended the color bar. They said that Negroes were illiterate; their votes were controlled; their concentration in key wards of New York City—one-third of the state's free Negroes lived in the city—was a disturbing element; they did not share the burdens of the state, being excluded by federal law from the militia and few of them paying taxes; many were still held in bondage in New York—under the gradual emancipation act of 1799 the last slaves would not be freed until 1846—public sentiment would not support a democratic suffrage embracing them; and so on. That the free Negroes had, as far as they could be qualified, generally voted the Federalist ticket of their former masters contributed to the hostility Republicans like Young and Van Buren felt for the Negro franchise. Underlying this political motive, however, was the conviction that democracy was for whites only. The example of Connecticut was before them: the constitution of 1818 had disfranchised the Negroes. And although the other New England states had not disfranchised them, the main advance of democracy north of the Mason-Dixon Line was clearly bound up with the subordination of the Negro. By 1840, 93 per cent of Northern Negroes lived in states where they were excluded from the polls.

Open and unmitigated disfranchisement was a distressing business. A majority of the delegates backed away from it, agreeing to Jay's motion. Other, more covert, means of disfranchisement would prove palatable, however. The question was included in the commitment of the suffrage article to the committee of thirteen, and it reported the freehold proposition for Negroes. Now Judge Platt moved to strike this proviso. The conservative corps voted 15 to 3 for striking; the radicals voted 3 to 19 for retaining the proviso. (Root, who preferred to shift the burden of disfranchisement to the federal government and its militia laws, was one of the three.) The total vote was 33 to 71. So New York enlisted in the movement for *white* democracy. Not until the Fifteenth Amendment to the federal Constitution would Negroes vote in New York.

No more troublesome problem faced the convention than the reform of the judiciary. The radicals aimed at a revolution in this branch of the government, and they very nearly succeeded in their object. There were two main complaints against the judiciary. First, it was over-centralized, over-burdened, and incapable of discharging the constantly expanding volume of business of the courts; yet the chancellor and the supreme court, whose five judges not only sat at Albany but rode circuit, steadfastly opposed any increase in their number or tampering with the judicial establishment. Second, the judges were political partisans; yet they were independent of the people and could not be removed except by impeachment. Their participation in the convention underscored this indictment, adding to the hatred old Republican enemies felt for the judges and turning the serious business of judicial reform into a political vendetta. In action on the report of the legislative committee, the convention gave the legislature the power to remove judges. Even Chancellor Kent, who was more open to reason than most of his brothers, concurred in the proposition. Root, whose proposition it was, kept up a relentless fire on the chancellor. Not only did he disbelieve in the high court and its powerful head, but he accused Kent of subverting New York law to English rules, particularly with regard to libel and blasphemy. The legislature had already attacked the salaries of judges—Kent's had been repeatedly reduced—and the convention refused to prohibit the practice.

The report of the judiciary committee came before the convention on October 22. Except for the addition of a vice-chancellor and a new tier of lower courts, with practically the same jurisdiction as the supreme court but limited to the trial of issues of fact, the report proposed no changes in the judicial system. It maintained judicial centralism, the division between equity and common-law jurisdiction, and—what was particularly galling to the radicals—it continued the old judges in their offices. Immediately, longing to see "the emancipation of the state from judicial thralldom," Root launched his attack. His substitute resolution called for the abolition of the existing courts, the creation of a new supreme court with jurisdiction in law and equity, the introduction of a system of circuit, or district, courts with the same jurisdiction, and the elimination at legislative discretion of the court of chancery. The substitute failed, 36 to 73; but the delegates were even less disposed to approve the committee's plan. So they committed the entire subject to a second committee of seven. Its members were sharply divided between maintaining the present system, as contemplated in the original report, and far-reaching reform modeled on Root's plan. There were two basic questions: (1) Should district courts be instituted? (2) Should the offices of the high courts be vacated? The chairman, Peter J. Munro, wavered on these issues, changing his mind between the drafting of the report and its presentation to the committee of the whole. There was, in effect, no majority report, and the convention was right back where it had started. Tompkins now moved to vacate the offices. He was, of course, supported by Root, a member of Munro's committee, and the radical contingent. The judges abstained from debate on a question so vital to themselves, but several moderate leaders, as well as conservatives, rose to their defense. The radicals had "thrown off all disguise," Van Buren charged, and had asked the convention to adopt an unprecedented vindictive measure solely to gratify their hatreds and prejudices against the judiciary. The delegates rejected Tompkins's motion by the vote of 44 to 64.

The convention seemed hopelessly deadlocked. Every other major issue had been resolved and the convention proceeded rapidly with the reports of the committee of the whole, but the question of the judiciary appeared no closer to settlement than before. Root was not a man to concede defeat. On November 1 an inconspicuous western delegate, Matthew Carpenter, suspected of being Root's tool, offered a motion to create a supreme court consisting of a chief justice and two judges, and a system of district courts with the same jurisdiction and such equity powers as the legislature might direct. This was Root's plan in a new form. It saved the chancery, at least, for a time, but vacated the supreme court, reduced its complement, and sought through the instrumentality of district courts to carry justice to the people's doorstep. Opponents thought it would be poor justice indeed. Chief Justice Spencer spoke for his colleagues in advocating Munro's solution—the addition of one or two circuit-court judges to the supreme court. Van Buren and other moderates tried to persuade the honorable delegates that, whatever changes were made in the judicial branch, the present incumbents should be retained in office. But the radicals had won many moderates to their cause, and they refused to listen. On November 4, only a week before adjournment, Carpenter's motion passed, 62 to 53.

The following day the delegates overrode the recommendation of a special committee to reduce the work of the convention to separate articles of amendment, after the Massachusetts plan, and voted instead to offer a totally revised constitution for the ratification of the people. Finally, after more than four months deliberation, the question was called: "Shall this Constitution pass?" The vote was 96 to 8.

Conservatives accounted for all but 1 of the negative votes; of the 22 delegates not voting or signing the constitution, nine belonged to that group, including all those from Albany and Columbia Counties and the chancellor and the judges, who had gone on circuit, where they might better have been all along. Ezekial Bacon, one of the handful of conservatives who signed, explained that though he thought the constitution worse than its predecessor, it nevertheless had the singular merit of being subject to correction by way of amendment. Rufus King, whose sympathies were as confused as his politics, approved of the constitution with deep reservations about the expanded suffrage and reformed judiciary. Ratification was a foregone conclusion. Apparently there was little public controversy or popular interest. Nearly twenty-eight thousand fewer people went to the polls in January, 1822, than had voted on the convention question nine months before. They ratified the constitution by an overwhelming majority.

It has sometimes been said that the New York convention was a conservative body. The characterization is misleading, even if applied to the majority of moderates in the convention. Actually, it produced more important reforms than any other convention of the time. It abolished the Council of Revision and the Council of Appointment; it reorganized the executive department, bringing it into line with prevailing American theory and practice; it made thousands of officers elective—sheriffs, county clerks, and others, as well as most militia officers—and decentralized the appointive power; it abolished property qualifications for the franchise, going almost to the limit of universal white manhood suffrage, and also impelled the movement in the Northern states for the disfranchisement of Negroes; it reformed the state judiciary, took the higher courts out of politics, and made the judges more responsible to the people. Finally, by Article IX of the constitution, the convention totally overturned the government. All legislative, executive, and judicial offices—all civil offices under the old government—became vacant on December 31, 1822. Incumbents would, of course, continue until replaced. Great numbers were. Spencer, Platt, and Van Ness were not reappointed to the supreme court, and Kent soon retired. Thus, with respect to the judiciary, and several other parts of the constitution as well, the radicals came closer to realizing their objectives than any other party in the convention. The constitution was as confusing and complex as the partisanship that produced it, but it gave New York a democratic frame of government. If its democracy was not complete and consistent in all details, the people might see to their correction. As early as 1826 they removed the last futile bar to the white suffrage and took to themselves the election of justices of the peace. The constitution of 1822 endured for a quarter-century, which was a long time in a state as politically turbulent, socially chaotic, and enterprising as New York.

1820

November 20   The Council of Revision returns a bill calling for a convention to amend the constitution of 1777.

1821

March 13   A statute provides for a referendum on the question of a convention and for the election of delegates if a majority of the electorate approves.

April 30   The enlarged electorate, as provided by law, approves of the convention. The vote is 109,346 to 34,901.

June 18   Delegates are elected from cities and counties in accordance with the apportionment of members to the lower chamber of the legislature.

August 28   The convention opens in Albany.

September 4   The convention resolves itself into committee of the whole to begin debate on the reports of the select committees.

September 25   Spencer's amendment to attach a $250 property qualification to electors for the senate is defeated in committee of the whole, 19 to 100.

October 27   The convention begins to act on amendments adopted in the committee of the whole and approves the suffrage article, 72 to 32.

November 4   Carpenter's amendment for the reform of the judiciary is adopted, 62 to 53.

November 10   The convention approves the revised constitution, 98 to 8, and adjourns *sine die*.

1822

January 15–17   The revised constitution is ratified by the electorate that called the convention into being, 75,422 to 41,497.

11.　The Council of Revision and the Veto Power

When the committee on the Council of Revision presented its report on December 5, Peter R. Livingston at once moved to lower the vote required in the legislature to override the governor's negative from two-thirds, as proposed, to a simple majority. Livingston was a wealthy gentleman farmer from Dutchess County, a philosophical democrat, and an ardent follower of his "political mentor," Erastus Root. Jonas Platt, the judge, answered Livingston. He made a defense of the council, only a portion of which is given in the part of his speech reproduced below. Platt was then fifty-four years old. After he was forced off the supreme court in 1823, he built up a lucrative practice. Root despised Platt and his brethren of the robe—the robe of despotism in his opinion. His stinging retort is a fair sample of his style. Root was Connecticut born, a lawyer, forty-eight years of age, with a record of service in Congress and the state assembly. He became the first lieutenant governor under the new constitution but would never in his later career surpass his performance in the convention. James Tallmadge, who scoffed at the radicals' "majesty of democracy," is best remembered as the Congressman whose resolution of 1819 precipitated the Missouri Compromise. A Dutchess County lawyer, and one of the leading moderates in the convention, Tallmadge remained for many years an important figure in New York politics. The Livingston amendment was rejected and the committee resolution adopted on September 8.

. . . MR. LIVINGSTON. . . . It is a fact not to be disguised, that a towering majority of this Convention represent the interests, feelings, and views of the friends of democratic government. In a republican government it will not be denied that all the power of the legislature is vested in, and emanates from, the people. If that maxim be not controverted, he was in favour of expunging every article in the constitution, which contravenes

From *Reports of the Proceedings and Debates of the Convention of 1821* (Albany, 1821), pp. 50–54, 56–57, 61–63, 65–69.

that great principle. He should propose a substitute in conformity with that principle. If the third article of the constitution, which relates to the council of revision, had been administered with integrity and wisdom, the amendment now proposed would never have been suggested. It would have excited the admiration of every jurist, and that feature would have been the pride of the constitution itself. If the construction of that great patriot and statesman, now living, and who once presided over the destinies of the state, had been followed, this amendment would never have been brought into contemplation. He gave the wise construction to it. When a law had passed both branches of the legislature, and was presented to the council, the only inquiry was, is it in violation of constitutional rights. If he found no defect in the constitutionality of the law, he did not extend his inquiries to its expediency, or its tendency to promote the public good; but he left that to the judgment, good sense, and patriotism, which have ever characterized the representatives of the people. He declared that the two branches of the legislature ought to be the judges of what conduced to the public good. But the moment they began to assume the power of judging as to the expediency of laws, the people became alarmed.

The wisdom of the remark cannot be questioned, that from experience we derive every thing, and from the want of it, we are exposed to every thing. Then let me for a moment turn the attention of the Convention to our sister states. You will find that seven states, viz. Maine, New-Hampshire, Massachusetts, Pennsylvania, Georgia, Louisiana, and Mississippi, have vested the veto in the hands of the governor, and in the event of a bill being returned, they require it to be passed by a majority of two thirds of each branch of the legislature. In the states of Rhode-Island, New-Jersey, Delaware, Maryland, Virginia, North Carolina, South Carolina, and Ohio, no veto is provided by their constitutions. In Connecticut, Kentucky, Tennessee, Indiana, Missouri, and Alabama, the principle for which he was contending had been adopted, and the veto was placed in the hands of the governor; but if he objected, a majority of all the members elected, could pass the bill notwithstanding. In Illinois, the veto was lodged with the governor and council; but a majority of the legislature could nevertheless pass any bill that might be sent back with objections. In Vermont, the veto is placed in the hands of the governor and council; and if objected to, a bill must lie over for consideration one year. And in New-York, if the governor and council of revision object to a bill, we require a majority of two thirds of both houses to pass it. What is the result from this exposition? Why, several of the states have no negative at all. Eight or nine only require a majority to confirm, in case of a negative. . . .

. . . Is there no danger to be apprehended from the chief magistrate, if you retain that article of the constitution, which permits him to hold his office for three years? And if the appointing power should so be disposed of, that he should have the right of nominations to the senate, you give him a vast patronage, which carries with it an overwhelming influence.— He asked the convention whether it would not be in the power of the chief magistrate, where the state of things might make it necessary to subserve his purposes, to prevent the passage of any law. The senate, he said, consisted of thirty-two members, and it will require twenty-two members in that branch, to pass a bill which may have received his negative.—When you come into the other branch, it will require more than eighty members.

What, asked Mr. L. has led to the destruction of the third article of the constitution? It was the violence of the executive and council of revision, in endeavouring to restrain the passage of some important bills. A bill passed by a majority of eight in the senate, and thirty in the house, was defeated by a contemptible minority with the executive at their head. It was these acts that agitated the feelings of the public. Is it not absurd to suppose that about forty members in this house, and eleven in the senate, with the chief magistrate, should possess more wisdom than more than one hundred men?

Another reason, sir, in the way of anticipation, is this—I know it will be urged—it will be said that if you require only a bare majority of members elected, you may as well not have a qualifying negative. Not so. I am to presume, and ever shall presume, that that body of men, who are to represent the interests of the state, and who will represent the talents, wealth, integrity, and good sense of the country, will not come here and persevere in the passage of a law which will be fatal to the public interest. Inasmuch as they are the creatures of the community, should they be guilty of such a procedure they would never darken the door of a legislative forum again. That is your security. Legislators may be guilty of an error once; but if shewn to them, they will have more magnanimity than to persist in it.

Many cases may be supposed, and they are not the creatures of the imagination, on which this power vested in an individual, would be highly dangerous. Such a state of things has existed in the union; nay, it has existed in our own state. It is but yesterday since the thunders of the cannon have ceased—since we were engaged in an awful war which was to determine whether our independence could be sustained by the patriotism and valour of the country. A proposition was made for raising a volunteer corps, necessary for our defence, and to save the state from destruction. You saw one branch of the government willing to raise the corps, but they would not let them pull a trigger out of the margin of the state. Suppose a like emergency should occur again, and both branches of the legislature should pass the necessary act for our defence, but a minority of one branch, of numbers enough, with a chief magistrate whose views were in accordance with that minority—how could you get along in that hour of peril? Your state must be ruined, and the national union shaken to its foundation. Our independence would be placed upon a barrel of gunpowder, liable at any moment to be blown up.

Mr. L. in conclusion, said he would not trust a man, place him where you will. In politics, as in dealings, he would consider every man a rogue. He was for going on the safe side. Keep the power with the people. They will not abuse it. With these views, sir, said he, I shall at present content myself, making this frank and candid confession, that if any views of this subject, of mine, shall be pointed out to me as erroneous, there will be no citizen in this Convention who would more readily retract them, and go with the majority.

JUDGE PLATT. Having the honour, Mr. chairman, of being one of the select committee who made the report now under discussion, it becomes my duty to aid in explaining the reasons which induced that report.

The first point which presented itself for the consideration of the committee, was, whether it was wise and expedient to retain any check over the legislative department by way of a qualified negative upon the acts of the senate and assembly. The committee deemed it unsafe to dispense entirely with the supervising power at present reposed in the council of revision. We deemed it essential to the public safety to vest somewhere in firm and independent hands, a *limited veto* upon the legislative will.

In a free representative government there is a strong and natural tendency to *excessive* legislation. That department must be composed of a very numerous body of men. In general we may hope, that they will possess sound and upright intentions; but a majority of them will probably possess little experience in framing laws: and the nature of man, and our own experience shew, that men, suddenly elevated to power, have a natural proneness to use their power immoderately. Our state, in common with others, has from time to time had many bold and rude reformers; who see evils and disorders all around them, in whatever does not accord with their own narrow views of public policy; and who often apply remedies with so unskilful a hand, and with so little wisdom and circumspection, that in curing one evil, they create many others. Such an inexperienced lawgiver has his eye intently fixed on some particular mischief which he supposes to exist, and then, with a strong hand he extirpates that evil; but in doing so he often throws down the fences erected for the security of private rights. Almost every man who comes to the legislature seems to suppose that he is bound to do something; and this propensity is so strong, that it is often excited into a passion and a rage. All change in the public laws of the state is in itself an evil. It renders the rule of action for a time unknown or uncertain. The stability of laws inspires confidence; and the success of all our prospective plans in the various business of life must essentially depend on that stability. Fickle caprice is the law of a tyrant's will; and in proportion as our laws are unstable, they partake of that characteristic feature of tyranny.

Besides, sir, it is not to be disguised, that we are at all times exposed to the arts and designs of ambitious demagogues, to selfish intriguers, who speculate on the public bounty, through means of party favouritism; and to that *esprit de corps*, which under strong party excitement, often infests with contagious influence, all who are within its immediate atmosphere. The pride of our nature is often humbled, when we see men, who in their private life and character are deserving of all our confidence and esteem; yet, when associated in large assemblies, and inflamed with party zeal, are induced to commit intemperate acts of outrage and violence under the false pleas of public necessity, or of retaliation and self-defence—acts of which any one of them, in a moment of calm reflection, would blush to think himself capable.

These, sir, are some of the infirmities and vices inherent in our form of government; and so long as man continues imperfect and depraved, these evils must ever attend the many blessings which we enjoy under our happy republic. But while this truth admonishes that perfection is unattainable in any human device; it solemnly warns us on this occasion, to retain or provide every suitable check and guard against those evils; so far as human sagacity and wisdom can discern and prevent them.

On this subject, sir, it is important to realize the distinction between the *actual* power of legislation, and a mere *negative veto*. The power of making or altering the law ought unquestionably to be confided to the two houses of the legislature exclusively. That power expands itself to all objects not forbidden by the constitution, or the fundamental and universal principles of justice.—Such vast powers are obviously liable to great abuse: and if abused, the injurious effects are permanent; and in a great measure incurable. If the legislature pass a law which is unconstitutional, the judicial tribunals, if the case be regularly presented to them, will declare it null and void. But in many cases, a long time elapses between the passing of the act, and the judicial interpretation of it; and what, let me ask, is the condition of the people during that interval? Who, in such a case, can safely regulate his conduct? In many cases a person is compelled to act in reference to such a statute, while he is necessarily involved in doubt as to its validity.

But where the legislature abuse their discretion, on questions of *expediency* merely, the mischief is often still worse. In all cases of *private* acts, which comprize three fourths of our statute book, the evil of an improvident act is incurable, because it usually vests private rights in individuals or corporations which no power under the government can afterwards repeal or annul. No matter how unequal, unwise, or inconvenient, such laws must be carried into effect. *Fieri non debet; factum valet.*[1]

---

[1] It should not happen, but the fact is it does happen [Ed.].

But in regard to the evils which might by possibility flow from the improper exercise of the qualified veto on the legislature, they are very limited in their effects, and of far less dangerous character. The council of revision, or the executive holding this check, can originate no bill, nor make nor alter any law. The effect of the objections where they prevail, can only produce the result of suspending the legislative will of the two houses. And the worst consequence which can ordinarily happen, is, that the people must remain under the law as it stood; until the voice of the people, through their new representatives, shall produce a change.

Having come to the conclusion that such a check is indispensable to the public safety; the next question in order, is, whether it shall be retained in the council of revision, or transferred to the governor alone? I yesterday voted for the abolition of the council of revision, but with an implied supposition, that a similar power vested in the executive, should be substituted, according to the report of the select committee. . . .

. . . The evils and inconveniences resulting from the council of revision are obvious and apparent, while its benefits are chiefly unseen and unacknowledged. Its operation consists not so much in doing positive good, as in preventing mischiefs. It has undoubtedly, as all confess, hindered many dangerous and pernicious bills from becoming laws: but how many schemes of profligacy; how many base speculations; and how many acts of party violence have been strangled and suppressed, because their authors dared not to present them to the test of such an ordeal, it is impossible to demonstrate; but there can be no doubt in the mind of any reflecting man, that much evil has been thus prevented. The very existence of such a power, in wise, firm, and independent hands, has in a thousand instances prevented the necessity of using it; and this silent and unseen operation has been most salutary and benign.

I owe it to myself, and to the public, to declare, that in my judgment such a power will never be exercised with so much wisdom and steady firmness in any other hands. In my opinion we shall by this change, injure the constitution, as it regards the legislative department: but it will improve the constitution as it relates to the judicial department. By removing the officers of the judiciary from all connexion and collision with the legislature, I hope that jealousies will be removed, and harmony restored and preserved between those departments. And so far as I may be supposed to have any personal interest in the question, I declare my heartfelt satisfaction at the complete separation. We are now called to revise the works of our fathers' hands. To a small number of us on this floor, this is *literally* true: and all I trust will recognize in the framers of our constitution, the fathers and founders of the state. I feel the solemnity of the occasion, and when I see the axe laid to the root of the tree which our fathers planted, and watered, and defended; a tree which has yielded much good and wholesome fruit; and has so long afforded to us its shade and shelter; I confess, sir, that I witness its destruction with no ordinary emotions.

Let the council of revision descend in silence to the grave. But let no man now write any inscription on its tomb. When the feelings, and interests, and passions of the day shall have subsided, if I do not greatly deceive myself, impartial posterity will inscribe an epitaph on that tomb, expressive of profound veneration.

In regard to the intent of the proposed power in the executive alone, I concur decidedly in the report of the select committee. Such a power is necessary to check usurpation in the legislature, which must ever be the strongest. The power is necessary as a shield to protect the weaker departments against the controlling influence of the legislature. The maxim of separating the departments, is of vital importance to the existence of civil liberty. But, sir, it is idle to separate them in form, on parchment, if in reality they are not made independent and capable of self defence against each other. No single elective magistrate can stand against the persevering and systematic assaults of a numerous body of popular and influential men who compose the legislature. They not only have the power over the subsistence of the officers of the judicial and executive departments; but in the plenitude of their power, they may so regulate the duties of those officers, as to render their situation uncomfortable in a variety of modes: and they may in fact thus indirectly legislate the governor, and chancellor, and judges out of office.

The best definition of tyranny is, any form of government in which all the powers, legislative, judicial, and executive, are united in the same hands. And in the same degree as the power, and strength of any one of the departments, bears an undue proportion to those of any other department; in that same degree, will the government partake in reality of the nature and character of despotism. It is in vain, sir, to mock the people with the form of separation in the departments; so long as any one is so disproportionate in strength as to compel the other to act in subserviency to its views. My fear is, sir, not that the governor will wantonly abuse this power; but that he will not exercise it with that firm and intrepid independence which the public interest and safety may require. . . .

. . . GEN. ROOT. It has been well observed, that it is an important question which is now submitted to the consideration of this Convention. It is important, because it involves the fundamental principles of government; and if, in its consequences, those principles of free government which it embraces, should be hastily trodden under foot, it will be cause for mourning. I say, sir, that if it shall be determined that neither the people nor their representatives have power to decide upon their own actions, it will be cause for mourning.

I have listened, sir, with much attention to the handsome encomium which the honorourable gentleman from Oneida (Mr. Platt) has been pleased to bestow upon the council of revision; and I had even travelled with him so far, that I had almost lost sight of the question before the committee.

It has been said, sir, by the honourable gentleman, that of

one hundred and twenty-eight bills which have been returned by the council with their objections, only seventeen have finally passed by the constitutional majority of two-thirds. What does this prove? It proves that in seventeen cases out of one hundred and twenty eight, a majority of two-thirds of both branches of the legislature have been of the opinion that the council of revision did not care for the people, or would not listen to their voice. We have been told, that on the return of bills, the legislature have often been unanimous in assenting to the objections which the council have made. What can we infer from this? That a disposition exists in the representatives of the people to acquiesce, whenever their attention is drawn to the unconstitutionality of a bill. It also shews, that it is not necessary to require the assent of two-thirds of the legislature, as is contemplated in the report before the committee, for if the legislature has been incautiously involved in error, they are ready to retract it.—But we are informed of a certain silent, secret operation of the council of revision, which has been extremely beneficial to the public welfare. The annals of the state, sir, and the recollections of gentlemen will shew, that the operations of that body have not been altogether of a *silent* and *negative* character. Witness the *informal amendments* of midnight. Witness the various other acts of a *positive* character, which have aroused the indignation of the people, and made even *Felix tremble.*[2] The inscription prepared for its tomb is written on the journals; and I am willing to leave it to posterity to weave those garlands which shall decorate its grave. It is gone, sir, and what is its substitute?

It is proposed to refer the powers of the council to the governor; and it seems to be feared that the executive will too far

---

[2] Felix was procurator of Judea and Galilee under Claudius. He is mentioned in Acts 24:25: "And as he [Paul] reasoned of righteousness, temperance, and judgment to come, Felix trembled, and answered, Go thy way for this time; when I have a convenient season, I will call for thee" [Ed.].

bend to popular opinion. Sir, I deprecate that firmness which grows out of an independence of the popular voice, to oppose the popular will. But before we discuss the manner in which this veto may be exercised, it may be proper to consider in what it consists, and what has been its history and progress. The framers of our constitution had received their education under the system of British government, and with a deep veneration for British law. It is not extraordinary, therefore, that we should find them talking of royal negatives. Indeed, sir, we ascertain indubitable traces of the British constitution throughout the whole of our own. The check here proposed is not positive, but qualified; for the experience of all states has shown the folly of permitting an unqualified veto to reside in any branch of the government. And we find constitutions of the states more perfect, the later the period in which they have been made.—That of Connecticut, which is the last, is in my judgment the most perfect. It has provided, that when a bill has been returned by the governor with his objections, the ayes and noes shall be recorded, and if a majority of both houses adhere to their vote, the bill shall become a law; the governor's objections to the contrary notwithstanding.

But in England, sir, from whence our idea of a negating power seems to be drawn, all laws are supposed to be derived from the king, and are enacted in the name of his most royal majesty. Many reigns intervened after the conquest, before there was any call of a parliament whatever. At length, by the interposition of the hardy barons, that call was obtained, and thenceforth laws were passed in the name of the king, by the lords spiritual and temporal and his faithful commons—subject, however, to his royal assent.

And why has this branch of the royal prerogative been preserved in England? To protect his majesty's rights from the encroachment of the lords and commons. But to preserve the analogy, and to apply the argument to this country, where it is acknowledged on all hands that the sovereignty resides in the people, this veto should be lodged with them, as they represent majesty, and not in the people's agents, to enable them to defeat the will of their masters.

The authority to be given to the governor should be supervisory only; the repose of confidence, not the delegation of power. It should be in the nature of a committee of enrolment, to see that the laws are correctly engrossed. Even in England, sir, there is no such thing as a direct and absolute veto. His majesty is too *modest* to assume that language; he only says, *Rex advisare vult*—the king will advise upon it.

The notion of a *veto* was derived from ancient Rome. It came from the tribunes of the people. After a long struggle between the patricians and plebeians, the latter obtained the power of hindering the passage of any law which the patrician senate should have enacted. The tribunes were the organ of their will, and whenever they thought proper to interpose, they pronounced the *veto—I forbid it*. And what, sir, is derivable from this authority? That the people, not the rulers, may refuse their sanction to a law which shall injure them. There is no analogy, therefore, of which the gentlemen opposed, can avail themselves, unless they resort to the maxim, that it is expedient to "save the people from their worst enemies—to save them from themselves."

It would seem from the remarks of my honourable friend near me, (Mr. Edwards) that it is necessary for the security of the people, that they should put a bridle into the mouths of their representatives to restrain them. And is it really so, that they require snaffles, and reins, and martingales, to keep them within the path of their duty? No, sir, they are members of their own body, subject to, and affected by, the same laws, and possess a common interest with those who elect them.

But it is said, sir, that if the governor does not possess a sufficient power to thwart the will of the people, his authority will dwindle to a mere shadow. In order, then, to decorate the governor with some of the trappings of royalty, you would deprive the people of one third of their power! You would impoverish them of their rights, to enrich the executive with prerogative; and the people are to be stripped of their privileges, to confer high powers upon the public functionaries! . . .

. . . It was charged upon the king of England in the declaration of independence, that he had "refused his assent to laws the most wholesome and necessary for the public good"; and if the same evil advisers continue to surround the executive chair, when the angry passions have survived his popularity, and give the same advice, we cannot but expect the same unfortunate and pernicious results.

In all ages, where free governments have existed, those have been found, who would transfer to the minister or executive, more power than was expedient for the good of the people. This tends to perpetuate the aristocracy that exists in the constitution, and instead of being fostered, should receive the firm opposition of those who advocate the cause of the people. . . .

. . . GEN. TALLMADGE. . . . Any government, he said, was a libel on man. If there were no weakness, no frailty, no corruption in human nature, governments would be unnecessary. The very idea of government, therefore, supposed that it was to operate as a restraint upon the vicious and the profligate, and that all its provisions should be based upon this fundamental principle.

He then went into an examination of the several departments of government, and the importance of keeping them distinct. The experience of all ages and all countries convinced us of the necessity of checks and balances in the organization of governments, and of giving to one branch a restraining power upon the others. Wherever this has not been done, the power of one department has become exorbitant, and invariably ended in tyranny. Such was the depravity of man, that restraints were in all cases found necessary to check him in his disposition to acquire power and to trample on the rights and liberties of others.

In the establishment of our system of government these

great principles were woven into our constitution. The several departments were intended to act as checks upon each other. In the organization of the legislature, it was thought advisable that there should be two branches—the senate and assembly, that the one might control and check the abuses of the other, and prevent either from acquiring an overwhelming and dangerous power, if such a disposition should ever be manifested. As an additional safeguard to the rights and liberties of the people, a third branch of the legislature, the council of revision, was instituted. Its object was to resist the encroachments of the senate and assembly, whether through error or corruption, upon the other branches of the government, as well as upon the rights of the citizen, to prevent all, all, from being swallowed up by the inordinate power of the legislature. This third and supervising power was not only defensive in its nature, but it was a power to guard the people against hasty and improvident legislation.

Without this power of a veto over the bodies of legislation, in vain may you boast of the independence of your judiciary, and in confirmation point to the fixed tenure of their places, till sixty years, or even for life. Remember that the power over the subsistence, is a power over the will of man. When you have secured to them the tenure of their places, you seem to have provided for their safety because you have placed them in a citadel which cannot be stormed: but yet you have artfully retained in the legislative body, the means of their subsistence, and the power to starve them into submission. Let them venture on the integrity of their conduct to come in collision, or to thwart the legislative will, and attempt to break down some law which may violate the constitution, or have for its object the destruction of the other branches of government, and the grasping at all power, it will be then that the legislative body will show to the judiciary its dependence, and that although holding a citadel which cannot be sacked, yet their subsistence and their existence while there, is at the pleasure of that body which they vainly attempt to withstand. When such a crisis shall arrive, some modern Caesar, with a senate at his heels, may control, by his cunning and his influence, the majority in your bodies of legislation, and thus throw down the fabric of your government. I beseech you to preserve the proposed check, and thus provide against the ascendant powers of either corruption or inordinate ambition.

He considered the sheet anchor of our safety to be the wholesome principle that the majority should govern, and to this he would hold.—But the will of the majority was to be fairly expressed by the representatives of the people, in the several departments of our government, and not by the democracy in its collective capacity. Found your government upon equal rights, and extended suffrage. Clothe its officers with all requisite powers, and provide for their direct and immediate accountability to the people themselves. Upon this system, the representatives of the people will rise like the wave of the ocean, which exists for a season, rolls onward until its functions are performed, and then again subsides into the great source from which it originated. There was in this respect a wide distinction between this country and the ancient republics. In the former, the interests and sentiments of the community are represented by delegates—in the latter, the people assembled en masse, to conduct their political affairs.—The fate of ancient republics should warn us against the danger of all democracies. Their liberties were lost by the licentiousness of the people, upon which their governments provided no check. The veto, and final adoption of laws was lodged in the collective mass of the people, and was exercised with that indiscretion and madness, which always characterize such tumultuous assemblies.

It was these popular assemblies where the laws received either the approving voice of the people, or were rejected, that called forth the powers of Demosthenes. These popular assemblies were the schools of the eloquence of ancient times, and the causes of their country's ruin. Let us avoid the rock on which other states have been wrecked; and while we manifest a becoming confidence in the intelligence and virtue of the people, let us never abolish those checks, which are necessary to preserve us from the encroachments of power.

His honourable colleague had enumerated several of our sister states, in whose governments no qualified negative on the acts of the legislature had been provided. The constitutions of those states had been cited as models for our own. But he would ask when these governments were adopted, and what had been their operation? Many of them, like our own, were established, to use the language of his colleague, amidst the noise of musketry and the thunder of cannon. Experience had proved them defective in many important points, and they ought not to be cited as precedents. Among others, the new constitution of Connecticut had been mentioned as an example for us. There was a wide difference between the population of that state and of this. They were emphatically one people, peculiar in their habits, customs, and manners. They were descended from one stock, and were united by an identity of interests and feelings. The people of this state, on the contrary, were descended from different states, and collected together from every country and every nation under heaven. There was an almost infinite variety of interests, sentiments, and feelings in the community; and hence the same government which was adapted to the people of Connecticut, would not answer for New-York. . . .

. . . Virginia, too had been introduced as a model; and her statesmen and patriots called up in splendid array. But after all, what had been the experience of that state? On this subject he begged leave to refer to the opinion of one of her greatest statesmen, he meant Mr. Jefferson. In his Notes on Virginia, that distinguished gentleman spoke freely of the defects of the constitution of that state. According to him, the government was administered by concurrent resolutions, and the governor was a mere creature of the legislature. If Virginia should ever call a convention to amend her constitution, this feature would undoubtedly be expunged; and yet we were called on to adopt these very defects. . . .

. . . I am to be told, said he, that my argument is founded on the corruption of the legislature; but remember that when I spoke of the legislature, I spoke of the members as being the representatives of the people. It is not the people themselves, but their agents, which are corrupt—and unfortunately, we have too many facts before us to justify a denial, that majorities in public bodies cannot always be trusted with safety. I will not say our own state affords any instances, either of corrupt, or of hasty, or unadvised legislation. To test the safety and prudence of reposing entire confidence in legislative bodies, turn your eyes to the state of Georgia. It will there be found, that one legislature elected by the people, enacted a law which the next succeeding legislature pronounced to be corrupt, and directed it to be burned by the common hangman. It was not for him to pronounce which was correct. But it abundantly proves the danger to the public welfare in trusting all power to legislatures, without a proper supervising authority. And let it not be said there is such immaculate purity in the representatives of the people. He wished the argument were a true one, but experience forbids us to believe it. We do not ask for a veto as in a regal government; but as our constitution has wisely provided, that our legislature shall consist of two branches, one in which bills generally originate, the other less numerous to reconsider them, and a third, the supervising power, less liable to encroach upon the rights of property, and the liberties of the people. It is necessary there should be a system of checks and balances, to prevent the legislature from monopolizing all power. Where this is not the case, and where the sole power of enacting laws is lodged with one body, or one individual, there must be tyranny. His honourable colleague (Mr. Livingston) had yesterday invoked 'the majesty of democracy.'—Sir, said Mr. T. I recognize no such majesty.

The majesty of democracy reigns not in this republican country; but we have a sovereign people, with whom, of right, all political power resides, and from whom alone it emenates. We have a government of laws, founded on equal rights, and based on the principle of representation. It was the distinguishing character incorporated into our governments, and the great feature wherein ours differed from the ancient republics. The rock upon which they were ruined, was marked on the chart before us—it was our business to avoid it—and the principle of representation must be adhered to as of vital importance. Secure to the people in your constitution, reasonable and proper rights—keep them from meddling with government in their collective capacity—let them enjoy freedom in their agricultural, commercial, and manufacturing pursuits, with the constant accountability of all officers to them, and then you will have a government whose ingredients will be stable and permanent. Without these precautions, we may see that majesty which has been so feelingly invoked—'The majesty of democracy.' It once reigned in Paris. It was the majesty of democracy in the consummation of its mad career, which inscribed upon accountable man, *Death is eternal sleep.* It should be the prayer of his life that no such majesty should ever reign over this now happy land.

His maxim was caution and moderation in approaching the constitution: avoid innovations in its principles. Let the work of our fathers be preserved, after undergoing wholesome amendments. Preserve the principle of proper checks and balances, as provided by them, and you may remedy the defects which experience has pointed out. Suppose for a moment, that the executive possessing this veto, should think proper to suspend the passage of a law and two-thirds of the legislature should be unwilling to pass it. The experience of the community shews, that no essential injury could result from such a suspension. If in the sequel it should prove that it was a wise and salutary law, which was thus suspended, and that the veto was injudiciously exercised, the evil would be only temporary, and the final passage of the law could not be defeated. If it be a bad law, and it be once passed, it can never be recalled—if it be a good one, there will be nothing to prevent its passage, when the representatives shall have been changed by a new election. Sir, suppose the most unimportant case—suppose a turnpike act be passed, and rights and property be vested under it. It was unfortunately passed, but cannot be repealed. But if the executive, by the exercise of his veto had suspended it, where would have been the injury of a temporary delay? And permit me to add, the history of the world will show, that the folly of republics has been an excess of legislation.

He must again urge the necessity of keeping the constitution properly balanced, and avoiding all innovations in its principles. . . .

12. The Term of the Governor

On September 12, in debate on the report of the executive committee, Root made the motion for annual election of the governor. When he finished, John Cramer of Saratoga County spoke for the motion. Cramer, at forty-two years of age, was already a veteran politician. According to Van Buren, this Bucktail "lived on political intrigue." He usually voted with the radicals in the convention. Van Buren's speech on the motion suggests the stance he maintained throughout the convention, except where patronage was the issue. He had been deep in politics since the election of 1800, when he was only eighteen years old. He had served in the state senate and as attorney general of New York for several years, until removed by the Clintonians in 1819. In 1821, having been elected to the United States Senate, he was on the threshold of a remarkable career in national politics. Judge Ogden Edwards, a Tammany leader from New York City, who in

1818 had introduced the first convention bill in the assembly, joined the conservatives on this issue and argued for the continuation of the triennial term, even after the delegates rejected it.

. . . MR. CRAMER. I must in duty to myself express my sentiments upon this subject. It is time for us to consider what powers we have given, and mean to give, to the governor, and for what purposes. He has the powers of veto, of pardon, and will probably have others of appointment. I have voted for the first two, not to give him power to protect himself, the judiciary, nor of any man in authority, nor for the sake of providing for hungry expectants of office; but to be exercised for the benefit of the people. I have not delegated this power, for the purposes of indulging the sympathies of his heart, or of rewarding contractors; but to protect the citizens against midnight murder, and the torch of the incendiary. I am willing to delegate the appointing power to him, not to reward sycophants and flatterers; but for the purpose of appointing to office men of talents and integrity, who will discharge their duty with a single eye to the public good.

I lay it down as a maxim, that as you increase power, you increase accountability. Let us render him accountable to the people, and frequently. Is this assembly less likely to act discreetly and wisely, because the people have a revision over us? No, sir; I rejoice at it—it will prevent many bad amendments— it will teach us to leave untouched that which the people have not complained of. Settle with your governor often—short accounts make long friends—but leave him in power two, four, or seven years, and both crimes and virtues are difficult to be tested. Frequency of election influences the habits and understandings of the people in a variety of ways. It enables them to discharge their duty with the same deliberation with which they discharge the ordinary business of life; and it renders

From *Reports*, pp. 138–139, 147–148, 154–156.

them less liable to the intrigues and misrepresentations of artful and designing men. Office is the mirror in which men are seen as they are; not as they profess to be. How often do we see men, who, in private life, make a boast of their attachment to our democratic institutions, when in power, belie their professions. Office is a political barometer, in which not only the intrinsic weight, but the value of the officer, is tested. If he stand the test—if he be a faithful shepherd—if he has honestly discharged his duty, the people are to be trusted—they will not be unjust to themselves, nor to a faithful servant. But if he has proved himself an unfaithful steward—if he be a cold, sordid, calculating wretch, without one generous emotion, without one tender sympathy, aiming at personal aggrandizement alone— if he should have removed from office men whom the people delight to honour, men whose talents and integrity would do honour to any age or country, and substitute men corrupt, profligate, and abandoned, literally wanting principle, and wanting bread—if he have disgorged that Pandora's box of the state prison on the people—if he have sanctioned unjust laws, or withheld his sanction from beneficial laws, which he himself had recommended, would it not be a consolation to every patriot in the country, that there was a redeeming power in the people, and that power near at hand?

It may be objected that a short term takes away the independence of the governor. There are two sorts of independence— one to be commended, the other to be deprecated. That which arises from a fearless boldness of doing right at all hazards; that which arises from a sense of moral obligation; that which arises from a still stronger and more sacred tie, that which arises from a religious obligation, which binds man to eternity, and whispers to him every step he takes, that there is an accountability hereafter. This is the independence I prize; the independence I wish to see exercised. But that independence which arises from the multiplication of power, from the perpetuity of office, and from independency of circumstances, is the same independence which a Bonaparte once wielded over his subjugated provinces; the same independence which the legitimate royal robbers of Europe, now wield over their degraded subjects. It is that independence, which I trust I shall never live to see any man wield over the destinies of this country. It is that independence, to resist which, every honest man in this community should place himself in the last bulwark of liberty, over which a Caesar or Cromwell must pass, ere he arrived at that fatal independence. I therefore am for the shortest period. . . .

. . . MR. VAN BUREN, before the question was taken, wished to explain the reasons of the vote he should give. There are three distinct propositions before this convention—one, for filling the blanks[3] with one year—another, with two—and a third, with three. He should consider each. One of the great objects of this Convention, to which the people looked with so much solicitude, is the hope that by the amendments which shall be adopted, party violence, in our politics, will in a great measure be done away. It is not to be denied, that very many of our own citizens, and those of other states, entertain an opinion, that the source of our discord is in the great favour and patronage of the governor; and they think this discord can only be allayed by making the governor a mere nominal head— a creature of the legislature. Though he did not assent in its extent to the propriety of this radical change, it would be unwise to neglect what public sentiment has so distinctly pointed at. Yet we must not disguise to ourselves the fact, that we have already augmented rather than diminished the power of the executive. We have given him the exclusive veto by an immense majority, and by the voices of the judiciary themselves, who formerly partook of this power. We have also invested him with the power of pardoning, and under these circumstances, he would have preferred waiting till we know

---

[3] Refers to the term of office of the governor [Ed.].

what other power will be given to the governor, before we
decided on this term. The majority of this committee had
decided otherwise; and the vote he should give on this question, would therefore be given under the expectation, that we
shall increase still more the power of the executive, by a vast
increase to his appointing power. The branch in which this
power formerly resided has been unequivocally condemned by
the public opinion; and there is no other hand, in which it
could be safely trusted, except the executive. With this feeling,
then, he could not but think, that as we increase the power of
the executive, we should also increase the responsibility of
the governor. We should bring him more frequently before
the people. His conflicts, if any, will not be with the legislature.
He was rendered by the provision now proposed, utterly and
entirely independent of the legislature. Of the people he did
not think he should be rendered so independent. In the exercise of the veto, which will only take place on important occasions, he will be supported, if he should have acted manifestly
for the public good. He had not experienced the evils of triennial elections; but as we had vastly increased the power of
the governor, a strong desire is manifested to abridge his
term, and in this sentiment he concurred. But how abridge it?
We wish the people to have an opportunity of testing their
governor's conduct, not by the feelings of temporary excitement, but by that sober second thought, which is never wrong.
Can that be effected if you abridge the term to one year? No,
sir: it is necessary that his power exist long enough to survive
that temporary excitement, which a measure of public importance must occasion, and to enable the people to detect the
fallacy with which the acts of the government may be veiled
as to their real motives. Can a fair judgment of motives, or of
the effect of measures, be made in a few months? No, sir—
even a term longer than three years, must sometimes be necessary to enable us to judge of the effect of measures. But we
must not go into extremes, or we shall arouse the jealousies of

the people, in weakening the responsibility to them, of their public officers. Let us test the question by reason. You have a state and population, whose concerns bear a strong analogy to the interests of the Union. Can a governor, in a term of one year, make himself acquainted with the interests, the wants, and condition of this great state? There was one remark he made with great deference—in all the eastern states, the tenure of the chief magistrate is for only one year; and the majority of this Convention have imbibed their notions under those constitutions, and naturally consider them wise. Others, who have lived under the constitution of this state, have preferred, as he had been accustomed to do, the tenure of three years; and he asked, if there was not some respect, some comity due, to those who have viewed this, among other provisions of our constitution, with reverence. For these reasons he hoped the blank would be filled with two years. . . .

. . . MR. EDWARDS. . . . Sir, what are the evils which the present term of the executive has produced? I can point to none. How was this government administered during the revolutionary war? Who then, as it were, "rode upon the whirlwind and directed the storm"? The venerable George Clinton; and he so administered it, that his name will ever be revered by the people of this state. During the late war, the government was again administered by a chief magistrate who held his office for three years, and who it will not be denied administered it to general satisfaction. Does not all this experience afford strong evidence of the utility of keeping the executive upon his present establishment? Sir, the views of the gentlemen who have advocated this limitation, seem to be limited to the "piping time of peace." If the expectation that peace is to endure forever, is not delusive, if the millennium has indeed commenced, then I will concede that there is weight in the arguments of those gentlemen. But, sir, while man remains as the history of the world has ever pourtrayed him, as ambitious, cruel, and rapacious—while his breast continues to be stormed by angry passions, wars will come; and every wise man, in establishing the form of government for his country, will so form it as to enable it to withstand the shock.

You must therefore have a governor whose powers and whose term of service will be such as to enable him to meet the emergency. The revolutionary war, as well as the late war, have both shewn, that such is our peculiar local situation, that whenever the United States are involved in a war, we shall be in a peculiar manner exposed to its depredations, and that this state must then put in requisition its own resources for its defence. The experience of the late war upon this subject, which is too recent to be forgotten, has demonstrated, that we have dealt out our power with so sparing a hand to the general government, that its arm is inadequate to the defence of every part of the country. Sir, it is but seven years, this very month, since I was summoned to attend in this hall as one of the representatives of the people, to provide for the defence of the state. The language which was then held out to the legislature was, that they must put in requisition the resources of the state for its defence, and rely upon the general government for remuneration at some future time—that the national treasury was exhausted, and that their forces were too feeble for the defence of the country. At this time we were threatened with invasion upon both the Atlantic and lake frontiers, and twenty thousand of our militia were in the field. These were then the sentiments of a decided majority of the legislature, and were in unison with the wishes of the people. The resources of the state were accordingly put in requisition, and the measures adopted were of so decided and so energetic a character, that they were attended with the most happy results. And will it be contended that it is expedient to put the executive of this state upon a one year establishment, when he may again be called upon to encounter scenes like these? What would become of all the plans for a campaign, all the military arrangements, all the organizations, and the infinite multiplicity of concerns, which must then necessarily engage his attention, provided he is cut short in his career by an annual election. Would the patriotic George Clinton have wielded, as effectually as he did, the power of this state, if his office had been kept dependent upon an annual election? Perhaps he might; but certain we are, that the government, during both wars, was administered to the satisfaction of the people.—How it might be under the contemplated organization, time alone can shew.

It will not be contended but that it is desirable that the government should be stable in all its departments. In the organization of the legislative and judicial departments, the requisite stability is provided for. Why, I would ask, is this stability requisite only in these departments? Why is it not equally requisite in the executive department? Why is whatever relates to the execution of your laws to be kept in an eternal state of fluctuation?

But, sir, the experience of other states, and especially of Connecticut, is appealed to, to shew that there is no necessity for extending the governor's term beyond one year. With respect to most of the states where this practice prevails, such is their interior situation, that they have nothing to apprehend from war.—And as it respects Connecticut, their steady habits preserve them from changes. The memory of man extends but to one change of party in that state, and that is of a recent date. Whoever is there elected governor, remains governor until the day of his death. The same stability characterizes all their proceedings. But recently an old man died there who had been fifty-six times elected a member of the legislature. If I was in Connecticut, I should as soon think of proposing that the Dey of Algiers should be imported to govern them, as to propose that their governor should be chosen for two years. The fact is, they are so firmly knit and bound together, that whether their governor is chosen monthly or yearly, or whether their government assume one form or another, the result will be nearly the same. You have all heard of the steady habits of Connecticut, but who ever heard of the steady habits of the state of New-York? Their steady habits is to keep in perpetual turmoil, and to rush from one extreme to another; and after they have accomplished one point, no son of Adam can tell what they will drive at next. Let us not, therefore, delude ourselves by relying upon the experience of other states, and above all, of Connecticut. The experience of our own state and of our own people, ought alone to govern. We are called upon to form a government for them, and not for a people essentially different from them.

Sir, I came not here to flatter the people. I came here to serve the people, by a faithful devotion of my faculties, such as they are, to a subject which most deeply concerns them and their posterity. To accomplish the end for which we are sent, we must form a correct estimate of the character of this people. We have heard much flattery delt out to them; and who would imagine from what we have heard, but that they were all wise, all honest, all, all honourable men. Sir, this is all folly. It is not true, and the people know that it is not true. The truth of the matter is, that the people of this state are like the people of other states. Some of them are wise and some are foolish; some honest and some are knaves. If the people are as they have been represented, how does it happen that your courts of justice are crowded with law-suits, and your state-prison so filled to overflowing, that it is necessary from time to time, to disgorge their foul contents upon the community? Sir, the very existence of civil government is a libel upon the human race. It is enough for us to know, that there is in the people of this, as well as of other states, a fund of good sense, of integrity, and of patriotism, which qualifies them in an eminent degree for the enjoyment of a free government. And it is our business so to organize the government, as that it will most effectually answer the end for which it is established, and that is to protect the virtuous and to punish the vicious; to cast a rampart around the deserving, and to restrain those who will not respect the laws of God or man. We must take things as we find them here. And I conjure the people from New-England not to be led away by the example of their native states, but to apply the experience of this state to its institutions. So long as we lean upon the staff of experience, so long we shall be preserved from wandering from the true path. And if we adhere to this, we shall find no reason for changing the government of this state in so fundamental a point as the duration of the office of the chief magistrate.

Sir, the science of government is above all sciences the most complex and difficult to be well understood. No human genius ever yet arrived at a full and complete comprehension of it. It is a subject upon which mankind have groped in darkness from the creation. Let us not, then, venture upon the field of experiment, but leave untouched all those parts of the constitution which have worn well. By a change in a particular which may be deemed unimportant now, we may in the lapse of time introduce evils of a most alarming character. Montesquieu has furnished us with numerous cases where a change in the form of government in a particular, which at the time appeared to be of small importance, in some instances changed the constitution, and in others overthrew the government. Now, although I do believe that nothing could deprive the people of this country of their free governments, yet, by an imprudent alteration, we may introduce evils which will be extremely mischievous. . . .

13. The Appointive Power

On October 1, after the suffrage debate, the delegates unanimously abolished the Council of Appointment and took up the report of Van Buren's committee. The Bucktail leader explained its provisions with great care. Nathan Williams, a Clintonian from Oneida County in the west, moved to strike the provision for local election of justices of the peace and, instead, include these petty magistrates under the new general appointive power, that is, the governor with the advice and consent of the senate. His motion never came to a vote. Chancellor Kent spoke briefly and cogently in favor of the committee's resolution. Other conservatives took the same position, as did such moderates as Rufus King and Ogden Edwards. Van Buren then presented his solution. He was answered by an old political enemy, the Columbia County Federalist, Jacob R. Van Rensselaer. Neither Van Buren's scheme nor local election could command a majority vote. On October 9 the delegates adopted the compromise offered by John Duer.

. . . MR. VAN BUREN. . . . The first question which presented itself for the consideration of the committee, was the propriety of abolishing the Council of Appointment. On this subject there was no difficulty; the same unanimity prevailed among the members of the select committee in this respect, as in the vote which had just passed in the committee of the whole, for the abolition of this power; and in this, they had only acted in accordance with public opinion, by which this feature of the old constitution had been condemned. He would not, he said, detain the committee by giving any reasons for this part of the report; after the unanimous vote just given, this would be a wanton waste of time.

The next and more important enquiry, was, with respect to what should be substituted in its stead; and here, as was to be expected, a diversity of sentiment prevailed, and many difficulties presented themselves. For the purpose, however, of lessening, as far as was practicable, the objections that would necessarily exist to any general appointing power, wherever placed, or however constituted, they had felt the propriety of reducing the patronage attached to it; and they had, with that view, separated from it the great mass of the officers of the

From *Reports,* pp. 297–300, 307–309, 319, 331–332.

state. Many of them, they had sent to be appointed, or elected, in the several counties or towns, and others they had left to the disposition of the legislature, to provide for their appointment or election, as experience might prove to be most advisable.

Of the 8287 military officers, they had recommended that all except 73, consisting of major generals, brigadier generals, and the adjutant general, should be elected by the privates and officers of the militia.

Of the 6663 civil officers, now appointed by the Council of Appointment, they recommended that 3643 should be appointed or elected as the legislature should direct—these were auctioneers, masters in chancery, public notaries, inspectors of turnpike roads, commissioners to acknowledge deeds, examiners in chancery, inspectors for commercial purposes, and some other officers. They also recommended that the clerks of counties, and district attorneys, should be appointed by the courts of common pleas, in the several counties. And that the mayors and clerks, of all the cities except New-York, should be appointed by the common council of the respective cities.

Thus far, no great diversity of sentiment had existed among the members of the committee, and there had been a general concurrence of opinion, on all the parts of the report already noticed.

This, together with the justices of the peace, which a majority of the committee had recommended to be elected, left only 453 officers for whose appointment, or election, it was necessary to provide.

In addition to the curtailment of the appointing power, to be retained at the seat of government; the committee, under a full conviction that much of the complaint against the existing Council of Appointment, had arisen from the circumstance of the concentration of power in one body, had thought it wise even here to distribute them; by giving the appointment of the heads of the different departments of this state to the legislature; they being officers entrusted with the public property, whose duties more immediately connected them with that body.

Still, some officers were left; small in number, it was true, but of considerable interest and importance. They were unanimously of opinion, that it would be improper for some of these officers to be elected by the people and a majority of them supposed that none of them ought to be so elected.

It became necessary, therefore, to provide for their appointment and to establish what may be called a general appointing power; though limited in the exercise of its functions, to the bestowment of a small number of offices.

Four plans presented themselves to the consideration of the committee.

1st. To create a new Council of Appointment, to be elected by the people.

2nd. To vest the power of Appointment in the Executive solely.

3rd. To give it to the Legislature. Or,

4th. To the Governor, by and with the advice and consent of the Senate.

These respective modes had been, he said, discussed and attentively considered by them. The project of electing a council, was thought liable to most of the objections which had been urged against the old council. There would be a want of responsibility, as now. And it was apprehended that their election would create a great excitement. The incumbents in office, and those desirous of obtaining offices, together with their respective friends, would, of course, feel a deep interest in the election of this council; and this would, of course, pervade every part of the state. Or, if such a council were to be chosen by the legislature, not from among the members of either house, though by being separated entirely from the business of legislation, would remove a part of the objections existing with respect to the present council. It was believed it would, notwithstanding, be attended with serious objections. It would necessarily produce some objection in the legislature, if they met at a different time or in a different place: yet the objection of irresponsibility, would remain in full force.

The Convention had already increased the powers of the executive, and the committee were unwilling to add to it the patronage of the sole power of appointment to office. Besides their own conviction that this was not advisable, they were perfectly confident that public opinion was opposed to such a regulation.

Nor were they satisfied that it would be proper to vest this power in the two branches of the legislature. They had already recommended that the appointment of some officers should be made by them, for reasons he had already explained; and these were all they thought ought to be appointed in this way.—In some of our sister states, this mode of appointment obtained, and had been found to operate beneficially; they were, however, differently circumstanced from us, having a less numerous population, and a smaller extent of territory. They had considered a connexion between the legislative and appointing power, as at best objectionable; the improper influence that such connexion was apt to have on legislation, was fully appreciated by them; and had induced them to recommend a mode, which, though not free from this objection, yet lessened the difficulty, by limiting the connexion to one branch only.

And this brought them to the fourth, and last plan mentioned, to wit: vesting the power in the governor and senate. This, he believed, they had unanimously considered as unaccompanied with the fewest objections; he might possibly be mistaken, but he was confident they were unanimously in favour of this project in the first instance.

The committee, he said, were fully aware of the objection to this mode, arising from the unfavourable effect which the possession of the power of appointment was calculated to produce upon the senate as a branch of the legislature; but more particularly from its being a court of the last resort. But they also knew that no plan could be adopted which would be free from objections of some kind—they knew that it was the fate of all human institutions to be imperfect, and they were therefore more content with the system they had recommended, than they otherwise would have been. They found, too, that they could not exempt the general appointing power from this objection, unless they gave it wholly to the governor, or to him in connexion with a council to be elected by the people; the former mode they had no reason to believe would be acceptable to any portion of the Convention; and the latter, they supposed, would not, in all probability, be relished by their constituents much better than the retaining of the old council.

They had not, he said, been able to derive any material benefit from an examination of the practice of other states. They had examined all their constitutions, and found that they varied greatly from each other. In Pennsylvania and Delaware, the power of appointment to office is vested in the governor singly. In Maine, Massachusetts, Maryland, North-Carolina and Virginia, the governor, and a council similar to ours. In Connecticut, Rhode-Island, Vermont, New-Jersey, South-Carolina, Georgia, Ohio, Tennessee, Mississippi, and Alabama, in the legislature. New-Hampshire was the only state in which they had a council chosen by the people. In Kentucky, Louisiana, Indiana, Illinois, and Missouri, the power is vested in the governor and senate as is proposed by the report.

The fact that the constitutions which had been recently formed, and might therefore be in some degree regarded as the most recent expression of the sense of a portion of the American people, were in unison with the plan they had reported, and calculated in a measure to recommend it. And so, likewise, was it, that a similar provision was contained in the constitution of the United States. But here, candour required the acknowledgment that there was an important difference between our state senate, and that of the Union—as the first was also a court of dernier resort; and the latter possessed no judicial power whatever.

Those considerations, together with the impracticability of devising any system, which in their opinion would be better, had induced them to recommend the constituting of the governor and senate the general appointing power. And they had given the exclusive right of nomination to the governor; this they thought very necessary, and the only way in which that would fix a responsibility for the appointments to be made; and because they were all convinced that the alteration which had been made to the constitution in 1801, had proved injurious, and such they firmly believed, was now the opinion of the people of this state. . . .

. . . Having, then, come to the determination to place the general appointing power in the governor, by and with the advice and consent of the senate; the next question to be settled was, what appointments should be conferred upon it.

The committee, he said, had all agreed, that the highest military officers should receive their appointments from this source, though some were of the opinion, that these might safely be entrusted with the executive alone, as commander in chief. They had *all* united in the opinion, that all judicial officers, except surrogates and justices of the peace, ought also to be appointed in this way; two members of the committee were in favour of having the surrogates elected by the people.

With respect to that section of the report, which provides for the election of justices of the peace by the people, a great contrariety of sentiment had existed among them. Neither that section, nor the next, which provided for the appointment of certain officers in the city of New-York, had received his assent.

He had, at every stage of the discussions before the committee, been decidedly opposed to the election of justices; and it had been to him a source of sincere regret, that in that respect, he had been overruled by the committee. Only four of the committee had agreed to the section making justices elective, and one of that number had consented to it, rather for the sake of agreeing upon something to report, than from a conviction of the propriety of the mode recommended. He would, he said, here observe, that the two sections just mentioned were the only parts of the report, of any moment, from which he had dissented. A minority of the committee, however, thought they had not gone far enough in curtailing the patronage of the general appointing power, and were for including sheriffs and surrogates; in this he had differed from them. His reasons, therefore, it would be more proper for him to give when these respective subjects should come under discussion in that committee. He would now content himself with stating, that the majority of the select committee, had not, on the question respecting sheriffs and surrogates, nor on that relating to justices of the peace, any strong personal predilections. They feel themselves entirely open to conviction on these, and on all other points, which might be raised respecting their report; and if, on a fair and deliberate examination, it should be thought that it would be better to have the sheriffs and surrogates elected by the people, they would cheerfully acquiesce in that decision. . . .

. . . MR. WILLIAMS . . . moved to strike out the words at the close of the second section, "*except justices of the peace,*" which would, as he said, leave their appointment to the general appointing power. He then proceeded to state, that it was a proposition assented to by all, that government was instituted for the good of the people, and like the sun, its benign influence ought to be felt in every part of the system. We ought to extend the principles of freedom to the utmost boundaries of the body politic; but at the same time to beware of doing any thing to excite a popular phrenzy. Of all the measures proposed in this Convention, I consider, sir, this one, of *electing* the magistrates of our towns, as fraught with the greatest mischief. It involves a principle the most pernicious to the peace of the community, and the most destructive to an orderly and correct course of justice. What, sir, elect your judges! For although some may think these magistrates of little consequence in society, I am of a very different opinion, and consider them of as much consequence in many respects, as any of the judges. And it may even be asserted that it would be safer and better to elect by the people, the justices of the supreme court, than the justices of the towns, by which you will eternise faction in every village and hamlet in the state. The judges of the supreme court are looked up to by the people of all grades, with great respect and veneration; and their residence and their decisions would be viewed as matters distant from the scenes of the election. But how would it be with your justices of towns? They would be engaged on the very spot where they reside, and would have to exercise their power in a contest with their constituents and neighbours, for an office which would give a controling influence over the reputation, liberty, and property of their very neighbours. Would such a contention be soon forgotten by even the most upright and virtuous magistrate? Would he be able to eradicate from his mind that his friends and his foes had been engaged, hand to hand, and foot to foot, in the contest?

But, sir, I would ask gentlemen to take another view of the subject. These judges in the several towns, are not only to adjudicate among their constituents when arrayed against each other, but as arrayed against the people of other towns and counties in the state. It cannot be expected that human nature in these magistrates would be so far elevated above all influence of this sort, that it would not be to be feared. Much less can this be expected, when we have so recently been told that some of the judicial officers, who fill the high stations of the supreme court, have been suspected of being influenced by their too warm interference in party politics.

I have said, sir, that the powers of these magistrates are very great: it is much greater than is generally imagined, and greater than they themselves are generally aware of. They have criminal jurisdiction to a very great extent. They can call any of their fellow-citizens, however high their standing, before them, for any offence whatever, on the accusation of any single individual, and whatever may be the risk of character or liberty. They can alone try some offences, and, associated with their fellows, can try, in a summary way, many misdemeanors. And indeed all prosecutions for offences of every name and nature, may be commenced before them. Then, sir, look at their civil power. Having jurisdiction of civil causes to the amount of fifty dollars, and having power to enter judgment in cases not litigated to the amount of one hundred dollars, they draw within the focus of their courts a greater amount of property than all the other courts in the state. In this point of view, it must be admitted, that they are the most important set of magistrates in the state; and it must be admitted also, that they would be able to put in motion a numerous and fearful corps of pettifoggers and retainers to secure their election. And it cannot be concealed, that, in some towns and villages, a single individual might be found, who would have a controling influence in the election of these officers.

I venture to assert, sir, that there is not to be found in the world, except in two instances in this country, a state or kingdom, in which this principle has been adopted. Having looked carefully into the constitutions of these United States, I am happy in being able to say, that Georgia and Ohio are the only states which have this pernicious plan in their constitutions: neither of which, when we take a survey of their judicial systems, and the state of their laws, shall we be solicitous to imitate. In the latter state, I have been informed, and have no doubt, that the people, I mean the more reflecting portion, are anxious to change the system. It need not astonish any one to be informed of the fact, that under such a system of justice, sap-troughs and basswood rails, are a tender upon executions, at the appraisal of men. Nor indeed will any one complain, that a judgment, induced by judges elected by the people, should be satisfied by such commodities.

It has been said, sir, I know, and there is great plausibility in the assertion, that the town officers generally, and especially the supervisors, all elected by the people, are very well selected. In general, the supervisors are men of integrity, and the board is highly respectable. But it ought to be remembered that this office excites very little interest in the community, as there is very little profit or power attached to it; and indeed, nothing is required of such an officer but integrity and economy, and he has not much to do but to reduce the accounts exhibited against the county as much as possible—say one-fourth or one-third. The election of such an officer will always be judicious, and excite very little commotion. We may say the same of the other officers of the town.

Upon the whole, I am bound to disapprove of this part of the report, considering it, as I do, very pernicious in principle, though in other respects the committee have presented us a very excellent plan. Let us strike out this provision, and then we shall be ready to act upon the appointing power with a full knowledge of what it is to perform. If these two or three thousand officers are to be thrown upon the senate, possibly it may occupy too much of their time and attention. But at any rate, I hope, sir, most anxiously, that this motion will prevail, and that some mode more salutary may be devised for the appointment of justices. . . .

. . . CHANCELLOR KENT. . . .The great value of these local appointments is, that they weaken by dividing the force of party. They will break down the scheme of one great, uniform, organized system of party domination throughout the state, and they will give to the minor party in each county, some chance for some participation in the local affairs of the county. They will disperse a great deal of the aliment of party spirit, and diminish its action, and consequently its intensity and its bitterness at the seat of government. This consideration cannot be too deeply impressed upon the minds of the committee. The future happiness, and, I might almost say, the future destiny of the people of this state, turn upon such an arrangement.

What have we to fear in future? We have no reason to appre-hend subjugation by foreign arms, nor conflicts between the states. We have no standing armies to menace our liberties. We have no hereditary aristocracy, nor privileged orders, nor established church to press upon our rights or our income: our liberties are to be assailed from other quarters and by other means. It is not to be disguised that our governments are be-coming downright democracies, with all their good, and all their evil. The principle of universal suffrage, which is now running a triumphant career from Maine to Louisiana, is an awful power, which, like gunpowder, or the steam engine, or the press itself, may be rendered mighty in mischief as well as in blessings. We have to fear the corrupting influence of con-stant struggles for office and power. We have to fear inflam-matory appeals to the worst passions of the worst men in society; and we have greatly to dread the disciplined force of fierce and vindictive majorities, headed by leaders flattering their weaknesses and passions, and turning their vengeance upon the heads and fortunes of minorities, under the forms of law. It requires all our wisdom, and all our patriotism, to sur-round our institutions with a rampart against the corruption and violence of party spirit. We must ingraft something like quarantine laws into our constitution, to prevent the introduc-tion and rage of this great moral pestilence. If we do not, then, take my word for it, we may expect to encounter the same disasters which have corrupted and shaken to the foundation so many popular states. What we have already done, will, as I greatly fear, give a freer operation and an increased impetus to the power of the evil genius of democracy. I need not surely inform this wise assembly, that all unchecked democracies are better calculated for man as he ought to be, than for man as he is, and as he has always appeared to be in the faithful page of history, and as he is declared to be in the volume of divine inspiration.

I hope, sir, I do not press this subject too far. I believe in my conscience, that unless we remove the means of concentrating, at the seat of government, or at any other given place, the elements of faction and the struggles for office, and unless we scatter them in fragments among the counties, our future career will be exceedingly tempestuous and corrupt. . . .

. . . GEN. J. R. VAN RENSSELAER rose to take a view of the different propositions before the Convention, and their probable effect if adopted. The Convention, he said, had unanimously agreed in abolishing the old council of appointment, from a conviction of its evil consequences and a knowledge of the desire of the people to try some other method of selecting and appointing officers. The people had for a long time been aware, that the appointments under our former council had been dictated by a few individuals at the seat of government, who were in no shape responsible to them, and were liable to be influenced by personal interests and motives. These are the reasons which led to the abolition of that method of appointment.

The proposition of the gentleman from Otsego, (Mr. Van Buren) would first receive his attention. He was of the opinion that the same evils would attend that method which had led to the destruction of the old council.

His method proposed that the judges of the court of common pleas in each county, should make out a list of the candidates for office within their respective counties, and that the supervisors of such counties should make out another. These lists shall be submitted to the governor, from which he shall appoint the justices of the peace for each county.

This board of supervisors, on an average, would consist of about thirteen members, who, together with the five judges in each county, would constitute a council of eighteen, for the nomination of the justices in each town, submitting to the governor the power of appointing and rejecting, as he may think proper, from these lists.

Sir, I want to know, said Mr. V. R. where, in this whole process, the people will be able to lay their hands on a single individual for the responsibility of a bad appointment? Should a person go to a supervisor, and enquire how such a man obtained his appointment, knowing him to be unfit for the office, and that in his own town he could not have obtained a nomination, the answer would be, I was opposed to that individual, still I was but one among thirteen—I was overpowered by the majority. The same would be the answer from the respective judges. When you come to the executive, and make the same enquiry, he would tell you he knew nothing about it. The constitution of the state has appointed a number of guardians over his conduct, and that he could do no other than comply with their recommendations.

Your magistrates are to hold for a considerable time, and it will be out of the power of the people to remove them.

In an early day of the session of this Convention, it was agreed to abolish the council of revision. One of the important reasons for which, was that the executive, legislative, and judicial departments should not be mingled. This was the principal reason which led to so unanimous a vote on that subject. Now what do you propose to do? You propose to make your court of common pleas the organ of executive power. The power of appointment is added to that of administering the laws. You take this power from the executive and cast it upon the judiciary. This is in violation of all sound doctrine, and the effect will be to make your judiciary necessarily the instruments of party. You compel them to take a part in the political squabbles of your counties. Is this wise, or is it discreet? It has been said, and truly said, that a party judiciary is the greatest curse that can be inflicted upon any community. With respect to the original proposition in the report of the select committee, and the amendment offered by the gentleman from Oneida [Mr. Platt], I am decidedly in favour of the report of the committee. I am anxious to carry home to the people the power of appointing.

But we are told one day that the people are capable of **voting** for governor, senators, and members of assembly; and the next day they are considered incapable of electing justices of the peace in the very towns where they live—today they are all enlightened and virtuous, to-morrow they are all ignorant and vicious, and unfit to manage the most trifling concern in which they are immediately interested—they are considered the tools of designing demagogues, and subservient to the will of petti-foggers and constables. He could not understand the force of such reasoning. He was not so great an advocate for the merits of the people as many, still he would not consent that they were unfit to manage their own trifling concerns as well as others could manage them for them.

The people are honest in intention; it is true they may be deceived, and led astray by demagogues from their duty and interest, but they will soon discover their danger, and return to both.—They are as capable of electing their own justices as they are of electing their chief magistrate and members of the legislature. Show me an instance of a magistrate in the country deciding a controversy from impure motives, and I will show you an individual who is held in universal detestation— an individual who cannot again obtain the patronage of a single man in the community. If there is a subject in the whole train of social concerns, in which the people ought to have a voice, it is upon that of electing those who are to decide be-tween individuals. With respect to these magistrates being elected by a political party—will not your supervisors be as likely to be elected by a party as your justices?

As to the effect to be produced by this method—you will produce the same party feelings in two distinct bodies of men in each county, and perpetuate it at the seat of government in your chief magistrate. These two lists of candidates are to be sent to the seat of government, where the same intrigue will be practised, and where the same irresponsibility exists as has been so much deprecated in our former council—and it would not be anticipating too much, to expect more deplorable conse-

quences to result from such a plan, than had resulted from
the former council. . . .

14. The Senate and the Suffrage

*The recently retired United States Senator, Nathan Sanford, pre-
sented the report of the committee on the suffrage on September 19.
Sanford, then forty-two, had had a brilliant career in the Republican
ranks for two decades; and in 1823 he would succeed James Kent as
chancellor. Kent made the most famous speech of the entire convention in support of Ambrose Spencer's motion to maintain a freehold
qualification for senatorial electors. It was a forthright statement of
conservative doctrine. This greatly learned jurist, the virtual creator
of equity jurisdiction in American law, had been chancellor for seven
years and might have continued for many more had the convention
seen fit to lift the constitution's mandatory retirement age of sixty.
The radicals were determined to cut down this "branching oak,
whose roots penetrated the union," and Kent's role in the convention,
"stationed at the straits of Thermopylae" against the onrushing
Jacobin horde, as Platt described it, merely strengthened their purpose. The best answer to Kent's speech came from a little-known
delegate, David Buel, Jr., a young lawyer representing Rensselaer
County, just east of Albany. But Van Buren's speech, on the third day
of debate, made the strongest impression on the delegates. Although
advocating a taxpaying qualification for the franchise, he could discover no basis in reason or in fact for perpetuating New York's dual
electorate. Two speakers followed him, summing-up for each side;
the delegates then conquered this last depleted outpost of aristocracy.*

Mr. N. Sanford took the floor. The question before us is the
right of suffrage—who shall, or who shall not, have the right to

From *Reports,* pp. 178–180, 219–222, 240–243, 257–261

vote. The committee have presented the scheme they thought best; to abolish all existing distinctions and make the right of voting uniform. Is this not right? Where did these distinctions arise? They arose from British precedents. In England, they have their three estates, which must always have their separate interests represented. Here there is but one estate—the people. To me, the only qualifications seem to be, the virtue and morality of the people; and if they may be safely entrusted to vote for one class of our rulers, why not for all? In my opinion, these distinctions are fallacious. We have the experience of almost all the other states against them. The principle of the scheme now proposed, is, that those who bear the burthens of the state, should choose those that rule it. There is no privilege given to property, as such; but those who contribute to the public support, we consider as entitled to a share in the election of rulers. The burthens are annual, and the elections are annual, and this appears proper. To me, and the majority of the committee, it appeared the only reasonable scheme that those who are to be affected by the acts of government, should be annually entitled to vote for those who administer it. Our taxes are of two sorts, on real and personal property. The payment of a tax on either, we thought, equally entitled a man to a vote, and thus we intended to destroy the odious distinctions of property which now exist. But we have considered personal service, in some cases, equivalent to a tax on personal property, as in work on the high roads. This is a burthen, and should entitle those subject to it to equivalent privileges. The road duty is equal to a poll tax on every male citizen, of 21 years, of 62½ cents per annum, which is about the value of each individual's work on the road. This work is a burthen imposed by the legislature—a duty required by rulers, and which should entitle those subject to it, to a choice of those rulers. Then, sir, the militia next presents itself; the idea of personal service, as applicable to the road duty, is, in like manner, applicable here; and this criterion has been adopted in other states. In Mississippi, mere enrolment gives a vote. In Connecticut, as is proposed here, actual service, and that without the right of commutation, is required. The duty in the militia is obligatory and onerous. The militia man must find his arms and accoutrements, and lose his time. But, after admitting all these persons, what restrictions, it will be said, are left on the right of suffrage? 1st. The voter must be a citizen. 2d. The service required must be performed within the year, on the principle that taxation is annual, and election annual; so that when the person ceases to contribute or serve, he ceases to vote.

A residence is also required. We proposed the term of six months, because we find it already in the constitution; but we propose this residence in the state, and not in the county or town, so that wherever a voter may be at the time of election, he may vote there, if he has been a resident of the state for six months. The object of this was to enable those who move, as very many do, in the six months preceding an election, out of the town or ward in which they have resided, to retain the right of voting in their new habitations. The term of six months is deemed long enough to qualify those who come into our state from abroad, to understand and exercise the privileges of a citizen here. Now, sir, this scheme will embrace almost the whole male population of the state. There is perhaps no subject so purely matter of opinion, as the question how far the right of suffrage may be safely carried. We propose to carry it almost as far as the male population of the state. The Convention may perhaps think this too broad. On this subject we have much experience; yet there are respectable citizens who think this extension of suffrage unfavourable to the rights of property. Certainly this would be a fatal objection, if well founded; for any government, however constituted, which does not secure property to its rightful owners, is a bad government. But how is the extension of the right of suffrage unfavourable to property? Will not our laws continue the same? Will not the administration of justice continue the same? And if so, how is private property to suffer? Unless these are changed, and upon them rest the rights and security of property, I am unable to perceive how property is to suffer by the extension of the right of suffrage. But we have abundant experience on this point in other states. Now, sir, in many of the states the right of suffrage has no restriction; every male inhabitant votes. Yet what harm has been done in those states? What evil has resulted to them from this cause? The course of things in this country is for the extension, and not the restriction of popular rights. I do not know that in Ohio or Pennsylvania, where the right of suffrage is universal, there is not the same security for private rights and private happiness as elsewhere. Every gentleman is aware that the scheme now proposed, is derived from the law calling this Convention, and in the constitution of this body, we have the first fruits of the operation of the principle of extensive suffrage—and will any one say that this example is not one evincing the discretion with which our people exercise this right? In our town meetings too, throughout the state, we have the same principle. In our town elections we have the highest proof of the virtue and intelligence of our people; they assemble in town meetings as a pure democracy, and choose their officers and local legislatures, if I may so call them; and if there is any part of our public business well done, it is that done in town meetings. Is not this a strong practical lesson of the beneficial operation of this principle? This scheme has been proposed by a majority of the committee; they think it safe and beneficial, founded in just and rational principles, and in the experience of this and neighbouring states. The committee have no attachment, however, to this particular scheme, and are willing to see it amended or altered, if it shall be judged for the interest of the people. . . .

. . . CHANCELLOR KENT. . . . I have reflected upon the report of the select committee with attention and with anxiety. We appear to be disregarding the principles of the constitution, under which we have so long and so happily lived, and to be changing some of its essential institutions. I cannot but think that the considerate men who have studied the history of republics, or are read in lessons of experience, must look with concern upon our apparent disposition to vibrate from a well balanced government, to the extremes of the democratic doctrines. Such a broad proposition as that contained in the report, at the distance of ten years past, would have struck the public mind with astonishment and terror. So rapid has been the career of our vibration.

Let us recall our attention, for a moment, to our past history.

This state has existed for forty-four years under our present constitution, which was formed by those illustrious sages and patriots who adorned the revolution. It has wonderfully fulfilled all the great ends of civil government. During that long period, we have enjoyed in an eminent degree, the blessings of civil and religious liberty. We have had our lives, our privileges, and our property, protected. We have had a succession of wise and temperate legislatures. The code of our statute law has been again and again revised and corrected, and it may proudly bear a comparison with that of any other people. We have had, during that period, (though I am, perhaps, not the fittest person to say it) a regular, stable, honest, and enlightened administration of justice. All the peaceable pursuits of industry, and all the important interests of education and science, have been fostered and encouraged. We have trebled our numbers within the last twenty-five years, have displayed mighty resources, and have made unexampled progress in the career of prosperity and greatness.

Our financial credit stands at an enviable height; and we are now successfully engaged in connecting the great lakes with the ocean by stupendous canals, which excite the admiration of our neighbours, and will make a conspicuous figure even upon the map of the United States.

These are some of the fruits of our present government; and yet we seem to be dissatisfied with our condition, and we are engaged in the bold and hazardous experiment of remodelling the constitution. Is it not fit and discreet: I speak as to wise men; is it not fit and proper that we should pause in our career, and reflect well on the immensity of the innovation in contemplation? Discontent in the midst of so much prosperity, and with such abundant means of happiness, looks like ingratitude, and as if we were disposed to arraign the goodness of Providence. Do we not expose ourselves to the danger of being deprived of the blessings we have enjoyed?—When the husbandman has gathered in his harvest, and has filled his barns and his graneries with the fruits of his industry, if he should then become discontented and unthankful, would he not have reason to apprehend, that the Lord of the harvest might come in his wrath, and with his lightning destroy them?

The senate has hitherto been elected by the farmers of the state—by the free and independent lords of the soil, worth at least $250 in freehold estate, over and above all debts charged thereon. The governor has been chosen by the same electors, and we have hitherto elected citizens of elevated rank and character. Our assembly has been chosen by freeholders, possessing a freehold of the value of $50, or by persons renting a tenement of the yearly value of $5, and who have been rated and actually paid taxes to the state. By the report before us, we propose to annihilate, at one stroke, all those property distinctions and to bow before the idol of universal suffrage. That extreme democratic principle, when applied to the legislative and executive departments of government, has been regarded with terror, by the wise men of every age, because in every European republic, ancient and modern, in which it has been tried, it has terminated disastrously, and been productive of corruption, injustice, violence, and tyranny. And dare we flatter ourselves that we are a peculiar people, who can run the career of history, exempted from the passions which have disturbed and corrupted the rest of mankind? If we are like other races of men, with similar follies and vices, then I greatly fear that our posterity will have reason to deplore in sackcloth and ashes, the delusion of the day.

It is not my purpose at present to interfere with the report of the committee, so far as respects the qualifications of electors for governor and members of assembly. I shall feel grateful if we may be permitted to retain the stability and security of a senate, bottomed upon the freehold property of the state. Such a body, so constituted, may prove a sheet anchor amidst the future factions and storms of the republic. The great leading and governing interest of this state, is, at present, the agricultural; and what madness would it be to commit that interest to the winds. The great body of the people, are now the owners and actual cultivators of the soil. With that wholesome population we always expect to find moderation, frugality, order, honesty, and a due sense of independence, liberty, and justice. It is impossible that any people can lose their liberties by internal fraud or violence, so long as the country is parcelled out among freeholders of moderate possessions, and those freeholders have a sure and efficient control in the affairs of the government. Their habits, sympathies, and employments, necessarily inspire them with a correct spirit of freedom and justice; they are the safest guardians of property and the laws: We certainly cannot too highly appreciate the value of the agricultural interest: It is the foundation of national wealth and power. According to the opinion of her ablest political economists, it is the surplus produce of the agriculture of England, that enables her to support her vast body of manufacturers, her formidable fleets and armies, and the crowds of persons engaged in the liberal professions, and the cultivation of the various arts.

Now, sir, I wish to preserve our senate as the representative of the landed interest. I wish those who have an interest in the soil, to retain the exclusive possession of a branch in the legislature, as a strong hold in which they may find safety through all the vicissitudes which the state may be destined, in the course of Providence, to experience. I wish them to be always enabled to say that their freeholds cannot be taxed without their consent. The men of no property, together with the crowds of dependants connected with great manufacturing and commercial establishments, and the motley and undefinable population of crowded ports, may, perhaps, at some future day, under skilful management, predominate in the assembly, and yet we should be perfectly safe if no laws could pass without the free consent of the owners of the soil. That security we at present enjoy; and it is that security which I wish to retain.

The apprehended danger from the experiment of universal suffrage applied to the whole legislative department, is no dream of the imagination. It is too mighty an excitement for the moral constitution of men to endure. The tendency of universal suffrage, is to jeopardize the rights of property, and the principles of liberty. There is a constant tendency in human society, and the history of every age proves it; there is a tendency in the poor to covet and to share the plunder of the rich; in the debtor to relax or avoid the obligation of contracts; in the majority to tyranize over the minority, and trample down their rights; in the indolent and the profligate, to cast the whole burthens of society upon the industrious and the virtuous; and *there is a tendency in ambitious and wicked men, to inflame these combustible materials.* It requires a vigilant government, and a firm administration of justice, to counteract that tendency. Thou shalt not covet; thou shalt not steal; are divine injunctions induced by this miserable depravity of our nature. Who can undertake to calculate with any precision, how many millions of people, this great state will contain in the course of this and the next century, and who can estimate the future extent and magnitude of our commercial ports? The disproportion between the men of property, and the men of no property, will be in every society in a ratio to its commerce, wealth, and population. We are no longer to remain plain and simple republics of farmers, like the New-England colonists, or the Dutch settlements on the Hudson. We are fast becoming a great nation, with great commerce, manufactures, population, wealth, luxuries, and with the vices and miseries that they engender. One seventh of the population of the city of Paris at this day subsists on charity, and one third of the inhabitants of that city die in the hospitals; what would become of such a city with universal suffrage? France has upwards of four, and England upwards of five millions of manufacturing and commercial labourers without property. Could these kingdoms sustain the weight of universal suffrage? The radicals in England, with the force of that mighty engine, would at once sweep away the property, the laws, and the liberties of that island like a deluge.

The growth of the city of New-York is enough to startle and awaken those who are pursuing the *ignis fatuus* of universal suffrage.

In	1773	it had	21,000	souls.
	1801	"	60,000	do.
	1806	"	76,000	do.
	1820	"	123,000	do.

It is rapidly swelling into the unwieldly population, and with the burdensome pauperism, of an European metropolis. New-York is destined to become the future London of America; and in less than a century, that city, with the operation of universal suffrage, and under skilful direction, will govern this state.

The notion that every man that works a day on the road, or serves an idle hour in the militia, is entitled as of right to an equal participation in the whole power of the government, is most unreasonable, and has no foundation in justice. We had better at once discard from the report such a nominal test of merit. If such persons have an equal share in one branch of the legislature, it is surely as much as they can in justice or policy demand. Society is an association for the protection of property as well as of life, and the individual who contributes only one cent to the common stock, ought not to have the same power and influence in directing the property concerns of the partnership, as he who contributes his thousands. He will not have the same inducements to care, and diligence, and fidelity. His inducements and his temptation would be to divide the whole capital upon the principles of an agrarian law.

Liberty, rightly understood, is an inestimable blessing, but liberty without wisdom, and without justice, is no better than wild and savage licentiousness. The danger which we have hereafter to apprehend, is not the want, but the abuse, of liberty. We have to apprehend the oppression of minorities, and a disposition to encroach on private right—to disturb chartered privileges—and to weaken, degrade, and overawe the administration of justice; we have to apprehend the establishment of unequal, and consequently, unjust systems of taxation, and all the mischiefs of a crude and mutable legislation. A stable senate, exempted from the influence of universal suffrage, will powerfully check these dangerous propensities, and such a check becomes the more necessary, since this Convention has already determined to withdraw the watchful eye of the judicial department from the passage of laws.

We are destined to become a great manufacturing as well as commercial state. We have already numerous and prosperous factories of one kind or another, and one master capitalist with his one hundred apprentices, and journeymen, and agents, and dependents, will bear down at the polls, an equal number of farmers of small estates in his vicinity, who cannot safely unite for their common defence. Large manufacturing and mechanical establishments, can act in an instant with the unity and efficacy of disciplined troops. It is against such combinations, among others, that I think we ought to give to the freeholders, or those who have interest in land, one branch of the legislature for their asylum and their comfort. Universal suffrage once granted, is granted forever, and never can be recalled.

There is no retrograde step in the rear of democracy. However mischievous the precedent may be in its consequences, or however fatal in its effects, universal suffrage never can be recalled or checked, but by the strength of the bayonet. We stand, therefore, this moment, on the brink of fate, on the very edge of the precipice. If we let go our present hold on the senate, we commit our proudest hopes and our most precious interests to the waves.

It ought further to be observed, that the senate is a court of justice in the last resort. It is the last depository of public and private rights; of civil and criminal justice. This gives the subject an awful consideration, and wonderfully increases the importance of securing that house from the inroads of universal suffrage. Our country freeholders are exclusively our jurors in the administration of justice, and there is equal reason that none but those who have an interest in the soil, should have any concern in the composition of that court. As long as the senate is safe, justice is safe, property is safe, and our liberties are safe. But when the wisdom, the integrity, and the independence of that court is lost, we may be certain that the freedom and happiness of this state, are fled forever.

I hope, sir, we shall not carry desolation through all the departments of the fabric erected by our fathers. I hope we shall not put forward to the world a new constitution, as will meet with the scorn of the wise, and the tears of the patriot. . . .

. . . Mr. Buel. . . .Of the twenty four states which compose this union, twelve states require only a certain time of residence as a qualification to vote for all their elective officers— eight require in addition to residence the payment of taxes or the performance of militia duty—four states only *require* a freehold qualification, viz. New-York, North-Carolina, Virginia, and Rhode-Island. The distinction which the amendment of the gentleman from Albany proposes to continue, exists only in the constitution of this state, and in that of North-Carolina.

In some of the states, the possession of a freehold, constitutes one of several qualifications, either of which gives the right of suffrage; but in four only, is the exclusive right of voting for any department of the government confined to landholders.

The progressive extension of the right of suffrage by the reformations which have taken place in several of the state constitutions, adds to the force of the authority. By the original constitution of Maryland, (made in 1776,) a considerable property qualification was necessary to constitute an elector. By successive alterations in the years 1802, and 1810, the right has been extended to all the white citizens who have a permanent residence in the state. A similar alteration has been made in the constitution of South-Carolina; and by the recent reformations in the constitutions of Connecticut and Massachusetts, property qualifications in the electors have been abolished; the right is extended in the former almost to universal suffrage, and in the latter to all the citizens who pay taxes. It is not in the smaller states only, that these liberal principles respecting suffrage, have been adopted. The constitution of Pennsylvania, adopted in the year 1790, extends the right of suffrage to all the citizens who pay taxes, and to their sons between the age of twenty-one and twenty-two years.

That constitution was formed by men, distinguished for patriotism and talents. At the head of them, we find the name of Judge [James] Wilson, a distinguished statesman, and one of the founders of the constitution of the United States.

The constitution of Pennsylvania was formed on the broad principle of suffrage, which that distinguished man lays down in his writings. "That every citizen whose circumstances do not render him necessarily dependant on the will of another, should possess a vote in electing those, by whose conduct his property, his reputation, his liberty, and his life may be almost materially affected." This is the correct rule, and it has been adopted into the constitution of every state which has been formed since the government of the United States was organized. So universal an admission of the great principle of general suffrage, by the Conventions of discreet and sober minded men, who have been engaged in forming or amending the different constitutions, produces a strong conviction that the principle is safe and salutary.

It is said by those who contend that the right of voting for senators should be confined to the landholders, that the framers of our constitution were wise and practical men, and that they deemed this distinction essential to the security of the landed property; and that we have not encountered any evils from it during the forty years experience which we have had. To this I answer, that if the restriction of the right of suffrage has produced no positive evil, it cannot be shown to have produced any good results.

The qualifications for assembly voters, under the existing constitution, are as liberal as any which will probably be adopted by this Convention. Is it pretended that the assembly, during the forty-three years experience which we have enjoyed under our constitution, has been, in any respect, inferior to the senate? Has the senate, although elected exclusively by free-holders, been composed of men of more talents, or greater probity, than the assembly? Have the rights of property, generally, or of the landed interest in particular, been more vigilantly watched, and more carefully protected by the senate than by the assembly? I might appeal to the journals of the two houses, and to the recollections and information of the members of the committee on this subject; but it is unnecessary, as I understand the gentlemen who support the amendment, distinctly admit, that hitherto the assembly has been as safe a depository of the rights of the landed interest, as the senate. But it is supposed that the framers of our constitution must have had wise and cogent reasons for making such a distinction between the electors of the different branches of the government. May we not, however, without the least derogation from the wisdom and good intentions of the framers of our constitution, ascribe the provision in question to circumstances which then influenced them, but which no longer ought to have weight?

When our constitution was framed, the domain of the state was in the hands of a few. The proprietors of the great manors were almost the only men of great influence; and the landed property was deemed worthy of almost exclusive consideration. Before the revolution, freeholders only were allowed to exercise the right of suffrage. The notions of our ancestors, in regard to real property, were all derived from England. The feudal tenures were universally adopted. The law of primogeniture, by which estates descended to the eldest son, and the rule of descent by which the male branches inherited the paternal estate, to the exclusion of the female, entails, and many other provisions of feudal origin were in force. The tendency of this system, it is well understood, was to keep the lands of the state in few hands. But since that period, by the operation of wiser laws, and by the prevalence of juster principles, an entire revolution has taken place in regard to real property. Our laws for regulating descents, and for converting entailed estates into fee-simple, have gradually increased the number of landholders: Our territory has been rapidly divided and subdivided: And although the landed interest is no longer controlled by the influence of a few great proprietors, its aggregate importance is vastly increased, and almost the whole community have become interested in its protection. In New-England, the inhabitants, from the earliest period, have enjoyed the system which we are progressively attaining to. There, the property of the soil has always been in the hands of the *many*. The great bulk of the population are farmers and freeholders, yet no provision is incorporated in their constitutions, excluding those who are not freeholders from a full participation in the right of suffrage. May we not trace the notions of the framers of our constitution, respecting the exclusive privilege of the freeholders, to the same source from whence they derived all their ideas of real property?

In England, from the earliest times, the superiority of the landed interest was maintained. To go no farther back than the Norman invasion, we find the domain of England parcelled out in great manors among the followers of the Conqueror. They and their descendants, for many years, were the only legislative and judiciary power in the kingdom. Their baronies gave them the right of legislation. It was a privilege annexed to the land which their vassals cultivated. Their vassals, in process of time, became freeholders, and formed the juries in the manor courts.

It was a long time before any other interests than that of the landholders was attended to. For some hundred years, the great cities and boroughs were not considered worthy of being represented in the great councils of the kingdom. And although numerous great interests have since arisen, the house of peers and the knights of the shire, are still supposed to represent the landed interest exclusively. It was not surprising that the framers of our constitution, though they in the main aimed to establish our government on republican principles, should have adopted some of the notions which they inherited, with their domains, from their ancestors. The force of habit and prejudice which induced those illustrious men to incorporate in the constitution absurd provisions, will manifestly appear by adverting to a single instance of the application of the rule established by them, to determine the right of voting for senators and governor.

A man who is possessed of a piece of land worth $250 for his own life, or the life of another person, is a freeholder, and has the right to vote for governor and senators. But one who has an estate in ever so valuable a farm, for 999 years, or any other definite term, however long, is not a freeholder and cannot vote. The absurdity of the distinction, at this day, is so glaring as to require no comment. Yet there are numerous farmers, in different parts of the state, who are excluded from the right of suffrage on this absurd distinction between freehold and leasehold estates. No person will now pretend that a farmer who holds his land by a thousand years lease is less attached to the soil, or less likely to exercise the privilege of freeman discreetly, than a freeholder. We shall not, I trust, be accused of want of respect to settled institutions, if we expunge such glaring absurdities from our constitution. It is supposed, however, by the honourable member before me (Chancellor Kent) that landed property will become insecure under the proposed extension of the right of suffrage, by the influx of a more dangerous population. That gentleman has drawn a picture from the existing state of society in European kingdoms, which would be indeed appalling, if we could suppose such a state of society could exist here. But are arguments, drawn from the state of society in Europe, applicable to our situation? I think the concessions of my honourable friend from Albany, who last addressed the committee, (Mr. Van Vechten) greatly weaken the force of the arguments of his honour the Chancellor.

It is conceded by my honourable friend, that the great landed estates must be cut up by the operation of our laws of descent; that we have already seen those laws effect a great change; and that it is the inevitable tendency of our rules of descent, to divide up our territory into farms of moderate size. The real property, therefore, will be in the hands of the *many*. But in England, and other European kingdoms, it is the policy of the aristocracy to keep the lands in few hands. The laws of primogeniture, the entailments and family settlements, all tend to give a confined direction to the course of descents. Hence we find in Europe, the landed estates possessed by a few rich men; and the great bulk of the population poor, and without that attachment to the government which is found among the owners of the soil. Hence, also, the poor envy and hate the rich, and mobs and insurrections sometimes render property insecure. Did I believe that our population would degenerate into such a state, I should, with the advocates for the amendment, hesitate in extending the right of suffrage; but I confess

I have no such fears. I have heretofore had doubts respecting the safety of adopting the principles of a suffrage as extensive as that now contemplated. I have given to the subject the best reflection of which I am capable; and I have satisfied myself, that there is no danger in adopting those liberal principles which are incorporated in almost all the constitutions of these United States.

There are in my judgment, many circumstances which will forever preserve the people of this state from the vices and the degradation of European population, beside those which I have already taken notice of. The provision already made for the establishment of common schools, will, in a very few years, extend the benefit of education to all our citizens. The universal diffusion of information will forever distinguish our population from that of Europe. Virtue and intelligence are the true basis on which every republican government must rest. When these are lost, freedom will no longer exist. The diffusion of education is the only sure means of establishing these pillars of freedom. I rejoice in this view of the subject, that our common school fund will (if the report on the legislative department be adopted,) be consecrated by a constitutional provision; and I feel no apprehension, for myself, or my posterity, in confiding the right of suffrage to the great mass of such a population as I believe ours will always be. The farmers in this country will always out number all other portions of our population. Admitting that the increase of our cities, and especially of our commercial metropolis, will be as great as it has been hitherto; it is not to be doubted that the agricultural population will increase in the same proportion. The city population will never be able to depress that of the country. New-York has always contained about a tenth part of the population of the state, and will probably always bear a similar proportion. Can she, with such a population, under any circumstances, render the property of the vast population of the country insecure? It may be that mobs will occasionally be collected, and commit depredations in a great city; but, can the mobs traverse our immense territory, and invade the farms, and despoil the property of the landholders? And if such a state of things were possible, would a senate, elected by freeholders, afford any security? It is the regular administration of the laws by an independent judiciary, that renders property secure against private acts of violence. And there will always be a vast majority of our citizens interested in preventing legislative injustice.

But the gentleman who introduced the proposition now before the committee, has predicted dangers of another kind to the landed interest, if their exclusive right of electing the senate shall be taken away. He supposes, that combinations of other interests will be formed to depress the landholders, by charging them exclusively with the burthen of taxation.

I cannot entertain any apprehension that such a state of things will ever exist. Under any probable extension of the right of suffrage, the landed interest will, in my view of the subject, always maintain a vast preponderance of numbers and influence. From what combinations of other interests can danger arise? The mercantile and manufacturing interests are the only ones which can obtain a formidable influence. Are the owners of manufacturing establishments, scattered through the state, as they always must be, likely to enter into a confederacy with the merchants of the great cities, for the purpose of depressing the yeomanry and landholders of this great state? Has our past experience shewn any tendency in those two great interests, to unite in any project, especially for such an one as that which I have mentioned? We usually find the merchants and manufacturers acting as rivals to each other: but both feel a community of interest with the landholders; and it will ever be the interest of the farmers, as it ever has been, to foster and protect both the manufacturing and mercantile interests. The discussions which the tariff has undergone, both in and out of congress, have demonstrated the feelings of rivalship which exist between our manufacturers and our merchants. But who has ever heard, in this or any other country, of a combination of those two classes of men, to destroy the interest of the farmers? No other combination, then, can be imagined, but that of the poor against the rich. Can it be anticipated, that those who have no property can ever so successfully combine their efforts, as to have a majority in both branches of the legislature, unfriendly to the security of property?

One ground of the argument of gentlemen who support the amendment is, that the extension of the right of suffrage will give an undue influence to the rich over the persons who depend upon them for employment; but if the rich control the votes of the poor, the result cannot be unfavourable to the security of property. The supposition that, at some future day, when the poor shall become numerous, they may imitate the radicals of England, or the jacobins of France; that they may rise, in the majesty of their strength, and usurp the property of the landholders, is so unlikely to be realized, that we may dismiss all fear arising from that source. Before that can happen, wealth must lose all its influence; public morals must be destroyed; and the nature of our government changed, and it would be in vain to look to a senate, chosen by landholders, for security in a case of such extremity. I cannot but think, that all the dangers which it is predicted will flow from doing away the exclusive right of the landholders to elect the senators, are groundless.

I contend, that by the true principle of our government, property, as such, is not the basis of representation. Our community is an association of persons—of human beings—not a partnership founded on property. The declared object of the people of this state in associating, was, to "establish such a government as they deemed best calculated to secure the rights and liberties of the good people of the state, and most conducive to their happiness and safety." Property, it is admitted, is one of the rights to be protected and secured; and although

the protection of life and liberty is the highest object of attention, it is certainly true, that the security of property is a most
interesting and important object in every free government.
Property is essential to our temporal happiness; and is necessarily one of the most interesting subjects of legislation. The
desire of acquiring property is a universal passion. I readily
give to property the important place which has been assigned
to it by the honourable member from Albany (Chancellor
Kent). To property we are indebted for most of our comforts,
and for much of our temporal happiness. The numerous religious, moral, and benevolent institutions which are every
where established, owe their existence to wealth; and it is
wealth which enables us to make those great internal improvements which we have undertaken. Property is only one of the
incidental rights of the person who possesses it; and, as such,
it must be made secure; but it does not follow, that it must
therefore be represented specifically in any branch of the government. . . .

. . . Mr. Van Buren. . . . By the census of 1814, it appeared,
that of 163,000 electors in this state, upwards of 75,000 were
freeholders, under $250, and all of them householders, who
may possess any amount of personal property—men who have
wives and children to protect and support; and who have
every thing but the mere dust on which they trod to bind them
to the country. And the question was, whether, in addition to
those who might, by this Convention, be clothed with the right
of suffrage, this class of men, composed of mechanics, professional men, and small landholders, and constituting the bone,
pith, and muscle of the population of the state, should be
excluded entirely from all representation in that branch of the
legislature which had equal power to originate all bills, and a
complete negative upon the passage of all laws; from which,
under the present constitution, proceeded the power that had
the bestowment of all offices, civil and military in the state:
and above all, which, in the language of an honourable mem-

ber from Albany, as a court of dernier resort, was entrusted with the life, liberty, and property, of every one of our citizens. This, said he, is, in sober truth, the question under discussion; and it would seem to him to be only necessary, that it should be fairly stated, and correctly understood, to secure its rejection. This was the grievance, under which so great a portion of the people of this state had hitherto laboured. It was to relieve them from this injustice, and this oppression, that the Convention had been called; and it was, and always had been, a matter of astonishment to him, that a reformation in this particular had been so long delayed.

There were two words, continued Mr. V. B., which had come into common use with our revolutionary struggle; words which contained an abridgment of our political rights; words which, at that day, had a talismanic effect; which led our fathers from the bosoms of their families to the tented field; which, for seven long years of toil and suffering, had kept them to their arms; and which finally conducted them to a glorious triumph. They were "TAXATION and REPRESENTATION"; nor did they lose their influence with the close of that struggle. They were never heard in our halls of legislation, without bringing to our recollections the consecrated feelings of those who won our liberties, or without reminding us of every thing that was sacred in principle.

It was, said he, but yesterday, that they afforded the strongest evidence of their continued hold upon our feelings and our judgments, by the triumph they effected, over the strongest aversions and prejudices of our nature—on the question of continuing the right of suffrage to the poor, degraded blacks. Apply, said he, for a moment, the principles they inculcate to the question under consideration, and let its merits be thereby tested. Are those of your citizens represented, whose voices are never heard in your senate? Are these citizens in any degree represented or heard, in the formation of your courts of justice, from the highest to the lowest? Was, then, representation in one branch of the legislature, which by itself can do nothing—which, instead of securing to them the blessings of legislation, only enables them to prevent it as an evil, any thing more than a shadow? Was it not emphatically "keeping the word of promise to the ear, and breaking it to the hope"? Was it not even less than the *virtual representation,* with which our fathers were attempted to be appeased by their oppressors? It was even so; and if so, could they, as long as this distinction was retained, hold up their heads, and, without blushing, pretend to be the advocates for that special canon of political rights, that taxation and representation were, and ever should be, indissoluble? He thought not.

In whose name, and for whose benefit, he inquired, were they called upon to disappoint the just expectations of their constituents, and to persevere in what he could not but regard as a violation of principle? It was in the name, and for the security of 'farmers,' that they were called upon to adopt this measure. This, he said, was, indeed, acting in an imposing name; and they who used it, knew full well that it was so. It was, continued Mr. V. B., the boast, the pride, and the security of this nation, that she had in her bosom a body of men who, for sobriety, integrity, industry, and patriotism, were unequalled by the cultivators of the earth in any part of the known world; nay, more, to compare them with men of similar pursuits in other countries, was to degrade them. And woeful must be our degeneracy, before any thing, which might be supposed to affect the interests of the farmers of this country, could be listened to with indifference by those who governed us.

He could not, he said, yield to any man in respect for this invaluable class of our citizens, nor in zeal for their support: But how did this matter stand? enquired Mr. V. B. Was the allegation that they were violating the wishes, and tampering with the security of the farmers, founded in fact, or was it merely colourable? Who, he asked, had hitherto constituted a majority of the voters of the state? The *farmers*—who had called for, and insisted upon the Convention. *Farmers and free-holders!* Who passed the law admitting those, who were not electors, to a free participation in the decision of the question of *Convention* or *No Convention,* and also in the choice of delegates to that body. A legislature, a majority of whom were farmers, and probably every one of them freeholders, of the value of two hundred and fifty dollars and upwards! The farmers of this state had, he said, by an overwhelming majority, admitted those who were not freeholders, to a full participation with themselves in every stage of this great effort to amend our constitution, and to ameliorate the condition of the people: Could he, then, ought he to be told, that they would be disappointed in their expectations, when they found that by the provisions of the constitution as amended, a great proportion of their fellow citizens were enfranchised, and released, from fetters which they themselves had done all in their power to loosen? He did not believe it. Again, enquired Mr. V. B. Who are we, that have been chosen to perform this great, and he could not but think, good work? A great majority of us are practical farmers; *all freeholders,* and of no small amounts. Were they their own worst enemies? Could they be suspected of a want of fidelity to the freehold interest? No! The farmers had looked for such an event; they earnestly desired it. Whatever ravages the possession of power might have made in the breasts of others, they at least had shewn that they could 'feel power without forgetting right.' If any thing, (said Mr. Van Buren,) could render this invaluable class of men dearer and more estimable than they were, it was this magnanimous sacrifice which they had made on the altar of principle, by consenting to admit those of their fellow citizens, who, though not so highly favoured as themselves by fortune, had still enough to bind them to their country, to an equal participation in the blessings of a free government. Thus, Mr. V. B. said he understood their wishes, and he would govern himself accordingly; having the consolation to know, that if he should have misunderstood them, they would have the power of rescuing themselves, from the effects of such mis-apprehension, by rejecting the amendments, which should be proposed for their adoption.

But let us, said he, consider this subject in another and different point of view; it was their duty, and he had no doubt it was their wish, to satisfy all, so that their proceedings might meet with the approbation of the whole community; it was his desire to respect the wishes and consult the interest of all; he would not hamper the rich nor tread upon the poor, but would respect each alike. He would, he said, submit a few con-siderations to the men of property, who think this provision necessary for its security, and in doing so, he would speak of property in general, dropping the important distinction made by the amendment offered between real and personal estate. Admitting, for the sake of argument, that the distinction was just, and wise, and necessary, for the security of property, was the object effected by the present regulation? He thought not; property was not now represented in the senate on the extent it was erroneously supposed to be. To represent *individual property*, it would be necessary that each individual should have a number of votes in some degree at least, in proportion to the amount of his property; this was the manner in which property was represented, in various corporations and in monied institutions. Suppose in any such institution one man had one hundred shares, another, one share, could you gravely tell the man who held one hundred shares, that his property was represented in the direction, if their votes were equal. To say that because a man worth millions, as is the case of one in this committee, has one vote, and another citizen worth only two hundred and fifty dollars in real estate, has one vote for senators, that therefore their property is equally represented in the senate, is, to say the least, speaking very incorrectly; it is literally substituting a shadow for a reality; and though the case he had stated by way of illustration, would not be a common one, still the disparity which pervaded the whole community, was sufficiently great to render his argument correct. . . .

. . . When the people of this state shall have so far degenerated; when the principles of order or of good government which now characterize our people, and afford security to our institutions, shall have so far given way to those of anarchy and violence, as to lead to an attack on private property, or an agrarian law; to which allusion had been made by the gentleman from Albany, (Mr. Kent); or by an attempt to throw all the public burthens on any particular class of men; then all constitutional provisions will be idle and unavailing, because they will have lost all their force and influence. In answer to the apprehension so frequently expressed, that unless this amendment prevails, there is nothing to prevent all the taxes being laid on the real estate, it is only necessary to state, that there is no more in the constitution of the United States, than there will be in ours, if the amendment fails, to prevent all the revenues of the union from being raised by direct taxation. And was such a fear ever entertained for the general government? How is it possible for gentlemen to suppose, that in a constitutional regulation, under which all the states are enjoying the most ample security for property, an individual state would be exposed to danger?

It is only (said Mr. V. B.) to protect property against property, that a provision in the constitution, basing the representation on property, is, or ought to be, desired in one branch of the government. It is when improvements are contemplated at the public expense, and when for those and for other objects, new impositions are to be put upon property, then it is that the interest of different sections of the state come in contact—and then it is that their respective weight in the legislature, becomes important to them. As for instance, the question of the canal, although the west, the north, and the south might unite in favour of that improvement, and its support by taxation, if that should ever become necessary, the middle and north western parts of the state might not feel that interest, and contemplate that advantage from the measure, as to induce them to consent to be taxed for its support or creation. Again— if it should be proposed to relieve the state from burthens, by calling in the public dues; in that case, that part of your state from which they are due, would have an interest in the question different from the others; in the imposition, increase or decrease of duties on salt, for instance, the effect would be the same; indeed, in all improvements at the public expense, the advantage must, more or less, be equal, while the monies to make them, are raised from the people at large. On such occasions the representation which the different sections of the state have, in proportion to the taxes they pay, may become material. To give to property its relative weight in such cases, in Massachusetts, where this subject has been examined and discussed with a degree of wisdom and research highly honourable to the character of the state, they have thought it wise to apportion their representation in the senate on the basis of the assessment list. Is this representation enjoyed in any reasonable sense, under the existing constitution? Let facts decide.

By the assessment lists in the comptroller's office, it appears that the southern district pays taxes on *one hundred and thirteen millions of dollars*—the western on *fifty-five millions* only —and yet the latter has *nine* senators, and the former only *six;* and after the next apportionment the disproportion will be still greater. Again—the western district, he said, paid one fifth more tax than the middle, which pays only forty-five millions, and yet their representation in the senate was equal. Again—the eastern and middle districts possessed only one third of the wealth, and about three-sevenths of the population of the state, and they elect a majority of the senators. And, to conclude, the city of New-York alone, pays taxes on *sixty-nine millions of dollars*, being *twenty-seven millions* more than the whole eastern district—*twenty-four millions* more than the middle district, and *fourteen millions* more than the western district, and the western district sends nine senators—the middle nine, and the eastern eight, and the city of New-York *one*.

The representation, then, of property in the senate, under the existing constitution, was, he said, as it respected individual estates, wholly delusive, and as it respected the interest of property in the different sections of the state so flagrantly unequal as to destroy practical advantage to property from a representation of it, and not only so, but made it infinitely worse than if property was not professed to be represented at all. . . .

. . . He had no doubt but the honourable gentlemen who had spoken in favour of the amendment, had suffered from the fearful forebodings which they had expressed. That ever to be revered band of patriots who made our constitution, entertained them also, and therefore they engrafted in it the clause which is now contended for. But a full and perfect experience had proved the fallacy of their speculations, and they were now called upon again to adopt the exploded notion; and on that ground, to disfranchise, if not a majority, nearly a moiety, of our citizens. He said he was an unbeliever in the speculations and mere theories on the subject of government, of the best and wisest men, when unsupported by, and especially when opposed to, experience. He believed with a sensible and elegant modern writer, "That constitutions are the work of time, not the invention of ingenuity; and that to frame a complete system of government, depending on habits of reverence and experience, was an attempt as absurd as to build a tree, or manufacture an opinion."

All our observation, he said, united to justify this assertion—when they looked at the proceedings of the Convention which adopted the constitution of the United States, they could not fail to be struck by the extravagance, and, as experience had proved, the futility of the fears and hopes that were entertained and expressed, from the different provisions of

that constitution, by the members. The venerable and enlightened Franklin, had no hope if the president had the qualified
negative, that it would be possible to keep him honest; that
the extensive power of objecting to laws, would inevitably
lead to the bestowment of doucers to prevent the exercise
of the power; and many, very many of the members, believed
that the general government, framed as it was, would, in a
few years, prostrate the state governments. While, on the
other hand, the lamented Hamilton, Mr. Madison, and others,
distressed themselves with the apprehension, that unless they
could infuse more vigour into the constitution they were
about to adopt, the work of their hands could not be expected
to survive its framers. Experience, the only unerring touch-
stone, had proved the fallacy of all those speculations, as
it had also those of the framers of our state constitution, in
the particular now under consideration; and having her records
before them, he was for being governed by them. . . .

15. The Negro and the Suffrage

*The question of the Negro franchise commanded as much attention
as the qualification for senatorial electors. The suffrage recommended
by the legislative committee was explicitly limited to white men.
Nathan Sanford passed over the ominous word in his exposition of
the report, but a member of his committee, John Z. Ross, promptly
supplied the omission. Stephen Van Rensselaer, the eighth patroon
of the great Hudson River manor, proposed a more modest extension
of the suffrage but without limitation as to color. Peter Jay and Robert Clarke, who stood at opposite poles of political opinion on every
other question, united in supporting it. Jay, a well-to-do Westchester
lawyer, had served in the legislature and, for a time, as a criminal
court judge in New York City. He had long been interested in the*

abolition of slavery and had endeavored to expedite the state's very
gradual emancipation law of 1799. Clarke, a physician by profession,
was Root's colleague from Delaware County and as radical a demo-
crat as any man in the convention. But Samuel Young, the prominent
Bucktail leader from Saratoga County, expressed the convictions of
most of the radicals on the issue of the Negro vote. When parliamen-
tary entanglements forced Van Rensselaer to withdraw his substitute,
Jay promptly moved to strike "white" from the committee's suffrage
resolution. The motion passed, after some debate, on September 20.
But the suffrage article was later committed to a select committee of
thirteen, which reported the freehold proposition for Negroes. Judge
Platt, an unblemished conservative, moved the elimination of the
proviso on October 8. His speech concludes the selections from the
debate on the Negro franchise.

. . . MR. Ross. . . .That all men are free and equal, according
to the usual declarations, applies to them only in a state of
nature, and not after the institution of civil government; for
then many rights, flowing from a natural equality, are necessarily abridged, with a view to produce the greatest amount
of security and happiness to the whole community. On this
principle the right of suffrage is extended to white men only.
But why, it will probably be asked, are blacks to be excluded?
I answer, because they are seldom, if ever, required to share
in the common burthens or defence of the state. There are also
additional reasons; they are a peculiar people, incapable, in
my judgment, of exercising that privilege with any sort of
discretion, prudence, or independence. They have no just con-
ceptions of civil liberty. They know not how to appreciate it,
and are consequently indifferent to its preservation.

Under such circumstances, it would hardly be compatible
with the safety of the state, to entrust such a people with this
right. It is not thought advisable to permit aliens to vote, neither

From *Reports*, pp. 180–181, 183–185, 187–191, 374–376.

would it be safe to extend it to the blacks. We deny to minors this right, and why? Because they are deemed incapable of exercising it discreetly, and therefore not safely, for the good of the whole community.—Even the better part of creation, as my honourable friend from Oneida (Mr. N. Williams,) stiles them, are not permitted to participate in this right. No sympathies seemed to be awakened in their behalf, nor in behalf of the aborigines, the original and only rightful proprietors of our soil—a people altogether more acute and discerning, and in whose judicious exercise of the right I should repose far more confidence, than in the African race. In nearly all the western and southern states, indeed many others, even in Connecticut, where steady habits and correct principles prevail, the blacks are excluded. And gentlemen have been frequently in the habit of citing the precedents of our sister states for our guide; and would it not be well to listen to the decisive weight of precedents furnished in this case also? It is true that in many of the states the black population is more numerous than in ours. Then, sir, if the exclusion be unjust or improper, that injustice would be of so much greater extent. The truth is, this exclusion invades no inherent rights, nor has it any connection at all with the question of slavery. The practice of every state in the union, is to make such exceptions, limitations, and provisions in relation to the elective privilege, under their respective constitutions, as are deemed to be necessary or consistent with public good—varied in each according to the existing circumstances under which they are made. It must therefore necessarily rest on the ground of expediency. And, sir, I fear that an extension to the blacks would serve to invite that kind of population to this state, an occurrence which I should most sincerely deplore. The petition presented in their behalf, now on your table, in all probability has been instigated by gentlemen of a different colour, who expect to control their votes. But whether this be so or not, next the blacks will claim to be represented by persons of their own colour, in your halls of legislation. And can you consistently refuse them? It would be well to be prepared for such a claim.

On the whole, sir, let your constitution, at a proper period, declare their emancipation; exempt them from military service as the United States government directs, and from other bur- thens as heretofore; give them the full benefits of protection; and there, in mercy to themselves, and to us, let us stay our hands. . . .

. . . Mr. Jay. . . .When this Convention was first assembled, it was generally understood that provisions would be made to extend the right of suffrage, and some were apprehensive that it might be extended to a degree which they could not approve. But, sir, it was not expected that this right was in any instance to be restricted, much less was it anticipated, or desired, that a single person was to be disfranchised. Why, sir, are these men to be excluded from rights which they possess in common with their countrymen? What crime have they committed for which they are to be punished? Why are they, who were born as free as ourselves, natives of the same country, and deriving from nature and our political institutions, the same rights and privi- leges which we have, now to be deprived of all those rights, and doomed to remain forever as aliens among us? We are told, in reply, that other states have set us the example. It is true that other states treat this race of men with cruelty and injustice, and that we have hitherto manifested towards them a disposition to be just and liberal. Yet even in Virginia and North-Carolina, free people of colour are permitted to vote, and if I am correctly informed, exercise that privilege. In Pennsylvania, they are much more numerous than they are here, and there they are not disfranchised, nor has any incon- venience been felt from extending to all men the rights which ought to be common to all. In Connecticut, it is true, they have, for the last three years, adopted a new constitution which prevents people of colour from acquiring the right of suffrage in future, yet even there they have preserved the right to all those who previously possessed it. . . .

. . . But we are told by one of the select committee, that people of colour are incapable of exercising the right of suffrage. I may have misunderstood that gentleman; but I thought he meant to say, that they laboured under a physical disability. It is true that some philosophers have held that the intellect of a black man, is naturally inferior to that of a white one; but this idea has been so completely refuted, and is now so universally exploded, that I did not expect to have heard of it in an assembly so enlightened as this, nor do I now think it necessary to disprove it. That in general the people of colour are inferior to the whites in knowledge and in industry, I shall not deny. You made them slaves, and nothing is more true than the ancient saying, "The day you make a man a slave takes half his worth away." Unaccustomed to provide for themselves, and habituated to regard labour as an evil, it is no wonder that when set free, they should be improvident and idle, and that their children should be brought up without education, and without prudence or forethought. But will you punish the children for your own crimes; for the injuries which you have inflicted upon their parents? Besides, sir, this state of things is fast passing away. Schools have been opened for them, and it will, I am sure, give pleasure to this committee to know, that in these schools there is discovered a thirst for instruction, and a progress in learning, seldom to be seen in the other schools of the state. They have also churches of their own, and clergymen of their own colour, who conduct their public worship with perfect decency and order, and not without ability.

This state, Mr. Chairman, has taken high ground against slavery, and all its degrading consequences and accompaniments. There are gentlemen on this floor, who, to their immortal honour, have defended the cause of this oppressed people in congress, and I trust they will not now desert them. Adopt the amendment now proposed, and you will hear a shout of triumph and a hiss of scorn from the southern part of the union, which I confess will mortify me—I shall shrink at the sound, because I fear it will be deserved. But it has been said that this measure is necessary to preserve the purity of your elections. I do not deny that necessity has no law, and that self-preservation may justify in states, as well as in individuals, an infringement of the rights of others. Were I a citizen of one of the southern states, I would not (much as I abhor slavery) advise an immediate and universal emancipation. But where is the necessity in the present instance? The whole number of coloured people in the state, whether free or in bondage, amounts to less than a fortieth part of the whole population. When your numbers are to theirs as forty to one, do you still fear them? To assert this, would be to pay them a compliment which, I am sure, you do not think they deserve. But there are a greater number in the city of New-York. How many? Sir, in even that city, the whites are to the blacks as ten to one. And even of the tenth which is composed of the black population, how few are there that are entitled to vote? It has also been said that their numbers are rapidly increasing. The very reverse is the fact. During the last ten years, in which the white population has advanced with astonishing rapidity, the coloured population of the state has been stationary. This fact appears from the official returns of the last and the preceding census, and completely refutes the arguments which are founded upon this mis-statement. Will you, then, without necessity, and merely to gratify an unreasonable prejudice, stain the constitution you are about to form, with a provision equally odious and unjust, and in direct violation of the principles which you profess, and upon which you intend to form it? I trust, I am sure, you will not. . . .

. . . Mr. R. Clarke. . . . Free people of colour are included in the number which regulates your representation in congress, and I wish to know how freemen can be represented when they are deprived of the privilege of voting for representatives. The constitution says, "representatives and direct taxes shall be apportioned among the different states, according to the inhabitants thereof, including all free persons," &c. All colours and complexions are here included. It is not free "white" persons. No, sir, our venerable fathers entertained too strong a sense of justice to countenance such an odious distinction.— Now, sir, taking this in connection with the declaration of independence, I think you cannot exclude them without being guilty of a palpable violation of every principle of justice. We are usurping to ourselves a power which we do not possess, and by so doing, deprive them of a privilege to which they are, and always have been, justly entitled—an invaluable right—a right in which we have prided ourselves as constituting our superiority over every other people on earth—a right which they have enjoyed ever since the formation of our government —the right of suffrage. And why do we do this? Instead of visiting the iniquities of these people upon them and their children, we are visiting their misfortunes upon them and their posterity unto the latest generation. It was not expected of us, that in forming a constitution to govern this state, we should so soon have shewn a disposition to adopt plans fraught with usurpation and injustice. Because we have done this people injustice, by enslaving them, and rendering them degraded and miserable, is it right that we should go on and continue to deprive them of their most invaluable rights, and visit upon their children to the latest posterity this deprivation? Is this just? Is it honest? Was it expected by our constituents? Will it not fix a foul stain upon the proceedings of this Convention which time will not efface.

My honourable colleague has told us "that these people are not liable to do military duty, and that as they are not required to contribute to the protection or defence of the state, they are not entitled to an equal participation in the privileges of its citizens." But, sir, whose fault is this? Have they ever refused to do military duty when called upon? It is haughtily asked, who will stand in the ranks, shoulder to shoulder, with a negro? I answer, no one in time of peace; no one when your musters and trainings are looked upon as mere pastimes; no one when your militia will shoulder their muskets and march to their trainings with as much unconcern as they would go to a sumptuous entertainment, or a splendid ball. But, sir, when the hour of danger approaches, your "white" militia are just as willing that the man of colour should be set up as a mark to be shot at by the enemy, as to be set up themselves. In the war of the revolution, these people helped to fight your battles by land and by sea. Some of your states were glad to turn out corps of coloured men, and to stand "shoulder to shoulder" with them. In your late war they contributed largely towards some of your most splendid victories. On Lakes Erie and Champlain, where your fleets triumphed over a foe superior in numbers, and engines of death, they were manned in a large proportion with men of colour. And in this very house, in the fall of 1814, a bill passed receiving the approbation of all the branches of your government, authorizing the governor to accept the services of a corps of 2000 free people of colour. Sir, these were times which tried men's souls. In these times it was no sporting matter to bear arms. These were times when a man who shouldered his musket, did not know but he bared his bosom to receive a death wound from the enemy ere he laid it aside; and in these times these people were found as ready and as willing to volunteer in your service as any other. They were not compelled to go, they were not drafted. No, your pride had placed them beyond your compulsory power. But there was no necessity for its exercise; they were volunteers; yes, sir, volunteers to defend that very country from the inroads and ravages of a ruthless and vindictive foe, which had treated them with insult, degradation, and slavery. Volunteers are the best of soldiers; give me the men, whatever be their complexion, that willingly volunteer, and not those who are compelled to turn out; such men do not fight from necessity, nor from mercenary motives, but from principle. Such men formed the most efficient corps for your country's defence in the late war; and of such consisted the crews of your squadrons on Erie and Champlain, who largely contributed to the safety and peace of your country, and the renown of her arms. Yet, strange to tell, such are the men whom you seek to degrade and oppress.

There is another consideration which I think important. Our government is a government of the people, supported and upheld by public sentiment; and to support and perpetuate our free institutions, it is our duty and our interest to attach to it all the different classes of the community. Indeed there should be but one class. Then, sir, is it wise, is it prudent, is it consistent with sound policy, to compel a large portion of your people and their posterity, forever to become your enemies, and to view you and your political institutions with distrust, jealousy, and hatred, to the latest posterity; to alienate one portion of the community from the rest, and from their own political institutions? I grant you, sir, that in times of profound peace, their numbers are so small that their resentment could make no serious impression. But, sir, are we sure; can we calculate that we are always to remain in a state of peace? that our tranquillity is never again to be disturbed by invasion or insurrection? And, sir, when that unhappy period arrives, if they, justly incensed by the accumulated wrongs which you heap upon them, should throw their weight in the scale of your enemies, it might, and most assuredly would, be severely felt. Then your gayest and proudest militiamen that now stand in your ranks, would rather be seen "shoulder to shoulder" with a negro, than have him added to the number of his enemies, and meet him in the field of battle.

By retaining the word "white," you impose a distinction impracticable in its operation. Among those who are by way of distinction called whites, and whose legitimate ancestors, as far as we can trace them, have never been slaves, there are many

shades of difference in complexion. Then how will you discriminate? and at what point will you limit your distinction?
Will you here descend to particulars, or leave that to the legislature? If you leave it to them, you will impose upon them a
burden which neither you nor they can bear. You ought not
to require of them impossibilities. Men descended from African
ancestors, but who have been pretty well white-washed by
their commingling with your white population, may escape your
scrutiny; while others, whose blood is as pure from any African
taint as any member of this Convention, may be called upon to
prove his pedigree, or forfeit his right of suffrage, because he
happens to have a swarthy complexion. Are you willing, by
any act of this Convention, to expose any, even the meanest,
of your white citizens, to such an insult? I hope not.

But it is said these people are incapable of exercising the
right of suffrage judiciously; that they will become the tools
and engines of aristocracy, and set themselves up in market,
and give their votes to the highest bidder; that they have no
will or judgment of their own, but will follow implicitly the
dictates of the purse-proud aristocrats of the day, on whom
they depend for bread. This may be true to a certain extent;
but, sir, they are not the only ones who abuse this privilege;
and if this be a sufficient reason for depriving any of your
citizens of their just rights, go on and exclude also the many
thousands of white fawning, cringing sycophants, who look up
to their more wealthy and more ambitious neighbours for
direction at the polls, as they look to them for bread. But
although most of this unfortunate class of men may at present
be in this dependent state, both in body and mind, yet we
ought to remember, that we are making our constitution, not
for a day, nor a year, but I hope for many generations; and
there is a redeeming spirit in liberty, which I have no doubt
will eventually raise these poor, abused, unfortunate people,
from their present degraded state, to equal intelligence with
their more fortunate and enlightened neighbours.

Sir, there is a day now fixed by law, when slavery must for-ever cease in this state. Have gentlemen seriously reflected upon the consequences which may result from this event, when they are about to deprive them of every inducement to become respectable members of society, turning them out from the protection, and beyond the control of their masters, and in the mean time ordaining them to be fugitives, vagabonds, and out-casts from society.

Sir, no longer ago than last winter, the legislature of this state almost unanimously resolved, that their senators be in-structed, and their representatives requested, to prevent any state from being admitted into this union, which should have incorporated in her constitution any provision denying to the citizens of "each state all the rights, privileges, and immunities of citizens of the several states." These instructions and re-quests, it is well known, particularly referred to Missouri; and were founded upon a clause in her constitution, interdicting this very class of people "from coming to, or settling in, that state, under any pretext whatsoever." Whether these instruc-tions and requests were proper and expedient at that time or not, is not necessary for me to inquire, and I only refer to them to shew, how tenacious the representatives of the people were, at that time, of even the smallest rights of this portion of their citizens—rights of infinitely less importance to the free people of colour of this state, than those of which you now propose to deprive them. About the same time, my honourable col-league, then a member of the assembly of this state, introduced a bill, declaring that, according to our declaration of inde-pendence and form of government, "slavery cannot exist in this state." I shall give no opinion upon the propriety of passing such a law at this day; but I will say, that even the advocating such a humane proposition, gave honourable testimony of the benevolence of his heart. And is it possible, that the represen-tatives of the same people should be found, in a few short months afterwards, entertaining a proposition, which virtually and practically declares, that freedom, that liberty cannot exist in this state; and this proposition receiving support from the same individual who last winter was the champion of African emancipation.

Sir, I well know that this subject is attended with embarrassment and difficulty, in whatever way it may be presented. I lament as much as any gentleman, that we have this species of population among us. But we have them here without any fault of theirs. They were brought here and enslaved by the arm of violence and oppression. We have heaped upon them every indignity, every injustice; and in restoring them at this late day, (as far as is practicable) to their natural rights and privileges, we make but a very partial atonement for the many wrongs which we have heaped upon them; and in the solemn work before us, as far as it related to these people, I would do them justice, and leave the consequences to the righteous disposal of an all-wise and merciful Providence.

The honourable gentleman from Genesee (Mr. Ross) has said that they were a *peculiar* people. We were told the other day that the people of Connecticut were a *peculiar* people. Indeed this is a *peculiarly* happy mode of evading the force of an argument. I admit that the blacks are a *peculiarly* unfortunate people, and I wish that such inducements may be held out, as shall induce them to become a sober and industrious class of the community, and raise them to the high standard of independent electors. . . .

. . . COL. YOUNG. . . . The gentleman who had just sat down had adverted to the declaration of independence to prove that the blacks are possessed of "certain unalienable rights." But is the right of voting a natural right? If so, our laws are oppressive and unjust. A natural right is one that is born with us. No man is born twenty-one years old, and of course all restraint upon the natural right of voting, during the period of nonage, is usurpation and tyranny. This confusion arises from mixing natural with acquired rights. The right of voting is adventitious. It is resorted to only as a means of securing our natural rights.

In forming a constitution, we should have reference to the feelings, habits, and modes of thinking of the people. The gentleman last up has alluded to the importance of regarding public sentiment. And what is the public sentiment in relation to this subject? Are the negroes permitted to a participation in social intercourse with the whites! Are they elevated to public office! No, sir—public sentiment forbids it. This they know; and hence they are prepared to sell their votes to the highest bidder. In this manner you introduce corruption into the very vitals of the government.

A few years ago a law was made requiring the clerks of the respective counties to make out a list of jurymen. Was a negro ever returned upon that list? If he were, no jury would sit with him. Was a constable ever known to summon a negro as a juror, even before a justice of the peace in a matter of five dollars amount? Never,—but gentlemen who would shrink from such an association, would now propose to associate with him in the important act of electing a governor of the state.

This distinction of colour is well understood. It is unnecessary to disguise it, and we ought to shape our constitution so as to meet the public sentiment. If that sentiment should alter—if the time should ever arrive when the African shall be raised to the level of the white man—when the distinctions that now prevail shall be done away—when the colours shall intermarry—when negroes shall be invited to your tables—to sit in your pew, or ride in your coach, it may then be proper to institute a new Convention, and remodel the constitution so as to conform to that state of society.

It has been urged, however, that it is not their fault that they do not serve in the militia. Granted—but state authority cannot compel them to serve. That subject is left to the general government, which directs the enrolment of *white* citizens only. *Expressio unius, est exclusio alterius.*[4]

An argument has been raised that the proposition in the report of the committee would deprive them of *vested rights.*

It has been correctly remarked in reply, by the gentleman from Delaware, (Mr. Root,) that you cannot vary or extend the rights of one class, without infringing upon those of another. Formerly, no residence was required for a voter. Now it is proposed to require the residence of a year; and perhaps by that provision the rights of four or five hundred emigrants may be affected, and by this, we may possibly exclude four or five hundred black freeholders. The argument in the one case will apply to the other.

If we look back to the time when our constitution was formed, we find that there were then few or no free blacks in the state. The present state of things was not contemplated, and hence no provision was made against it. The same was the case in Connecticut. In their recent constitution they have provided for the exclusion of the blacks.

If you admit the negroes, why exclude the aborigines? They have never been enslaved. They were born, free as the air they breathe. That want of self-respect which characterises the negroes, cannot be imputed to them.

It is said that the negroes fought our battles. So did aliens— the French. But were the French on that account entitled to vote at our elections? No, sir. It is a question of expediency; and believing as I do, that the blacks would abuse the privilege if granted, I am disposed to withhold it. . . .

. . . It had been objected that this measure would be a hardship upon the blacks. But it had been recently and soberly done in the land of "steady habits." And are we more wise, more sober, more correct, than they? We ought to make a con-

---

[4] When some members of a class are mentioned, others of the same class are excluded [Ed.].

stitution adapted to *our* habits, manners, and state of society. Metaphysical refinements and abstract speculations are of little use in framing a constitution. No white man will stand shoulder to shoulder with a negro in the train band or jury-room. He will not invite him to a seat at his table, nor in his pew in the church. And yet he must be placed on a footing of equality in the right of voting, and on no other occasion whatever, either civil or social.

It had been said that there was no criterion to determine questions of fact in relation to the various shades of colour. That will be left for the legislature to define and settle. And although there may be some difficulty in individual cases, yet that circumstance furnishes no argument against the establishment of the principle.

The minds of the blacks are not competent to vote. They are too much degraded to estimate the value, or exercise with fidelity and discretion that important right. It would be unsafe in their hands. Their vote would be at the call of the richest purchaser. If this class of people should hereafter arrive at such a degree of intelligence and virtue, as to inspire confidence, then it will be proper to confer this privilege upon them. At present emancipate and protect them; but withhold that privilege which they will inevitably abuse. Look to your jails and penitentiaries. By whom are they filled? By the very race, whom it is now proposed to clothe with the power of deciding upon your political rights.

If there is that natural, inherent right to vote, which some gentlemen have urged, it ought to be further extended. In New-Jersey, females were formerly allowed to vote; and on that principle, you must admit *negresses* as well as *negroes* to participate in the right of suffrage. Minors, too, and aliens must no longer be excluded, but the "era of good feelings" be commenced in earnest. . . .

. . . Mr. Platt moved to expunge the proviso in the first section, which declares that no person, "*other than a white man*," shall vote, unless he have a freehold estate of the value of $250. He said, I am not disposed, sir, to turn knight-errant in favour of the men of colour. But the obligations of justice are eternal and indispensable: and this proviso involves a principle which, upon reflection, I cannot concede, or compromise as a matter of expediency. I am aware of the intrinsic difficulty of this subject. The evils of negro slavery are deep rooted, and admit of no sudden and effectual remedy. In the act of doing justice, we are bound to consider consequences. With such a population as that of Virginia, or the Carolinas, a sudden emancipation, and permission to the negroes to vote, would be incompatible with the public safety: and necessity creates a law for itself. But, sir, in this state there is no grounds for such a plea. I admit, that most of the free negroes in our state, are unfit to be entrusted with the right of suffrage; they have neither sufficient intelligence, nor a sufficient degree of independence, to exercise that right in a safe and proper manner. I would exclude the great mass of them, but not by this unjust and odious discrimination of colour. We are under no necessity of adopting such a principle, in laying the foundation of our government. Let us attain this object of exclusion, by fixing such a uniform standard of qualification, as would not only exclude the great body of free men of colour, but also a large portion of ignorant and depraved white men, who are as unfit to exercise the power of voting as the men of colour. By adopting the principle of universal suffrage, in regard to white men, we create the necessity, which is now pleaded as an excuse for this unjust discrimination. Our republican text is, that all men are born equal, in civil and political rights; and if this proviso be ingrafted into our constitution, the practical commentary will be, that a portion of our free citizens shall not enjoy equal rights with their fellow citizens. All freemen, of African parentage, are to be constitutionally degraded: no matter how virtuous or intelligent. Test the principle, sir, by another example. Suppose the proposition were, to make a discrimination, so as to exclude the descendants of German, or Low Dutch, or Irish ancestors; would not every man be shocked at the horrid injustice of the principle? It is in vain to disguise the fact; we shall violate a sacred principle, without any necessity, if we retain this discrimination. We say to this unfortunate race of men, purchase a freehold estate of $250 value, and you shall then be equal to the white man, who parades one day in the militia, or performs a day's work on the highway. Sir, it is adding mockery to injustice. We know that, with rare exceptions, they have not the means of purchasing a freehold: and it would be unworthy of this grave Convention to do, *indirectly*, an act of injustice, which we are unwilling openly to avow. The real object is, to exclude the oppressed and degraded sons of Africa; and, in my humble judgment, it would better comport with the dignity of this Convention to speak out, and to pronounce the sentence of perpetual degradation, on negroes and their posterity for ever, than to establish a test, which we know they cannot comply with, and which we do not require of others.

The gentleman from Saratoga, who, as chairman of the committee, reported this proviso, (Mr. Young,) has exultingly told us, that ours is the only happy country where freemen acknowledge no distinction of ranks—where real native genius and merit can emerge from the humblest conditions of life, and rise to honours and distinction. It sounded charmingly in our republican ears, and I have but one objection to it, which is that, unfortunately for our patriotic pride, it is not true. I abhor the vices and oppressions which flow from privileged orders as much as any man, but it is a remarkable truth, that in England, the present *Lord Chancellor Elden,* and his illustrious brother, *Sir William Scott,* are the sons of a *coal-heaver;* and the present *Chief Justice Abbot,* of the Kings Bench, is the son of a *hair-dresser.* The gentleman from Saratoga, (Mr. Young,) began his philipic in favour of universal suffrage, by an eulogium on liberty and equality, in our happy state. And what then? Why, the same gentleman concluded by moving a resolution, in substance, that 37,000 of our free black citizens, and their posterity, for ever, shall be degraded by our constitution, below the common rank of freemen—that they never shall emerge from their humble condition—that they shall never assert the dignity of human nature, but shall ever remain a degraded caste in our republic.

The same gentleman recited to us on that occasion, an elegant extract from an admired poet, (Gray's Elegy,) describing in melting strains, the effects of humble poverty, and mental depression. Let me ask, sir, who is it, that now seeks to "repress the noble rage"; and to "freeze the genial current of the soul"? I must be permitted, to express my deep regret, that the gentleman's *poetry*, and his *prose*, do not agree in sentiment. I confess sir, I feel some apprehension, when I anticipate, that the speeches of that honourable member, will be read by the proud English critic;[5] who will boast, that "slaves cannot breathe English air"; that "they touch his country, and their shackles fall." The gentleman from Saratoga will be justly considered, as a leading patriot and statesman in our republic; and if his text and his commentary, his precept and his practice, are at variance; we shall be nakedly exposed to the lash of criticism, from the hand of retaliation.

Before we adopt this proviso, I hope gentlemen will take a retrospect of the last fifty years. Consider the astonishing progress of the human mind, in regard to religious toleration; the various plans of enlightened benevolence; and especially the mighty efforts of the wise and the good throughout Christendom, in favour of the benighted and oppressed children of Africa.

In our own state, public sentiment has been totally changed

---

[5] Probably the Reverend Sydney Smith (1771–1845), author of a famous attack on American culture in *The Edinburgh Review* in 1820 [Ed.].

on the subject of negro slavery. About sixty years ago, an act of our colonial assembly was passed, with this disgraceful preamble: "whereas justice and good policy require, that the African slave-trade should be liberally encouraged." And within the last forty years, I remember, in the sale of negroes, it was no uncommon occurrence to witness the separation of husband and wife, and parents and children, without their consent, and under circumstances which forbid all hope of their ever seeing each other again in this world. And this was done without apparent remorse or compunction, and with as little reluctance on the part of buyer and seller, as we now feel in separating a span of horses, or a yoke of oxen. But I thank God, that a sense of justice and mercy has in a good measure regenerated the hearts of men. A rapid emancipation has taken place; and we approach the era, when, according to the existing law, slavery will be abolished in this state.

But, sir, we owe to that innocent and unfortunate race of men, much more than mere emancipation. We owe to them our patient and persevering exertions, to elevate their condition and character, by means of moral and religious instruction. And I rejoice that by the instrumentality of Sunday schools, and other benevolent institutions, many of them promise fair to become intelligent, virtuous, and useful citizens. Judging from our experience of the last fifty years; what may we not reasonably expect, in the next half century? Sir, if we adopt the principle of this proviso, I hope and believe, that our posterity will blush, when they see the names recorded in favour of such a discrimination.

I beseech gentlemen to consider the enlighted age in which we live! Consider how much has already been accomplished by the efforts of Christian philanthropy! During the last forty years, we have brought up this African race from the house of bondage: We have led them nearly through the wilderness, and shewn them the promised land. Shall we now drive them back again into Egypt? I hope not, sir. The light

of science, and the heavenly beams of Christianity, are dawn-
ing upon them. Shall we extinguish these rays of hope? This
is not a mere question of expediency. Man has no right to deal
thus with his fellow man; except on the ground of necessity
and public safety. It is not pretended that such a reason exists
in this case. We shall violate a sacred principle, to avoid, at
most a slight inconvenience:—and, if I do not deceive myself,
those who shall live fifty years hence, will view this proviso in
the same light as we now view the law of our New-England
fathers, which punished with death all who were guilty of being Quakers, or the law of our fathers in the colonial assembly
of New-York, which offered bounties to encourage the slave
trade.

As a republican statesman, I protest against the principle of
inequality contained in this proviso. As a man and a father,
who expects justice for himself and his children, in this world;
and as a Christian, who hopes for mercy in the world to come;
I can not, I dare not, consent to this unjust proscription. . . .

16. Blasphemy and Libel

*On October 17, when the report of the legislative committee was
under consideration, Erastus Root moved to add an amendment that
would prohibit the judiciary from declaring "any particular religion"
to be the law of the land and from excluding witnesses on account of
religion. The next day he withdrew the latter clause, introducing it
separately at a later time but without success. The former clause was
clearly aimed at Chancellor Kent, who in a much disputed blasphemy
case,* People vs. Ruggles (1811) *had returned a conviction under the
rule of English common law that Christianity is "part and parcel of
the laws of the land." Kent defended his opinion against Root's attack, though he supposed the amendment "perfectly harmless" and*

actually voted with the majority on its passage in committee of the whole. But the judges, Senator King, and others did not think it harmless. Chief Justice Spencer, who moved to strike the amendment when it came before the convention, held that the words "particular religion" would place Judaism, Mohammedanism, and other faiths on an equality with Christianity and thus prohibit punishment of blasphemy. Kent now supported his friends, but he confused the issue by saying that blasphemy was punishable only as an offence against good morals, which was certainly not the doctrine of People vs. Ruggles. Spencer's motion prevailed. Fortunately, because the character of American institutions would not support Kent's rule, trials for blasphemy became exceedingly rare or nonexistent in New York and the other states.

Another minor but significant issue touching the judiciary concerned the law of libel, which of course had a direct bearing on freedom of the press. The committee on personal liberties proposed a constitutional guarantee that in cases of libel the truth might be admitted in evidence if published from good motives and for justifiable ends, but it left the determination of motive to the discretion of the court. Nathan Sanford moved an amendment to require decision by the jury. Root supported the amendment. Kent objected, though in the opinion of several delegates the amendment only gave constitutional standing to the existing statute. In fact, Jacob Sutherland implied that the Chancellor had actually set his own discretion above the law, which was further reason for writing the guarantee into the constitution. It passed, 97 to 8.

. . . GEN. ROOT moved to add to the section as just passed, or as a distinct section, the following:

"The judiciary shall not declare any particular religion, to be the law of the land; nor exclude any witness on account of his religious faith."

From *Reports*, pp. 462–464, 574–576, 488–493.

The supreme court, as Mr. Root contended, had brought into this state the common law of England, in defiance of what he (Mr. R.) considered to be the constitution of the state. Indictments had been sustained for blasphemy—particularly in the county of Herkimer, and in the county of Washington, as contained in Johnson's Reports. In the latter case it had been declared that Christianity was a part of the law of the land— and this was borrowed from the common law of England. The common law of that country was established during the prevalence of the Roman Catholic religion. It was then that they issued writs *de heretico comburendo*[6]—and this was the law that had been introduced into this state. If this was correct, punishment for blasphemy should now be inflicted on such as would not acknowledge the supremacy of the mother church, and on those who should ridicule the eating of wafers, or the doctrine of transubstantiation.

With respect to the part of the amendment relative to the exclusion of witnesses, he would observe—that when brought forward they were to be interrogated and catechised as to their articles of faith. If it was not held to be correct, they were excluded. This was calculated to produce falsehood and hypocrisy. Indeed if suffered to prevail, hypocrisy and lies would become the chief qualifications for a witness. And yet in a city, large enough in its population for a state, you have a Jew for a sheriff. As the law now is, he is guilty of blasphemy every time he enters the synagogue. Suppose a Musselman reads the Koran for his edification; he is guilty of blasphemy! He wished for freedom of conscience. Where that existed, true religion would flourish. But where such punishments were inflicted, commiseration would be excited for the accused, and execration for the ministers of the law. If judges undertake to support religion by the arm of the law, it will be brought into abhorrence and contempt.

---

[6] Concerning the burning of heretics [Ed.].

CHANCELLOR KENT said that the gentleman from Delaware (Mr. Root) had not stated correctly the decision of the supreme court which he arraigned. The court had never declared or adjudged that christianity was a religion established by law. They had only decided that to revile the author of christianity in a blasphemous manner, and with a malicious intent, was an offence against public morals, and indictable. The case to which the gentleman referred, arose in the county of Washington, in 1811. A person was indicted in that county for having uttered in a wanton manner, and with a malicious disposition, in the presence and hearing of divers people, that *Jesus Christ was a bastard and his mother a whore.* He was found guilty by a jury at the Oyer and Terminer, and the cause was removed into the supreme court, and the question submitted to the court was, whether the uttering of these words, in the manner and with the intent and disposition charged, was not a misdemeanor? He had the honour at that time to be chief justice of that court; and after argument and consideration, the court, consisting besides himself of judges Thompson, Spencer, Van Ness, and Yates, unanimously decided that the indictment was good, and the conviction valid in law.

This is the true state of the case. The court considered those blasphemous words, uttered with such an intent, as a breach of public morals, and an offence against public decency. They were indictable on the same principle as the act of wantonly going naked, or committing impure and indecent acts in the public streets. It was not because christianity was established by law, but because christianity was in fact the religion of this country, the rule of our faith and practice, and the basis of the public morals. Such blasphemy was an outrage upon public decorum, and if sanctioned by our tribunals would shock the moral sense of the country, and degrade our character as a christian people.

The authors of our constitution never meant to extirpate christianity, more than they meant to extirpate public decency.

It is in a degree recognized by the statute for the observance of the Lord's Day, and for the mode of administering oaths. The reasons of the judgment are in print, and before the public, and to them he referred. The court never intended to interfere with any religious creeds or sects, or with religious discussions. They meant to preserve, so far as it came within their cognizance, the morals of the country, which rested on christianity as the foundation. They meant to apply the principles of common law against blasphemy, which they did not believe the constitution ever meant to abolish. Are we not a christian people? Do not ninety-nine hundredths of our fellow citizens hold the general truths of the Bible to be dear and sacred? To attack them with ribaldry and malice, in the presence of those very believers, must, and ought, to be a serious public offence. It disturbs, and annoys, and offends, and shocks, and corrupts the public taste. The common law, as applied to correct such profanity, is the application of common reason and natural justice to the security of the peace and good order of society.

The supreme court is likewise charged by the gentleman from Delaware, (Mr. Root,) with rejecting the testimony of witnesses who had no religious belief. I do not know to what case the gentleman alludes. The act concerning oaths contained the only test or belief ever required of a witness, which was, that he believed in the *existence of a supreme being, and a future state of rewards and punishments*. He was persuaded that the court had never gone further in their inquiries of a witness. He had no knowledge of any case calling for such animadversion. This was all that the courts had done, as far as he knew, to check atheists and blasphemers: and could this Convention possibly think that the gentleman's amendment to the constitution was wanting to give them further protection? We should endanger the security of life, liberty, and property, and the comfort and happiness of our families. . . .

. . . MR. KING. With doubts on the subject, which I desire

rightly to understand, I hesitate in agreeing to the legal doctrine now recommended to our acceptance, and which seems to deny to the Christian religion the acknowledgment, protection, and authority, to which I have believed it to be by law entitled.

We are urged to amend the constitution, by adding an article thereto, "that no *particular religion* shall ever be declared, or adjudged to be the law of the land." We all know that the constitution of the state provides, "that such parts of the common and statute law of England, and of the acts of the colony of New-York, as together formed the law of the colony on the 19th of April, 1775, shall continue to be the law of the state, subject to such alterations as the legislature shall make concerning the same: and that all such parts of the common and statute law, and of the acts of the colony, as may be construed to establish or maintain any particular denomination of Christians, or their ministers, were, and are, abrogated and rejected."

It is not stated that the legislature have made any alterations in this law; and it is only necessary to ascertain its just interpretations, in order to determine how far the Christian religion may be declared and adjudged to be recognized as a portion of the law of the land.

The laws of every nation in Christendom have for ages acknowledged and protected the Christian religion—and in virtue of the laws and statutes of England, the Christian religion, for many centuries, has been acknowledged and established in that nation.

While the Christian religion, by force of the common and statute laws of England, and the acts of the colony of New-York, was fully acknowledged, and as respected the Episcopalians, was even established in the colony, the constitution provides that all such parts of these laws, as might be construed to establish or maintain any particular denomination of Christians, or their ministers, should be abrogated and rejected.

The object of this provision was to abolish the discrimination, by which the Episcopalians were alone deemed to be established in the colony, and thereby to place every denomination of Christians on the same, and upon an equal footing. Another clause of the constitution, to guard against spiritual oppression and intolerance, ordains that the free exercise and enjoyment of religious profession and worship, shall for ever *be allowed* within this state to all mankind. The fair import of the several provisions, taken in connection with each other, must be, that the laws of the state do so far recognize and establish the Christian religion, (comprehending all denominations of Christians, without distinction or preference,) as portion of the law of the land, that defamatory, scandalous, or blasphemous attacks upon the same, may and should be restrained and punished.

While all mankind are by our constitution tolerated, and free to enjoy religious profession and worship within this state, yet the religious professions of the Pagan, the Mahomedan, and the Christian, are not, in the eye of the law, of equal truth and excellence.

According to the Christian system, men pass into a future state of existence, when the deeds of their life become the subject of rewards or punishment—the moral law rests upon the truth of this doctrine, without which it has no sufficient sanction. Our laws constantly refer to this revelation, and by the oath which they prescribe, we appeal to the Supreme Being, so to deal with us hereafter, as we observe the obligation of our oaths.

The Pagan world were, and are, without the mighty influence of this principle, which is proclaimed in the Christian system— their morals were destitute of its powerful sanction, while their oaths neither awakened the hopes, nor the fears which a belief in Christianity inspires.

While the constitution tolerates the religious professions and worship of all men, it does more in behalf of the religion of the gospel—and by acknowledging, and in a certain sense, incorporating its truths into the laws of the land, we are restrained from adopting the proposed amendment, whereby the Christian religion may lose that security which every other Christian nation is anxious to afford it.

The provisions of the constitution, having served to preserve the purity of the religion which is professed by our fellow citizens, and not having in any case proved intolerant to those who have dissented from their worship; is it not a matter of prudence, as well as duty, that we leave this part of the constitution unaltered?

COL. YOUNG replied to the remarks of the gentleman from Queens, (Mr. King,) and was unable to see the force of his arguments. Jews, Mahomedans, and persons of all religions, were recognized as competent witnesses in courts of law. He related an instance where a Hindoo was admitted to swear in an English court.

CHANCELLOR KENT said, that the gentleman from Otsego, (Mr. Van Buren,) had given what he thought the just exposition of the case of the *People* vs. *Ruggles*, in VIIIth Johnson's Reports. He never intended to declare Christianity the legal religion of the state, because that would be considering Christianity as the established religion, and make it a civil or political institution. The constitution had declared that there was to be "no discrimination or preference in religious profession or worship." But Christianity was, *in fact*, the religion of the people of this state, and that fact was the principle of the decision. The Christian religion was the foundation of all belief and expectation of a future state, and the source and security of moral obligation. To blaspheme the author of that religion, and to defame it with wantonness and malice, was an offence against public morals, and injured the social ties and the moral sense of the country; and in that view the offence was punishable. The legislature had repeatedly recognized the Christian religion, not as the religion of the country established by law, but as being in truth the actual religion of the people of this state. The statute directing the administration of an oath, referred to the Bible as a sanction to it, and on the ground that the Bible was a volume of divine inspiration, and the oracle of the most affecting truths that could command the assent, or awaken the fears, or exercise the hopes, of mankind. So the act for the religious observance of the Lord's day, equally recognized the universal belief in Christianity, and the moral obligation and eminent utility of its precepts. In this sense, we may consider the duties and injunctions of the Christian religion as interwoven with the law of the land, and as part and parcel of the common law; and maliciously to revile it, is a public grievance, and as much so as any other public outrage upon common decency and decorum. The present constitution had gone quite far enough with the freedom of toleration of religious opinion. We had better leave it as it is, without any new provision on the subject, and especially any that might be construed to allow of still increasing latitude of discourse and action. We cannot now, without a statute provision, punish any attacks, by words or actions, or writings or prints, upon Christianity, any further than they may be considered as offences *contra bonus mores,*[7] and breaches of those public morals, and of that universal sense of fitness and duty, which rest as their basis on the belief of the Bible. . . .

. . . CHANCELLOR KENT said there were cases, in which the truth ought not to be heard in evidence; he would suppose for instance, that a publication had been made, charging a female with some personal defect, which might subject her to ridicule and wound and harass her feelings, and the feelings of her family; the injury might be so gross, as to require a resort for legal redress; and he would ask, whether it would be proper, that in such a case, a court and jury should be compelled to hear evidence, which must necessarily be very indecent and indelicate, and such as must tend to vitiate the public taste,

---

[7] Against good morals, i.e., harmful to the moral welfare of society [Ed.].

and to corrupt the public morals. The truth in such a case, so far from being a justification, ought to be considered an aggravation. Libels of that description could not possibly be published from a good motive or for any justifiable end; the publishers could have no other object in view, than to gratify the vile passions of envy or malice; and to permit them to give the truth in evidence, would be to degrade courts of justice into vehicles, for propagating most effectually, the most detestable slanders. Mr. K. referred to a case, which had happened in England. A suit had been brought on a wager, relating to a French minister at the English court, the Chevalier D'Eon; the case was noticed for trial before Lord Mansfield, and it was proposed to enter into an examination, to prove before the jury, that the minister was a female. The judge threw the record from him with indignation, and declared that he would not permit the sanctuary of justice to be profaned with a proceeding so indecent.

To permit the truth to be given in evidence in such cases, would be affording to malice an opportunity to glut its vengeance; a defendant who had libelled a female of a family, would call as witnesses perhaps the mother and sisters; and would degrade them, by an examination, which could not be listened to, without shocking the moral sense of all decent people.

He had, he said, always been opposed to what was once considered the law of libels, to wit: that on indictments for libels, the truth could not, under any circumstances be given in evidence; and gave the history of a case which had been tried in this state in 1804. It was an indictment for a libel against Mr. H. Croswell. The trial was had before the then Chief Justice Lewis. The defendant offered to give the truth in evidence: the judge decided, that it could not be received. The question was brought up for argument before the supreme court of this state, and was argued for the defendant by the late general Hamilton, and a more able and eloquent argument was perhaps never heard in any court.

Mr. [Alexander] Hamilton, counsel for the defendant on that occasion, contended that the truth might be given in evidence, provided the matter charged to be libellous was published with good motives and for justifiable ends, and such was his (Mr. Kent's) opinion. There were only four judges on the bench at the time, and being equally divided, the matter rested there. It was, he said, in consequence of this trial, that the statute was passed on this subject, permitting the truth to be given in evidence under the above restriction. He wished, he said, to preserve the principles of this statute, but considered the amendment of the gentleman from New-York as going much farther.

If a way could be devised by which the jury could be enabled to judge of the motives from which the publication had sprung, without a previous examination of the witnesses, he would have no objection to leave it to them. But that, he said, could not be done. And the only way in which such indecent and indelicate examinations could be excluded, was to leave with the judge to say, whether the testimony could be received: He did not believe that this power would be abused; it was necessary for the due administration of justice, that confidence should be placed in them. If such enquiries were permitted, there would always be some unworthy members of the bar, who would press them upon courts and juries: He hoped, therefore, that the amendment would not prevail. . . .

. . . GEN. ROOT said a mistaken notion had arisen in this country, from the strong predilection which the judges and lawyers feel for the law of England. In England it was a maxim that the king can do no wrong. That maxim and law might do in a monarchical government, where the ministers are subjects of the ridicule and recrimination; but in a republican government, to say that your president and governor can do no wrong, would not be endured. In England, the public officers, who live upon public plunder, are to be shielded from popular animadversion through the medium of the papers, or any other medium, even that of caricature. It is for the purpose of keeping up their monarchy, and therefore the greater the truth there, the greater the libel. In this country, where our governor and other great men are the subjects of scrutiny, we are told that the judges must be entrusted with the exercise of this power, which the honourable gentleman from Montgomery, (Mr. Dodge) has told us was exercised in a case which he had the honour of defending; when the judge determined that the truth should not be given in evidence, and that he was exclusively authorised to seal irrevocably and irremediably, the fate of his fellow-citizens.

Give me, said Mr. R. a Turkish bashaw, who directs the head of an individual to be stricken off, and then proceeds to determine his guilt. This bashaw does not condemn without he has a strong belief that the circumstances will warrant the measure; but our judge can consign to infamy and distress the victim of his caprice, without any regard to truth or justice. If these judges are to be trusted in all cases, where is the boasted privilege of trial by jury, so much eulogised in this country? If all is to be trusted to the judges, why not abolish the form of trial by jury at once? A defendant is summoned to appear at court, he goes with the most perfect confidence in the justice of his cause, supposing that the truth given in evidence will acquit him; but when he comes into the court he is told that the truth cannot be given in evidence. Sit down, sir, is the language which I have frequently heard come from the bench. The man is thus deprived of his defence, and the jury are compelled to pass upon his guilt, after hearing a more powerful and eloquent harangue from the bench than it is in the power of counsel to offer; and they are told that they must give exemplary damages, on account of the audacity and temerity of this defendant, in publishing the truth, and bringing it to be recorded in the journals of the court. Is this the way that justice is to be administered in a free country? It is insisted that the judges must be made independent of the people, and then trust them with the disposal of our lives, liberty, and property. Why are these judges to be rendered independent of the people? It is that they may play the tyrant under the sanction of a constitutional law.

The Dey of Algiers will hesitate before he plays the tyrant, because if his conduct is not justifiable, he knows that strangling is his fate; but our judges are safe; they know that political strangulation cannot be enforced upon them. . . .

. . . How many libels were published for years against the sage of Monticello, and what was their effect? They recoiled on their authors, whilst the object of their slander, and the patriot of his age, became more and more endeared to his country. Whilst his venerable predecessor was surrounded by sedition laws, and sanctioned prosecutions for libels, he sunk far below the common level; but since he has retired to private life, his character has been elevated and he again stands endeared to his countrymen. When he was surrounded by all this machinery, and when his friends were enforcing the penalty of the law, by prosecuting and immuring in dungeons, from one part of the union to another—how his character sunk! From a patriot, he became a despot; and instead of a republican, he was considered a tyrant!

Are gentlemen anxious for a like state of things at the present day, and in this great and patriotic state?

We are told by the honourable Chancellor, that the character of a female may be assailed. Would not the publisher of a slander against one of the fair ones receive his punishment, whether it was true or false? In either case, let it be determined by a jury: they are the most competent to determine whether his motives are good or bad.

The Chancellor has again referred us to a case which came before Lord Mansfield, in England, when the Chevalier D'Eon was publicly represented as a female, although he appeared in the character of a French ambassador to the court of St. James'. Can the provision which we are about to make affect such a case as that? No: the action could not lie, and the evidence would not be admitted to prove the fact which should so wantonly wound the feelings of this man or woman, as the case might be. He should hope that all such actions might fail; and in all actions of assumpsit, for the recovery of wages, the evidence ought to be rejected.

Mr. R. said he should vote for the amendment offered by the gentleman from New-York, although he did not think it went far enough. He would go further, and say that when a man considered himself libelled, he should not make use of a grand jury and public officers, at public expense, to vindicate his character. Let him bring his action as for verbal slander. He should not make a proposition to that effect, because he knew the attachment to the English libel system was so great that he should not succeed if he attempted it.

Mr. SANFORD said, that he conceived it to be of great importance that the freedom of speech and of the press should be secured by the constitution. The freedom of the press is the best security of public liberty; and this truth, so familiar to us all, has become an acknowledged maxim, which requires no discussion. The liberty of the press in this state, now depends upon the pleasure of the legislature. The existing law of the state upon that subject may be at any time repealed, and any other regulation abridging the rights of the citizens in this respect, may be substituted. The point now under consideration, is a very precise question. The provision reported by the select committee is, that in prosecutions for libels, the truth may be given in evidence, if it shall appear that the matter charged as libellous was published with good motives and for justifiable ends. The amendment of this provision, which he, Mr. S. proposed, was, that in all prosecutions for libels, the truth may be given in evidence to the jury, and that if it shall appear to the jury that the matter charged as a libel was published with good motives and for justifiable ends, the truth shall be a complete defence. According to the first proposition, the judge is to decide upon the motive and purpose of the person charged as a libeller. According to the second proposition, the jury are to hear the evidence, and to decide upon the motive and purpose of the publisher of the alleged libel. Mr. S. would never agree that the judge should have the sole power of deciding whether the truth of the libel should be received as a defence or not. Is a citizen prosecuted for a libel, to be tried and condemned by the judge alone? And is no evidence to be given even to that judge? According to this project, no inquiry into the truth of the case can take place, unless the judge shall first decide that the intentions of the party accused were good. How is the judge to decide upon the purpose with which the alleged libel was published? He is to hear no proof of facts, to show a purpose of good or ill; but he is to decide by divination, or arbitrary discretion, whether the charge in question was published from good or from bad motives. The true motives of the publisher are always a matter of fact; they seldom appear from the supposed libel itself; and they often form the principal question in such prosecutions. Thus the judge is to decide the most difficult question in the cause, upon the mere perusal of the supposed libel. If the judge should think the motives of the publisher unjustifiable, all evidence of the truth of the charges would be excluded, and the party accused would be condemned, even though he might be able to prove both the purity of his motives, and the truth of his charges. If our laws allowed an appeal from the decision of a judge in such a case, to a superior court, the objection would still remain. That objection is, that the party accused is tried upon an important fact in his cause, without evidence and without a jury. It was Mr. S's. object that the whole question of libel and every part of it, should be tried and decided by a jury, upon evidence given to that jury. But it is said that indecent disclosures of facts unimportant to the public, and painful to individuals may sometimes take place. Such disclosures are often necessary, and often occur before the courts of justice in various other cases. In questions of libel, as in other cases where facts are asserted by one party, and denied by the other, the proofs must be heard in order to arrive at the justice of the case. When the publisher of an alleged libel offers to prove the truth of his charges, and his adversary objects to that proof, the suppression of the evidence offered may be justly considered to be quite as scandalous and injurious to the party complaining of the libel, and objecting to the proof, as any exposition of the truth of the charges. If the cause were to be tried by the judge alone, the proofs of all disputed facts should be heard. But the great question is, whether the liberty of the press shall depend upon judges or juries. Mr. S. entertained no unreasonable distrust of judges; but he wished to confide this great trust of protecting the freedom of the press, and deciding upon its abuses, to the juries of the state. In their hands it will be safe. Under their control, it will be efficacious, both in correcting mischief and effecting good. Here is at once the best security for the freedom of the press, and the best security against its licentiousness. Let the jury have the aid of the judge in these, as in other cases; but let the truth of the charges be proved in all these cases. Let the jury decide upon the motives of the publisher, as well as upon the truth of his charges; and with a full knowledge of all the facts of the case, pronounce him guilty or innocent.

CHANCELLOR KENT replied to the remarks which had fallen from the gentleman from Delaware, (Mr. Root,) and the gentleman from New-York, (Mr. Sanford). The latter gentleman was mistaken in supposing that the effect of his amendment would be, to rescue the liberty of speech and of the press from the hands of the court, and place it in the hands of the jury. Its tendency was to sanction the publication of calumnies, and to disturb the peace of society, by dragging before the public gross indecencies, which ought not to be made the subject of investigation, whether true or false. He had uniformly been in favour of the liberty of the press; and he challenged any gentleman to point to an official act in the whole course of his public life, which contravened this declaration. But he was in favour of rational freedom, not of licentiousness. . . .

. . . Mr. I. Sutherland was surprised to hear such sentiments expressed, as had fallen from the gentleman from Albany [Chancellor Kent], in whose integrity and purity of motives, he had the fullest confidence. The doctrines advanced by him restricted the law, as it now stood, in evidence of which Mr. S. read from the statute, and claimed that the law of this state, as it now stood, does not give to the judge the power of deciding the *quo animo* of the libel. And if such power had been assumed, it was clearly a usurpation. The judge is to determine the law, and the jury the evidence; and to determine whether a publication was made from good motives and for justifiable ends, was matter of evidence, of which the jury only are competent to decide. He was in favour of the amendment, and thought it was placing the subject upon just grounds. . . .

17. Reform of the Judiciary

In the confusion produced by the second report on the judiciary, Vice-President Tompkins introduced his substitute, which would vacate the offices of the high courts. Ogden Edwards was one of several moderates who spoke against this Draconian measure. It was defeated on October 25, 1821, but returned a few days later as part of the Carpenter resolution on the judiciary. Robert Clarke opened the debate for the radicals. Chief Justice Spencer followed with a tired speech addressing the sympathies of the delegates but, in effect, conceding the inadequacy of the present court system he was reluctant to change. The moderate, David Buel, made the most cogent argument against the Carpenter plan. Erastus Root, who surely merits the last word on these debates, renewed his fierce assault until

the judicial ramparts of the old constitution fell. The Carpenter reso-
lution passed on the third day of debate, November 4, 1821.

MR. EDWARDS. I do not conceive it proper that a subject of such deep concern should be passed upon without being more thoroughly discussed and seriously considered. However lightly our judicial system may be held by some, yet if we fail in establishing a good one, the community will sooner or later be made to feel that it is a thing of no ordinary importance. A little reflection must satisfy every man, that in a country which is governed solely by laws, as every free government must be, and where those laws can be brought to bear upon the people only through the instrumentality of judges, that the men who are to administer those laws should be extremely well qualified to perform those duties.

The common law, sir, is so framed as to afford a reasonable rule for the regulation of every question which can arise relative to the rights of persons and the rights of things. As it embraces all the transactions which occur in civil society, its rules must necessarily be extremely multifarious. A thorough knowledge of those laws is only to be acquired by long and laborious study; and to enable the community to enjoy the full benefit of them, it is necessary that they should avail themselves of the services of learned men. When our ancestors came to this country, although they fled from the persecutions they experienced in their native land, yet such was their attachment to the common law, that they brought it along with them, and subjected their conduct to its regulation. We have been long flourishing under it, administered as it has been by institutions similar to those under which it was nurtured. The mother country is indebted to it for whatever of liberty remains among them: and it is generally admitted, that the judicial establishments are the only sound parts of their government.

From *Reports*, pp. 529–531, 602–604, 606–610, 616–617.

By the wisdom of the founders of the English government in this state, those institutions were here established, and the consequence has been, that while other states have gone on in a course of experiments, our judicial establishments have remained firm and stable: revered by the people of this state, and admired by those of our sister states. Now, sir, with all this blaze of experience in favour of maintaining those institutions, shall we rudely prostrate them? What oracle is there among us who can afford us a sufficient assurance that we shall benefit by the change? As it respects myself, sir, I know of none: and I doubt whether any thing short of inspiration could satisfy me of the expediency of making it.

Let it not be said, sir, that the change contemplated by the report on your table, is not material. True, the supreme court is to be continued, but how is it to be with the circuits? Let no gentleman deceive himself into a belief that it is matter of trifling concern who presides there. Who, sir, I would ask, consigns your fellow beings to the gloomy recesses of your state prisons? Who dooms them to the scaffold? Under whose presiding genius is it that your juries proceed in the investigation of facts which are to regulate the disposition of your property? Is it not the circuit judges? If ignorance and stupidity there preside, what will be the consequence? I entreat you, gentlemen, while bending your minds to this subject, not to let them glance for a moment from the grand object to be obtained—the faithful and intelligent administration of the laws—the faithful administration of justice.

But it will be urged that under the contemplated system, you may have as intelligent judges upon the circuits, as you would ordinarily have under the present arrangement. But, sir, will this be the case? If this power is delegated to the legislature, they will be passed upon from time to time, by two-penny lawyers, who will confederate to secure these places. The legislature never can be induced to give adequate salaries to ten or a dozen circuit judges to command the services of suitable men, and the consequence will be, that those places will be usurped by ignorance.

Although, sir, I cannot give my consent to the adoption of the present plan, yet, sir, it is apparent that some enlargement of the judiciary is necessary to enable the courts to despatch the business. There is such an accumulation of it, and so much delay has ensued in consequence of it, that it amounts almost to a denial of justice. The system originally reported by the committee, met with my entire approbation, but that has been voted down. The plan now proposed by the honourable gentleman from Westchester (Mr. Munro) I also highly approve of. It simply contemplates the adding of three judges to the supreme court, and vesting the legislature with the power of authorizing one half of the judges to hold the terms. Under this arrangement, ten terms could be held in New-York and in Albany, Utica and Canandaigua, and abundance of time would be left to enable the judges to hold the circuits. The advantages of this system over that proposed, of creating circuit judges, are very great. The peculiar duties of circuit judges are to investigate facts, and do not lead them to pay that attention to the study of the laws which the public welfare requires. Judges, on the other hand, who both sit at the terms and hold the circuits, must of necessity give much of their attention to their books. By this arrangement, therefore, you will have able men, and at a much less expense than you will be subjected to by the plan reported by the committee. In the one case your laws will be administered in their true spirit, by learned and able men; and in the other, not unfrequently by ignorant men, who, from lack of knowledge, must substitute their own discretion. Discretionary power in the hands of a judge is but another term for arbitrary power; and under such an order of things, your judges might ride the circuits the terror of the land.

It appears, sir, from the motion made by the honourable gentleman from Richmond, (Mr. Tompkins,) that another object in view, is so to frame the constitution as to drive the present judges from their stations. Justice to myself, and to the station I here occupy, demands from me some remarks on this subject. I have, sir, so freely and so frequently expressed myself in terms of reprehension of the political course pursued by some of those gentlemen, that my sentiments respecting them cannot be unknown to many of the members of this Convention. But, sir, I was sent here to assist in revising the constitution of this state, and to establish fundamental laws for its future government, and not to try any man or set of men for their transgressions: and I should be for ever ashamed of myself, if I could for a moment be brought to avail myself of a "little brief authority," for the purpose of gratifying any hostile feelings. You have provided tribunals, and invested them with power to animadvert upon the conduct of your judicial officers. Turn them over to those tribunals; it is not our business to pass upon their conduct. Such a proceeding would fix a blemish, a stain upon the character of this Convention. It is, to be sure, urged, that we have dismissed the senate and the first judges of the counties. But, sir, the new organization of the senatorial districts, which the public good demanded, rendered the proceeding, with respect to the senators, indispensable. As to the first judges, it was matter of general complaint, that the permanent duration of their offices, owing to the appointment of incompetent men, was a source of serious inconvenience in many of the counties. You were also led to believe, that the welfare of the state would be promoted by shortening the terms of their offices. You, therefore, made their private interest yield to the public good. But, sir, no alteration has been made in the organization of the supreme court to render this change necessary. There is not a veil to conceal the motive which induces to the adoption of this amendment. It stands naked before the world, that the motive, and the only motive, is to dismiss the judges. This cannot be concealed from the people, and it may as well be frankly acknowledged at once. I have nothing to say in justification of their conduct: but I repeat it, that we are out of the line of our duty in inflicting punishment upon them. It is unbecoming the dignity of this honourable body. You have established tribunals who are invested with the necessary power: leave it to them to do what justice may require. . . .

. . . Mr. R. Clarke moved that the proposition of the honourable gentleman from Tioga (Mr. Carpenter) submitted yesterday, be received therefor as a substitute.

In support of the motion, Mr. Clarke remarked, that a proposition of this sort was loudly called for by the necessities of the people.

It contemplated, in the first place, a reduction of the supreme court. And on this point he would observe, that the object was not merely to remove the present incumbents—but to establish an useful system for the state. We had already removed from them a part of their burthens. We had abolished the council of revision, which had been an ungracious, but heavy burthen upon them; and it was contemplated to establish them as a court of appellate jurisdiction only. Being thus relieved, he thought there would be no necessity for more than three judges to constitute that court; and it was deserving of much consideration, how far it was expedient from feelings of delicacy, to retain a greater number of officers than the public necessities required, and to tax the community for their support.

In the second place, the substitute proposed to establish district courts. There were imperiously called for by the exigencies of the public. The judges of the supreme court had probably done as much and as well as they could, but it was notorious that the short space allowed for the sittings on the circuits, did not admit of an opportunity for that careful and patient investigation, and deliberate discussion and decision of the causes before them which the fair and complete administration of justice demanded. It was true that the number of judges would be increased; but he believed it would be favourable to the solid economy and interest of the state. At present it is often necessary for suitors, and their witnesses, to go home from the court because their causes cannot be tried, owing to the pressure of time upon the judge. This would be remedied by the system proposed. Certain justice, and prompt justice, would then be extended to all the people of the state.

In the third place, the equity powers that are proposed to be given to the district courts, are important. It might, perhaps, be thought presumptuous in him to express an opinion on this subject; but this he did know, that to a large part of the state, the present chancery system was worse than useless. By this remark he intended no disrespect to the honourable gentleman who now fills that station. He believed that the chancellor had performed the duties of his office as well as any man could perform them. But the defect lay in the system; and indeed he almost despaired of another chancellor who would perform his duties as well as the present incumbent, and this very fact convinced him (Mr. C.) of the necessity of an alteration in that court. The fact was, that the chancellor cannot carry equity into the various counties in the state. Those who are remote, especially, cannot maintain their equitable rights, except at an expense that is equivalent to a denial of them. Mr. C. alluded to a case of ejectment, in which a party, to obtain justice, had resort to the court of chancery. In winning his farm by a decree, he lost his farm in the costs. This was but one in the many instances that exist. The people are disheartened and discouraged. If they have no other than an equitable claim, they are induced to succumb, for by pursuing it they are certain to be the losers.

CHIEF JUSTICE SPENCER remarked, that it would perhaps be expected that the judges should express those views in relation to the judicial department which their experience had suggested. With regard to the specific substitute before the Convention, it could affect him personally but little. In less than five years his office would expire by constitutional limitation;

and it was known for sometime past to his friends, that he had contemplated resigning it. He had received it under the administration of the venerable first governor of this state, under the present constitution. He had held it eighteen years—and during a very tempestuous period of our public affairs. Although he had perhaps possessed strong party feelings, yet he had always endeavoured to suppress them as a judge.

In the station in which judges were placed, it was to be expected that they would be best able to discern the defects of the present system, and most competent to devise an adequate remedy. It had occupied their deliberate attention for some years. There were at first but three judges of the supreme court. Another was afterwards added, and the number was ultimately increased to five. When there were four judges the population of the state did not exceed one half of its present number. There were then but twenty counties—there were now fifty-two; and it was not to be disguised, that the judges had not sufficient time for the performance of their duties. They held four terms in a year, and usually for three weeks in each term. They were sometimes obliged to break up before the business could be disposed of, to go on the circuit. He had been six months on the circuits in the course of a year, and had sometimes not returned until within a fortnight before the term—and then all the intervening time was necessarily occupied in examining and preparing for decision the cases that had been argued at the preceding term. This had often occasioned them pecuniary loss, and he could say, that if ever men had been devoted to public business, with a desire to discharge the duties of an office with integrity and despatch, it has been the judges of your supreme court; but the increasing population of the state, together with the addition of new counties, have rendered it almost impossible for them longer to discharge the duties of that office. At the last session of our legislature, there were three or four new counties erected, in which there must hereafter be circuits holden, which will necessarily

require so great a share of time in addition to that now required to attend the different circuits of the state, that no time
will be left for study or deliberation. There had already been
a number of propositions submitted to the consideration of this
Convention, one of which was to increase the number of supreme judges, and to divide them into two classes; another to
reduce their number, and appoint circuit judges. It had been
his opinion, and the opinion of his associates, that with the
addition of one or two circuit judges, the present court would
be able to do all the business that would be required for many
years. They never had been desirous of being released from
their circuit duties entirely, because they had considered it for
the best that they should mingle with the people in the different counties of the state. It is rational to suppose that such a
plan is best calculated to give satisfaction among the people;
as a judge coming from a remote part of the state must be
supposed to be a stranger to the parties who are called before
him. They had, therefore, only wished to be released from
that part of this duty which it was not convenient for them
to perform. The objections raised to this plan have been, that
no man well qualified for that station, (and it must be a man
well read in the law to discharge the duties of that office)
would accept of it, unless he could be placed out of the reach
of a removal at every change of party. It would be, indeed,
hazarding too much, for a gentleman of the profession to abandon his business for this office, when he has no assurance of
holding it any longer than a particular party may predominate,
and thus rendering himself liable to fall a sacrifice to their
ambition, when perhaps he has not been appointed two years.
—This evil can be remedied by giving them a tenure of office
equal to that of the chancellor and judges of the supreme
court, and leaving it to the legislature to provide such salaries
as they may think proper. . . .

. . . Mr. S. remarked, that he took a seat upon the bench of
the supreme court eighteen years ago, since which his whole

time had been devoted to a discharge of the duties incumbent on him in that station. The salary of that office, had barely enabled him to support his family and educate his children, without laying up a dollar from that source, more than he had when he accepted the office. He had abandoned his profession, which was far more lucrative than the office which he accepted, and he had received that appointment under the sanction of the constitution, with a pledge, that he should hold it till he arrived at the age of sixty, unless removed for mal-conduct. His term of service by that limitation, would expire in about four years; but if the public good required his removal, amen, to it. The Convention had an undoubted right to do it if they thought proper, notwithstanding it would appear rational, that those who had received that office under the old constitution should continue till their term expired by law. . . .

. . . Mr. Buel. . . . It appears to me that the full extent of the alteration in our judiciary system, which the adoption of the plan will produce, is not duly considered. There is more in it than at first view meets the eye. It proposes to divide the state into districts, and for each district a judge is to be appointed, who is to reside within the district after his appointment. I have no doubt the intention of the framer of the proposition is, to create district courts, possessing original jurisdiction in law and equity. This I understand to be the import of the second section. These judges, therefore, are not to be created merely to hold circuits for the trial of issues joined in the supreme court, and to preside in courts of oyer and terminer. These powers it is true, the legislature may confer upon them, as incidental to their other powers; but I believe the great object of the proposed plan to be the erection of a new species of courts, with general jurisdiction in law and equity within the districts. Although this prominent feature of the plan has not been spoken of, I am persuaded the honourable gentleman who introduced the proposition, will admit, that such is his intention; and that it will be competent for the legislature to give original jurisdiction to these district judges, cannot, I think, be well doubted. . . .

. . . But whence the necessity of our adopting a new system of judicature? What are the defects complained of in our system? Besides our court of chancery, we have a supreme court, whose decisions have usually commanded the confidence of the citizens and the respect of our neighbours. Our circuit courts are well calculated for the trial of questions of fact; and the county courts are susceptible of much improvement, and may be made adequate to the administration of justice in local causes of limited amount. Is it not safer to renovate and improve our old system, than to hazard the introduction of a new and untried one? The time has been, when much of the litigation of the state was carried on in the county courts. Unfortunately, however, the fluctuations of party produced such frequent changes of the judges as to bring those courts into disrepute. It became so much a matter of course to displace the judges upon each change of party, that a seat on the bench was not desired by those who were best qualified to fill it. Hereafter, it is to be hoped, this evil will be remedied; a more stable tenure is to be secured to the county judges, and if care is used by the appointing power in making selections for the bench, these courts may be restored to their former consequence.

With respect to the supreme court, I believe no complaints were made until within a few years. Since my acquaintance with the proceedings of that court, it was able to clear the calendar at its terms, and the causes which were ready for trial were almost always disposed of at the circuit.

For several years past, it is true, the five judges have not been always able to despatch the business of the bench, and of the circuits. This, I apprehend, has not been owing to the great increase of business so much as to other causes. Counties have been multiplied, and many more circuits are requisite to be held than formerly. The connexion of the judges of the supreme court with the legislature, as members of the council of revision, has occupied a large portion of their time. They are about to be released from this duty, and will therefore be able to devote two or three months more to their judicial duties. I think it not improbable that this alteration in our constitution would of itself remedy the evil complained of. But certainly the addition of a single judge, as proposed by the honourable member from Westchester (Mr. Munro) or the appointment of a circuit judge, as proposed by the chief justice, would amply provide for all the exigencies of the case, without disturbing the order of our system.

And in regard to *expense*, such a provision would be much preferable to the adoption of the plan under consideration. That plan contemplates the appointment of eight district judges, and it must be presumed, that the advocates of it will desire to place men of some distinction in their courts. To secure the acceptance of the office by such men, competent salaries must be provided. The salaries of these eight judges, with those of the three judges of the supreme court, will necessarily increase the expense much beyond that of the existing system. And is it not to be apprehended, that whilst the proposed plan will be much more expensive than the old system, it will not be as acceptable to the people? It appears to me that gentlemen aim at impossibilities. They wish to bring justice nearer home, to make it cheaper, and to have courts which shall have a more homely appearance, and yet possess equal intelligence, and command equal confidence. Why have the county courts been deserted by suitors? Certainly because the judges were not men of as much capacity and independence as the judges of the supreme court. Because he who was judge to-day might be displaced to-morrow.

These local courts have, therefore, gradually lost their consequence, and all business of importance is done in the supreme court. The attempt is now to be made to call suitors back; not indeed to the county courts, but to new local tribunals. But will these courts probably be as respectable, and acquire the confidence of the community, as much as the supreme court? The very circumstance of their being local courts, limited in jurisdiction, as it regards territory, will at once give them the character of inferior subordinate courts.

Perhaps, in some instances, men of competent talents will be induced to accept the office of district judge; but it is to be feared this will not always, perhaps not generally, be the case.

Is the residence of the judge within the district of any advantage? Too often the feelings of neighbourhood and intimacy will be apt to influence him; nor will his residence in one part of the district, tend much to promote the convenience of the inhabitants of the whole district; nor are the avocations of the district judges calculated to improve their capacity for administering justice in a very high degree. It will be a principal part of their duty to try questions of fact. These must necessarily be conducted with despatch. The crowd of suitors, witnesses, and jurors, pressing on the court, leaves no time for deliberate discussions of questions of law. Such questions must be hastily decided, and the remedy against a wrong decision must be sought in the supreme court. The judge, whose principal employment is that of presiding at trials by jury, may acquire habits of despatch, considerable acuteness in analysing testimony, and an acquaintance with the rules of evidence; beyond this not much can be expected. He can make but small advances in legal learning, and his decisions on intricate questions of law, must be crude and unsatisfactory. And is it not to be feared, on the other hand, that the change proposed by the plan under discussion, will equally affect the character and reputation of the supreme court? The judges of that court will be confined to the bench to hear appeals and decide questions of law; lawyers alone will frequent the court. The habits of promptness acquired by holding circuit courts will be lost; and although they may acquire a more profound knowledge of the principles and cases, they will probably have less acuteness, and certainly less mental activity. The experience of ages has demonstrated that the most accurate and accomplished judges have been formed under that system which combines the trial by jury at the circuit, with the decision of questions of law in bench by the same judges. This system, pruned of some excrescences, was brought by our ancestors from the land of their forefathers. There it had been reared and perfected by able and upright judges. It grew up with the exigencies of the people of England. And let us not reject it because it is of British origin. With as much reason might we change our language. If any thing is to be admired in the institutions of England, it is its jurisprudence. That bulwark of freedom, the jury trial, is derived from England.

If we adopt the proposed plan, we shut up our supreme court from public view. Lawyers alone will see it. The names of the judges will scarcely be heard of beyond the hall in which it holds its terms; and it is to be feared that public confidence will desert it. The district judges, whose decisions come under its review, will not be very much disposed to reverence it. Having no connexion with the supreme court—perhaps no personal acquaintance with the judges—a frequent reversal of the decisions of the district courts by the supreme court, will be much more likely to produce hostility than respect. It is among the manifest advantages of the system which we have enjoyed, that the judge who has tried the cause at the circuit, sits with his brethren on the review of his own decision. Habits of candour and liberal scrutiny of the decisions of each other, are by this means produced, and if mistakes have been made in the statement of the proceedings which took place at the trial, the judge who held the circuit is present to correct them. And although it is not proper that judges who have deliberately settled questions of law, should sit on the review of their own decisions in a court of last resort, we are authorized by our own experience, and by the history of the English courts, to assert that the decisions made by a judge, in the progress of a trial at the circuit, do not disqualify him from sitting with his brethren on the re-examination of the questions on deliberate argument at the term.

I am strongly opposed to changing our system of administering justice, by the consideration of the high comparative reputation which our courts have long enjoyed in this country. Many gentlemen in this Convention know, that the decisions of our courts have long been held in the highest respect in the other states. I believe I hazard nothing in saying that the character of our courts has been as high as that of any state in the union. And may I not add, that the people of this state, during almost the whole time which has elapsed since the adoption of our constitution, have had as much confidence in the decisions of their highest courts, and have been as well satisfied with the administration of justice, as the people of any other state? If the excellence of our system is acknowledged abroad, and if it has generally inspired confidence at home, why are we called on to change it for another, which has not, in any state where it has been adopted, proved to be better than our own? And in some respects, our system evidently possesses a decided superiority over the one proposed to be substituted. The excellence of our plan of administering justice, arises, in the first place, from the separation of our courts of law and equity. In a former discussion, the excellence of this part of our plan was made so manifest, that the Convention, by a most decisive vote, rejected the project of uniting the two branches of jurisprudence in the same court.

Nor does the plan under consideration propose to destroy this feature in our system in the highest courts. The next trait of excellence in our system, is the one to which I have already adverted—that of employing the same judges to try issues of fact at the circuit, and to decide questions of law on the bench. It is by this means that the unity of our system and a uniformity of proceedings in all parts of the state, is preserved.

Every part of the state, by means of the rotation in holding circuits among the judges, enjoys, in turn, the talents of every member of the court; and the united decisions of the same judges in term, ensures to every part of the state uniform rules of law and of legal proceedings, whilst the certain effect of discharging their various duties, is to increase the experience and improve the capacity of the judges. These advantages, I apprehend, will in a great measure be lost, if the proposed plan should be adopted; and I much fear that our tribunals of justice would sink in character and usefulness. By confining the jurisdiction of a judge within narrow limits, the idea of inferiority is produced, although it may not exist in fact. District judges, it is to be feared, will often be men of less capacity than many members of the bar—I presume this will be so, because I do not believe the legislature will be disposed to give to such a number of judges a salary sufficient to induce men of the first standing at the bar to accept the office; and whenever the counsel are greatly superior to the court, the confidence of suitors, and of the citizens in general, in the courts, will be impaired. The suspicion of weakness in a court, has almost as bad an effect as a suspicion of its integrity. . . .

. . . MR. ROOT. . . . The supreme court, as now constituted, appeared to be the object not only of the special care, but of the adoration of the members of the Convention. It was the fashion, when speaking of our courts, to laud the Chancellor and judges, and to set them forth as the most perfect patterns of piety and legal learning in the world. How often had we been told that Johnson's Reports were quoted not only from Maine to New-Orleans, but that the decisions they contained were regarded with reverence in the legal sanctuary of Westminster Hall? The Chancellor, too, had been described as a branching oak, whose roots penetrated the union, whilst its branches afforded shelter to all those who were fortunate enough to obtain access to its shade. Strange, however, as it might seem, it had been even made a question in this body, whether that oak should be preserved. It was, indeed, finally determined that it should not be rooted up; although it was admitted by the honourable gentleman from Westchester, (Mr. Munro) that it often cast a baleful political pestilence around it, and that, like the Bohon Upas[8] of Java, it carried death and desolation to the extent of its atmosphere. If it was really so pestiferous, he (Mr. R.) could see no reason why that gentleman, or others, should refuse to nurture a few *sapling oaks* near the margin of its shade, that might soften and diffuse, and thereby render less baleful, this political pestilence.

But the judges of the supreme court, it was said, must not be disturbed. They hold their offices as a matter of *right,* and that, too, in despite of the people, for whose benefit they were elevated. This was a doctrine that he could never admit. But it had been urged that the judges had abandoned lucrative professions on the faith of the state, that they should hold until sixty years of age. He would reply, that there were few professions so lucrative, that the persons engaged in them can obtain a greater average compensation than $4,500 per year, which the judges had for many years received. If there were, the people ought to know it, and be on their guard against paying such extravagant fees. Four thousand five hundred dollars a year, was as much as many of our farmers, who are esteemed affluent, are enabled to accumulate by the hard earned industry of a whole laborious life. Again, we were told that by thus rendering the tenure of the office insecure, we should not find candidates willing to accept it. But when, he would ask, was the time ever known, in which a vacancy had happened, or was ever foreseen, when activity was not awake and at work to fill it. The rooms of members who were supposed to be influential, were always thronged with applicants. And whence did this proceed?—Were these applicants inspired

---

[8] Pohon Upas, a tall Asiatic and East Indian tree with a poisonous latex used as an arrow poison [Ed.].

with the *mens sibi conscia recti;*[9] or were they actuated by the snug profits of four thousand five hundred dollars a year?

Feudal vassalage, said Mr. R. has been done away in our country—but there was another kind of vassalage from which we had not yet escaped. And he could not omit to notice the phraseology of the honourable gentleman from Oneida, (Mr. N. Williams) who hoped that the system would be *abolished gradually.* He seemed to have in his mind the *gradual abolition* of *slavery;*—and, indeed, that association of ideas was very natural. But as we had already determined upon the one, he hoped we should not shrink from the other. For his part, he longed to see the emancipation of the state from judicial thraldom.

Under this kind of slavery, has this state groaned ever since I have been a member of it; and whenever a member of the bar has undertaken to lift his voice, he has had cause to rue the day that he undertook it. The gentlemen of the bar in the country have seen and felt the evils of this system; and, as you have been already told, it is important that your high judicial officers be above suspicion; otherwise they are worse than useless. If they are suspected, they cannot render to the people justice and equity to their satisfaction. Then bring them before the proper appointing power, and see whether they are free from suspicion, and whether the people are willing to reappoint them. See whether they can look upon the multitude with the same averted eye as heretofore. See whether they respond with an artificial importance to the Roman poet—*odi profanum vulgus*—and add with a frown, *et arceo.*

I am willing, sir, that this profane vulgar should be permitted to gaze on them through the medium of the constituted author-ities; and let them see whether they will bear this popular gaze, with as much fortitude as they have heretofore mani-fested. They may have occasion to hide their heads in shame

---

[9] Mind conscious of its own rectitude [Ed.].

and confusion; and perhaps they will not be able to find a fig leaf to cover their nakedness in the garden.

Let us put them to the test: three judges are enough. But we are told by the gentleman from Oneida, that it will not do to reduce the number to three, because there must always be three on the bench. Yet we have been told by the chancellor, that in a court of equity *one* is enough. Why is it that law and equity are so much at variance, that they cannot be administered by the same number of individuals? [Mr. N. Williams explained.] The reason for having them upon the bench at all times, is probably for the purpose of inspiring the people with more awe; but sometimes another way is preferred to inspire awe and terror, than by aggregate numbers. A ponderous wig, a black gown and band are placed upon the judge, thereby making him appear artificially wise.

Now, if we could do with a less number of judges, by placing on their heads these wise wigs, it would be a great relief to our treasury, and perhaps law and equity would be full as well administered as with the present number of judges.

The gentleman from Westchester, (Mr. Munro) who was so frightened yesterday at a single proposition, is desirous of establishing two courts; because, forsooth, old Scotia in her high courts, had divided the jurisdiction of the judges into branches of coequal authority. Mr. R. did not much reverence the example of Scotland; yet he had no special objection to a certain species of ramification, if the branches are not as large, or larger than the main trunk: but we should not like to have them like an old split or crooked oak, sundered from the very ground. This kind of ramification would not be so desirable.

It has been a great question to know, whether the judges of the supreme court belong to the people, to the few, or to themselves; and does this gentleman suppose it necessary to have the wisdom of Solomon to ascertain the truth of this proposition? That we should divide the court in twain, to see who the agonized parent would be, to claim it? I imagine we can get along without this extraordinary wisdom. The gentleman from Westchester (Mr. M.) had likened the system proposed to the gun-boat system; and that honourable gentleman, said Mr. R. would have nothing but seventy-fours upon the ocean of this state, armed with nothing but great guns, and long toms upon the decks, or under the decks. The people have too long feared, and trembled at their sound; but by dividing them, you may call them gun-boats if you please. Such a kind of judicial gun-boats would not strike so great a terror, even if they should happen to be in the neighbourhood of a corn-field: and if these judicial gun-boats will defend the rights of the people, God speed them.

These large ships of war have carried terror and dismay throughout the state: they are calculated to float in deep water, to attack but not defend; and from these deep waters, the rights and privileges of the people have been attacked, by these great ships of war!! Let us then, in heaven's name, prepare ourselves for defence in the shoal waters, and the remote regions of the state—then let us establish an armament for our security.

In the proposition of the gentleman from Albany, it is required, that a man, to be competent to become a circuit judge, must be of the degree of counsellor; as if the criterion of a man's fitness to discharge the duties of that office, could be no way determined, but by the particular quality of a piece of sheepskin. Does this proposition propose to give us any right which we do not now possess? By the old constitution, we are not limited to any particular number of judges; the only limitation is in the minutes of the council of revision, and in the statute books, by which five only can receive pay. The legislature are competent to increase the number of judges, but cannot provide for their payment.

The plan proposed by the gentleman from Tioga, will remedy every evil, and enable the legislature so to organize the system, as to bring justice and equity into every county in the state. . . .

TABLE 2.1

The Vote by Districts on the Convention Bill, Suffrage, and Judicial Reform, and the Revised Constitution, in the New York Convention

DISTRICT	NUMBER OF DELEGATES	CONVENTION BILL, APRIL 30		SUFFRAGE ARTICLE, OCTOBER 27	
		Yea	*Nay*	*Yea*	*Nay*
Southern	29	15,906	8,409	14	10
Middle	30	20,158	12,764	16	10
Eastern	31	25,465	9,278	17	8
Western	36	47,817	4,450	25	4
Totals	126	109,346	34,901	72	32

DISTRICT	JUDICAL REFORM, NOVEMBER 4°		REVISED CONSTITUTION, NOVEMBER 10		
	Yea	*Nay*	*Yea*	*Nay*	*No Vote*
Southern	7	20	24	2	3
Middle	14	12	19	3	9
Eastern	19	11	24	3	4
Western	22	10	29	0	6
Totals	62	53	96†	8	22

° The Carpenter Amendment.

† On the roll-call vote as reported, two of the affirmative votes cannot be assigned to delegates.

TABLE 2.2

The Vote of Radicals and Conservatives on Selected Questions in the New York Convention

QUESTION	RADICALS*		CONSERVATIVES†	
	Yea	*Nay*	*Yea*	*Nay*
On Livingston's amendment to restrict the governor's veto power, September 8	20	3	0	19
On Spencer's amendment to attach a property qualification for senatorial electors, September 25	0	25	16	0
On Platt's motion to strike the Negro proviso from the suffrage article, October 8	3	19	15	3
On Root's amendment to abolish the court of chancery, October 24	22	3	0	13
On the motion to approve the suffrage article, October 27	23	0	0	15
On the motion to establish a two-year term for governor, October 27	0	25	17	0
On Carpenter's amendment for the reform of the judiciary, November 4	24	1	0	13
On the final motion to approve the revised constitution, November 10	21	0	4	7

---

* *The Radicals:* Brooks, Burroughs, Carver, Case, R. Clarke, Howe, Humphrey, Hunting, A. Livingston, P. R. Livingston, McCall, Park, Pike, Price, Richards, Root, Rosebrugh, R. Sanford, Starkweather, Swift, Taylor, Townley, Townsend, Van Fleet, Young—25.

† *The Conservatives:* Bacon, Fish, Hees, Hunter, Huntington, Jay, James, Kent, Platt, Rhinelander, Rose, Spencer, Sylvester, Van Horne, Van Ness, J. R. Van Rensselaer, S. Van Rensselaer, Van Vechten, E. Williams—19.

III

THE VIRGINIA CONVENTION
OF 1829–1830

INTRODUCTION

The Virginia Convention of 1829–1830 was the last of the great constituent assemblies in American history. As an arena of ideological
encounter it was unexcelled. It was a seemingly inexhaustible exercise in political erudition—the last gasp of Jeffersonian America's
passion for political disputation. It was a dazzling forensic display of
more than three months' duration. "The Old Dominion," one of the
delegates observed, "has long been celebrated for producing great
orators; the ablest metaphysicians in policy; men that can split hairs
in all abstruse questions of political economy." And the convention of
1829–1830 was the acme of Virginia fame. The presence of illustrious
personages gave an éclat to its proceedings far beyond Virginia's
borders. Former Presidents James Madison and James Monroe, Chief
Justice of the United States John Marshall, Speaker of the House of
Representatives Philip P. Barbour, vintage Jeffersonians John Randolph and William B. Giles, governors, Senators, and judges in number, past, present, and future, even a later President, John Tyler,
were among its members. In the choice of delegates the people had
laid aside party animosities and qualifications of residence in order
to send the state's ablest men to Richmond. The result was not only
a spectacle to behold but a classic struggle between democratic and
conservative forces in a developing American state.

Virginia's venerable constitution of 1776 had been under attack for several decades. Except in the executive department, that document made no significant change in the colonial frame of government. Thomas Jefferson at once became its leading critic, attacking the constitution openly in his *Notes on the State of Virginia* (1785) and repeatedly, over several decades, endeavoring to bring about a convention for its reform. After the War of 1812, formidable opposition appeared west of the Blue Ridge. These low-lying mountains divided the state politically, socially, and economically. Two well-defined physiographic regions lay on either side: on the east, the Tidewater stretching from Chesapeake Bay to the fall line, thence the Piedmont to the Blue Ridge; on the west, the narrow, fertile Shenandoah Valley, beyond which lay the Trans-Allegheny section, comprising the greater part of the present state of West Virginia. The older, eastern sections, representing successive stages in the growth of a uniform plantation society, were united in their determination to preserve it. Although the east still held most of the wealth and population of the state, together with a disproportionate share of political power, it suffered chronic economic ills and steadily lost ground to the flourishing new society west of the Blue Ridge. Free labor and independent farming prevailed in the west, giving a distinct cast to its society. Paths of commerce ran north and west into adjacent states, breaking the crust of provincialism. As a developing section—the tramontane more so than the valley—the west had strong interests in banks, internal improvements, and other aids to industry from either the state or the federal government. But existing constitutional arrangements, particularly the inequality of representation in the legislature, left the westerners virtually helpless in state affairs. And the advocacy of measures tending to increase the power of the federal government brought the westerners into conflict with the Jeffersonian canons of state rights in Virginia politics.

Yet it was Jefferson, the venerable Sage of Monticello, democrat as well as state rightist, who supplied the westerners with a reform ideology and platform. In 1816 he expounded his views in two remarkable letters to Samuel Kercheval, a westerner then agitating constitutional reform. Recalling his long-standing objections to the constitution, he confessed that even his own earlier proposals for reform had contained "gross departures . . . from genuine republican canons." Governments, he said, "are republican only in proportion as they embody the will of the people, and execute it." Applying this "mother principle," he called for several far-reaching reforms. First, equality of representation in the state legislature. Second, the enfranchisement of every man who paid taxes or served in the militia. Third, the abolition of the executive council; popular election of the governor and of judges, too, or, at least, their appointment by the governor alone, subject to removal on the concurrence of both chambers of the legislature. Fourth, the overthrow of the oligarchical "monopolies of county administration," the county courts, and the transfer of their functions to the people in newly constituted local units called wards. Finally, believing that "laws and institutions must go hand in hand with the progress of the human mind," Jefferson assailed the exaggerated respect for the historic constitution and called for regular amendment and revision. The publication of these letters propelled the convention movement on its course; so widely circulated were Jefferson's opinions that, in the words of a contemporary observer, they were "at once stereotyped in the public voice." Jefferson supplied the westerners with democratic theory and precept to support their grievances against the conservative east, an ideology that fixed the lines of debate and enabled a conflict of interests to be conducted as a conflict of principles. When the convention finally came in 1829, the reform leader Philip Doddridge could fairly claim "that every principle for which we contend is supported by the deliberate opinions of Mr. Jefferson."

By then Jefferson was safely in his grave. For a dozen years the conservatives had fought a delaying action. In 1816 the reformers had met at Staunton, thirty-eight counties being represented, and demanded a constitutional convention. Representation was the principal issue. The system of representation for the dominant house of the general assembly, two delegates for each county, took no account of population and was grossly unfavorable to the west. Little Warwick in the Tidewater, with 620 free whites, had the same power in the assembly as Shenandoah County with 17,000. The freehold suffrage was an important, if secondary, issue. The assembly staved off reform in 1817 by reapportioning the senate, a body notoriously subservient to the house of delegates, so as to increase the representation of the western districts from 4 to 9 of the 24 members. But the reformers mobilized again in 1824—a second Staunton convention followed. Prominent converts to their cause in the east, such as the Richmond editors Thomas Ritchie and John Hampton Pleasants, who disagreed on every other political question, gave further impetus to reform. The conservatives held their ground. In three successive years they defeated convention bills in the general assembly. Then, in the 1827–1828 session, the assembly approved submission of the question to the vote of the freeholders. They favored the convention, 38,533 going to the polls, by a majority of 5,000. In 1829 the same electorate chose 4 delegates in each of the 24 senatorial districts. Since only 36 of the 96 delegates came from west of the Blue Ridge, this solid reform bloc was vitally dependent on the support of eastern friends. They were roughly a dozen, most of them from upland counties close to the Blue Ridge and economically depressed counties in northern Virginia. These friends, in fact, held the balance of power in the convention. Some, like some westerners, were of Federalist backgrounds. It was only a question of whether they would overcome the conservative defenses or give way before them.

The delegates assembled on October 5, 1829 in the house chamber of the splendid porticoed capitol of Jefferson's design. James Monroe was chosen president—when illness forced him to retire, Philip P. Barbour took the chair—and the convention got down to business. It was agreed to divide the constitution among four committees, one on each of the three branches of government and a fourth on the declaration of rights. The last was the first to report, on October 19. It recommended no change in the world-famous charter of liberties; but several days later its chairman, General William P. Taylor of Norfolk, moved to add guarantees of equality of suffrage and of representation to the bill of rights. The whole purpose of the instrument, he said, was "to set up certain landmarks for the framing of a Constitution," and yet, on the crucial questions before the convention, the declaration of rights gave no reliable guidance. Reformers and conservatives freely interpreted it to suit themselves. What it seemed to concede to the reformers with one hand, as in the first article's declaration of the natural freedom and equality of all men, it took away with the other, by asserting in article six that only men "having sufficient evidence of permanent common interest with, and attachment to the community have a right of suffrage." What this "evidence" consisted in was subject to different interpretations. The reformers made as little distinction as possible between "interest" and "right," while the conservatives demanded the old statutory evidence of a freehold. They rejected Taylor's position that these questions of suffrage and representation were matters of right and, therefore, capable of settlement in the bill of rights. His motion was tabled. In the words of one reformer, the convention "set sail without compass, rudder or pilot" to guide it.

Everyone recognized that nothing could be accomplished until the first and decisive question of the basis of representation was settled. So on October 26, after hearing the report of the legislative committee, the convention went into committee of the whole, where it remained except for day-to-day formalities of parliamentary procedure until December 16. The committee of twenty-four recommended no change in the composition of the senate but asked that the house be established on the basis of the white population. The reformers had won the first round behind the closed doors of the senate chamber where the legislative committee met for two weeks. There, seated around a long table—all except John Randolph, who pouted and stared in a corner—and presided over by an old man in a threadbare "snuff-colored" overcoat, James Madison—the only survivor of the Virginia convention of 1776—the committee members debated the issue at length and finally voted for the white basis 13 to 11. Since there were only 8 westerners on the committee, the winning margin was provided by the 5 votes of the small but pivotal reform element east of the Blue Ridge. Madison, though he was not an ardent reformer and later retreated, was one of these. His vote proved decisive on this question, as well as on the lesser one of senatorial representation.

Immediately, in the committee of the whole, John W. Green of Culpeper moved to amend the first resolution of the report so as to base representation in the house on population and taxation combined. The fight was on. Delegates scurried to the tax books to discover precisely what this compound basis would mean. Since eight-tenths of the state taxes fell on land and slaves, this greater eastern wealth would be reflected in the system of representation. Calculations differed, but it was clear that under the white basis the west would receive something over 45 per cent of the delegates, while under the compound basis the share would drop to roughly 35 per cent (see Table 3.1). The reformers, led by Philip Doddridge, John R. Cooke, and Chapman Johnson, pitched their case on the Jeffersonian ground of natural rights, republican virtue, and popular sovereignty. In a free society, they said, a representation founded on property was as unnecessary as it was unjust. The principle was unknown to the Virginia constitution and, as was pointed out, to every other state of the Union, except South Carolina, where it did indeed throw the control of the government to the coastal aristocracy.

The conservatives were led in debate by two of the most promising men of the new generation in Virginia, Abel P. Upshur and Benjamin Watkins Leigh. Like their peers in the west, they were learned and celebrated lawyers for whom planting and even politics were secondary occupations. Upshur put their favorite doctrine in a nutshell: "There is a majority in *interest,* as well as a majority in number." Planter interests in land and slaves could not be left to the mercy of an approaching western majority in unholy alliance with the commercial and propertyless classes of the eastern towns. Lavish projects of internal improvement would bankrupt the planters already overburdened with taxes. (Actually, as Johnson pointed out, the conflict of interest in regard to internal improvements crossed the state in several directions; and, unlike in New York, the clash of local interests was so great as to "present almost an insuperable barrier to any improvement at all.") Moreover, the rule of a popular majority in Virginia councils portended "the annihilation of all state rights." It was perhaps the principal object, Leigh said, "of those who set this ball of revolution in motion, to overturn the doctrine of state rights, of which Virginia has been the pillar . . . by so reorganizing the legislature that Virginia, too, may be hitched to the Federal car." Should the movement succeed, the whole plantation edifice would be put in jeopardy, and "old" Virginia would stand to the state government as the commonwealth then stood to the federal government—exploited, after the manner of the protective tariff and internal improvements. Thus the Jeffersonian doctrine of state rights was transmuted into the doctrine of minority concurrence and employed to check the progress of democracy in Virginia.

Green's resolution met defeat on the casting vote of the president, Monroe, on November 14. The delegates then took up Leigh's resolution to base representation on "federal numbers," that is, the white population plus three-fifths of the slaves. The effect would be little different from the compound ratio; but being founded on the clause of the federal Constitution that accorded the states representation for three-fifths of their slaves, it was not liable to the same objection of principle. In fact, conservatives argued, it was positively recommended as a means of buttressing the institution of slavery and Virginia's power in the Union. Every delegate recognized the truth of Monroe's observation that "if no such thing as slavery existed . . . the people of our Atlantic border, would meet their brethren of the east, upon the basis of a majority of the free white population." But slavery existed, largely as an eastern institution, and it demanded protection. Again the reformers protested. The principle was unknown to the historic constitution. It would enslave the west or sever the state along the Blue Ridge. They dared not attack slavery. About some of them, Randolph detected the odor of abolitionism; they denied it, of course, and took pains to demonstrate the increase of the slave population west of the Blue Ridge, concluding that eastern fears on this count were groundless. Leigh's plan was defeated 47 to 49. The convention then passed over the first resolution of the legislative committee in order to dispose of the rest of the report.

The delegates returned to the obstinate problem on November 30. "Temper has heretofore maintained her uncertain empire," a reporter wrote, "but many symptoms portend stormy debates. What will be the issue no one can tell." In the two week interval leaders of both parties endeavored to work out compromise plans to break the stalemate. Five such plans were presented, all employing the principle of federal numbers. Upshur proposed to fix representation on an average of the three ratios: the white basis, the compound basis, and federal numbers. Leigh proposed an average of the white basis and federal numbers. Marshall offered a slight modification of the same plan, which while somewhat more favorable to the west still kept it a poor relation. None of these plans was acceptable to the democratic leaders. But two others, both originated by moderate reformers of the Albemarle district in the upper Piedmont (near the Blue Ridge), were seriously considered. The plan of James Pleasants called for the white basis in the house and federal numbers in the senate. William Fitzhugh Gordon, seeing that no rule or principle could be agreed upon, abandoned principle altogether and proposed to "sink the question" by an arbitrary but equitable apportionment of representatives and senators to each of the four sections—Tidewater, Piedmont, Shenandoah Valley, and Trans-Allegheny. This so-called mixed basis gave the west about one-half the increased representation expected under the favored-white basis. John R. Cooke and several of his friends thought it a reasonable compromise, provided the defect of the rule for reapportionment could be overcome. The Pleasants plan, on the other hand, embodied the vicious principle that "every five slaves in the East were equal to three citizens in the West."

On November 27, while both plans still lay on the table, the reform party caucused. To Cooke's surprise most of the delegates preferred Pleasants' compromise over Gordon's. They appointed Cooke and Richard H. Henderson, of the Loudoun district in northern Virginia—the main center of reform outside the west—to confer with the liberal element of the east. These delegates advised support of the Gordon plan, though they would not pledge their votes. Cooke and Henderson concurred, but when they reported to the reform caucus they, with Gordon himself, were its only advocates. So they united on the Pleasants compromise, now called the "Western plan." Cooke himself offered it to the convention on November 30. Doddridge was its principal champion, however. "Further than this I will never go," he stoutly declared, "and here I nail my flag." The conservatives were equally firm. Control of the senate was worthless and the reformers knew it, Leigh said. "They know that if they get the white basis in the Lower House, it is a matter of no sort of consequence what basis you adopt in the Senate—none, Sir—none at all." The eastern leaders were now reconciled to the Gordon plan.

Finally, on December 5, the delegates, in committee of the whole, voted down the Pleasants plan and approved the mixed basis. The decision was later ratified in convention on a record vote, 50 to 46. The western delegates, supported by their staunch friends in northern Virginia, voted unanimously against the Gordon plan. The three votes that furnished the winning margin came from reformers of Gordon's own Albemarle district. A select committee filled in the details of the new system; and after much wrangling on the equities of the apportionment between one county and another and a net addition of seven to the total number of delegates, the convention brought it to completion. There only remained the problem of a rule for reapportionment. Actually, no rule was agreed upon. The legislature was obligated to reapportion the delegates after each census, never allowing the total to exceed 150, and except on a two-thirds vote no changes could be made in the *total* representation assigned to the four "great districts" or, for senators, to the two "great divisions" of the commonwealth. Again it was Cooke who came forth from the reform ranks as a conciliator. The proposition offered a static solution to a dynamic situation. It was a crushing defeat for the west.

During the stalemate on representation, the delegates reached a compromise on the suffrage. Only in Virginia and North Carolina— in the election of the house—had the historic freehold suffrage withstood the advance of democracy. The constitution of 1776 had left it intact. The franchise belonged to freeholders of one-quarter-acre lots in towns, twenty-five acres and a dwelling in the country, or one hundred acres of unimproved land. In 1785 the legislature lowered the last requirement to fifty acres. Thus the law stood in 1829. Estimates of the number of freeholders varied, though not by much. Doddridge, who was a veritable fountainhead of facts and figures, concluded that no more than one-half the adult white males had the franchise. But how well the law was enforced is a matter of conjecture. Madison said it was ignored in the west. Complaints of fraudulent voting, leading to contested elections, regularly came before the general assembly from 1800 forward. The practical problem of enforcing the freehold requirement, and thus keeping elections honest, was repeatedly emphasized by the friends of reform. They also pointed to the gross injustices worked by the freehold qualification. Thousands of militiamen responsible for the protection of their communities—there were nightly patrols in areas thickly populated with slaves—had no voice in public affairs. Changes in the leasehold system, from leases for life, which were deemed freeholds, to short-term leases, which were not, deprived great numbers of farm tenants of the franchise. Similarly excluded were growing numbers of artisans and tradesmen in the towns. They naturally joined hands with the westerners; unfortunately, however, they could furnish no votes. The division on the suffrage in the convention, as on representation, was largely sectional, the reform ranks numbering the same few delegates in the upper Piedmont and northern Virginia counties who voted with the west on other issues.

"Who is the Commonwealth?" Doddridge asked the delegates. "According to some, it consists of certain freeholders alone; according to others, of all tax-paying citizens; while others again, compose it of the whole white population." The reform leaders adhered to the third position, which entailed universal white manhood suffrage; but they quickly realized it was unattainable and retreated to the second. Even here they were in advance of the legislative committee, which proposed to extend the franchise only to leaseholders and householders. The conservatives fought this change. They identified the freehold suffrage with all that was glorious in Virginia life and states-manship. In their hands the Jeffersonian ideal of a freeholders' re-public became a shield of aristocracy rather than a sword of democracy. Any departure from the freehold suffrage, Leigh and his friends warned, would lead to the conquest of the state by the "pot-boilers of the towns" and "the peasantry of the West" under that *"ignis fatuus* of French politics and French irreligion," universal suffrage. These conservatives continued, with their forebears of the Revolutionary generation, to view the American people in European terms and democracy as a demented Jacobinic innovation. The re-formers answered with a litany of Jeffersonian phrases.

On November 17 a delegate from beyond the mountains, Eugenius M. Wilson, offered the taxpaying qualification as a basis of com-promise. The majority spurned it, first in the great committee and later in the convention. Faintly discernible in this debate was the interpolation of proslavery ideas in the democratic argument. The presence of slavery demanded the elevation of all white men to the highest privileges of citizenship, it was said. This logic of democracy thus led to the doctrine of white supremacy—in time, Virginia and the entire South would heed the call. On November 23, after seven weeks in which the convention had agreed on no substantive resolu-tion and Randolph was advising them to go home, the delegates ap-proved the motion of the northern Virginia reformer Charles F. Mercer to admit housekeepers to the suffrage. The next day lease-holders were added. The compromise, such as it was, was carried by the reform party. It broke the freehold suffrage, but fell far short of general or universal suffrage. When the convention finished its work, probably one-third the adult white males still lacked the vote. The modest extension of the franchise had no significant effect on the politics and government of the Old Dominion.

The Virginia executive under the Revolutionary constitution was perhaps the weakest of any state. The governor was a puppet of the general assembly, receiving his appointment annually from that body and being required to act jointly with an executive council similarly appointed. Jefferson had experienced the trials of this system as wartime governor. He had bitterly denounced it, and the reformers added little to what he had said in their advocacy of a popularly elected governor and abolition of the council. The report of the executive committee, which Giles headed, provided for the latter but left the former question open. The convention repeatedly changed its mind on both questions. The reformers, though they spoke much of the theory of separation of powers, wished to strengthen the governor's office and to make it responsible to the people. The conservatives, on the other hand, though they dredged up old fears of monarchial prerogative—Giles called the federal executive "monarchical"—wanted a weak governor, fettered by a council, and both responsible to the legislature, which they controlled. Twice in committee of the whole Doddridge's motion for popular election failed; then, in convention, it succeeded, only finally to be overturned when Gordon's eleventh hour amendment for election of the governor by the general assembly for a term of three years passed, 50 to 46. Only one western delegate voted with the majority. Ten of the reform party in the east and, surprisingly, the conservative Upshur voted in the minority. The defection of three of the four reformers from the Albemarle district proved decisive. The story was much the same for the council, abolished in the great committee. This decision was twice sustained in the convention. But when a conservative delegate moved, three days before adjournment, to revive the council as an advisory body, the amendment carried, 51 to 44.

The debate on the judiciary is especially interesting with respect to local government. Local government centered in the county courts. Many eulogies had been passed upon these oligarchical bodies, and the convention's defenders of the old order added to the store. The courts consisted of the justices of the peace, who nominated—to the governor—or appointed local officials, assessed taxes, issued licenses, managed roads and police, and dispensed justice. As self-perpetuating bodies, neither the people nor any other authority could control them. Not only did they monopolize county administration—the only elective body in a county was the overseers of the poor, a relic of the old vestry—but they also had great influence in state politics. They were not secured in the constitution, which merely took them for granted, but were sanctioned by unassailable tradition. Even Jefferson had made no objection to this institution in his *Notes on the State of Virginia*. Later, his hostility was aroused, possibly because of the courts' failure to levy taxes and implement the optional county system of education authorized by statute in 1796, and he came to regard the county courts as the worst feature of Virginia government.

In the judiciary committee a narrow majority first voted to deny constitutional status to the county courts. Marshall, the chairman, asked for reconsideration at a subsequent meeting when one of the reformers was absent, and the vote was reversed. Ironically, what Marshall proposed was exactly what Jefferson had proposed in his draft Virginia constitution of 1783—the inclusion of the county courts in the constituted judicial power of the commonwealth. From the reformers' standpoint, this was a step backward. When the judiciary committee reported, the Reverend Alexander Campbell, one of the western minority on that committee, moved an amendment to make justices of the peace elective of the people. The amendment was premature; it was never called up. Subsequently, Thomas M. Bayly, an easterner, moved to deny constitutional recognition of the courts, thereby leaving their future to the legislature. The debate centered on this motion. It was defeated, with only 22 votes cast in its favor; renewed in the convention, it received 27 votes. The west was almost evenly split on the question. Obviously, the courts functioned with varying success among the counties regardless of sectional lines.

Other reforms proposed in county administration met the same fate. Popular election of the sheriffs was first approved overwhelmingly, then defeated. Lewis Summers, from Kanawha, ably championed Jefferson's ward scheme of local democracy, but the delegates turned it down without debate.

The convention finished its work on January 15, 1830. A select committee headed by Madison had been appointed to draft a new constitution by grafting the resolutions adopted upon the old fabric. This document, reported on January 4, had then been thrown open to amendment, again revised by Madison's committee, again amended, and finally engrossed for passage on the third reading. It passed 55 to 40. Cooke was the sole westerner recorded in the majority, while six delegates from east of the Blue Ridge—four from the Loudoun district—stood by the reformers to the dismal end. It was, in fact, a crushing defeat for the west and all friends of reform. The apportionment of representation, though not in itself sanctioning the anti-majoritarian principles championed by the conservatives, ensured the continued dominance of "old" Virginia in the affairs of the commonwealth. Despite extension of the suffrage, over 30,000 adult white males remained outside the circle of political competence. The general assembly continued to elect the governor, triennially, to be sure, and with an advisory council. The undemocratic system of local government survived untouched. Judges were made somewhat more removable, but none was admitted to election by the people. Finally, the defects of the constitution were without remedy, since the convention refused to make provision for its amendment. The proposition, when introduced, was promptly buried under John Randolph's scorn.

This eccentric genius, who then represented what today would be called the "radical right," was also responsible for the convention's failure to adopt a democratic instrument of ratification of the constitution. He would as soon the document be ratified by the people of Japan as by the whole people of Virginia, or even by those newly admitted to the franchise. (Exercising to the end his talent for perversity, Randolph advised his constituents to reject the constitution.) The electorate approved the convention's work by a decisive majority. The Trans-Allegheny counties polled nearly 40 per cent of the negative vote. There was talk of secession—talk that had been hushed in the convention. Secession would come eventually, with the Civil War. The Shenandoah Valley, however, would gradually be assimilated to the east. The result was predictable in 1830. The Valley vote was surprisingly favorable to the constitution. Those delegates who had pointed, whether in fear or in confidence, to the growth of slavery in the Valley accurately forecast its future. Within twenty years the east had less reason to fear the democracy of the west, for the latter had become increasingly mixed with slavery. Democracy triumphed at last in the convention of 1850–1851, when the reformers won nearly everything they had asked for two decades before.

"We are engaged, Mr. Chairman," Chapman Johnson had solemnly addressed the house,

in a contest for power—disguise it as you will—call it a discussion of the rights of man, natural or social—call it an enquiry into political expediency . . . still, Sir, all our metaphysical reasoning and our practical rules, all our scholastic learning and political wisdom, are but the arms employed in a contest, which involves the great and agitating question, whether the sceptre shall pass from Judah. . . .

The student of these debates must agree with Johnson, adding, however, that discussions of the rights of man always involve contests of power. As an exhibition of political theory in the thick context of practical political life, as a study of democratic and conservative ideologies, the Virginia debates of 1829–1830 are unexcelled in American political discourse. In the final analysis, the convention signalized the division in the house that Jefferson built. The two main factors that had given rise to the Jeffersonian order in Virginia politics—the ideas of natural rights and popular sovereignty, together with the defensive and decentralizing doctrines of state rights—no longer worked in unison, and the dominant power in the state was forced to deny one in order to secure the other.

1827

December 14   The house of delegates passes a bill submitting the question of convention to the freeholders.

1828

April   The freeholders endorse the convention by a vote of 21,896 to 16,637.

1829

February 10   The general assembly enacts a law calling the convention into being. The vote—114 to 93 in the house of delegates, 17 to 7 in the senate.

May   The delegates are elected by the freeholders in senatorial districts.

October 5   The convention opens in Richmond.

October 26   The convention resolves itself into committee of the whole to commence debate on the reports of the select committees.

December 5   The Gordon plan for the apportionment of senators and representatives is adopted in committee of the whole, 49 to 43.

December 16   The convention begins consideration of the report of the committee of the whole.

1830

January 4   The select committee of seven, Madison chairman, reports the draft of an amended constitution.

January 14   The proposed constitution, after further amendment, is adopted, 55 to 40.

January 15   The convention adjourns *sine die.*

April   The constitution is ratified in the counties, 26,055 to 15,563.

Representation

18. Cooke on Democratic Representation

On October 27, at the opening of debate on the compound versus the white basis, Benjamin Watkins Leigh presumptuously challenged the reformers to prove their case. John R. Cooke responded at length in a speech his foes derided as "speculative." Forty-three years old, from the prosperous Shenandoah Valley county of Frederick, Cooke was little known in the east, though he had been in the forefront of the reform movement since 1816. As the west's principal conciliator in the later stages of the convention, he played a crucial role in its outcome. He was, or soon became, one of Virginia's most distinguished lawyers. The novelist John Esten Cooke and the poet Philip Pendleton Cooke were his sons.

MR. LEIGH of Chesterfield, said, that he did hope that the friends of the proposition reported by the Legislative Committee, would assign their reasons in support of a plan which proposes, in effect, to put the power of controlling the wealth of the State, into hands different from those which hold that wealth; a plan, which declares that representation shall be regulated by one ratio, and contribution by another: that representation shall be founded on the white population alone, and contribution on a ratio double, treble, and quadruple in proportion. He hoped the friends of these new propositions, new at least in our State, if not new throughout the world, would give to those who differed from themselves, some reasons in support of their scheme; some better reasons than that such principles were unknown to our English ancestors, from whom we have derived our institutions; better than the rights of man as held in

---

From *Proceedings and Debates of the Virginia State Convention of 1829-30* (Richmond, 1830), pp. 53-62.

the French school; better than that they were calculated in their nature to lead to rapine, anarchy and bloodshed, and in the end, to military despotism: a scheme, which has respect to numbers alone, and considers property as unworthy of regard. Give us, said Mr. L. some reasons; reasons which may excuse us in our own self-esteem, for a tame submission to this (in my opinion) cruel, palpable and crying injustice. Let us have at least some plausible reason; something which has at least the colour of reason, which may excuse us to ourselves: something which may gild the pill and disguise its bitterness: something to save us from the contempt of this present time, and the assured curse of posterity, if we shall betray their interest. Give us something which we may at least call reasons for it: not arithmetical and mathematical reasons; no mere abstractions; but referring to the actual state of things as they are; to the circumstances and condition of this Commonwealth; why we must submit to what I cannot help regarding as the most crying injustice ever attempted in any land. I call upon gentlemen for these reasons.

MR. COOKE of Frederick, rose in reply.

Mr. Cooke said, that he could not but express his unfeigned astonishment, that the able gentleman from Chesterfield (Mr. Leigh) should have ventured to say to that assembly, that the principle of representation recommended by the Legislative Committee, was "new to him, and new in the history of the world." Can the gentleman have forgotten, (said Mr. Cooke,) that the principle which he treats as a novelty, and an innovation, is asserted in the "Declaration of the Rights of the people of Virginia"? And does he not know, that when the Convention of 1776 promulgated, in that instrument, the principles of Government on which their infant Republic was founded, they did but announce, in solemn form, to the people of Virginia, principles which had received, *a century before,* the deliberate sanction of the most enlightened friends of liberty, throughout the world?

Sir, the fathers of the Revolution did but *reiterate* those great and sacred truths which had been illustrated by the genius of Locke, and Sydney, and Milton: truths for which [John] Hampden, and a host of his compatriots, had poured out their blood in vain.

Driven from Europe, by Kings, and Priests, and Nobles, those simple truths were received, with favour, by the sturdy yeomanry who dwelt on the western shores of the Atlantic. The love of liberty, aye, Sir, and of *equality* too, grew with the growth, and strengthened with the strength, of the Colonies. It declared war, at last, not only against the *power* of the *King,* but against the *privilege* of the *Noble,* and laid the deep foundations of our Republic on *the sovereignty of the people* and *the equality of men.*

The sacred instrument, for sacred I will dare to call it, notwithstanding the sneers which its very name excites in this assembly of *Republicans,* the sacred instrument in which those great principles were declared, was ushered into existence under circumstances the most impressive and solemn. The "Declaration of the Rights of the people of Virginia," was made by an assembly of sages and patriots, who had just involved their country in all the horrors of war, in all the dangers of an unequal contest with the most powerful nation on earth, for the sake of the noble and elevated principles which that instrument announces and declares. For the sake of those principles, they had imperilled their lives, their fortunes, their wives, their children, their country; and, in one word, all that is dear to man. For the sake of those principles, they had spread havoc and desolation over their native land, and consigned to ruin and poverty a whole generation of the people of Virginia.

And for what did they make these mighty sacrifices! For wild "abstractions, and metaphysical subtleties!" No, Sir. For principles of eternal truth; as practical, in character, as they are vital, in importance; for principles deep-seated in the nature of man, by whose development, alone, he can attain the happiness which is the great object of his being. Those principles are,

"That all power is vested in, and consequently derived from, *the people.*"

"That all men are, by nature, *equally* free." And

"That *a majority of the community* possesses, by the law of nature and necessity, a right to control its concerns."

These are the principles which the gentleman from Chesterfield regards as "wild and visionary;" as "abstractions and metaphysical subtleties;" and which are contemptuously styled by others, who think with him, "*mere* abstract principles." Passing by, without comment, the curious fact, that these "abstract principles" received but yesterday the sanction of an unanimous vote of this body (so far, at least, as a *nemine contradicente*[1] vote can be called unanimous): passing by the fact, I say, that the resolution of a special Committee declaring that the Bill of Rights requires *no amendment,* was but yesterday adopted, without a dissenting voice, I will pause, for a moment, to enquire what these gentlemen mean by their favourite phrase, "mere abstract principles?" If I rightly apprehend the import of the term "abstract," when applied, in *a disparaging sense,* to any general principle, it means that the principle, though true, *as expressed,* is, nevertheless, expressed in terms so general, that when an attempt is made to apply it to any given subject, it is almost always found that the subject is included, not within the principle itself, but within one or other of those *exceptions,* which detract from the *universal* correctness of *all* general principles. That the principle is an unmeaning generality, and scarcely susceptible of application to the every-day business of men. In short, that it is wild, visionary and *unpractical.*

Let us see, then, whether the principles which are announced

---

[1] With no one contradicting [Ed.].

by the Declaration of Rights, as the "basis and foundation of Government," are of this wild and visionary character. Let us see whether they do not, on the contrary, come home to the "business and bosoms of men."

It declares, then, in the first place, "that all power is vested in, and consequently derived from, *the people*."

Look to the situation and circumstances of those who made this declaration, to the occasion on which it was made, and to its bearing and operation on the existing institutions of Virginia, and then say whether it was not a *practical* principle, and one too, of great pith and moment. The colonies had long been smarting under the tyrannical exercise of power, *not derived from the people:* Under the exercise of power assumed, by the King and Parliament of Great Britain, *without the consent of the people.* Here, then, is a bold denunciation of this usurped authority; an abolition of kingly power; a declaration that *the people* of Virginia are the only *sovereigns* of Virginia, and that they would tolerate, in all time to come, neither foreign Parliaments, nor Kings, nor Caesars. A declaration that the only legitimate Government, is a Government of *magistrates,* deriving their power *from* the people, and responsible *to* the people.

With whatever colour of plausibility this might have been called an abstract principle, in Europe, in the time of Locke and Sydney,[2] who first maintained and supported it, thanks to the indomitable spirit of our ancestors, it became *practical* in Virginia, in 1776; was gallantly sustained through all the vicissitudes of the war, and received the sanction of royalty itself, at the peace which ensued. It was then that the slavish doctrine of the *jus divinum*[3] of Kings, openly supported, but a century before, in the country from whence we sprung, re-

---

[2] Algernon Sidney (1622–1683), early republican theorist, author of *Discourses Concerning Government* (1698) [Ed.].

[3] Divine right [Ed.].

ceived its *practical* refutation; and it might have been hoped, in *Virginia* at least, *its final doom.* From the period of the revolution *till the meeting of this Convention,* the doctrine "that all power is vested in, and consequently derived from, the people," was considered *a great practical truth. Now,* it is an *"abstract principle,"* a wild and visionary speculation!

But again, Sir. The Bill of Rights declares, "that all men are, by nature, *equally* free." And this is considered an abstraction *par excellence;* the very abstraction of abstractions. It is even pronounced to be "absurd on the face of it," because it amounts, as it is said, to a declaration, that "all men, all women, and all children, are entitled to an equal share of political power."

I shall briefly examine this principle, Sir, in connexion with that which stands by its side in the Declaration of Rights, which is, in effect, that the sovereign power, the supreme control of its affairs, is vested in the majority of every free community. And I hesitate not to say, that taken in connexion, and they *must* be taken in connexion, they are so far from being speculative and abstract truths, much less absurd speculations, that they constitute in fact, a compendium of the whole law of rational and practical liberty, and were peculiarly appropriate and practical in their application to the actual condition of Virginia. Taking first the insulated proposition, that "all men are, by nature, *equally* free"; I pronounce it to be a great practical truth; a self-evident proposition; the primary postulate of the science of Government. Sir, what does this proposition mean, but that no *one* man is born with a natural right to control any *other* man; that no one man comes into the world with a mark on him, to designate him as possessing superior rights to any other man; that neither God nor nature recognize, in anticipation, the distinctions of bond and free, of despot and slave; but that these distinctions are artificial; are the work of man; are the result of fraud or violence. And who is so bold as to deny this simple truth?

But is it a mere *"abstract"* truth? Was it not, when declared by the authors of the Declaration of Rights, replete with *practical* meaning? What was their actual situation? The Government of England, against which this principle was directed, was incumbered with privileged orders; there was the King with his *hereditary prerogative*, and the noble with his *hereditary privilege*. The colonists had found, to their cost, in the earlier stages of their struggle, that *prerogative* and *privilege*, derived from birth, were the sworn and mortal foes of liberty. In announcing and reinstating the original *equality of men*, they declared war against both, and from that time, neither privilege nor prerogative derived from birth, have been tolerated in the Commonwealth which they established. And is there nothing practical in this? Is this a mere abstract principle; a mere "metaphysical subtlety"?

But it is said, that if it be true that "all men are by nature equally free," then all men, all women, and all children, are entitled to equal shares of political power; in other words, that they are all entitled to the right of suffrage, which is, practically, political power.

Sir, no such absurdity can be inferred from the language of the Declaration of Rights. The framers of that instrument did not undertake to write down in it all the rules and all the exceptions which constitute political law. They did not *express* the self-evident truth that the Creator of the Universe, to render woman more fit for the sphere in which He intended her to act, had made her weak and timid, in comparison with man, and had thus placed her under his *control,* as well as under his protection. That children, also, from the immaturity of their bodies and their minds, were under a like control. They did not say, *in terms,* that the exercise of political power, that is to say, of the right of suffrage, necessarily implies *free-agency* and *intelligence;* free-agency, because it consists in *election* or *choice* between different men and different measures; and *intelligence,* because on a *judicious* choice depends the very safety and existence of the community. That nature herself had therefore pronounced, on women and children, a sentence of incapacity to exercise political power. They did not say all this; and why? Because to the universal sense of all mankind, these were self-evident truths. They meant, therefore, this, and no more: that all the members of a community, of mature reason, and free agents by situation, are originally and by nature, *equally* entitled to the exercise of political power, or a voice in the Government.

But at the same time that they recognized and expressed the general principle, the general right, they recognized and *expressed* a limitation of that general right imposed by *nature* and *necessity*. In affirming and declaring the *jus majoris*[4] to be the law of all free communities, they did but declare the simple and obvious truth, that the essential character of a free Government, of a Government whose movements are regulated by numbers, involves the *necessity* of a submission by the *minority* to the *majority*. For the right of deliberation and *election* necessarily involves some *decision* between the men or the measures which are the subject of deliberation and election. All deliberation must come to a close, and every exercise of the right of election must terminate in a choice. To bring deliberation to *some* close, and election to *some* choice, it must of necessity be adopted as a rule, either that the majority or the minority must put an end to the deliberation, by pronouncing a decision: And the necessity of adopting the rule that the majority shall so pronounce, is founded on the necessity of a *sanction* to every law, on the fact that the majority possesses, in its superior physical force, *that sanction,* and on the certainty that it would not permanently submit to the opposite regulation. I say, *permanently:* Because, though the majority may be deluded for a time, by the artificial and vicious institutions of society, into a submission to the voice of the

---

4 Right of the majority [Ed.].

minority, they will arise, at last, and assert and enforce their natural superiority.

Neither did the framers of the Declaration of Rights carry out the *jus majoris* into certain other plain and obvious results: for they were not writing a treatise on political law, but merely announcing, in a brief and compendious form, its leading principles. They declared, for example, that the majority of every community has a right to adopt such a form of Government, and such a fundamental law, as to them seems best. They left unexpressed the plain and obvious propositions, that in forming that fundamental law, the majority have a right to act, and ought to act, on the principles, that the safety of the people is the supreme law; that the legitimate object of all Government, is to promote the greatest happiness of the greatest number; and that the perfect and entire protection of life, property, and personal liberty, constitutes the essential basis of the greatest happiness of the greatest number. That to effect these essential objects, the majority have a perfect right to prescribe, by a fundamental law, still further limitations to the universality of the right of suffrage. That they have a right to exclude, and ought to exclude, by their fundamental law, from the exercise of the right of suffrage, all those, who in the honest and deliberate opinion of the majority, cannot *safely* be entrusted with the exercise of it; or in other words, all those whose exercise of this right would be, in the honest and deliberate opinion of the majority, incompatible with the safety and well-being of the community, which is the supreme law. They did not set down, in express terms, all these distinct and consecutive propositions. But they *did* state the result to which they lead, when they said, in effect, that, in a well regulated community, those alone should be permitted to exercise the right of suffrage, who have "a permanent common interest with, and attachment to, the community."

I say, then, Sir, with a confidence inspired by a deep conviction of the truth of what I advance, that the principles of the *sovereignty of the people*, the *equality of men*, and the *right of the majority*, set forth in the "Declaration of the Rights of the people of Virginia," so far from being "wild and visionary," so far from being "abstractions and metaphysical subtleties," are the very principles which alone give a *distinctive* character to our institutions, are the principles which have had the *practical* effect in Virginia, of abolishing *kingly power*, and *aristocratic privilege*, substituting for them an elective magistracy, deriving their power *from* the people, and responsible *to* the people.

But it has been said that the authors of the Declaration of Rights themselves, admitted, in effect, the abstract and *unpractical* character of the principles which it contains, by establishing a Government whose practical regulations are wholly inconsistent with those theoretical principles. That while, in the Declaration of Rights, they asserted that all power is vested in *the people*, and should be exercised by *a majority* of the people, they established a Government in which *unequal counties*, expressing their sense by the representatives of a *selected few* in those counties, to wit, the *freeholders*, were the real political *units*, or essential *elements* of political power. That the right of the majority, in this frame of Government, was violated in two different modes: First, by vesting the power, within each county, in the freeholders, who are a minority of the people, and next by investing small masses of people in the small counties, and large masses in the large counties, with equal power in the Government.

Sir, the argument would be a good one if the premises which support it were correct. But it is *not true* that the authors of the Declaration of Rights *established* the anomalous Government under which we have lived these fifty years and more. There can be no grosser error than to suppose that the Constitution of Virginia was *formed* in 1776. Its two great distinctive features, the *sectional*, and the *aristocratic* had been given to it a century before. The *equal representation of the counties*, which was the remote cause of its sectional character, was established, in 1661, by a General Assembly representing a population residing exclusively in the tide-water country, and consequently, at that time, homogeneous in character and identical in interest. The *limitation of suffrage to freeholders* which gave to it an aristocratic character, was imposed on the Colony in 1677, without any act of Assembly, by a letter of instructions from the King of England to his Governor in Virginia, backed and enforced by two regiments of British soldiers, who had been sent to the Colony for the express purpose of suppressing a popular insurrection. At the aera of the revolution, then, these two provisions had been the constitutional law of the Colony for more than one hundred years. The freeholders had learned to pride themselves on their superior power and privileges, and the smaller counties on their equality with the larger. The body of the people were reconciled by habit to their actual condition.

What, then, was the situation in which the framers of the Constitution were placed?—While they framed that instrument they were almost within hearing of the thunder of hostile cannon. The invader was at the door. They were in continual danger of being driven from the very hall of legislation by the bayonets of the enemy. The whole undivided physical force of the country was barely sufficient to defend it against the superior force of a foreign enemy. It was utterly *impossible,* under such circumstances, to pull down, and erect anew, the whole fabric of Government. And it would have been to the last degree unwise and impolitic, at such a fearful crisis, to distract the minds of the people by attempting a new distribution and arrangement of political power. It would have been the very height of folly, at such a crisis, to create disaffection in the minds of the *freeholders,* by stripping them of their exclusive powers, and to exasperate the smaller *counties* by degrading them from the rank which they had held under the royal Government. In leaving the *freeholders* and the *counties*

as they found them, the framers of the Constitution bowed to
the supreme law of necessity, and acted like wise and *practical*
statesmen. Weak and unstable, then, is the argument which
infers the *unpractical* character of the principles contained in
the Declaration of Rights from the inconsistency of the actual
Government formed, with those principles. The very language
resorted to in disposing of a subject of such vital importance
as the regulation of the right of suffrage, the brief and summary
way in which it is disposed of, would shew, in the absence of
all other evidence, that it was a subject which the framers of
the Constitution *scarcely dared to touch.*—"The right of suffrage shall remain as at present exercised."

No, Sir, it was not reserved for *us* to discover the inconsistency between their theoretical principles, and their practical regulations. They saw it themselves, and deplored it. In
the very heat of the war which was waged for these "abstractions"—in the hurly-burly of the conflict, *one* statesman, at
least, was found, to point out those inconsistencies, and to
urge home on the people of Virginia the "new and unheard
of" principle, that in the apportionment of representation, regard should be had to the white population only. As early as
1781, Mr. Jefferson exhorted the people of Virginia, in the
most earnest and impressive language, to reduce the principle
to practice, "so soon as leisure should be afforded them, for
intrenching, within good forms, the rights for which they had
bled."

From that time to this, the spirit of reform has never slept.
From that time to this, the friends of liberty have continually
lifted up their voices against the inequality and injustice of our
system of Government. Incessantly baffled and defeated, they
have not abandoned their purpose; and after a struggle of
fifty years, that purpose seems at length on the eve of accom-
plishment. The Representatives of the people of Virginia have
at length assembled in Convention, to revise the Constitution
of the State. A special committee of this Convention has recom-

mended, among other measures of reform, the adoption of a resolution.

"That in the apportionment of representation, in the House of Delegates, regard should be had to white population exclusively."

It is this resolution which has called forth the denunciations of the gentleman from Chesterfield. It is this proposition, "new in the history of our Government, if not throughout the world; new certainly to him," which he calls on us to support.

Sir, I have ventured to assert, in the commencement of the remarks which I have had the honour to address to the Committee, that this proposition, so far from being *"new and unheard of,"* is but a reiteration, a practical enforcement, of those principles of political law which were solemnly announced by the fathers of the revolution, in that noble paper, the "Declaration of the Rights of the people of Virginia," which rights do pertain to them and their posterity, as the basis and foundation of Government. I proceed to redeem the pledge.

The Bill of Rights declares, that *the people* are the only legitimate source and fountain of political power.—The resolution of the Committee affirms this doctrine, by proposing, that in apportioning representation, or political power, regard shall be had to *the people* exclusively. Not to wealth, not to overgrown sectional interests, not to the supposed rights of the counties; but to the white population; to *the people* only.

The Bill of Rights asserts the political equality of the citizens. —The resolution proposes to give to that principle a practical existence in our Government, by abolishing the inveterate abuse of the *equal* representation of *unequal* counties, and equalizing, as nearly as may be, the electoral districts throughout the Commonwealth, on the basis of free white population alone.

The Bill of Rights pronounces the *jus majoris* to be the law of all free communities, by attributing to the majority of a community, the power to reform, alter or abolish, at its will and pleasure, the very Government itself, and consequently the lesser power of deciding, without appeal, in all matters of *ordinary legislation.*—The resolution proposes to give practical effect to the *jus majoris*, by making each Delegate the representative of an *equal number* of the people, so that the voice of a majority of the Delegates, will be the voice of a majority of the people. It proposes, in short, to establish that beautiful harmony between our theoretical principles and our practical regulations; the want of which, has been, for fifty years, the reproach of Virginia.

The resolution of the Committee, then, proposes no new and unheard of scheme; no innovation on the established principles of our Government. It calls on you to listen to the warning voice of the fathers of the revolution, who, in this despised "declaration," have told you, "that no free Government, or the blessings of liberty, can be preserved to any people, but by a frequent recurrence to fundamental principles."

But the accordance of the resolution with these great fundamental principles, has not obtained for it, the approbation of the gentleman from Culpeper, (Judge Green). He proposes to amend it by striking out the word "exclusively," and adding the words "and taxation combined"; so that the resolution, as amended, would be,

"That in the apportionment of representation in the House of Delegates, regard should be had to white population *and taxation combined.*" . . .

. . . It will be perceived, on the slightest examination, that it violates, not one only of those principles, which I have mentioned, but *every one.*

1. It repudiates the doctrine that *the people* are the *only* legitimate source and fountain of political power, and that "all power is derived from the people," and makes property *one* of the sources of power, and declares it to be derived, in part, *from* property.

2. It denies the correctness of the principle, that all the electors in the Commonwealth are equal in political rights, by conferring on *a small number of wealthy electors,* congregated in one electoral district, the same power that it confers on *a large number of poor electors,* congregated in another electoral district.

3. It subverts the *jus majoris,* the third great principle alluded to, and which is, in fact, but a corollary from the first, that the sovereignty is vested in *the body of the people,* and substitutes for it the control of the wealthy few; or in other words, the most odious, pernicious and despicable of all aristocracies—an aristocracy of wealth.

And for what purpose, I pray you, are we thus to dilapidate the very foundations of our free institutions?—For what purpose are we to make this retrograde movement in the science of Government, and in the practical institutions of our country, which should rather keep pace with the improvements of that science, and the march of intellect?—While human liberty is making a progress, which, though slow, is yet certain, even in countries where the *jus divinum* of Kings is still the prevailing doctrine, why should we alone run counter to the spirit of the age, and disavow and repudiate the doctrines consecrated by the blood of our fathers?—While most of the old, and all the new Republics of this extensive confederacy, are carrying out the principle of the sovereignty of the people to its full extent, why should we alone, seek to narrow, and limit, and restrain its operation?—What mighty good is to be attained by this abandonment of the principles of the revolution? . . .

. . . It is alleged, then, Sir, that the principles of Government contained in the Declaration of Rights, I mean those elevated and elevating principles which, in an assembly of *Virginia Statesmen,* I have this day been compelled to defend, are little better than mere abstractions. That whether they are correct or not, as "abstract principles," there is a great *practical* principle, wholly overlooked in the resolution of the Select Committee, of vital and *paramount* importance. . . .

. . . To this argument I answer that, like most unsound arguments, it is founded on a bold assumption of false premises. It is founded on the assumption that men are, by nature, *robbers*, and are restrained from incessant invasions of the rights of each other, only by fear or coercion. But, is this a just picture of that compound creature *man?* Sir, I conceive it to be a libel on the race, disproved by every page of its history. If you will look there you will find that man, though sometimes driven by stormy passions to the commission of atrocious crimes, is by nature and habit neither a wolf nor a tiger. That he is an *affectionate,* a *social,* a patriotic, a conscientious and a religious creature. In him alone, of all animals, has nature implanted the feeling of *affection for his kindred,* after the attainment of maturity. This alone is a restraint on the excess of his natural desire for property as extensive as the ties of blood that bind him to his fellow man. Designing, moreover, that man shall live in *communities,* where alone he can exist, nature has given to him the *social feeling;* the feeling of attachment to those around him. Intending that for the more perfect development of his high faculties, and for the attainment of the greatest degree of comfort and happiness of which he is susceptible, man should associate in *nations,* she implanted in him a feeling, the glorious displays of which have shed lustre around so many pages of his history. I mean *the love of country or patriotism.* Designing that he should attain to happiness through the practice of virtue, and in that way only, she erected in each man's bosom the tribunal of *conscience,* which passes in review all the actions of the individual, and pronounces sentence of condemnation on every manifest deviation from moral rectitude. To add sanctions to the decisions of conscience, she also implanted in his bosom an intuitive belief in the existence of an intelligence governing the world, who would reward virtue and punish vice in a future state of being. Man is therefore, by nature a *religious* creature, whose conduct is more or less regulated by the love or fear of the unknown governor of the Universe. Above all, the light of revealed religion has shone for ages on the world, and that Divine system of morals which commands us "to do unto others as we would have them do unto us," has shed its benign influence on the hearts of countless thousands, of the high and the low, the wise and the foolish, the *rich* and the *poor*. But we are asked to believe that all these natural feelings, all these social affections, and all these monitions of conscience, all these religious impressions, all these Christian charities, all these hopes of future rewards and fears of future punishments, are dead, and silent, and inoperative in the bosom of man. The love of property is the great engrossing passion which swallows up all other passions, and feelings, and principles; and thus not in particular cases only, but in all men. The poor man is fatally and inevitably the enemy of the rich, and will wage a war of rapine against him, if once let loose from the restraints of the fundamental law. A doctrine monstrous, hateful and incredible!

But, Sir, if I were even to admit, for a moment, the truth of the revolting proposition that the desire for property swallows up all the other feelings of man, does it follow that the aspirants after the enjoyments that property confers, will seek to attain their object in the manner which the argument in question supposes? If it be contended that man is a greedy and avaricious, it will, still, not be denied, that he is a reasoning and calculating, animal. When he desires to *attain* property it is in order that he may *possess and enjoy it.* But if he join in establishing the rule that the right of the strongest is the best right, what security has he that he, in his turn, will not soon be deprived of his property by some one stronger than himself? Sir, the *very* desire for property implies the desire to possess it *securely.* And he who has a strong desire to possess it, and a high relish, in anticipation, of the pleasure of enjoying it securely, will be a firm supporter of the laws which secure that possession, and a decided enemy to every systematic invasion of the rule of *meum* and *tuum*.[5] In other words, man is sagacious enough to know that as a general and public rule of action, the maxim that honesty is the best policy, is the safest and best maxim. And when he deviates from that rule he always hopes that the violation will go undiscovered, or otherwise escape punishment. So true is this, that I am persuaded that if a nation could be found consisting exclusively of rogues and swindlers, there would not be found in the legislative code of that nation a systematic invasion of the right of property, such as the argument for the proposed amendment apprehends and seeks to provide against.

Communities of men are sagacious enough to know and follow their *real* interest. And, Sir, I do not, and cannot believe that it is, or ever was the real interest of any class in the community, or of any community to commit gross and flagrant abuses of power, to disregard the monitions of conscience, to break down the barriers and obliterate the distinctions between right and wrong, and thus to involve society in all the horrors of anarchy. The principles of justice are the foundation of the social fabric, and rash and foolish is he and blind to his true interest, who undermines the foundation and tumbles the fabric in ruins. . . .

. . . But I know, Sir, incidentally, that the mover of this amendment entertains the opinion, that the case of Virginia is, from peculiar circumstances, a case *sui generis*. His opinion is that the comparatively non-slave-holding population of Virginia, must ere long constitute, if it does not now constitute, a decided majority of the people, and *that* majority inhabiting

---

[5] Mine and yours [Ed.].

a particular section of the State, alienated from their slave-holding fellow-citizens, by distance, localities and dissimilar views on questions of general policy.—That it will be, or what amounts to the same thing, that they will suppose it to be, their interest to lay the burthens of Government almost exclusively on the slave property of their eastern brethren. And that it is, therefore, necessary to invest the slave-holding minority with *factitious power,* under the new Constitutions, to enable it to protect itself against the injustice and oppression of the comparatively non-slave-holding majority.

Supposing the *facts* which I have just stated to be as he imagines them to be, I do not see any thing in the case stated, which takes it out of the operation of the principles of security which I have supposed to exist in regard to property in general. He *will not* contend that the people of the west are less operated on by the principle of honor, by sentiments of justice, and by a sense of their *real* interests, than the people of the east.— And if this be so, his fears are groundless. For the people of the east, under similar circumstances, have repelled the base suggestions of a sordid and short-sighted interest, and have been governed by nobler and more enlarged views of expediency and right. But, Sir, his premises fail him.—Look at the map of Virginia, and at the tables of population which have this day been reported by the Auditor. He estimates the white population east of the Blue Ridge of mountains, at 362,745, and the white population west of those mountains at 319,516. The people of the east have, therefore, a majority of 43,229 over those of the west. I need scarcely, Sir, tell this assembly, that the whole white population east of the Ridge is a slave-holding population. The black population is even more dense along the eastern base of the Ridge, than along the shore of the Atlantic. For while the two senatorial districts bordering on the ocean, contained, by the Census of 1820, one of them but 17,416, and the other but 18,363, three of the districts along the eastern base of the Ridge contained, one of them 27,417, another 27,514, and the third 30,621. Thus you perceive, Sir, that the slave population is crowded up to the very foot of the mountain. But this is not all. The slave-holding population extends *beyond* the Ridge. The district which I have the honor in part to represent, contains about 12,000 slaves. The four western counties of Berkeley, Jefferson, Frederick and Botetourt contain 17,070. They are therefore, fairly to be considered as slave-holding counties, to the practical intent of being interested in exempting slaves from undue taxation. These four counties are estimated to contain, at present, a white population of 47,013. Add this slave-holding population, west of the mountain, (to say nothing of other western counties which contain slaves to the amount of several thousands more,) to the slave-holding population east of the mountains, and you have an aggregate of 409,758. The comparatively non-slave-holding population in all the remaining counties of Virginia, is but 272,503. There is, therefore, a majority of slave-holding population, amounting to 137,255.

And yet, strange to tell, an apprehension is entertained, that if representation be *equally* apportioned among the white population, slave property will be burthened by unequal and oppressive taxes!—If the resolution of the Committee be adopted, the slave-holding population will possess, in the House of Delegates, a majority of representatives in the proportion of 409,758 to 272,503; and yet a fear is entertained, that the representatives of the 272,503 non-slave-holders will overtax the property of the 409,758 slave-holders! And to avert this imminent peril and flagrant injustice, you are asked to invest the 409,758 with *factitious Constitutional power*—to destroy the great landmarks of natural right, established at the aera of the revolution—to repudiate all the principles of Government which have been, until now, held sacred and inviolable. Such, Sir, is the argument by which the proposed amendment is supported.

19. Upshur on Majorities and Minorities

Abel P. Upshur of Northampton replied to John R. Cooke in a speech extending over two days. It was a brilliant first statement of the conservative theory of state. In the opinion of one who heard it: "It was as conclusive on the branch of the subject which it discussed as ever speech could be, and hermetically sealed a fountain which had been gushing for years." Upshur, a forty-year-old judge of the general court, previously a member of the house of delegates, was actually less totally committed to the conservative cause than his words would suggest. He favored a taxpaying qualification for the suffrage and a popularly elected governor, voting with the reformers on these issues. Years later, when secretary of state in President Tyler's cabinet, Upshur was killed in an explosion aboard the warship Princeton.

It is contended by our opponents, that the proper basis of representation in the General Assembly, is white population alone, because this principle results necessarily from the right which the majority possess, to rule the minority. I have been forcibly struck with the fact, that in all the arguments upon this subject here and elsewhere, this right in a majority is assumed as a postulate. It has not yet been proved, nor have I even heard an attempt to prove it. It is for this proof that I was desirous to wait. Assuming this right as conceded, the whole scope of the argument has been to prove, that in the application of the right to the practical Government, we must of necessity, graduate political power according to white population alone. It may not perhaps, be more curious than profitable, to examine somewhat in detail, the grounds upon which this pretension rests.

There are two kinds of majority. There is a majority in *interest*, as well as a majority in number. If the first be within the contemplation of gentlemen, there is an end of all discus-

From *Proceedings,* pp. 66–71, 74–79.

sion. It is precisely the principle for which we contend, and we shall be happy to unite with them in so regulating this matter, that those who have the greatest stake in the Government, shall have the greatest share of power in the administration of it. But this is not what gentlemen mean. They mean, for they distinctly say so, that a majority in number only, without regard to property, shall give the rule. It is the propriety of this rule, which I propose to examine.

If there be, as our opponents assume, an original, *a priori,* inherent and indestructible right in a majority to control a minority, from what source permit me to inquire, is that right derived? If it exist at all, it must I apprehend, be found either in some positive compact or agreement conferring it, or else in some order of our nature, independent of all compact, and consequently prior to all Government. If gentlemen claim the right here as springing from positive compact, from *what compact* does it spring? Not certainly from that Constitution of Government which we are now revising; for the chief purpose for which we have been brought together, is to correct a supposed defect in the Constitution, in this very particular. Not certainly from any other Constitution or form of Government, for to none other are we at liberty to look, for any grant of power, or any principle which can bind us. The right then, is not conventional. Its source must be found beyond all civil society, prior to all social compact, and independent of its sanctions. We must look for it in the law of nature; we have indeed been distinctly told, that it exists in "necessity and nature"; and upon that ground only, has it hitherto been claimed. I propose now to inquire whether the law of nature does indeed, confer this right or not.

Let me not be misunderstood, Sir. I am not now inquiring whether, according to the form and nature of our institutions, a majority ought or ought not to rule. That inquiry will be made hereafter. At present, I propose only to prove that there is *no original a priori* principle in the law of nature, which gives to a majority a right to control a minority; and of course, that we are not bound by any obligation *prior to society*, to adopt that principle in our civil institutions.

If there be any thing in the law of nature which confers the right now contended for, in what part of her code, I would ask, is it to be found? For my own part, I incline strongly to think, that, closely examined, the law of nature will be found to confer no other right than this: the right in every creature to use the powers derived from nature, in such mode as will best promote its own happiness. If this be not the law of nature, she is certainly but little obeyed in any of the living departments of her *empire*. Throughout her boundless domain, the law of force gives the only rule of right. The lion devours the ox; the ox drives the lamb from the green pasture; the lamb exerts the same law of power over the animal that is weaker and more timid than itself; and thus the rule runs, throughout all the gradations of life, until at last, the worm devours us all. But, if there be another law independent of force, which gives to a greater number of right to control a smaller number, to what consequence does it lead? Gentlemen must themselves admit, that all men are by nature *equal*, for this is the very foundation of their claim of right in a majority. If this be so, each individual has his rights, which are precisely equal to the rights of his fellow. But the right of a majority to rule, necessarily implies a right to impose restraints, in some form or other; either upon the freedom of opinion or the freedom of action. And what follows? Each one of three, enjoys the same rights with each one of four, and yet it is gravely said, that because four is a majority of the seven, *that* majority has a right to restrain, to abridge, and consequently, to destroy all the rights of the lesser number. That is to say, while all are by nature equal, and all derive from nature the same rights in every respect, there shall yet be a number, only one less than a majority of the whole, who may not by the law of nature possess any rights at all!

If, Sir, it be possible to carry our minds back to such a state of existence, let us suppose that the wild children of nature are for the first time, assembling together for the purpose of forming a social compact. Each one of them would bring with him all the rights which he derived from nature, and among these rights, would be found the right to say *whether a majority* should rule him or not. And, suppose a civil compact should be entered into by every member of the savage assembly, save one. Is that one bound by what the rest have determined? If he has originally a right to say whether he will agree to the compact or not, at what time does that right cease to exist, and by what authority is it taken away? *Until* the compact is formed, there is no majority in existence; and *after* it is formed, he is *no* party to it; and therefore not bound by its majority.

Again.—How is this majority to be ascertained? Who shall appoint the tellers, and who shall announce on which side the majority is? All these are necessary operations, without which the idea of a majority, is indeed, an "abstraction"; and yet these very operations presuppose a degree of order and arrangement inconsistent with a state of nature, and which cannot exist except in a state of society.

Again.—Within what limits is this majority to act? Is it a majority of the whole world, or only of a part of it? If of the whole world, then two millions of savages who range the forests of America, may prescribe the law to one million who inhabit the Asiatic Islands; two millions who live by hunting the elk and the buffaloe with a bow and arrow, have authority to say that one million, among whom these animals of the chase may not be found, shall not draw their subsistence from the ocean which surrounds them! Is this the law of nature? Has the Creator really ingrafted upon the nature of man, a principle which gives sanction to such monstrous cruelty and injustice?

But suppose, instead of looking to the whole world, you limit your majority to particular districts of it. It is impossible to do this, according to any fixed rule, except by supposing that the world is divided into separate and distinct communities, possessing separate and distinct interests. And this is precisely what we understand by a state of society, as contra-distinguished from a state of nature; and of course, the majority which is to be found there, is not the majority which the proposition supposes.

But again. If nature really gives this right to a majority; if as the clear-minded gentleman from Frederick (Mr. Cooke) supposes, there be impressed upon us by nature, a principle of this sort, which is mandatory upon us, and which we are not at liberty to disregard, in what does the right consist? Is it in mere numbers? If so, every creature must be counted, men, women and children; the useless as well as the useful; the drone who lives upon the industry of others, as well as the most profitable member of the human family. The law of nature knows no distinction between these classes, and indeed, one of the very postulates on which gentlemen rely, is that "*all* are by nature equal." In point of rights, nature does not own any distinction of age or sex. Infancy has equal rights with mature age; and surely it does not consist with the gallantry of the present day, to say that the ladies are not at least the equals of ourselves. Nay, more Sir, nature as strongly disowns all invidious distinctions in complexion: in her eye, there is no difference between jet and vermilion. A distinction does indeed prevail here, Sir, and a wide one it is. But the same rule of taste would not answer in Africa; for the African paints the devil white. According to your rule of numbers, all of these various classes and descriptions of persons must count. And if so, what estimate have gentlemen themselves put upon their own rule? If in the estimate of numbers, all are counted, why exclude any from the right of suffrage? Why are not women, and children, and paupers, admitted to the polls? The rule, even if it *exists* in nature, is worth nothing, unless its fair analogies will hold in a state of society. And how can gentlemen venture to limit themselves to *white* population alone, and yet found their claim on a law of nature which knows no distinction between white and black? By *their* rule, we are entitled to representation of every slave in our land; and if they will give us this, we shall dispute with them no longer. The majority will then be with us. God forbid, Sir, that I should propose this seriously. I am as ready as any gentleman here, to disclaim every idea of the sort. I use the argument only to shew to what consequences this demand, founded on a supposed law of nature, must inevitably conduct us. Gentlemen may not claim the benefit of a rule, which will not bear to be pushed to its legitimate results; a rule which they themselves are compelled to abandon, at the very first step which they take into practical Government.

If then, there be no inherent virtue in *numbers* which confers this right, in what else does it consist? I have heard elsewhere, of another ground on which gentlemen have been pleased to rest it, and it is now distinctly announced by the able gentleman from Frederick. It is a *physical power.* I do not understand the gentleman from Frederick in the objectionable sense, of which his language was probably susceptible. He did not mean that this power in a majority would or ought to be applied, in the actual Government; it is impossible to attribute to the clear head and sound principles of that gentleman, any meaning so uncourteous as a threat. I understood him, as he meant to be understood, in this sense only: Every law implies the necessity of some sanction; force is the only sanction in the case before us, and as this force is presumed to reside in the greatest degree, in a majority, it follows that a majority only can apply the sanction, and of course that a majority ought to give the law.

Here, Sir, we are under the necessity of looking back upon the preceding proposition. From what sources are we to derive this majority? I have endeavored to shew that by nature, all are equal and possess equal rights. Then women and children must·be counted *here* also, as well as men. Now, we learn from good authority, that throughout the universe, the sexes rank to each other as thirteen and fourteen. Suppose then, the females to be all ranged on one side of the question, with a few children in their laps, and a few superannuated and decrepid men, at their sides. They may thus very well constitute a majority of the whole *number*; but will the *physical power* be with them? No Sir. That power has ever been found with personal strength, and intrepidity and skill. These qualities have at all times, and in all places, been an overmatch for mere undisciplined numbers. Here then is a case in which the majority do *not* possess the power of applying the sanction; and of course, the right to rule, which is supposed to follow the sanction, is in this case, with the *minority*. The case is quite as apt to occur, and quite as easy to be supposed, as that state of existence to which it refers, and from which gentlemen borrow their argument. And the necessary conclusion, upon the hypothesis assumed, is, that in one state of things a *majority* may have a right to rule, and in another state of things a *minority* may have that right; and this too, by the very same fixed and uniform law of nature!

To such absurdities are we inevitably driven when we attempt to apply principles deduced from a state of nature, to a state of society; a state which pre-supposes that nature with all her rights and all her laws, has been shaken off! Indeed, Sir, the whole reasoning is fallacious, because it is founded on a state of things which in all probability, never had existence at all. It goes back to a state prior to all history, and about which we know nothing beyond mere conjecture. The first accounts which we have of man, are of man in a social state. Wherever he has been found, and however rude his condition, he has been bound to his fellows by some form of association, in advance of a state of nature. If we may indulge any conjecture upon such a subject, the probability is that he was first urged into society, by a strong *feeling of property* implanted in his nature; by a feeling that he had, or at least, that he ought to have, a better title than another, to whatever his own labour had appropriated. The necessity of securing this right and protecting him in the enjoyment of it, in all probability, first suggested the idea of the social compact. Although property therefore, is strictly speaking the creature of society, yet a *feeling of property* was probably its creator. The result would be, that at the very moment that two human beings first came together, the social compact was formed. And gentlemen have fallen into another error also, of a kindred nature. They build their systems upon the notion of an abstract equality, for which there is no warrant in any thing we know of the history of man. Sir, I am about to use a borrowed idea; but it is valuable for its truth, and perfectly applicable to the subject. The first account that we have of man, is that contained in the Bible; and how will this notion of original equality stand, when tested by the orthodox book? Adam was the first of created beings; Eve was created next; and the very fiat which brought her into existence, subjected her to the dominion of her husband. Here then was no equality. Cain was the first born of men, and at what period did he become the equal of his father? Was it at the moment of his birth, while he was yet scarcely conscious of his own existence, a helpless dependent upon the care of his parents? And if not *then*, at what age did this equality first attach? Was it at ten, or fifteen, or twenty-five, or thirty-five years of age? Where is the law, or the *doctrine* of nature, which enables us to say with certainty and precision, at what age the child becomes the equal of his father? Sir, the true meaning of the equality of men, as applicable to this subject, was happily expressed by the gentleman from Culpeper (Mr. Green) when he said that "all men are so far equal by the law of nature, that when they enter into a state of society, no one can claim a natural right to rule over another." And for the same reason, no ten men can claim a natural right over any nine men.

This subject, Mr. Chairman, is scarcely worth the examination it has received. I will pursue it no farther, since I have no intention to give you a treatise on nature law, instead of an argument upon the practical subject of Government. I have thought it necessary to go thus far into an examination of the subject, because gentlemen have founded themselves upon what they are pleased to consider an axiom, that there is in a majority, an *a priori, inherent* and indestructible right to rule a minority, under all circumstances, and in every conceivable condition of things. And one of them at least has been understood by me, as referring this right to the law of nature; a law which he supposes, no society cannot repeal, and which therefore, is of original and universal authority. Surely this is a very great mistake. Nay Sir, there is proof enough before us that gentlemen themselves, who claim this right, and who seek to give it solemnity by referring it to the very law of our being, do not venture to carry it into the details of their own system. If there be a right in a majority of persons or of *white* persons, to rule a minority, upon what principle is it that the right of suffrage is restricted? *All* are counted, in making up the majority; and each one of the majority, ought of consequence, to possess a share in its rights. Why then do you not admit women to the polls? Nature has stamped no such inferiority upon that sex, as to disqualify it under all circumstances, for a safe and judicious exercise of the right of suffrage. And why exclude minors? Infants who have not acquired language, or whose intellects are not sufficiently unfolded to enable them to understand their own actions, may be excluded from the necessity of the case. But at what time, in the ordinary course of nature, do these disabilities cease? Gentlemen say, at the age of twenty-one years. And why so? Not certainly because nature declares it; for the faculties attain maturity at different periods, in different latitudes of the earth. In one latitude we are ripe at sixteen; in another, not until 30; and even among ourselves, we see many, under the age of twenty-one, who possess more wisdom and more power of general usefulness, than can be found in others of fifty; far more than in those who have approached their second childhood. What is there then, which indicates the precise period of twenty-one years, as the earliest at which these members of the ruling majority, may exercise the rights which belong to them? This, and this only: that the rule which is furnished by nature, is unfit for a state of society, and we are compelled, in our own defence, to adopt an arbitrary rule of our own, which is better suited to our actual condition. There is no one among us so wild and visionary, as to desire universal suffrage; and yet it is perfectly certain that, at the moment when you limit that right, in however small a degree, you depart from the *principle* that a majority shall rule. If you establish any disqualification whatever, there is no *natural necessity*, nor even a moral certainty, that a majority in any given community, will not come within the exception. And this state of things may by possibility, exist within every election district in the Commonwealth: and thus you establish a rule, with reference to the *entire body*, which is rejected in every *constitutent member* of that body. Surely, gentlemen cannot claim the benefit of a principle, which will not bear to be pushed to its practical consequences; a principle which they themselves are obliged to desert as unwise, unsafe and impracticable, in the details of actual Government.

In truth, Mr. Chairman, *there are no original principles of Government at all*. Novel and strange as the idea may appear, it is nevertheless, strictly true, in the sense in which I announce it. There are no original principles, existing in the nature of things and independent of agreement, to which Government must of necessity conform, in order to be either legitimate or philosophical. The principles of Government are those principles only, which the people who form the Government, choose to *adopt and apply to themselves*. Principles do not *precede*, but spring out of Government. If this should be considered a dangerous novelty in this age of improvement, when all old fashioned things are rejected as worthless; let us test the doctrine by reference to examples. In Turkey, the Government is centered in one man; in England, it resides in King, Lords, and Commons; and in the Republics of the United States, we profess to repose it in the people alone. The principles of all these Governments are essentially different; and yet will it be said that the Governments of Turkey and England are no Governments at all, or not legitimate Governments, because in them, the will of a majority does not give the rule? Or, will it be said, that our own Governments are not legitimate, because they do not conform to the despotic principles of Turkey, nor recognise the aristocracy of England? If there be these original principles at all, we must presume that they are uniform in themselves, and universal in their application. It will not do to say that there is one principle for one place, and another principle for another place. The conclusion resulting from the reasoning of gentlemen will be, that there is one Government in the world which is *really* a Government, rightful and legitimate; and all other forms of social compact, however long, or however firmly established, are no Government at all. Every Government is legitimate which springs directly from the will of the people, or to which the people have consented to give allegiance. And I am not going too far, in asserting that Governments are freer or otherwise, only in proportion as the people have been consulted in forming them, and as their rulers are directly responsible to them for the execution of their will. It matters not what form they assume, nor who are the immediate depositories of political power. It may suit the purposes of the people, as it once suited those of Rome, to invest all authority in a Dictator; and if the people choose this form of Government; if their interest and safety require that they shall submit to it, what original principle is there which renders it illegitimate? If the majority possess all power, they possess the power to *surrender* their power. And if it be just and wise that they should do so, it is still their own Government, and no one can impugn its legitimacy.

I have thus, Mr. Chairman, endeavored to prove, that there

is not in nature, nor even in sound political science, any fundamental principle applicable to this subject, which is mandatory
upon us. We are at perfect liberty to choose our own principle;
to consult all the circumstances which attend our condition,
and to mould our Government as our interests and necessities
may require. We are now to ascertain what rule of representation, those interests and those necessities suggest, as wise, just
and expedient.

I admit, as a general proposition, that in free Governments,
power ought to be given to the majority; and why? The rule
is founded in the idea that there is an identity, though not an
equality of interests, in the several members of the body
politic: in which case the presumption naturally arises, that
the greater number possess the greater interest. But the rule
no longer applies, when the reason of it fails. And here we
should be careful to remember, that the question does not
relate to the administration of an actual Government. It is
not contended that the Legislature, when the Government shall
go into operation, ought not to adopt the rule of a majority
in acts of ordinary Legislation. The question before us, is prior
to actual Government: it is not whether a majority shall rule
in the Legislature, but *of what elements that majority shall
be composed.* If the interests of the several parts of the Commonwealth were identical, it would be, we admit, safe and
proper that a majority of *persons only* should give the rule of
political power. But our interests are not identical, and the
difference between us arises from property alone. We therefore contend that property ought to be considered, in fixing
the basis of representation.

What, Sir, are the constituent elements of society? Persons
and property. What are the subjects of Legislation? Persons
and property. Was there ever a society seen on earth, which
consisted only of men, women, and children? The very idea
of society, carries with it the idea of property, as its necessary
and inseparable attendant. History cannot show any form of

the social compact, at any time, or in any place, into which property did not enter as a constituent element, nor one in which that element did not enjoy protection in a greater or less degree. Nor was there ever a society in which the protection once extended to property, was afterwards withdrawn, which did not fall an easy prey to violence and disorder. Society cannot exist without property; it constitutes the full half of its being. Take away all protection from property, and our next business is to cut each other's throats. All experience proves this. The safety of men depends on the safety of property; the rights of persons must mingle in the ruin of the rights of property. And shall it not then be protected? Sir, your Government cannot move an inch without property. Are you to have no political head? No Legislature to make laws? No Judiciary to interpret them? No Executive to enforce them? And if you are to have all these departments, will they render their services out of mere grace and favor, and for the honor and glory of the thing? Not in these money loving days, depend on it. If we would find patriotism thus disinterested, we must indeed, go back to a period prior to Bible history. And what are the subjects upon which the law-making power is called to act? Persons *and property.* To these two subjects, and not to one of them alone, is the business of legislation confined. And of these two, it may be fairly asserted that property is not only of *equal,* but even of *more* importance. The laws which relate to our personal actions, with reference to the body politic; which prescribe the duties which we owe to the public, or define and punish crime, are comparatively few in number, and simple in their provisions. And one half of these few find their best sanctions in public opinion. But the ramifications of the rights of property, are infinite. Volume upon volume, which few of us, I fear, are able to understand, are required to contain even the leading principles relating to them, and yet new relations are every day arising, which require continual interpositions of the Legislative power. If then,

Sir, property is thus necessary to the very being of society; thus indispensable to every moment of Government; if it be that subject upon which Government chiefly acts; is it not, I would ask, entitled to such protection as shall be above all suspicion, and free from every hazard? It appears to me that I need only announce the proposition, to secure the assent of every gentleman present.

Sir, the obligations of man in his social state are two-fold; to bear arms, and to pay taxes for the support of Government. The obligation to bear arms, results from the duty which society owes him, to protect his rights of person. The society which protects me, I am bound to protect in return. The obligation to pay taxes, results from the protection extended to property. Not a protection against foreign enemies; not a protection by swords and bayonets merely; but a protection derived from a prompt and correct administration of justice; a protection against the violence, the fraud, or the injustice of my neighbor. In this protection, the owner of property is alone interested. Here, then, is the plain agreement between Government on the one hand, and the tax-paying citizen on the other. It is an agreement which results, of necessity, from the social compact; and when the consideration is fairly paid, how can you honestly withhold the equivalent? Indeed, gentlemen admit that property is entitled to protection; and that *our* property *is* entitled to it, when they offer us guarantees. I shall have occasion to speak of these by and by; at present I will only say, that although they are certainly offered in good faith, they would prove in practice, wholly unavailing.

Let us now inquire of *what kind,* this protection must be, if we would give it any value. I agree with the gentleman from Culpeper (Mr. Green) that it cannot be any thing short of a direct influence in the Government.

There is one consequence, supposed to result from our doctrine on this subject, which all the gentlemen opposed to us, seem to contemplate with a sort of horror: "What," say they, "will you balance money against the bone and sinew of the country? Will you say that fifty men on this side of the mountain, shall be counted against one hundred and fifty on the other?"

Sir, no man supposes that property should be represented *eo nomine;*[6] it would be grossly absurd to place a bag of guineas upon your table, and call it a constituent entitled to representation. We do not propose to represent money, but the *right and interests which spring from the possession of money.* This is not a metaphysical refinement, an unmeaning distinction. It is easily comprehended, and it ought to remove every shadow of odium from our proposition, considered in this view. If men enter into the social compact upon unequal terms; if one man brings into the partnership, his rights of person alone, and another brings into it, equal rights of person and all the rights of property beside, can they be said to have an equal interest in the common stock? Shall not he who has most at stake; who has, not only a *greater* interest, but a *peculiar* interest in society, possess an authority proportioned to that interest, and adequate to its protection? I certainly do not mean to say, that the right of suffrage in the *individual* ought to be in proportion to his property; that if a man owning one thousand dollars is entitled to one vote, a man owning two thousand is entitled to two votes. I do not expect to be so understood after the admission which I have already made, in announcing the precise limit to which my proposition extends. Where there is an identity of interest, no difference should be made in the rights of the voter, in consequence of a difference in the extent or degree of that interest. But where there is *not* this identity; where there are different and *distinct* interests, existing in masses sufficiently large to form important objects in the Government, . . . there the rule emphatically applies. . . .

---

[6] Under that name [Ed.].

. . . Every view, Mr. Chairman, which I am capable of taking of this subject, has led me to the conclusion that property is entitled to its influence in Government. But if this be not true as a *general proposition, it is true as to us.*

Gentlemen have fallen into a great error both in their reasoning and in their conclusion, by considering the subject before us, as if we were now for the first time, entering into a social compact. If we stood in the nakedness of nature, with no rights but such as are strictly personal, we should all come together upon precisely equal ground. But such is not the case. We cannot now enter into a new compact upon the basis of original equality; we bring more than our fair proportion, into the common stock. For fifty-four years we have been associated together, under the provisions of an actual Government. A great variety of rights and interests, and a great variety of feelings dear to the heart and connected with those rights and interests, have grown up among us. They have grown up and flourished under a Government which stood pledged to protect them; that Government itself, was but a system of pledges, interchangeably given among those who were parties to it, that all the rights and all the interests which it invited into existence, should be protected by the power of the whole. Under this system, our property has been acquired; and we felt safe in the acquisition, because under the provisions of that system, we possessed a power of self-protection. And by whom was that system ordained? Not indeed by the same *men* who are now here assembled, but by the same *community,* which is now here represented. It was the *people of Virginia* who gave us these pledges; and it is the people of Virginia who now claim a right to withdraw them. Sir, can it be fair, or just, or honourable, to do this? The rights and interests which you are now seeking to prostrate, you yourselves invited into being. Under your own distributions of political power, you gave us an assurance that our property should be safe, for you put the protection of it into our own hands. With what justice or propriety then, can you now say to us, that the rights and interests which you have thus fostered until they have become the chief pillars of your strength, shall now be prostrated; melted into the general mass, and be re-distributed, according to your will and pleasure? Nay, Sir, you do not even leave us the option whether to come into your measures or not. With all these rights, and all these interests, and all these feelings, we are to be *forced*, whether willing or unwilling; we are to be *forced* by the unyielding power of a majority, into a compact which violates them all! Is there not, Sir, something of *violence* and *fraud* in this? Gentlemen are too courteous to suppose me capable of charging iniquity of this sort, upon them. They have too just an estimate, both of themselves and of me, to attribute to me so offensive a thought. If I really intended to express it, it might indeed expose me to just censure; but it would be worthless as an argument. I urge this view of the subject, because I feel entirely assured, that if gentlemen can discern either fraud or violence in their measures, they will themselves, be the first to abandon them.

I am sensible, Sir, that there is nothing in this view of the subject, unless the rights and interests to which I have alluded, are of a peculiar and distinctive character. What then are they? I purposely wave all subjects of minor importance, as too inconsiderable to give any rule. But a peculiar interest, and a great, and important, and leading interest, is presented in our slaves; an interest which predominates throughout the Eastern divisions of the State, whilst it is of secondary consequence West of the Blue Ridge. And what, let us now inquire, are its claims to consideration?

Will you not be surprised to hear, Sir, that the slave population of Virginia pays 30 per cent. of the whole revenue derived from taxation? Did there ever exist in any community, a separate and peculiar interest, of more commanding magnitude? But this is not all. It affords almost the whole productive labour of one half of the Commonwealth. What difference does it make whether a certain amount of labour is brought into the common stock, by four hundred thousand slaves, or four hundred thousand freemen? The gain is the same to the aggregate wealth; which is but another name for the aggregate power, of the State. And here permit me to remark, that of all the subjects of taxation which ever yet existed, this has been the most oppressively dealt with. You not only tax our slaves as property, but you also tax *their labour.* Let me illustrate the idea by an example. The farmer who derives his income from the labour of slaves, pays a tax for those slaves, considered as property. With that income so derived, he purchases a carriage, or a horse, and these again are taxed. You first tax the slave who makes the money, and then you tax the article which the money procures. Is not this a great injustice; a gross inequality? No such tax is laid upon the white labourer of the West, and yet the product of his labour is of no more importance to the general welfare, than the same product from the labour of slaves. Here then, is a striking peculiarity in our property; a peculiarity which subjects it to double impositions, and which therefore, demands a double security.

There is yet Sir, another view of this subject which is not only of importance with reference to the immediate topic under consideration, but which furnishes a strong argument against the change which gentlemen contemplate. One eleventh[7] of the power which we possess in the national councils, is derived from slaves. We obtain that power by counting three-fifths of the whole number, in apportioning representation among the several States. Sir, we live in time of great political changes. Some new doctrine or other is broached almost every day; and it is impossible to foresee what changes in our political condition, a single year may bring about.

---

[7] Judge Upshur corrects a mistake in his calculation. The proportion is about one sixth.

Suppose a proposition should be made to alter the Constitution of the United States in the particular now under consideration; what could Virginia say, after embracing such a basis as gentlemen propose? Would she not be told by those who abhor this species of property, and who are restive under the power which it confers, "you have abandoned this principle in your own institutions, and with what face can you claim it, in your connexions with us?" What reply could she make to such an appeal as this? Sir, the moral power of Virginia has always been felt, and deeply felt, in all the important concerns of this nation; and that power has been derived from the unchanging consistency of her principles, and her invincible firmness in maintaining them. Is she now prepared to surrender it, in pursuit of a speculative principle of doubtful propriety, at best, and certainly not demanded by any thing in her present condition? If you adopt the combined basis proposed by the amendment, this danger is avoided. You may then reply to the taunting question above supposed, "we have *not* abandoned our principle; on the contrary, we have extended it. Instead of three-fifths, *all* our slaves are considered in our representation. It is true, we do not count them as *men,* but their influence is still preserved, as *taxable subjects.* The principle is the same, although the modes of applying it may be different. We are *not* inconsistent with ourselves." To my mind, there is much force in this argument, and I think that the gentlemen opposed to us, to whom the influence of our common State is as dear as it is to us, cannot but feel and acknowledge it. The topic is fruitful of imposing reflections; but I will not pursue it farther.

I have thus endeavored to prove, Mr. Chairman, that whether it be right as a general principle or not, that property should possess an influence in Government, it is certainly right as to us. It is right, because *our* property, so far as slaves are concerned, is *peculiar;* because it is of imposing magnitude; because it affords almost a full half of the productive labour of the State; because it is exposed to peculiar impositions, and therefore to peculiar hazards; and because it is the interest of the whole Commonwealth, that its power should not be taken away. I admit that we have no danger to apprehend, except from oppressive and unequal taxation; no other injustice can reasonably be feared. It is impossible that any free Government, can establish an open and palpable inequality of rights. Resistance would be the necessary consequence; and thus the evil would soon cure itself. But the power of taxation often works insidiously. The very victim who feels its oppression, may be ignorant of the source from which it springs.

Gentlemen tell us that our alarms are unfounded; that even if we should give them power to tax us at their will and pleasure, there is no danger that they will ever abuse it. They urge many arguments to prove this; and among the rest, they tell us that there is no *disposition* among them, to practice injustice towards their eastern brethren. Sir, I do firmly believe it. It gives me pleasure to say, that in all my associations with the people of the west, I have never had reason to doubt either their justice or their generosity. And if they can give us a sure guarantee that the same just and kind feelings which they now entertain, shall be transmitted as an inheritance to their posterity forever, we will ask no other security. But who can answer for the generations that are to come? It is not for this day only, but I trust for distant ages, that we are now laboring; we are very unwisely employed, if we are not making provision for far distant times. And can gentlemen feel any assurance, that under no change which time may work in our political condition, there shall be found any clashing of interests, or any conflict of passions? Will they, who are just *now* be *always* just, under whatever temptations of interest, or whatever excitements of the feelings? Shall there be no jealousies in time to come? No resentments? Nothing to *mislead the judgment,* even if it does not corrupt the feelings? Even if no *disposition* to oppress us should exist, how can we be assured that the people of the west shall view their own acts in all time to come, in the same light in which they may appear to us? That which *they* may consider mere justice, may appear to us as the worst oppression. Surely it is not surprising that we should claim a right to say, whether we are oppressed or not.

Again.—We are told that slave-holders cannot be in danger, because in point of fact, they comprise a majority of our white population. If so, it would seem to follow that no good objection could be urged to the basis proposed by us; it is the basis required by the interests of the majority, and therefore right by our opponents' own rule. But while the fact as stated, is literally true, the conclusion deduced from it, is not so. How is this majority made up? By counting the slave-holders in all parts of the State; by taking a few, scattered here and there, through the western counties, where slaves are scarcely considered at all, and if considered, are absorbed in other and greater interests, and adding them to the numbers on this side the mountain[s], where slaves constitute the leading and most important interest. I need not press this view of the subject. It must be manifest to all, that the slave-holder of the east cannot calculate on the co-operation of the slave-holder of the west, in any measure calculated to protect that species of property, against demands made upon it by other interests, which to the western slave-holder, are more important and immediate concern.

We are told also, that slave population is rapidly increasing to the west, and that in a few years it will constitute a predominant interest there. If so, Sir, the same few years will, upon the principles of our own basis, transfer to the west, the very power which they are now seeking through another channel. They cannot lose more by waiting for this power, than we shall lose in the same time, by surrendering it. But, Sir, although it is admitted that slave population is increasing to the west, yet its increase is by a *continually decreasing ratio*. In the period between 1800 and 1810, the ratio of increase was sixty-five and a half; between 1810 and 1820, it was forty-six; and between 1820 and 1829, it was twenty-eight. Whence is this? It arises from causes which cannot for ages be removed. There exists in a great portion of the west, a rooted antipathy to this species of population; the habits of the people are strongly opposed to it. With them, personal industry, and a reliance on personal exertion, is the order of society. They know how little slave labour is worth; while their feelings as freemen, forbid them to work by the side of a slave. And besides, Sir, their vicinity to non-slave-holding States, must forever render this sort of property precarious and insecure. It will not do to tell me that Ohio no longer gives freedom, nor even shelter, to the runaway; that Pennsylvania is tired of blacks, and is ready to aid in restoring them to their owners. The moral sentiment of these States is against slavery; and that influence will assuredly be felt, notwithstanding the geographical line or narrow river, which may separate them from us. And again, Sir, the course of industry in the west, does not require slave labour; slaves will always be found in the grain-growing and tobacco country alone. This is not now the character of the western country, nor can it be, until a general system of roads and canals, shall facilitate their access to market. And when that time shall arrive, the worst evils which we apprehend will have been experienced; for it is to *make* these very roads and canals, that our taxes are required.

I think, Sir, it must be manifest by this time, unless indeed, my labour has been wholly thrown away, that property is entitled to protection, and that *our* property imperiously demands *that kind of protection* which flows from the possession of power. Gentlemen admit that our property is peculiar, and that it requires protection, but they deny to it the power to protect itself. And what equivalent do they offer to us? The best, I own, which it is in their power to devise; and it cannot be doubted that they offer it in perfect sincerity and good faith. It is due to them to say this, but it is also due to us to say that they can give us *no* security, independent of political power. They offer us Constitutional guarantees; but of what value will they be to us in practice? No paper guarantee was ever yet worth any thing, unless the whole, or at least a majority of the community, were interested in maintaining it. And this is a sufficient reply to an idea of the gentleman from Norfolk, (Mr. Taylor). "Will you," said he, "trust your lives and liberties to the guarantees of the Constitution, and will you not also trust your property?" Sir, every man in the community is interested in the preservation of life and liberty. But what is the case before us? A guarantee is offered us by that majority who claim to possess all power, and who have a direct and strong interest to violate their own pledges. In effect, it amounts to this. Gentlemen are indeed, ready to give us their bond, provided we will permit *them* to say whether they shall pay it or not. No guarantee can be worth a rush, if the very men who give it, have the power to take it away. Suppose your guarantee shall be violated, to whom are we to look for redress? Will the majority hold themselves responsible to the minority, for an abuse of their powers? To whom shall our complaints be addressed; on whom shall we call to relieve us from the unjust burthens which bear us down to the earth? On none, Sir, but the very men who have imposed them. We may appeal from Caesar to Caesar himself, and that is the only sanction which is given to this law for our security. . . .

. . . The conclusion to which I have arrived, (and I congratulate the Committee that I am fast drawing to a close,) is this: It is necessary to the well being, and even to the very existence of society, that property should be protected; it cannot in any case, and least of all, in *our own case,* hope for protection, except in the power of protecting itself; and no adequate substitute for that power, has been, or can be offered, in any other form of Constitutional provision. And now, permit me to ask, with whom can this power be most *safely* deposited? I grant, Sir, that gentlemen opposed to us, are equally patriotic in their feelings; equally just in their purposes, and equally sincere in their declarations, with ourselves. Still, I ask, even upon the very principle of this equality, where can the political power of this Commonwealth, be most *safely* deposited? So far as rights of person are concerned, we are all precisely equal, and the slave-holder can have no imaginable motive to do injustice in this respect. In the exercise of the tax-laying power, from which alone, injustice is to be apprehended, he has not the power to make any injurious discrimination. Among all the articles which have ever yet been made the subjects of taxation within this Commonwealth, which of them is not found on this side of the mountain, in just and fair proportion, at least? How, then, can we tax the west, without also taxing ourselves, in the same mode, and in just proportion? But reverse the case. There is not in the west, in any considerable degree, *one* species of property which constitutes the full half of our wealth, and which has always presented a ready subject for taxation. Give the power to the west, and will there be no temptation to abuse it? no temptation to shake off the public burthens from themselves, and throw an unjust proportion of them upon the slave-holder? Sir, there is much in this view of the subject. I am not indulging in mere speculation and conjecture. The experiment has been actually tried. For fifty-four years, the taxing power has been with us, and who can say that it has ever been abused? The gentleman from Frederick (Mr. Cooke) himself, has admitted that we have never abused it. I heard the admission with great pleasure; it was honourable to his candour, and valuable to us, for the source from which it sprung. Why, then, change this deposit of power, which has been thus justly and safely exercised for more than half a century? Shall we, for the sake of mere theoretical principles, or speculative doctrines, throw our interests and our safety, upon new and hazardous experiments? Let us not forget, Sir, that after all, Government is a practical thing, and *that* Government is best which is best in its practical results. There is no end of speculative systems. The world has been full of them, from Plato, down through Harrington and Moore,[8] and a host who succeeded them, even to the prolific bureaux of the French revolutionists. Of all their schemes, not one has ever been reduced to practice, in any part of the world. Experience is the best guide in Government. That guide we have; let us not shut our eyes to the lights which it affords us. For more than half a century, the political power of this Commonwealth, has been in the hands which now hold it. During all that time, it has not been abused. Is it then without cause, that I ask for a good reason why it should now be taken away?

20. Doddridge in Rebuttal

According to Hugh Blair Grigsby, a Norfolk delegate and first historian of the convention, its existence owed more to Philip Doddridge than to any other man living. From the far northwest county of Brooke, he was near sixty years of age, a lawyer, twice a delegate in the legislature, where he had in 1816 helped to put the senate on a white basis, and currently the Congressman from his district. A fellow westerner wrote a vivid description of him in 1829: "He has none of the bland and polished manner belonging to the South. He is a low thick broad shoulder'd uncouth looking man having an uncommonly large head & face with cheaks [sic] over-loaded with flesh. . . . He speaks in the broad Scotch-Irish dialect although he is an excellent scholar & man of extensive and profound research." This "Patrick Henry of the West" replied with some acerbity to Abel P. Upshur and John W. Green, whose motion was on the floor. After first dis-

---

[8] Sir Thomas More (1478–1535), author of *Utopia* (1516) [Ed.].

*cussing the history of the reform movement and the declaration of
rights, he proceeded to confront "old" Virginia with the challenge of
"new" Virginia.*

. . . In our course we have not exactly followed in the foot-
steps of our predecessors who made the present Constitution.
They acted as master builders: we have not. They laid the
foundation first, and then proceeded to the superstructure.
After they had declared the Government of the King of England at an end, the first thing they did was to appoint a Committee to prepare and report a *Declaration of Rights.* For what
purpose? To *serve as a* basis of Government. They first determined the powers they would surrender, and the powers they
would retain, and they acted upon and passed the Declaration
of Rights first, and then, and not until then, they proceeded
to erect upon their declared principles, the Constitution. If it
must be so called, they made the preface first, and then the
book.

In the course of his very eloquent argument, the gentleman
from Northhampton admitted, that it was the safest rule that
a majority of the units of the community should govern, but
only when property was equal. Unless property was equal he
did not admit the principle at all.

[MR. UPSHUR rose to explain. He said the gentleman from
Brooke had mistaken his meaning. He had not said that the
rule was only safe when the property of one individual was
equal to that of another. He disclaimed, alike, the principle,
and the effect that might be deduced from it. He applied the
remark to large masses of population having not only unequal
but discordant interests.]

MR. DODDRIDGE proceeded. I must have misunderstood the
gentleman yesterday, but I did not misunderstand him to-day,

From *Proceedings,* pp. 85–88.

and this, had he listened a little longer, he would have discovered. The gentleman from Northampton has laboured, and I am sure he thinks successfully, to maintain that, in Virginia the majority of free white persons have not the right (and he almost denies their power) to govern the State. This *jus majoris,* he says, is not derived to them, from the law of nature; ("that, with all its principles, is swept away,") nor from the exigencies of society; nor from the nature and necessities of Government; nor yet from any Conventional source, which can only be by an express provision in the present Constitution. *Argumenti gratia,*[9] let the gentleman be right, and for this purpose let it be conceded that the majority could only derive this right, if at all, from some one of those repudiated sources. His conclusion then is, that a majority of freemen in this free land are not possessed of the right or power to govern. But Government there must be, or we instantly sink into anarchy. Pray whence, then, will the gentleman derive the power in question to the minority?

Surely he will not go back to the natural state, where force prevailed. That state of things "with all its principles, was swept away," when the present Government was formed. He cannot deduce this right from the exigencies of society; nor from the nature or necessities of Government; nor if not from these sources, can he claim the right from any thing written in the Constitution or Bill of Rights. These look to, and declare the rights of the majority. Every source by which the right of governing could be derived to the majority, is repudiated by the gentleman's argument, and the same argument, conclusively denies the right claimed for the minority; and if the gentlemen are right, we are now in a perfect state of anarchy, which, we know, is not true.

Both gentlemen have, as I have before stated, admitted, that, but for the possession of slaves, in great masses, by the

---

[9] For the sake of argument [Ed.].

minority, residing mostly in a particular part of the State, the rule of the majority would be safe now. But this property they fear to subject to the Legislation of a majority, lest it might be oppressively taxed. Against this abuse the majority had labored to suggest a satisfactory guarantee; but nothing which their ingenuity could invent was satisfactory. Each plan was denounced as mere paper work, which the majority might disregard when invested with power, and that to complain of this, would be like appealing from Caesar to Caesar. . . .

We are complimented, it is true, with many expressions of kindness; of confidence in our integrity; in our generous and liberal feelings. But then the most serious fears are entertained of our children. It is feared, that forsaking the example of their fathers, they will become freebooters; not that they will plunder their immediate neighbors, nor that they will have courage enough to attack the minority with open force. The fear is, that the rights of the minority may be invaded by a system of Legislative rapine, because "there are no principles in Government."

Were we disposed to act in that manner, or should our children be so disposed, it would only be necessary to look at the census of 1790, and the tabular statements since made, to enable you to discover how feeble would be the resistance you would shortly be able to make to such violence. You may there see, that a race is rising up with astonishing rapidity, sufficiently strong and powerful to burst asunder any chain by which you may attempt to bind them, with as much ease as the thread parts in a candle blaze. I refer gentlemen to the documents furnished us, to shew them how vain must be the attempt to impose a yoke, and how illusory the hope that it will be long worn.

In 1790, the whole white population east of the Blue Ridge, was 314,523, and the whole population west, 127,594; 1800, east of the Ridge, 336,389, and west, 177,476; 1810, east of the Ridge 338,837, and west 212,726; 1820, east of the Ridge 348,873, and west 254,308; 1829, by estimate, east 362,745, and west 319,516. . . .

. . . In 1790 the whole slave population was 292,627, and in 1829, 448,294. By which it appears that during a period of thirty-nine years, the white population has increased at a ratio of 36⅓ per cent. only, and slave population 44⅔, notwithstanding the drains made from the latter by sale and otherwise. The increase of free people of colour is yet more surprising. In 1790 this class amounted to only 12,866, and in 1829 to 44,212. This increase of coloured population, is a subject of regret and alarm. I looked over these statements of population last evening, and noted them down, with the different principles disclosed in this debate. This I did both for present and future use. A view of them will enable my constitutents to appreciate the arguments and claims of the minority, and to discern, if we should be successful in reforming the Government as we hope, the depth of that gulph of political degradation, which was prepared for them, and from which they will have, happily, escaped! The arguments of the friends of the minority here, look to our perpetual slavery; for they maintain that the great mass of slave property, not only is, but always must be, in the east, because, they say, both the physical and moral constitutions of the western people, forbid the adaptation of that species of property to their uses. At the same time, it is admitted, that if a majority of white population is not now in the west, it will soon be there, and there increase forever. It will not vary their principles in the least, if at a future time, ten white men should be found west for one in the east. Their principle is, that the owners of slave property must possess all the powers of Government, however small their own numbers may be, to secure that property from the rapacity of an overgrown majority of white men. This principle admits of no relaxation, because the weaker the minority becomes, the greater will their need for power be, according to their own doctrines. This, to be sure, is pushing their argument *in absurdum,* but the fault is in the argument, that it admits this criticism. It applies to a case far distant, in point of time, I own, when the tide-water population will be, to the whole, but as a drop in the bucket. East of the mountain, slaves are increasing more rapidly than whites. Between tide and the Ridge, this increase is truly alarming. In a short time, such will be the preponderance of numbers in the west, that the citizen will scarcely know where to find the power that rules him, and will be induced to ask with astonishment, to whom it is that he must submit? I say again, this western increase must proceed. It cannot be checked; it will go on while the east oppressed by the increasing weight of another race will be stationary; and if you have cause to fear us now, that cause will increase, and with it your fears and desires for power. . . .

. . . We have long been in the habit of considering this Ancient Commonwealth, as the freest and happiest in the world; our Constitution as the best on earth, and ourselves the most fortunate of men. What would the citizen of another State think, or how would he feel, at the sight of an hundred wretches exposed to sale, singly or in families, with their master's lands, if in addition to the usual commendations of the auctioneer to encourage bidders, he should hear him tell them, that if they should purchase his goods, they would instantly become Sovereigns in this free land, and the present possessor would become their slave? Do I misrepresent or exaggerate when I say your doctrine makes me a slave? I may still live in the west; may pursue my own business and obey my own inclinations, but so long as you hold political dominion over me, I am a slave. We are a majority of individual units in the State, and your equals in intelligence and virtue, moral and political. Yet you say we must obey you. You declare that the rule of the minority has never oppressed us, nor visited us with practical evil; but of this, we are the best judges. We have felt your weight and have suffered under misrule. We never expected you to acknowledge this. You are not competent judges. It was not expected that you would make this acknowledgment, or part with power willingly. To do either, would be to furnish a precedent of the first impression.

We do not know to a certainty, what districts may vote with us, but if the results of the public polls furnish any sure indications, our strength in the community is to the minority as 402,000 to 280,000 souls. And if this be so, the heroic resistance made to our claims, proves a degree of moral firmness, equalled only by the moral worth of those who make it. . . .

21. Leigh on Power and Property

Benjamin Watkins Leigh, representing Chesterfield, was the outstanding spokesman of the conservative party and a thorn in the flesh of reformers throughout the convention. A prominent lawyer at the height of his powers, he had first made a name for himself two decades before in enunciating the doctrine of legislative instruction to Virginia's Senators in Washington and later as compiler of the Revised Code of 1819. "Leigh was eloquent, bold, uncompromising," Grigsby wrote, "yet there was something in his manner that displayed a childish fretfulness, that ill became a man of his distinguished excellence." In this he took after his master, John Randolph. He earned the west's hatred. When he compared the slaves in the east to the "peasantry of the West," the entire "peasantry" of Harrisonburg hanged and burned him in effigy.

. . . Sir, the resolution reported by the Legislative Committee, in effect, proposes to divorce power from property—to base representation on numbers alone, though numbers do not quadrate with property—though mountains rise between them—to transfer, in the course of a very few years, the weight of power over taxation and property to the west, though it be admitted, on all hands, that the far greater mass of property is now, and

From *Proceedings*, pp. 156–162, 164.

must still be held in the east. Power and property may be separated for a time, by force or fraud—but divorced, never. For, so soon as the pang of separation is felt—if there be truth in history, if there be any certainty in the experience of ages, if all pretensions to knowledge of the human heart be not vanity and folly—property will purchase power, or power will take property. And either way, there must be an end of free Government. If property buy power, the very process is corruption. If power ravish property, the sword must be drawn —so essential is property to the very being of civilized society, and so certain that civilized man will never consent to return to a savage state. Corruption and violence alike terminate in military despotism. All the Republics in the world have died this death. In the pursuit of a wild impracticable liberty, the people have first become disgusted with all regular Government, then violated the security of property which regular Government alone can defend, and been glad at last to find a master. License, is not liberty, but the bane of liberty. There is a book—but the author was a tory, an English tory, and he wrote before the American Revolution, so that I am almost afraid to refer to it—yet I will—there is an Essay of Swift on the dissentions of Athens and Rome, in which the downfall of those Republics, is clearly traced to the same fatal error of placing power over property in different hands from those that held the property. The manner of doing the mischief there, was the vesting of all the powers of judicature in the people; but no matter how the manner may be varied, the principle is the same. There has been no change in the natural feelings, passions and appetites of men, any more than in their outward form, from the days of Solon to those of George Washington. Like political or moral causes put in action, have ever produced, and must forever produce, every where, like effects— in Athens, in Rome, in France, in America.

The resolution of the Legislative Committee, proposes to give to those who have comparatively little property, power

over those who have a great deal—to give to those who contribute the least, the power of taxation over those who contribute the most, to the public treasury—and (what seems most
strange and incongruous) to give the power over property to
numbers alone, in that branch of the Legislature which should
be the especial guardian of property—in the revenue-giving
branch. To my mind, Sir, the scheme is irreconcilable with the
fundamental principle of representative Government, and mili-
tates against its peculiar mode of operation, in producing
liberty at first, and then nurturing, fostering, defending and
preserving it, for a thousand years. My friend from Hanover,
(Mr. Morris) has already explained to the Committee, how the
institution of the House of Commons in England, grew out of
the necessities of the Crown to ask aids from the people. The
free spirit of the Saxon laws, mingling with the sterner spirit
of the feudal system, had decreed that property was sacred.
The lawful prerogative of the Crown at no time extended to
taxation; and if violence was sometimes resorted to, the supplies it collected were scant and temporary. Originally, the
whole function of the House of Commons, was to give money;
but the money being theirs, it belonged to them to say, when,
how much, for what purpose, they would give it. From the
first, and invariably to this day, the Commons have been the
sole representative of property—the Lords never have been
regarded in that light. And from this power of the Commons
to give or withhold money, have sprung all the liberties of
England—all that has distinguished that nation from the other
nations of Europe. They used their power over the purse, to
extort freedom from the necessities of the King—and then to
secure and defend it—they made his ambition, his waste, his
very vices, work in favor of liberty. Every spark of English
liberty was kindled at that golden lamp. "I ask money"—said
the Crown—"money to resist or to conquer your enemies and
mine"—"give us privileges then" (was the constant answer,)
"acknowledge and secure our rights; and in order to secure

them, put them into our own keeping."—Sir, I know it is the fashion to decry every thing that is English, or supposed to be so; I know that in the opinion of many, it is enough to condemn any proposition, in morals, or in politics, to denounce it as English doctrine; but that is neither my opinion nor my feeling. I know well enough that the sentiment is unpopular—but I laid it down as a law to myself when I entered this Convention, to conceal no feeling and no thought I entertain, and never to vary in the least from an exact exhibition of my opinions, so far as it is in the power of words to paint the mind—and I have no hesitation in saying, in the face of the whole world, that the English Government, is a free Government, and the English people a free people. I pray gentlemen to cast their eyes over the habitable globe, survey every form of civil Government, examine the condition of every society—and point me out one, if they can, who has even so much as a conception, and much more the enjoyment, of civil liberty, in our sense of it, save only the British nation and their descendants. England was the inventor, the founder of that representative Government we so justly and so highly prize. I shall, therefore, still study her institutions; exercise my judgment in ascertaining what is vitious, or rotten, or unsuitable to our condition; and rejecting that, hold fast to all that is sound and wise and good, and proved by experience to be fit and capable to secure liberty and property; property, without which liberty can never exist, or if it could, would be valueless. Give me liberty in the English sense—liberty founded on law, and protected by law—no liberty held at the will of demagogue or tyrant (for I have no choice between them)—no liberty for me to prey on others—no liberty for others to prey on me. I want no French liberty—none; a liberty which first attacked property, then the lives of its foes, then those of its friends; which prostrated all religion and morals; set up nature and reason, as Goddesses to be worshipped; afterwards condescended to decree, that there is a God; and, at last, embraced iron despotism as its heaven-destined spouse. Sir, the true, the peculiar advantage of the principle of representative Government, is, that it holds Government absolutely dependent on individual property—that it gives the owner of property an interest to watch the Government—that it puts the purse-strings in the hands of its owners. Leave those who are to contribute money, to determine the measure and the object of contribution, and none will ever knowingly give their money to destroy their own liberty. Give to those who are not to contribute, the power to determine the measure and object of the contribution of others, and they *may* give it to destroy those from whom it is thus unjustly taken. From this false principle, the scheme of representation in question, is variant only in degree—it only proposes to give one portion of the people, power to take three dollars from another, for every dollar they contribute on their own. I say, therefore, that the plan is at war with the first principle of representative Government—and if it prevail, must destroy it—how soon, depends not on the wretched finite wisdom of man, but on the providence of God.

The resolution of the Legislative Committee, proposes to give the west power of taxation over the east, though it be apparent, that, in some respects, concerning as well the objects of taxes as the subjects of appropriation, the west has not only no common interest with the east, but a contrary or different interest. The interest of the west is contrary to ours, in regard to *slaves* considered as a subject of taxation, certainly and obviously. The unavoidable inequality of taxation upon all subjects, and the unavoidable equality of benefit from the revenue, give the west an interest to augment, and the east an interest to reduce, the amount of taxes. And, as to those internal improvements, those roads and canals, which seem, in the opinions of many, to be the only objects of Government, let any man survey the face of the country, and deny, if he can, that different, more extensive, and more expensive, works of the kind, are wanted, and even projected, in the west and in the north, than are wanted or have ever entered into the imagination of the east and the south. They would expend thousands where we would expend hundreds; that is, of our money; for if the expenditure was to be of their own, I cannot doubt they would grudge it as much as we do, or more. . . . We are asked, gravely and importunately asked, and in a tone as if they thought the request the most reasonable in the world, to give them power to tax us three times as much as themselves, when their great object can only be, to apply the revenue (after providing for, perhaps stinting, the civil list) to those internal improvements they have so much at heart. Let it be always remembered, that as the east has never hitherto imposed any burdens, which have not borne more heavily on ourselves than on our western brethren, so neither will it ever be possible for the east, if the taxes be uniform they must be, to levy any exactions on the west, which will not be more grievous to ourselves, so long as we hold a so much larger mass of taxable property: whereas the west may, by a uniform taxation, impose oppressive burdens on the east, which its own population will hardly feel the weight of. I should be sorry to say any thing offensive to gentlemen from any quarter—but I must follow the lights of my own mind, and declare it as my opinion, that the cunning of man, or of the devil, cannot devise a more vexatious and grinding tyranny for any people, than to subject them to taxation by those, who have not the same interest with them, much more who have interests contrary to or different from theirs.

The resolution of the Legislative Committee, proposes to give full representation to the labour of the west, with an exemption from taxation, while the labour of the east will be subjected to taxation deprived of representation.

The complaint seems to shock gentlemen—I shall repeat my words. (He repeated them)—In every civilized country under the sun, some there must be who labour for their daily bread, either by contract with, or subjection to others, or for themselves. Slaves, in the eastern part of this State, fill the place of the peasantry of Europe—of the peasantry or day-labourers in the non-slave-holding States of this Union. The denser the population, the more numerous will this class be. Even in the present state of the population beyond the Allegheny, there must be some peasantry, and as the country fills up, they will scarcely have more—that is, men who tend the herds and dig the soil, who have neither real nor personal capital of their own, and who earn their daily bread by the sweat of their brow. These, by this scheme, are all to be represented—but none of our slaves. And yet, in political economy, the latter fill exactly the same place. Slaves, indeed, are not and never will be comparable with the hardy peasantry of the mountains, in intellectual power, in moral worth, in all that determines man's degree in the moral scale, and raises him above the brute—I beg pardon, his Maker placed him above the brute— above the savage—above that wretched state, of which the only comfort is the natural rights of man. I have as sincere feelings of regard for that people, as any man who lives among them. But I ask gentlemen to say, whether they believe, that those who are obliged to depend on their daily labour for daily subsistence, can, or do ever enter into political affairs? They never do—never will—never can. Educated myself to a profession, which *in this country* has been supposed to fit the mind for the duties of the Statesman, I have yet never had occasion to turn my mind to any general question of politics, without feeling the effect of professional habits to narrow and contract the mind. If others are more fortunate, I congratulate them. Now, what real share, so far as mind is concerned, does any man suppose the peasantry of the west—that peasantry, which it must have when the country is as completely filled up with day-labourers as ours is of slaves—can or will take in affairs of State? Gentlemen may say, their labourers are the most intelligent on earth—which I hope is true—that they will rise to political intelligence. But, when any rise, others must supply the place they rise from. What then, is the practical effect of the scheme of representation in question? Simply, that the men of property of the west, shall be allowed a representation for all their day-labourers, without contributing an additional cent of revenue, and that the men of property of the east, shall contribute in proportion to all the slave-labour they employ, without any additional representation. Sir, I am against all this—I am for a representation of every interest in society—for poising and balancing all interests—for saving each and all, from the sin of oppressing, and from the curse of being oppressed.

Sir, the amendment offered by my honorable friend from Culpeper [Mr. Green], is a scheme for balancing the various interests of the Commonwealth with exact and equal justice— not depriving *numbers* of their due weight, for it allows them full representation—yet allowing property also that fair, due and just share of representation, which is essential to its protection and security. It proposes to build up Government on the interests of society with due regard to the rights both of persons and property; and to confide power to those whose self-love will forever prevent them from abusing it. If gentlemen prefer the federal number as the basis of representation, I shall be content. If they prefer a county representation, founded on any fair principle, respecting peculiar interests, and balancing the powers of Government accordingly—though I am sensible that this will be a more difficult operation—I shall be content. But I must forever contend, that a principle, which, in a Government professedly instituted for the protection and security of property as well as mere personal rights, disclaims all regard to the interests of property, and allows representation to numbers only, is dangerous and vicious, contrary to all the dictates of prudence and justice, and incompatible with the nature of representative Government, its wholesome operation and all its ends. . . .

. . . Then gentlemen urge our own Bill of Rights upon us, as perfectly conclusive—and to the amazement of some and the amusement of others of this Committee, gentlemen, founding their whole argument on the Bill of Rights, deny the competency of the Convention of '76—and, by consequence, one would think, the authority of the Bill of Rights. Mr. Jefferson was the first person that brought this charge of usurpation against that Convention—and (so important are great men's errors) tho' with him it seemed rather matter of curious speculation only, yet ever since, when our old Constitution has been assailed for its supposed defects, this opinion of Mr. Jefferson has been referred to as conclusive authority.[10] I had implicit faith in the opinion myself when I was at College—how long after I cannot say, not being able to fix the date when my mind came to maturity. At what period Mr. Jefferson discovered the incompetency of the Convention of '76, it were vain to conjecture—but I apprehend, it was not during the session of that body—for I know that Mr. J. himself prepared a Constitution for Virginia, and sent it to Williamsburg that it might be proposed to the Convention, during the session, from which the preamble and nothing more, was taken and prefixed to the present Constitution. Any one may see, at a glance, that that preamble was written by the author of the Declaration of Independence. I have seen the projet of the Constitution, which Mr. J. offered, in the council chamber, in his own hand writing, tho' it cannot now be found—and I have since cursed my folly that I neglected to take a copy of it, in order to compare Mr. J's democracy *of that day,* with George Mason's practical republicanism. But, Sir, the validity of the Constitution, as such, has

---

[10] Jefferson always insisted the Constitution had no higher authority than a statute, because it was formed by what was, in effect, the legislative body [Ed.].

been maintained by Pendleton, Wythe, Roane,[11] by the whole Commonwealth for fifty-four years. If the Convention of '76 was incompetent to that act, it was incompetent also to abolish the Colonial Government, and that yet remains in force, in like manner as the Colonial form of Government of Connecticut was retained for years; and all the objections to the authority of our Convention of '76, might be urged with equal force, against all the Constitutions established in our sister States during the revolution. It is said the existing Constitution is not a lawful Government, because it was ordained by the representatives of the freeholders only, and never submitted to the great body of the people. To whom is it intended, that *our* amended or new Constitution shall be submitted? To those, I presume, to whom we shall allow the right of suffrage—that is, if gentlemen succeed according to their wishes in that particular, to lease-holders, house-keepers and taxpayers, as well as freeholders. It is a remarkable truth, in the natural history of man in this country, that the sons are invariably wiser than their fathers, such is the march of mind! Our sons may allege, hereafter, that our acts never had the sanction of the people— why did we exclude women and children? Why minors, tho' enrolled in the militia, and bound to bear arms? Why paupers, whose only sin is poverty? Nay, why the felons in the Penitentiary? All are part of the great body of the people. Sir, if we shall acknowledge, that we are at this moment in a state of nature; that men have resumed their natural rights, and are entitled to insist on them to the uttermost; we may live to see the day, when it will be claimed as matter of right, that the keeper of the Penitentiary shall bring his prisoners to the polls.

Now, as to the Bill of Rights—The first article declares, that

---

[11] George Mason (1725–1792), Edmund Pendleton (1721–1803), George Wythe (1726–1806) were members of the Virginia convention of 1776; Spencer Roane (1762–1822) was a state rights jurist on the Virginia supreme court of appeals [Ed.].

"all men are by nature equally free and independent, and have certain inherent rights, of which, when they enter into a state of society, they cannot, by any compact, deprive or divest their posterity; namely, the enjoyment of life and liberty, with the means of acquiring and possessing property, and possessing property, and pursuing and obtaining happiness and safety."— The article enumerates *property* as equally dear and sacred with *life* and *liberty*, and as the principal means of happiness and safety—and with good reason—for, in order to live free and happy it is necessary that we live, and property is necessary to sustain life, and just as necessary to maintain liberty. Yet property is to be wholly disregarded in our fundamental institutions!—But, not to repeat what has been better said by others, I shall desire the committee to remember, that this article is expressed in the language of Locke's theory of government, then familiarly known; and that Locke, no more than the Convention of '76, understood the proposition in the broad sense now ascribed to it. Locke has had a singular fate. He was a zealous advocate of mixed monarchy—his Essay on Government was written to maintain the throne of William and Mary —his notions of practical Government, are exhibited in the Constitution he made for North Carolina, with its caciques and land-graves: yet, from *his* book, have been deduced the wildest democracy, and demented French jacobinism. He exploded the *right divine* of *Kings*—he showed that all Government is of human institution; yet he is supposed to have established the *divine right of democracy*. So, he was a pious Christian of the Church of England—of the low Church, however—yet, from his chapter on innate ideas, in his Essay on the Human Understanding, infidels have deduced the doctrines of materialism, infidelity and atheism. The truth is, that there is no proposition in ethics or politics, however true when duly measured and applied, which, if pushed to extremes, will not lead to absurdity or vice. It does not follow, that, because all men are born equal, and have equal rights to life, liberty, and the property they can acquire by honest industry, therefore, all men may rightly claim, in an established society, equal political powers—especially, equal power to dispose of the property of others.

It is very remarkable, Sir, that both the gentlemen from Frederick, (Mr. Cooke and Mr. Powell,) in founding the argument, they endeavoured to deduce from the third article of the Bills of Rights, read to the Committee, only the first and third sentences of it, which seem to suit their purposes, and omitted the intermediate sentence, so material to the just understanding of the doctrine the article inculcates, and so opposite to the conclusions at which they were aiming. I acquit them of all wilful unfairness—the respect I bear them, would not endure any suspicion of the kind—but the omission is a striking instance, how prone are the minds of men, studiously bent on maintaining a favorite point, to overlook, rather than to meet, difficulties, however obvious. The whole article reads,—"That Government is, or ought to be, instituted for the common benefit, protection and security of the people, nation or community. —Of all the various modes and forms of Government, that is best, which is capable of producing the greatest degree of happiness and safety, and is most effectually secured against the dangers of mal-administration—and when any Government shall be found inadequate or contrary to these purposes, a majority of the Commonwealth hath an indubitable, unalienable, and indefeasible right to reform, alter, or abolish it, in such manner as shall be judged most conducive to the public weal."—From the first sentence, the gentlemen deduced the perfect equality of men in a social state—not as to civil rights only, but political powers; and from the last, the absolute despotic right of bare majority, to change the fundamental laws, and to assume to themselves under a new form of polity, the sovereign power to govern without limitation or check. Read the whole article, and it will be seen, that it means to declare, that when the existing Government fails to produce happiness and safety; fails to protect *property* as well as *liberty*, which in the first article are recognized, as the means of happiness and safety; and appears not to be effectually secured against the dangers of mal-administration: then, and not till then, the majority has the right to reform, alter or abolish it, and to substitute another, better calculated to produce happiness and safety; better suited to secure life, liberty, and *property* without which neither life nor liberty can be enjoyed or maintained; and more effectually secured against the dangers of mal-administration. But so long as the established Government answers those cardinal purposes of its institution, the majority may, indeed, have the *physical power,* but it can have no *moral right,* to overturn it. Now, we have the authority of the venerable gentleman from Loudoun, (Mr. Monroe) that under our present Government, in the course of fifty-four years, there has been no wrong, no oppression—Again: the sentence which the gentlemen overlooked, distinctly affirms the great principle for which we are so earnestly contending, that it behoves men engaged in framing a Government, to establish a just and wise Government—not a Government founded on theoretical principles, and squared according to the exact model of the natural rights of man, which, being necessarily the same in all societies of mankind, would, if followed, eventuate every where in the same form of civil polity—but a just and wise Government, adapted to the peculiar circumstances of the people for whom it is intended. No Government can be just, or wise, or safe, which, either wholly or in any material degree, gives one portion of the people the principal power of taxation, and imposes on the other, the principal duty of contribution—no Government can produce the greatest degree of happiness and safety, or fail to destroy them, which does not provide the most jealous security for property, which does not wed power to property, which disclaims, in the first principle of its organization, all regard to property. No Government can be just, or wise, or safe for Virginia, which shall place the property of the East in the power and at the disposal of the West. Whenever they shall take away the little earnings of my labour, or any part of them—whenever they shall seize the bread I earn for my children—for their own local purposes —against my consent, and the consent of all those who represent my interests—and I shall be bound to submit to such exaction, without means of redress; I shall be obliged to them, sincerely obliged to them, to take away my life too; I shall not desire to survive an hour. . . .

. . . Sir, we the people of the East demand of our fellow-citizens of the West, the same principle of representation for the security of our property, which the Southern States demanded of the Northern, and these conceded, in framing the Federal Government. Look to the experience of the Federal Government; and it will be found, that the representation apportioned to the Southern States has not been more than adequate to the security of their interests—no, not adequate. A gigantic system of protecting duties is proposed—the Southern States in vain exclaim against its partial and oppressive operation—in vain deprecate, remonstrate, struggle—a bare majority hesitates not to impose the tariff. Of the constitutionality of that system of measures—of its policy considered by itself, with a view to political economy—I shall give no opinion now: all I have to say, is, that in a Government constituted like ours, it never can be wise to persist in any system of measures, against which a large portion of the nation, though it be a minority, separated from the rest by geographical and political divisions, and by political interests too, so far as the proposed measures are concerned, raises its united voice. In my poor opinion, every commercial operation of the Federal Government, since I attained to manhood, has been detrimental to the Southern, Atlantic, slave-holding, planting States. In 1800, we had a great West India and a flourishing European trade— We imported for ourselves, and for a good part of North Carolina, perhaps of Tennessee—where is all that trade now? annihilated.—Where is the capital which carried it on? gone. Sir, we have not an adequate representation in the Federal Government. And as to that which we have, I have heard one gentleman doubt the wisdom and justice of the principle which gave it to us—the gentleman from Albemarle. [Mr. Gordon explained—he thought he had said, that wise statesmen might doubt the wisdom of that principle of representation.] If the gentleman does not doubt himself, I have only to ask his attention to another consideration. Suppose the Legislature of this State reformed and based upon white population; the time comes for making a new apportionment of our representation in Congress; the West insists, that that too shall be apportioned according to white population; the Loudoun district joins the West, as it does now; and Albemarle, in its zeal for the rights of man, forgets her old love and abandons State Rights—then shall we see Virginia, like Kentucky, hitched to the car of the Federal Government, for Internal Improvement and protecting duties.

22. Randolph on the Federal Issue

John Randolph's first speech was in reply to Chapman Johnson's marathon address of two and one-half days duration. "The word passed through the city in an instant that Randolph was speaking, and soon the house, the lobby, and the gallery, were crowded almost to suffocation." This tall "unearthly-looking figure," the unaccountably brilliant eyes, melodic voice, venomous tongue, and fantastic gestures—this half-crazed aberration of Virginia Republicanism—cast an almost hypnotic spell over the convention. It was his last public performance—many of his admirers thought it his greatest.

From *Proceedings,* pp. 316–319.

Mr. Chairman, since I have been here, the scene has recalled many old recollections. At one time, I thought myself in the House of Representatives, listening to the debate on the Tariff; at another time, I imagined myself listening to the debate on the Missouri Question; and sometimes I fancied myself listening to both questions debated at once. Are we men? met to consult about the affairs of men? Or are we, in truth, a Robinhood Society? discussing rights in the abstract? Have we no house over our heads? Do we forget, that we are living under a Constitution, which has shielded us for more than half a century—that we are not a parcel of naked and forlorn savages, on the shores of New Holland; and that the worst that can come is, that we shall live under the same Constitution that we have lived under, freely and happily, for half a century? To their monstrous claims of power, we plead this prescription; but then we are told, that *nullum tempus occurrit Regi*[12]— King whom? King Numbers. And they will not listen to a prescription of fifty-four years—a period greater, by four years, than would secure a title to the best estate in the Commonwealth, unsupported by any other shadow of right. Nay, Sir, in this case, prescription operates *against* possession. They tell us, it is only a case of long-continued, and therefore, of aggravated injustice. They say to us, in words the most courteous and soft, (but I am not so soft as to swallow them,) "we shall be—we will be—we must be your masters, and you shall submit." To whom do they hold this language? To dependents? weak, unprotected, and incapable of defence? Or is it to the great tobacco-growing and slave-holding interest, and to every other interest on this side the Ridge? "We are numbers, you have property." I am not so obtuse, as to require any further explanation on this head. "We are numbers, you have property." Sir, I understand it perfectly. Mr. Chairman, since the

---

[12] Time does not run against the king, i.e., no lapse of time bars the rights of the crown (concerning statutory limitations) [Ed.].

days of the French Revolution, when the Duke of Orleans, who was the richest subject, not only in France, but in all Europe, lent himself to the *mountain* party in the Convention, in the vain and weak hope of grasping political power, perhaps of mounting the throne, still slippery with the blood of the last incumbent—from that day to this, so great a degree of infatuation, has not shown by any individual, as by the tobacco-grower, and slave-holder of Virginia, who shall lend his aid to rivet this yoke on the necks of his brethren, and on his own. Woe betide that man! Even the Duke of Orleans himself, profligate and reprobate as he was, would have halted in his course, had he foreseen in the end, his property confiscated to the winds, and his head in the sack of the executioner.

I enter into no calculations of my own, for I have made none, nor shall I follow the example which has been set me. I leave that branch of the argument, if argument it can be called, of the gentleman from Augusta [Mr. Johnson], to be answered by himself.

The gentleman told us, the day before yesterday, that in fifteen minutes of the succeeding day, he would conclude all he had to say; and he then kept us two hours, not by the Shrewsbury clock,[13] but by as good a watch as can be made in the city of London. [*Drawing out and opening his watch.*] As fifteen minutes are to two hours—in the proportion of one to eight—such is the approximation to truth, in the gentleman's calculations. If all the calculations and promises of the gentleman from Augusta, which he held out to gull us—I speak not of his intentions, but only of the effect that would have ensued—shall be no nearer the truth than these, where then should we be who trust them?

In the course of what I fear will be thought my very weari-

---

[13] Alluding to the ludicrous boast of Shakespeare's Sir John Falstaff that he "fought a long hour by Shrewsbury clock" (*King Henry IV, Part I,* Act V, Scene 4, Line 148) [Ed.].

some observations, I spoke of the Tariff Law. When the people of the United States threw off their allegiance to Great Britain, and established Republican Governments here, whether State or Federal, one discovery since made in politics, had not yet entered into the head of any man in the Union, and which, if not arrested by the good sense and patriotism of the country, will destroy all Republican Government, as certainly and inevitably as time will one day destroy us. That discovery is this: that a bare majority—(the majority on the Tariff was, I believe, but two—my friend, behind me, (Mr. P. P. Barbour,) tells me that I am right—and on one important branch of that law, that I mean, which relates to cotton bagging, the majority was but one, and that consisted of the casting vote of the Speaker,) that a bare majority may oppress, harass, and plunder the minority at pleasure, but that it is their interest to keep up the minority to the highest possible point consistent with their subjugation, because, the larger that minority shall be, in proportion to the majority, by that same proportion are the profits of the majority enhanced, which they have extracted and extorted from the minority. And after all our exclamations against this crying oppression; after all our memorials and remonstrances; after all our irrefragable arguments against it, (I refer not to the share I had in them, I speak of the arguments of other gentlemen, and not of my own,) shall we in Virginia, introduce this deadly principle into our own Government? and give power to a bare majority to tax us *ad libitum*,[14] and that when the strongest temptation is at the same time held out to them, to do it? It is now a great while since I learned from the philosopher of Malmesbury,[15] that a state of nature is a state of war; but if we sanction this principle, we shall prove that a state, not of nature, but of society, and of Constitutional Government, is a state of interminable war. And it will not stop

---

[14] At your pleasure [Ed.].

[15] Thomas Hobbes (1588–1679) [Ed.].

here. Instructed by this most baneful, yes, and most baleful example, we shall next have one part of a county conspiring to throw their share of the burden of the levy upon the other part. Sir, if there is a destructive principle in politics, it is that which is maintained by the gentleman from Augusta.

But we are told that we are to have a stay of exception. "We will give you time,|"] say the gentlemen: ["]only give us a bond binding all your estate, secured by a deed of trust on all your slaves." Why, Sir, there is not a hard-hearted Shylock in the Commonwealth, who will not, on such conditions, give you time. Are we so weak, that, like the spend-thrift who runs to the usurer, we are willing to encounter this calamity, because it is not to come upon us till the year 1856? A period not as long as some of us have been in public life? Sir, I would not consent to it, if it were not to come till the year 2056. I am at war with the principle. Let me not be told, that then I am at war with the Bill of Rights. I subscribe to every word in the Bill of Rights. I need not show how this can be. It has been better done already by the gentleman from Spottsylvania, (Mr. Stanard,) to whom I feel personally indebted as a tobacco-planter and a slave-holder, for the speech he has made. The Bill of Rights contains unmodified principles. The declarations it contains are our lights and guides, but when we come to apply these great principles, we must modify them for use; we must set limitations to their operation, and the inquiry then is, *quousque?* How far? It is a question not of principle, but of degree. The very moment this immaculate principle of their's is touched, it becomes what all principles are, materials in the hands of men of sense, to be applied to the welfare of the Commonwealth. It is not an incantation. It is no Talisman. It is not witchcraft. It is not a torpedo to benumb us. If the naked principle of numbers only is to be followed, the requisites for the Statesman fall far below what the gentleman from Spottsylvania rated them at. He needs not the four rules of arithmetic. No, Sir, a negro boy with a knife and a tally-stick, is a Statesman complete in this school. Sir, I do not scoff, jeer or flout, (I use, I think, the very words of the gentleman from Augusta; two of them certainly were employed by him,) at the principles of the Bill of Rights, and so help me Heaven, I have not heard of any who did. But I hold with one of the greatest masters of political philosophy, that "no rational man ever did govern himself by abstractions and universals." I do not put abstract ideas wholly out of any question, because I know well that under that name I should dismiss principles; and that without the guide and light of sound, well understood principles, all reasonings in politics, as every thing else, would be only a confused jumble of particular facts and details, without the means of drawing out any sort of theoretical or practical conclusion. . . .

. . . If there is any country on earth where circumstances have a more important bearing than in another, it is here, in Virginia. Nearly half the population are in bondage—yes, Sir, more than half in the country below the Ridge. And is this no circumstance? Yet, let me say with the gentleman from Accomac, (Mr. Joynes,) whose irresistible array of figures set all figures of speech at defiance, that if there were not a negro in Virginia, I would still contend for the principle in the amendment. And why? Because I will put it in the power of no man or set of men who ever lived, or who ever shall live, to tax me without my consent. It is wholly immaterial whether this is done without my having any representation at all, or, as it was done in the case of the Tariff Law, by a phalanx stern and inexorable, who being the majority, and having the power, prescribe to me the law that I shall obey. Sir, what was it to all the Southern interest, that we came within two votes of defeating that iniquitous measure? Do not our adversaries, (for adversaries they are,) know that they have the power? and that we must submit? Yes, Sir. This whole slave-holding country, the whole of it, from the Potomac to Mexico, was placed under the ban and anathema of a majority of two. And will you introduce such a principle into your own State Government? Sir, at some times during this debate, I doubted if I were in my right mind. From the beginning of time till now, there is no case to be found of a rational and moral people subverting a Constitution under which they had lived for half a century—aye, for two centuries, by a majority of *one*. When revolutions have happened in other countries, it was the effect of a political storm, a Levanter, a tornado, to which all opposition was fruitless. But did any body ever hear of a revolution affecting the entire condition of one half of a great State, being effected by a majority of one? Did it ever enter the head of the wildest visionary, from the days of Peter the Hermit, to— a day I will not name—to accomplish a revolution by a majority of *one*? Sir, to change your Constitution by such a majority, is nothing more than to sound the tocsin for a civil war. It may be at first, a war of words, a weaponless war, but it is one of those cases in which, as the lawyers tell us, fury supplies arms. Sir, this thing cannot be: it must not be. I was about to say, it *shall* not be. I tell gentlemen now, with the most perfect deliberation and calmness, that we cannot submit to this outrage on our rights. It surpasses that measure of submission and forbearance, which is due from every member of an organized Government, to that Government. And why do I so tell them? Sir, we are not a company of naked savages on the coast of New Holland, or Van Diemans Land[16]—we have a Government; we have rights; and do you think that we shall tamely submit, and let you deprive us of our vested rights, and reduce us to bondage? Yes, vested rights! that we shall let you impose on us a yoke hardly lighter than that of the villeins regardant of the manor? We are now little better than the trustees of slave-labour for the nabobs of the East, and of the North, (if there be any such persons in our country,) and to the specu-

---

[16] Tasmania was originally named Van Diemans Land in honor of the governor of the Dutch East Indies, sometimes called New Holland [Ed.].

lators of the West. They regulate our labour. Are we to have *two* masters? When every vein has been sluiced—when our whole system presents nothing but one pitiful enchymosis[17]— are we to be patted and tapped to find yet another vein to breathe,[18] not for the Federal Government, but for our own? Why, Sir, the richest man in Virginia, be that man who he may, would make a good bargain to make you a present of his estate, provided you give him bond upon that estate, allowing him to tax it as he pleases, and to spend the money as he pleases. It is of the very essence of property, that none shall tax it but the owner himself, or one who has a common feeling and interest with him. It does not require a plain planter to tell an Assembly like this, more than half of whose members are gentlemen of the law, that no man may set his foot on your land, without your permission, but as a trespasser, and that he renders himself liable to an action for damages. This is of the very essence of property. But he says, "thank you, for nothing—with all my heart, I don't mean to set my foot on your land; but, not owning one foot of land myself, I will stand here, in the highway, which is as free to me as it is to you, and I will tax your land, not to your heart's content, but to *mine,* and spend the proceeds as I please. I cannot enter upon it myself, but I will send the Sheriff of the county, and he shall enter upon it, and do what I cannot do in my own person." Sir, is this to be endured? It is not to be endured. And unless I am ignorant of the character and the feelings, and of what is dearer to me than all, of the prejudices of the people of the lower country, it will not be endured. You may as well adjourn *sine die.* We are too old birds to be taken with chaff, or else we are not old enough, I don't know which. We will not give up this question for the certainty, and far less for the hope, that the evil will be rectified in the other branch of the Legislature. We know, every

---

[17] Decay [Ed.].

[18] To open a vein, or let blood [Ed.].

body knows, that it is impossible. Why, Sir, the British House of Peers, which contains four hundred members, holding a vast property, much more now, it is true, than when Chatham said, they were but as a drop in the ocean, compared with the wealth of the Commons: If they, holding their seats for life, and receiving and transmitting them by hereditary descent, have never been able to resist the House of Commons, in any measure on which that House chose to insist, do you believe that twenty-four gentlemen up-stairs, can resist one hundred and twenty below? especially when the one hundred and twenty represent their own districts, and are to go home with them to their common constituents? Sir, the case has never yet happened, I believe, when a Senator has been able to resist the united delegation from his district in the lower House.

Mr. Chairman, I am a practical man. I go for solid security, and I never will, knowingly, take any other. But, if the security on which I have relied, is insufficient, and my property is in danger, it is better that I should know it in time, and I may prepare to meet the consequences, while it is yet called to-day, than to rest on a security that is fallacious and deceptive. Sir, I would not give a button for your mixed basis in the Senate. Give up this question, and I have nothing more to lose. This is the entering wedge, and every thing else must follow. We are told, indeed, that we must rely on a restriction of the Right of Suffrage; but, gentlemen, know, that after you shall have adopted the report of the Select Committee, you can place no restriction upon it. When this principle is in operation, the waters are out. It is as if you would ask an industrious and sagacious Hollander,[19] that you may cut his dykes, provided you make your cut only of a certain width. A rat hole will let in the ocean. Sir, there is an end to the security of all property in the Commonwealth, and he will be unwise, who shall not

---

[19] Looking to the Chevalier Huygens, the Dutch Minister, who was in the Hall.

abandon the ship to the underwriters. It is the first time in my life, that I ever heard of a Government, which was to divorce property from power. Yet, this is seriously and soberly proposed to us. Sir, I know it is practicable, but it can be done only by a violent divulsion, as in France—but the moment you have separated the two, that very moment property will go in search of power, and power in search of property. "Male and female created he them"; and the two sexes do not more certainly, nor by a more unerring law, gravitate to each other, than power and property. You can only cause them to change hands. I could almost wish, indeed, for the accommodation of the gentleman from Augusta, that God had ordained it otherwise; but so it is, and so it is obliged to be. It is of the nature of man. Man always has been in society—we always find him in possession of property, and with a certain appetite for it, which leads him to seek it, if not *per fas*,[20] sometimes *per nefas;*[21] and hence the need of laws to protect it, and to punish its invaders. . . .

23. Marshall on Compromise

Chief Justice Marshall, then in his seventy-fifth year, first addressed the house in a plea for compromise on the basis question. Marshall, representing Richmond, invariably voted with the conservative bloc, but so did his old Republican enemies, William B. Giles, John Randolph, Littleton W. Tazewell, and—with insignificant exceptions— James Madison. A homely appearing man, with none of the showy

---

[20] Lawfully [Ed.].
[21] Unlawfully [Ed.].

attributes of an orator, he was nevertheless reputed among his con-
temporaries for his eloquence. According to one of them, "The char-
acteristic of his eloquence is an irresistible cogency, and a luminous
simplicity in the order of his reason." This "cogency" comes through
in his brief speech on December 4 addressed to the defeat of the
"Western plan."

Two propositions respecting the basis of Representation have
divided this Convention almost equally. One party has supported the basis of white population alone, the other has supported a basis compounded of white population and taxation;
or which is the same thing in its result, the basis of Federal
numbers. The question has been discussed, until discussion has
become useless. It has been argued, until argument is exhausted. We have now met on the ground of compromise. It
is now no longer a question whether the one or the other shall
be adopted entirely, but whether we shall, as a compromise,
adopt a combination of the two, so as to unite the House on
something which we may recommend to the people of Virginia,
with a reasonable hope that it may be adopted.

Now, when on the subject of compromise, two propositions
are again submitted to the Committee; one of them is, that the
two principles originally proposed shall remain distinct; one of
them constituting the basis of the House of Delegates, and the
other of the Senate. The other proposition is, that the two principles shall be combined and made the basis of both Houses.
This latter proposition presents the exact middle ground between white population exclusively, and the basis of white
population combined with taxation, or what has been denominated the basis of Federal numbers.

The motion of the gentleman from Augusta, (Mr. Johnson)
to strike out the word "Resolved," from the proposition offered

From *Proceedings,* pp. 561–562.

by the gentleman from Northampton, (Mr. Upshur,) is intended to substitute for the combined ratio, which is the foundation of that gentleman's scheme, the proposition of the
gentleman from Frederick, (Mr. Cooke,) which is to introduce
white population exclusively as the basis of the House of Delegates, and white population and taxation combined as the basis
of the Senate. This is the question now before the Committee.

We are engaged on the subject of compromise,—a compromise of principles which neither is willing to surrender. The
very term implies mutual concession. Some concession must
be made on both sides, but the quantum to be made by each
must depend on the relative situation of the parties, and this
must be considered before a right judgment can be formed on
the subject. Let us enquire, then, what is the real situation of
the parties on this question. On this enquiry will depend the
reasonableness of any compromise that may be proposed.

The past discussion shows conclusively the sincerity with
which each principle has been supported. There can be no
doubt of the honest conviction of each side, that its pretensions
are fair and just. The claims of both are sustained with equal
sincerity, and an equally honest conviction, that their own
principle is correct, and the adversary principle is unwise and
incorrect. On the subject of principle, nothing can be added,
no advantage can be claimed by either side; for, no doubt can
be entertained of the sincerity of either. To attempt now to
throw considerations of principle into either scale, is to add
fuel to a flame which it is our purpose to extinguish. We must
lose sight of the situation of parties and state of opinion, if we
make this attempt. . . .

. . . The endeavor would be vain to conceal the fact, that in a
part of the Eastern country—that lying upon and South of
James river near the Blue Ridge, there are interests which must
and will operate with great force, unless human nature shall
cease to be what it has been in all time. It is impossible to say
what may be the influence on those interests abroad, though
they may exert none on the members of this Convention. It is

impossible to say, how far they may affect the adoption or rejection of the Constitution. But it is by no means certain, that this change in public opinion will not be felt in this body also. Admitting gentlemen to retain their theories—theories which they maintain with perfect sincerity, still there exists another theory equally Republican, and which they equally respect, the theory that it is the duty of a Representative to speak the will of his constituents. We cannot say how far this may carry gentlemen. Neither can we say what will be the ultimate decision of this House or of the people.

Taking this view of the state of parties, it is manifest that to obtain a just compromise, concession must not only be mutual —it must be equal also. The claims of the parties are the same. Each ought to concede to the other as much as he demands from that other, and thus meet on middle ground. There can be no hope that either will yield more than it gets in return.

What is that middle ground?

One party proposes that the House of Delegates shall be formed on the basis of white population exclusively, and the Senate on the mixed basis of white population and taxation, or on the Federal numbers. The other party proposes that the white population shall be combined with Federal numbers, and shall, mixed in equal proportions, form the basis of Representation in both Houses. This last proposition must be equal. All feel it to be equal. If the two principles are combined exactly, and thus combined, form the basis of both Houses, the compromise must be perfectly equal.

Is the other proposition equal? I ask the gentlemen who make it, if they think it so?

The party in favor of the compound basis in both Houses have declared their conviction, that there is no equality in the proposition. They at least think it unequal. How can they accede to a proposition as a compromise which they firmly believe to be unequal? Do gentlemen of the opposite party think it equal? If they do, why refuse to take what they offer to us?

They consent that the Senate shall be founded on the mixed basis, and the House of Delegates on the white basis. If this be equality, why will they not take the Senate? There can be only one reason for rejecting it—they think the proposition unequal. If the Senate would protect the East, will it not protect the West also? If the proposition is equal when the Senate is tendered by them to us, is it not equal when tendered by us to them? If it is equal, it must be a matter of absolute indifference to which party the Senate is assigned. If a difficulty arises, it is because the proposition is unequal; and if it be unequal, can gentlemen believe that it will be accepted? Ought they to wish it?

After the warm language (to use the mildest phrase) which has been mingled with argument on both sides, I heard with inexpressible satisfaction, propositions for compromise proposed by both parties in the language of conciliation. I hailed these auspicious appearances with as much joy, as the inhabitant of the polar regions hails the re-appearance of the sun after his long absence of six tedious months. Can these appearances prove fallacious? Is it a meteor we have seen and mistaken for that splendid luminary which dispenses light and gladness throughout creation? It must be so, if we cannot meet on equal ground. If we cannot meet on the line that divides us equally, then take the hand of friendship, and make an equal compromise; it is vain to hope that any compromise can be made.

24. Summers on the Gordon Plan

On December 18, the Gordon plan, having been approved in committee of the whole, was upheld in the convention. Before the vote

*Lewis Summers, from Kanawha on the western-flowing waters, ex-
plained why his party could not accept the proffered compromise.
Summers, a judge of the general court, was one of the strongest reform voices in the convention. He alone championed far-reaching
reform of local government. Two years later, in the famous Virginia
slavery debate, he again occupied Jeffersonian ground as an advocate
of gradual emancipation.*

The proposition of the gentleman from Albemarle, (Mr. Gordon,) concurred in by the Committee of the Whole, gave as the
present apportionment in a House of one hundred and twenty-
seven members, the following proportions:

Western District,	29
Valley,	24
Midland,	40
Eastern,	34

Placing a majority in the hands of the country east of the Blue
Ridge, of twenty-one, while the basis of white population, denied to that country a majority larger than eight. It proposed
a Senate of thirty-two members, distributing thirteen West of
the Blue Ridge, and nineteen East of that range of mountains—
while the present apportionment of that body, enlarging it to
thirty-two members, gives a Representation equal to twelve
and twenty. He said, that contrasting this scheme with the
results of white population in the House of Delegates, and the
present condition of the Senate, it sacrifices thirteen delegates
in the West, and yields one additional Senator to that district.
Should the future Senate be composed with references to Federal numbers, the relative apportionment of that body, he said,
would undergo no sensible change, as he had found upon
computation that the West would be entitled to eleven and a
quarter Senators, in the present state of the population. Mr. S.
proceeded to remark upon the effect of the proposed apportion-

From *Proceedings*, pp. 662–665.

ments, upon the district West of the Allegheny mountains. That country, he said, was divided into twenty-six counties, now sending fifty-two delegates, to a House composed of two hundred and fourteen members, equal to thirty-one in a House composed of one hundred and twenty-eight mumbers [*sic*]; that it now sent four and a half Senators, nearly equal to six in a Senate of thirty-two—and what were the inducements, he asked, for gentlemen representing that country, to reduce its present influence in the House of Delegates, without any acquisition in the Senate; a sacrifice not called for, in support of any principle connected with Representative Government, but on the contrary avowedly supported on the ground, that it was founded on no principle whatever, except the equitable notions of its author? If, said he, the Western delegation can be justified, in accepting a present apportionment, so unequal and unjust, in relation to their constituents, that justification must be found in the salutary operations of a future rule of apportionment. The gentleman from Albemarle, he said, had given them none to appeal to: that presented by the gentleman from Northampton, (Mr. Upshur,) as it stands now amended by the Committee of the Whole, was alone pressed upon the acceptance of the West, by either of the gentlemen.

He said, it came to us recommended by the votes and advice of the most revered and respected members of the House. It was urged as a measure of conciliation and compromise, as one that called for equal concession of the different grounds sustained here; that while one side had contended for taxation and population combined, or Federal numbers as its equivalent, the other had insisted on white population alone as the true basis of Government: That taking those two as the extreme rules, their combination, and the average of both, ought to be occupied as the middle ground: That here equal, and only equal sacrifices of opinion, were made on the altar of concord. So strong was this appeal, so ably was it enforced by the highest reasoning powers of this country, that he said he had been for some time in deliberation as to the vote which he ought to give. An examination of the whole ground, and a comparison of the concessions required, had been necessary to convince him of the unequal, and consequently unjust abandonment, which was asked at his hand.

The principle affirmed on one side was, that the people were capable of self-government, and ought to participate equally in its formation, and that a majority ought to give the direction of its action. On the other side it was contended that a portion of the people ought to hold an increased influence in the formation and direction of Government, either in proportion to the taxes paid by the different quarters of the State, or to the number of slaves held in the different portions of the Commonwealth, by the application of which rule a minority of the people from the adventitious circumstances of wealth or situation, might, and probably would, have the Government in their hands, and exercise it independent of, and uncontrouled by, the majority. He denied, that the proposed accommodation attained middle ground, and insisted, that it only increased the numbers of the minority to whom it proposed to confide the Government, and illustrated the effects of the proposed compromise of the question of future apportionments by supposing three hundred thousand free white citizens to reside West of the Blue Ridge, and two thousand East of that Ridge. He said, the slave population in the East exceeded that of the West, three hundred and seventy-two, and if three tenths were introduced into the body politic, it would give an increase of political units to the East of one hundred and four thousand; with the aid of which, two Eastern men would balance three Western men, as long as their relative state of the population remained, and this pernicious element of power continued. Its influence would not, he said, be limited to the controul of the action of the majority, when that action might be at variance with the interests or wishes of the minority, but would place the entire lawmaking power in the hands of the minority, to be exercised independent of the majority, and uncontrouled by their unanimous wishes and entire interests. If it was determined to perpetuate power in lowland hands, and to balance three of his constituents, with two of the favoured district, it was of but little consequence on what pretext the injurious and degrading policy was made to rest; no gilding could induce him to swallow the pill; it must produce nausea in whatever combination it may be given—and cannot long be retained by those upon whom you force it.

With this view of the subject, he said, he never could consent to the proposed measure of compromise; he never could affirm a principle that denied to the people of Virginia the capacity of self-government, and from which resulted the republican rule, that the interests of society could only be confided to a majority of its members. He thought, that it was fully as objectionable to give one part of the State increased political power over another, by reason of its wealth, as it would be to give the inhabitants of the same county unequal portions of political power in consequence of the disparity of their fortunes. On turning his mind to what would be an equal concession by the rival parties, he called to his recollection what had been affirmed by distinguished gentlemen in the past debate, (Mr. Giles and Mr. P. P. Barbour). By those gentlemen the right of the majority, to give the direction of the Government, was defended: they then only contended, that the rights of the minority ought to be respected in all just Governments, and that a sufficient portion of political power ought to be exercised by the minority, to stay the action of the majority, when not directed by the interest of all—A rule so just in itself, so salutary in practice, readily met with his assent: he was desirous of carrying it into effect by restrictions on the Legislative powers of the Government. He had supposed, that restraining clauses would as amply protect property in all its various relations, as the freedom of religion; the freedom of the press; and the great shield of civil liberty, the writ of habeas corpus; but so earnest, and so pervading seemed the fears of the Eastern gentlemen, that he had at length come to the conclusion of giving them security on their own principles of controuling power by power. Upon this hypothesis, he had consented to give in connection with the House of Delegates flowing from white population, a Senate based on Federal numbers. In doing so, he had satisfied himself that the fears of the East, whether real or imaginary, must be buried in a branch of the Government flowing in an eminent degree directly from themselves, charged with their peculiar interests and safety, and immediately responsible to Eastern constituents. This principle of security and of compromise had the further recommendation of calling into existence the Legislative part of the Government from two rival elements. To the people it gave the popular branch; to the slave-holders it gave the supervising and controuling body—it equally denied the powers of the Government to numbers alone, or to the wealth of the country in the hands of its holders. Although it was objected with much force, that this compromise of interests would enable the minority, to paralize the will of the majority, yet, it was unquestionably more in unison with the equal rights of all, that the action of the majority should be stayed, when the consent of the minority should be denied, than commit the Government to a minority of the people, with the power of applying its action to all persons, and all things, regardless of the interests, the feelings, or the wishes to the majority.

If protection is really the object of Eastern gentlemen, they will not hesitate to accept a Senate so formed—its members returning to Eastern constituents, will possess their confidence in the degree in which Eastern interests have been the objects of their care. The influence claimed for the slave property will be doubled in this branch of the Legislature—one hundred thousand white persons of the East, with their political influence increased in the Senate, by three-fifths of the slaves, may reject bills which unite in their favour three hundred thousand of the white population of the West.

Should this division of the power of Legislation be rejected, can the people of Lower Virginia suppose—can the world believe, that the protection of property has been the object sought for here? Will not the disguise be thrown off? Will not this question shew the most determined effort ever made in the American States, to render the *many* the vassals of the *few?*

For the safety of the State he hoped this lust of power would be abandoned, and a spirit of compromise and conciliation really adopted—a compromise, which giving to one branch of the Legislature, the principles contended for on one side, embodies in the other, the elements attempted to be infused throughout. . . .

. . . Beyond this, he could not go; other or further sacrifices of the just rights of his constituents he could not make. If it should be the pleasure of gentlemen to force upon them the cruel and galling yoke with which they were threatened, he took leave to assure them, that the polls would show its indignant rejection.

If the rights of the Western people are now to be denied to them, he would do no act to bar their future claims to an equal participation in the Government. He had fully weighed the subject, and was prepared to await the growing influence of wealth, numbers, and intelligence in the West, and a returning sense of justice and equality in the East, rather than take a Constitution affording but a meagre and inadequate relief, and which might hereafter be holden to release all that is not now obtained. He begged gentlemen to consider, that a majority in Convention represented a minority of the people, and how extremely idle and futile it must be, to offer a Constitution for acceptance, which could not be received by those who are seeking reform without placing themselves in colonial inferiority, if not in a state of vassalage: How vain it was for a Government like ours, to offer, on the demand of reform, less than the people would accept. They will not be appeased by such an illusory answer to their claims, they will but reiterate their demands in language which must be heard and cannot be disobeyed.

He asked, if the protection now offered in the Senate should be refused, will not even the people of Eastern Virginia perceive that it is the lust of power, and not the protection of property, for which the rights of their fellow-citizens of the West have been sacrificed. Such discovery, he thought, must unquestionably follow the present artificial and groundless excitement, and bring with it that calm sense of justice, which will secure to the people of every part of the Commonwealth, their equal and unalienable rights.

If, however, these anticipations should not be realized, and the cold-hearted and cruel policy should prevail, which holds the Western Virginians unsafe depositories of equal portions of the political power of the Commonwealth, they may, and I trust, will submit as men who know their duties to their country, although they may feel most sensibly its injustice.

He said, it had been the pride of the men of the mountains to witness the metropolitan honors of the lowlands. They have contributed freely from a common treasury to the enlargement and embellishment of the Eastern towns—for all the public works of the East, they have voted freely—they have regarded the genius and talents of Eastern men, as shedding equal glory and renown on every part of the Commonwealth. But what must be their future feelings, under the deprivations of political rights with which they are now threatened!

He begged gentlemen to pause before they severed those cords of affection, which had so long and so strongly bound the people of the West to those of the East.

25. Gordon on the Gordon Plan

Although the convention had adopted Gordon's plan, he felt called upon to defend it against expressions of dissatisfaction on both sides. In the work of compromise, William Fitzhugh Gordon of Albemarle was unquestionably the leading figure in the convention, just as the district he represented played a pivotal role. He was a reformer, like the other delegates from the district, but he felt no allegiance to the west and was naturally inclined to moderation. A lawyer and a general of the militia, he had represented Jefferson's county in the house of delegates for ten years, during which he had labored diligently for the establishment of the University of Virginia. His remarks on December 19 help to explain the motives and the reasoning behind his mixed-basis plan.

Mr. President,—I greatly regret the excitement, either of expression or manner, apparent in this debate. I shall endeavour to avoid either, in what I may say. The proposition I submitted for the consideration of the Convention, was made in the hope of sinking the *discussion* on the basis of *future* apportionment of Representation. My own opinion was, and is, that the white population, gave a fair criterion for a just arrangement of power among the several parts of the Commonwealth. We have, however, found the Convention equally divided in opinion; each positive and pertinacious, in opposing any plan of Representation founded in the views of the other. This discussion had greatly agitated our councils, distracted our deliberations, and disturbed the quiet of the country. We had nothing to hope from prolonging it: nor can there now be any other purpose in continuing it, unless to rupture the Convention and send us home to a distracted and dissatisfied community, divided by a geographical line, into two great hostile parties. Sir, it was in the hope of healing these divisions, that I ventured to propose to this Convention a plan for the *present* division of Representative power in the State.

I thought long and anxiously on the subject. I made various calculations on the condition of the Commonwealth, drawn from statistics within my reach. Sir, the proposition which I have submitted, was not *guess work;* much less was it a *scheme*

From *Proceedings,* pp. 672–674.

to give to one part of the Commonwealth a disproportionate and unjust power over the rights and interests of any other. It was proposed in a spirit of conciliation and compromise, violating no principle deemed correct by myself, and those with whom I had thought and acted; and, above all, in strict regard to what I considered just to every part of the State.

I found by calculations on the Census of 1820, the only authentic document of population within our power, that the present apportionment of Representation in the House of Delegates was greatly unequal throughout the State, and among its several parts: That in a House of Delegates of two hundred and fourteen members, the twenty-six counties West of the Allegheny mountains, composing the first Western district, had fifty-two delegates, when, by the white numbers of 1820, they were entitled to only forty-seven: That the section of the State, below tide-water, with thirty-six counties and four towns, had seventy-six delegates, whilst they were entitled to but fifty-nine: That the Valley or second Western district, with fourteen counties and twenty-eight delegates, was entitled to forty-two, and that the middle country from which I come, with twenty-nine counties, had fifty-eight delegates, and was entitled to sixty-six: That the two last mentioned subdivisions of the State, the Valley and middle sections, had a majority of seven thousand, seven hundred and forty-two white population, of twenty-two thousand, five hundred and sixty-two slaves, and paid of the taxes of 1828, $17,926 more than the other two, or the extreme West and Eastern divisions: That these two central contiguous districts of country, containing a majority of whites, a majority of slaves, and paying greatly more than half the revenue of the State, had a vote in the House of Delegates, as eighty-six is to two hundred and fourteen. Sir, the glaring inequality of Representation, has not, and cannot be met by any argument, and challenges universal assent to its injustice. Do gentlemen suppose that I, as one of the Representatives from one of the largest and most populous districts in Virginia, both as to white and Federal numbers, was insensible of its true interests, or was disposed to abandon them? I assure gentlemen the proposition I have submitted for their consideration, was not a leap in the dark. My first proposal was to reduce the House of Delegates to one hundred and twenty, (I added seven members to satisfy the wishes of some of the Convention). I made various estimates on the different propositions for apportionment, suggested to the Convention by others, or that presented themselves to my own mind. I found that if taxation alone was the basis of Representation in a House of one hundred and twenty members, the twenty-nine counties composing the first Western district, would have eleven and a half. The second Western or Valley district, seventeen and a half. The first Eastern or Middle district, forty-six and a half. The second Eastern or Lower district, forty-four and a half. If the Federal number, the first district, twenty; the second, nineteen; the third, forty-three and a half; and the fourth, thirty-seven and a half. If the combined ratio of numbers and taxation, the first district, nineteen; the second, twenty and three-quarters; the third, forty-two; the fourth, thirty-eight and a quarter members. On the Federal numbers of the Auditor's estimate of the present population, the first district would have twenty-four; the second, twenty-one; the third, forty-four; and the fourth, thirty-eight members. Sir, I made other estimates from the Auditor's statement of the taxes of 1828. Dividing the whole amount of taxes or revenue, by the whole number of delegates in our present House of Delegates, I found that if all parts of the State paid equally, the average for each member, should be $1,872. I then made a comparative estimate of the taxation and Representation of each section of the State—I found that the first Western section paid $751 per member; the second Western or Valley District, paid $2,233 per member; the third or middle district, $2,830, and the fourth or second Eastern district, paid $1,684 per member. Sir, I give these estimates in no spirit of reproach to that Western district, for the small contributions to the Treasury, in proportion to their actual Representative power in the Government, but to admonish gentlemen who complain that my proposition does injustice to their country, that they should not forget, that in Committee of the Whole, forty members of this Convention rose in favour of a proposition to base Representation on taxation alone. Sir, when it is conceded on all hands, that without a spirit of temperance and moderation, no good can result from our deliberations, I ask what injustice my proposition can do to the West? On the contrary, is it not fair and liberal? It gives to the whole country West of the Blue Ridge, within a very few members of what it would be entitled to upon the present uncertain estimate of the Auditor of the white population of the State; and it gives to the Valley *all*, all it claims for the present on any scheme of Representation, and to the Trans-Allegheny country, three more than it would be entitled to by the Census of 1820, on white population alone. Sir, is not this a fair and liberal estimate for the West? Does it not give all that it may fairly claim for the present? What do gentlemen ask: that we should give a rule of *future* apportionments: without fixing the Representation for the present? Can our brethren of the West think it would be right or reasonable in us of the East, who represent a country containing nearly half a million of bondsmen, whilst they have, comparatively but few, to return to our constituents the *masters* of these slaves, without being able to tell them what will be the actual state of their Representation in the Legislature? What will be the actual and relative power of each section of the State in regard to this great and delicate interest? Sir, the people of Virginia would ratify no Constitution, looking to a prospective Census, which did not fix the *present* Representation of its respective districts. The very anxious suspense and uncertainty on that subject, after the agitations which have been excited here and elsewhere, would make them reject any Constitution you can propose, and content them to live under the present Constitution, unequal as the distribution of power under it, undoubtedly is. Sir, when I first presented my plan of Representation, I thought it would be acceptable to the

West, because, I was sure, it did them ample justice, and was not subject to be criticised, from containing in its principles any element peculiarly objectionable to them. In presenting it I looked to the rights and interests of the whole State—acknowledging as I always do, my peculiar obligations and duties to my immediate constituents. I feel and have felt that their interests will on this occasion be best subserved by looking with an enlarged view to the rights and interest of the whole, rather than to a perpetuation of sectional strife, in which they, nor any who love their country, can take delight. With these views, the proposition was submitted and has been sustained. The first proposition was the result of an estimate of the white population of 1820—modified from one hundred and twenty members to one hundred and twenty-seven, to accommodate the views and to endeavour to *sink* the *debate* on that vexed question. Sir, one great objection I always had to bringing this Federal number or mixed basis under discussion, was an anticipation of the heat and unhappiness it would engender; and a strong objection to fixing it in the Constitution, was, that it would be an element of faction; a seed of discord; fatal to the permanence of the Constitution. If you do put it in the Constitution, cannot the non-slave-holding part of that State, excite you on this subject whenever they may have a purpose to answer by it—and you may have a Missouri question, of perpetual recurrence in the heart of your institutions. Sir, no Constitution you can form, situated as Virginia is, can endure with such a provision in it.

The non-freeholders and non-slave-owners, who are excluded from the Right of Suffrage, will be the lever to wrench your institutions from such foundations—they will not be insensible to the appeal, that this fair domain of Virginia, was conquered by their fathers in many a battle bravely won—that they established a republican form of Government, leaving its administration in the hands of the freeholders—that after fifty-four years of possession of this exclusive power, they delegated their men of age and wisdom, who met in council to liberalize their institutions and fix the foundations of future Government, but that such had been the influence of long submission to unequal power, that they not only refused to extend the Right of Suffrage to the freemen of the country, but they infused a new element of power—they made their slaves the basis, in part, of representation, whilst those who guard them in their subjugation, are denied a voice in their councils and in elections. Sir, I will not pursue this subject, but ask gentlemen to reflect. Can a Government so based, be permanent? Will it not contain within itself the fatal germ of its own destruction, after years of strife and confusion? Sir, is it wise in a slave-holding community to keep up this discussion? If we do not put this ingredient in our cup, may we not fairly appeal to the just sympathies of our Western brethren? Not from any apprehension of danger personal to ourselves. Those who have commanded slaves, can never become so themselves; the spirit of command endures through life. But when they reflect that we are hereditary masters of men born in slavery; that our condition is unalterable at present; that theirs is every day more and more assimilated to ours; that their interests and ours equally combine to allay this excitement and look to Virginia as one great united Commonwealth, I am sure the appeal will not be in vain. Sir, we ought to meet on this middle ground of the Census of 1820, notwithstanding the West sets up a higher claim. . . .

The Suffrage

26. The Non-Freeholders' Memorial

The best statement of the case for a broad suffrage was "The Memorial of the Non-Freeholders of the City of Richmond." John Mar-

shall dutifully presented it to the convention on October 13, and it was referred to the legislative committee.

Your memorialists, as their designation imports, belong to that class of citizens, who, not having the good fortune to possess a certain portion of land, are, for that cause only, debarred from the enjoyment of the right of suffrage. Experience has but too clearly evinced, what, indeed, reason had always foretold, by how frail a tenure they hold every other right, who are denied this, the highest prerogative of freemen. The want of it has afforded both the pretext and the means of excluding the entire class, to which your memorialists belong, from all participation in the recent election of the body, they now respectfully address. Comprising a very large part, probably a majority of male citizens of mature age, they have been passed by, like aliens or slaves, as if destitute of interest, or unworthy of a voice, in measures involving their future political destiny: whilst the freeholders, sole possessors, under the existing Constitution, of the elective franchise, have, upon the strength of that possession alone, asserted and maintained in themselves, the exclusive power of new-modelling the fundamental laws of the State: in other words, have seized upon the sovereign authority.

It cannot be necessary, in addressing the Convention now assembled, to expatiate on the momentous importance of the right of suffrage, or to enumerate the evils consequent upon its unjust limitation. Were there no other than that your memorialists have brought to your attention, and which has made them feel with full force their degraded condition, well might it justify their best efforts to obtain the great privilege they now seek, as the only effectual method of preventing its recurrence. To that privilege, they respectfully contend, they are

From *Proceedings*, pp. 25–31.

entitled equally with its present possessors. Many are bold enough to deny their title. None can show a better. It rests upon no subtle or abstruse reasoning; but upon grounds simple in their character, intelligible to the plainest capacity, and such as appeal to the heart, as well as the understanding, of all who comprehend and duly appreciate the principles of free Government. Among the doctrines inculcated in the great charter handed down to us, as a declaration of the rights pertaining to the good people of Virginia and their posterity, "as the basis and foundation of Government," we are taught,

"That all men are by nature equally free and independent, and have certain inherent rights, of which, when they enter into a state of society, they cannot, by any compact, deprive or divest their posterity: namely, the enjoyment of life and liberty, with the means of acquiring and possessing property, and pursuing and obtaining happiness and safety.

"That all power is vested in, and consequently derived from, the people.

"That a majority of the community hath an indubitable, unalienable, and indefeasible right to reform, alter or abolish the Government.

"That no man, nor set of men, are entitled to exclusive or separate emoluments or privileges, but in consideration of public services.

"That all men, having sufficient evidence of permanent common interest with, and attachment to, the community, have a right of suffrage, and cannot be taxed, or deprived of their property, without their consent, or that of their representative, nor bound by any law, to which they have not, in like manner, assented, for the public good."

How do the principles thus proclaimed, accord with the existing regulation of suffrage? A regulation, which, instead of the equality nature ordains, creates an odious distinction between members of the same community; robs of all share, in the enactment of the laws, a large portion of the citizens, bound by them, and whose blood and treasure are pledged to maintain them, and vests in a favoured class, not in consideration of their public services, but of their private possessions, the highest of all privileges; one which, as is now in flagrant proof, if it does not constitute, at least is held practically to confer, absolute sovereignty. Let it not be urged, that the regulation complained of and the charter it violates, sprung from the same honored source. The conflict between them is not on that account the less apparent. Nor does it derogate from the fair fame of the Convention of '76, that they should not have framed a Constitution perfect in all its parts. Deliberating amid the din of arms, not merely on a plan of Government, but on the necessary means for conducting a most unequal struggle for national existence, it was not to be expected, that the relative rights of the citizens, could be maturely considered, or adjusted in detail. From any change of the regulation, in regard to suffrage, a subject prolific, always, of much dissention, they might have feared to generate feuds among those, upon whose harmony of feeling and concert of action, depended the salvation of their country. They left it, therefore, as they found it. The non-freeholders, moreover, unrepresented in the Convention, and for the most part, probably, engaged in resisting the common enemy, it is fair to infer, in the actual condition of the country, had neither the opportunity nor the inclination to press their claims. Nor should it be forgotten, that the Convention having been chosen by the freeholders, whose political power was derived from the abrogated Government, many of our wisest Statesmen regarded the Constitution itself, as wanting in authority, or at least as repealable by a succeeding Legislature: and, accordingly, it has, in point of fact, since undergone a material change, in the very provision now in question, touching the right of suffrage.

If the Bill of Rights may not challenge respect, the opinions of any individual, however eminent, will be still more lightly regarded. Yet your memorialists cannot but exult in the countenance their cause has received from him, who was ever fore-most to assert the rights of his fellow men; the venerated author of the Declaration of Independence, and of the Act of Religious Freedom. When those rights are brought in question, they know of none whose sentiments are worthy of higher estimation. To none among the founders of our Republic, are we indebted for more in its institutions, that is admirable in theory, or valuable in practice. His name is identified with the independence of his country; with all that is liberal and enlightened in her policy. Never had liberty an advocate of more unaffected zeal; of more splendid abilities; of purer principles. Nor is there in ancient or modern times, an example to be found of one, who in his life and conduct, more strongly exemplified the sincerity of his faith, or more brightly illustrated the beauty of its tenets. . . .

But not to the authority of great names merely, does the existing restriction upon suffrage stand opposed: reason and justice equally condemn it. The object, it is presumed, meant to be attained, was, as far as practicable, to admit the meritorious, and reject the unworthy. And had this object really been attained, whatever opinions might prevail as to the mere right, not a murmur probably would have been heard. Surely it were much to be desired that every citizen should be qualified for the proper exercise of all his rights, and the due performance of all his duties. But the same qualifications that entitle him to assume the management of his private affairs, and to claim all other privileges of citizenship, equally entitle him, in the judgment of your memorialists, to be entrusted with this, the dearest of all his privileges, the most important of all his concerns. But if otherwise, still they cannot discern in the possession of land any evidence of peculiar merit, or superior title. To ascribe to a landed possession, moral or intellectual endowments, would truly be regarded as ludicrous, were it not for the gravity with which the proposition is maintained, and still more for the grave consequences flowing from it. Such possession no more proves him who has it, wiser or better, than it proves him taller or stronger, than him who has it not. That cannot be a fit criterion for the exercise of any right, the possession of which does not indicate the existence, nor the want of it the absence, of any essential qualification.

But this criterion, it is strenuously insisted, though not perfect, is yet the best human wisdom can devise. It affords the strongest, if not the only evidence of the requisite qualifications; more particularly of what are absolutely essential, "permanent common interest with, and attachment to, the community." Those who cannot furnish this evidence, are therefore deservedly excluded.

Your memorialists do not design to institute a comparison; they fear none that can be fairly made between the privileged and the proscribed classes. They may be permitted, however, without disrespect, to remark, that of the latter, not a few possess land: many, though not proprietors, are yet cultivators of the soil: others are engaged in avocations of a different nature, often as useful, presupposing no less integrity, requiring as much intelligence, and as fixed a residence, as agricultural pursuits. Virtue, intelligence, are not among the products of the soil. Attachment to property, often a sordid sentiment, is not to be confounded with the sacred flame of patriotism. The love of country, like that of parents and offspring, is engrafted in our nature. It exists in all climates, among all classes, under every possible form of Government. Riches oftener impair it than poverty. Who has it not is a monster.

Your memorialists feel the difficulty of undertaking calmly to repel charges and insinuations involving in infamy themselves, and so large a portion of their fellow-citizens. To be deprived of their rightful equality, and to hear as an apology that they are too ignorant and vicious to enjoy it, is no ordinary trial of patience. Yet they will suppress the indignant emotions these sweeping denunciations are well calculated to excite. The freeholders themselves know them to be unfounded: Why, else, are arms placed in the hands of a body of disaffected citizens, so ignorant, so depraved, and so numerous? In the hour of danger, they have drawn no invidious distinctions between the sons of Virginia. The muster rolls have undergone no scrutiny, no comparison with the land books, with a view to expunge those who have been struck from the ranks of freemen. If the landless citizens have been ignominiously driven from the polls, in time of peace, they have at least been generously summoned, in war, to the battle-field. Nor have they disobeyed the summons, or, less profusely than others, poured out their blood in the defence of that country which is asked to disown them. Will it be said they owe allegiance to the Government that gives them protection? Be it so: and if they acknowledge the obligation; if privileges are really extended to them in defence of which they may reasonably be required to shed their blood, have they not motives, irresistible motives, of attachment to the community? Have they not an interest, a deep interest, in perpetuating the blessings they enjoy, and a right, consequently, to guard those blessings, not from foreign aggression merely, but from domestic encroachment?

But, it is said, yield them this right, and they will abuse it: property, that is, landed property, will be rendered insecure, or at least overburthened, by those who possess it not. The freeholders, on the contrary, can pass no law to the injury of any other class, which will not more injuriously affect themselves. The alarm is sounded too, of danger from large manufacturing institutions, where one corrupt individual may sway the corrupt votes of thousands. It were a vain task to attempt to meet all the flimsy pretexts urged, to allay all the apprehensions felt or feigned by the enemies of a just and liberal policy. The danger of abuse is a dangerous plea. Like *necessity,* the detested plea of the tyrant, or the still more detestible plea of the Jesuit, *expediency;* it serves as an ever-ready apology for all oppression. If we are sincerely republican, we must give our confidence to the pri[n]ciples we profess. We have been taught by our fathers, that all power is vested in, and derived from, the people; not the freeholders: that the majority of the community, in whom abides the physical force, have also the political right of creating and remoulding at will, their civil institutions. Nor can this right be any where more safely deposited. The generality of mankind, doubtless, desire to become owners of property: left free to reap the fruit of their labours, they will seek to acquire it honestly. It can never be their interest to overburthen, or render precarious, what they themselves desire to enjoy in peace. But should they ever prove as base as the argument supposes, force alone; arms, not votes, could effect their designs; and when that shall be attempted, what virtue is there in Constitutional restrictions, in mere wax and paper, to withstand it? To deny to the great body of the people all share in the Government; on suspicion that they may deprive others of their property, to rob them, in advance of their rights; to look to a privileged order as the fountain and depository of all power; is to depart from the fundamental maxims, to destroy the chief beauty, the characteristic feature, indeed, of Republican Government. . . .

. . . The right of suffrage, however, it seems, is not a natural right. If by natural, is meant what is just and reasonable, then, nothing is more reasonable than that those whose purses contribute to maintain, whose lives are pledged to defend the country, should participate in all the privileges of citizenship. But say it is not a natural right. Whence did the freeholders derive it? How become its exclusive possessors? Will they arrogantly tell us they own the country, because they hold the land? The right by which they hold their land is not itself a natural right, and by consequence, nothing claimed as incidental to it. Whence then did they derive this privilege? From grant or conquest? Not from the latter. No war has ever been waged to assert it. If from the former, by whom was it conferred? They cannot, if they would, recur to the Royal Instructions of that English monarch, of infamous memory, who enjoined it upon the Governor of the then Colony of Virginia, "to take care that the members of the Assembly be elected *only by the freeholders,* as being more agreeable to the custome of England:" he might have added more congenial also with monarchical institutions. If Colonial regulations might properly be looked to, then the right, not of freeholders merely, but of *freemen,* to vote, may be traced to a more distant antiquity, and a less polluted source. But, by our ever-glorious revolution, the Government whence these regulations emanated, was annulled, and with it all the political privileges it had conferred, swept away. Will they rely on the Constitutional provision? That was the act of men delegated by themselves. They exercised the very right in question in appointing the body from whom they profess to derive it, and indeed gave to that body all the power it possessed. What is this but to say they generously conferred the privilege upon themselves? Perhaps they may rely on length of time to forestal enquiry. We acknowledge no act of limitations against the oppressed. Or will they disdain to shew any title; and, clinging to power, rest on force, the last argument of Kings, as its source and its defence? This were, doubtless, the more politic course.

Let us concede that the right of suffrage is a social right; that it must of necessity be regulated by society. Still the question recurs, is the existing limitation proper? For obvious reasons, by almost universal consent, women and children, aliens and slaves, are excluded. It were useless to discuss the propriety of a rule that scarcely admits of diversity of opinion. What is concurred in by those who constitute the society, the body politic, must be taken to be right. But the exclusion of these classes for reasons peculiarly applicable to them, is no argument for excluding others to whom no one of those reasons applies.

It is said to be *expedient,* however, to exclude non-freeholders also. Who shall judge of this expediency? The society: and does that embrace the proprietors of certain portions of land only? Expedient, for whom? for the freeholders. A harsh appellation would he deserve, who, on the plea of expediency, should take from another his property: what, then, should be said of him who, on that plea, takes from another his rights, upon which the security, not of his property only, but of his life and liberty depends?

But the non-freeholders are condemned for pursuing an abstract right, whose privation occasions no practical injury.

Your memorialists do not, perhaps, sufficiently comprehend the precise import of this language, so often used. The enjoyment of all other rights, whether of person or property, they will not deny, may be as perfect among those deprived of the privilege of voting, as among those possessing it. It may be as great under a despotism, as under any other form of Government. But they alone deserve to be called free, or have a guarantee for their rights, who participate in the formation of their political institutions, and in the control of those who make and administer the laws. To such as may be disposed to surrender this, or any other immunity, to the keeping of others, no practical mischief may ensue from its abandonment; or if any, none that will not be justly merited. Not so with him who feels as a freeman should; who would think for himself and speak what he thinks; who would not commit his conscience or his liberty to the uncontrolled direction of others. To him the privation of right, of that especially, which is the only safeguard of freedom, is practically wrong. So thought the fathers of the republic. It was not the oppressive weight of the taxes imposed by England on America: it was the assertion of a right to impose any burthens whatever upon those who were not represented; to bind by laws those who had no share, personal or delegated, in their enactment, that roused this continent to arms. . . .

27. The Freehold Suffrage Defended

Philip N. Nicholas, son of the wealthy former treasurer of the colony Robert Carter Nicholas, was described by Hugh Blair Grigsby as "a singular compound of buffonery and good sense." Although a Richmond banker, he seemed to think that virtue did indeed spring from the soil. His speech on the suffrage may be read as an answer to the Richmond "Memorial."

. . . Mr. N. said, he should proceed to discuss what was the real question before the Committee, stripped of those extraneous considerations, which do not bear upon it, and which are rather calculated to mislead, than to enlighten. This subject has received from me, Mr. Chairman, my anxious consideration; not only since it has been agitated in this Convention, but whilst during the canvass, which preceded the elections, it was discussed in the public prints, in speeches to the people, and in the addresses of various gentlemen who were called on to declare their sentiments. Amongst the arguments relied upon by the advocates of a very extended Suffrage, one of the most fallacious, is, that which attempts to found the right upon principles of natural equality. This pre-supposes that Suffrage is a conventional, and not a natural right. In a state of nature, (if such state ever existed except in the imagination of the poets,) every man acts for himself, and is the sole judge of what will contribute to his happiness. When he enters into the social state, which he is compelled to do, to guard himself against violence, and to protect him in the enjoyment of the fruits of his industry, he gives up to the society the powers of Government, and surrenders to it, so much of his natural rights as are essential to secure to him such portion of those rights which he retains, or such other rights as grow out of the new relations in which he is placed.

In the rudiments of society, and whilst the people are few, the making laws and the decision on the most important concerns, such, for instance, as war and peace, were exercised by

From *Proceedings,* pp. 363–367.

the body of the people in their collective capacity. Such was the ancient republic of Athens, and some of the other Grecian States, and such is said to be the little republic of St. Marino. When the community became large, it was found impracticable to exercise their sovereignty in their primary Assemblies. These were too numerous for deliberation, and were too much under the control of violent passions, and too liable to be influenced by the seductions of artful men, who flattered the people only to destroy them. It was found absolutely necessary, to entrust the making of laws and the management of the public affairs to agents, or deputies, and this gave rise to representation. The power of voting for these agents or deputies constitutes the Right of Suffrage. This plain exposition of the origin and formation of society, incontestibly shows that both Representation and Suffrage are social institutions. It proves that it is a solecism to insist, that it is proper to refer back to a state of nature, for principles to regulate rights which never existed in it—which could only exist after mankind abandoned it, rather than by a correct estimate of those relations, which are to be found in a state of society, of which, both Representation and Suffrage are the offspring. It has been attempted to sustain almost unlimited suffrage . . . by reference to those general phrases in the Bill of Rights, which declare, "that all men are by nature equally free and independent." But the same section of the Bill of Rights plainly discriminates between the state of nature, and the social state, and admits the modification which natural rights may receive by entering into society. It is true it speaks of inherent rights, of which men, when they enter into society "cannot by any compact deprive or divest their posterity"; "namely, the enjoyment of life and liberty, with the means of acquiring and possessing property, and pursuing and obtaining happiness and safety." But it is most obvious that this last clause does not comprehend suffrage, or representation, or any fancied rights growing out of them; first, because these are not natural rights; and next, if they were, as the clause last referred to enumerates the rights which a man in a social state cannot alienate, and that enumeration has nothing to do with suffrage or representation, it must in candour be admitted, that these subjects are surrendered (so far as the Bill of Rights is concerned) to the regulation of society. These considerations, Mr. Chairman, appear to me clearly to prove, that in deciding upon suffrage, we are deciding a question of expediency and policy, and that we ought so to regulate it, as will best promote the happiness and prosperity of society. Our opponents have themselves afforded unequivocal evidence of the truth of what we contend for, by advocating schemes of suffrage which profess to impose restrictions on the exercise of the right, though those restrictions (in my humble judgment) are totally inadequate and illusory.

. . . It is much, however, to be deplored, that whilst these gentlemen pay such adoration to the Bill of Rights, and its authors, they should in the same breath deny that they understood their own principles, and assert, that in the formation of every essential part of the Constitution, they were guilty of a flagrant violation of them! What then, is the rule laid down by the authors of our Constitution on this subject? It is, "that all men having sufficient evidence of permanent, common interest with, and attachment to, the community, have the Right of Suffrage." Every part of this definition, Mr. Chairman, is highly important. First, there must be "sufficient evidence," and next, it must be the evidence "of permanent, common interest with, and attachment to, the community." Now, I contend that this sufficient evidence of common, permanent interest, is only to be found in a lasting ownership of the soil of the country.

This kind of property is durable, it is indestructible; and the man who acquires, or is the proprietor of it, connects his fate by the strongest of all ties, with the destiny of the country. No other species of property has the same qualities, or affords the same evidence. Personal property is fluctuating—it is frequently invisible, as well as intangible—it can be removed, and can be enjoyed as well in one society as another. What evidence of permanent interest and attachment, is afforded by the ownership of horses, cattle, or slaves? Can it retard or impede the removal from the State, in times of difficulty or danger impending over it? What security is the ownership of Bank or other stocks, or in the funded debt? None. A man may transfer this kind of property in a few moments, take his seat in the stage, or embark in the steamboat, and be out of the State in one day, carrying with him all he possesses.

The same objection applies to admitting persons who have only a temporary interest in the soil: besides, that these temporary interests give a control to others, over the votes of the holder, just as certainly, as that "a control over a man's subsistence, is always a control over his will." In vain do gentlemen refer to the example of other States. Here we have a safe rule laid down, by the wisdom of our ancestors, whom gentlemen unite in canonizing, and tested and approved by the experience of more than half a century. Sir, I always thought I was a republican, but gentlemen would argue me out of my belief. I have always supposed, that our Right of Suffrage was so constructed, as to protect both persons and property. God forbid that I should wish to exclude any, who I can be convinced ought to be admitted, or that I would oppress any portion of my fellow-citizens. My principles would lead me to admit all I could, consistently with what I believe the welfare of society requires. I am no enemy to the non-freeholder; but I must vote for that rule, which by securing the tranquillity and happiness of society, secures those inestimable blessings to every member of it. I do not deny to the advocates of greatly extended suffrage, either in this House or out of it, perfect rectitude and sincerity of motive. Enthusiasm is always sincere—but that truth does not at all mitigate the evils and desolations, which it has often inflicted on mankind.

Sir, I know it has become fashionable to represent those who are opposed to many of the innovations which are contemplated, as the enemies of the people. . . . Gentlemen argue this question as if it was one between the Satraps, (the existence of whom they choose to suppose) and the poor of the land. Instead of making war upon the middling or even the poorer classes, we believe we are defending their best interests. We go not for the interests of wealth, when we say, that we are of opinion that an interest in the soil is the best evidence of permanent attachment. This idea of an aristocracy of freeholders, is not only incorrect but ludicrous. Are we contending for giving wealth in the distribution of suffrage, a weight in proportion to its extent? The answer is, that a freeholder, whose farm is worth fifty dollars, has as available a suffrage as one who has land worth two hundred thousand dollars. Are we for fixing a high property qualification? We reply, that it appears from this debate, that a man can get a freehold in almost any county in the State for fifty dollars, and in some (indeed many) for twenty-five dollars, or for a smaller sum. . . . But it is said, that every man who pays a tax ought to vote—now, what evidence of interest in the community, is furnished by the payment of four cents upon a horse, or paying a poor rate and county levy? Is it even the semblance of testimony, that the person paying it, intends to remain in the Commonwealth? It is also contended that service in the militia, is a proper and valid claim to a vote. It is said the non-freeholder fights your battles—but does not the freeholder do so too? And does he not do another thing, pay for the support of the non-freeholder? War cannot be carried on by men alone: you require munitions of war, provisions and every thing necessary to equip and sustain an army. Without these, numbers are of no avail, indeed injurious. Your army would soon be disorganized without them. In time of peace, the militia service which is common to freeholder and non-freeholder, is light, if not nominal. In time of war, you draw heavily on the property of the country, and then the freeholder is not only bound to fight, but to pay.

We have a strong example of this during the last war. During that war, Virginia was thrown very much upon her own resources, and having found that the keeping very large bodies of militia in the field, was very harassing to the people, very expensive, and not very efficient, the Assembly determined on raising ten thousand men for the defence of the State. The law provided, that the expenses of these troops should be assessed on the property of the country, and it would have fallen with great and oppressive weight on the land and slave-owners. Happily, the intervention of peace saved the country from the severe burthens, to which the property-holders would have been subjected. But it serves to show, what ever will be the case, when we are exposed to the calamities incident to war.

The gentleman from Loudoun [Mr. Henderson] has stated, that he knows of no particular virtue attached to the soil, that we should select the owners as the sole depositories of political power. All professions are on a par in his estimation. I do not pretend that great virtues may not be found in all the professions and walks of life. But I do believe, if there are any chosen people of God, they are the cultivators of the soil. If there be virtue to be found any where, it would be amongst the middling farmers, who constitute the yeomanry, the bone and sinew of our country. Sir, they are men of moderate desires, they have to labor for their subsistence, and the support of their families; their wishes are bounded by the limits of their small possessions; they are not harassed by envy, by the love of show and splendor, nor agitated by the restless and insatiable passion of ambition. When they lay their heads at night upon their pillows under the consciousness of having spent the day in the discharge of their duties to their families, they enjoy a sweeter sleep under their humble roofs, than frequently do those who repose in gilded palaces. Amid the same description of persons, I should look for independence of character. It is a fact, that our voters are less exposed to influence and intrigue, than any, I believe, in the United States. A man may be popular enough to be elected himself, but he cannot dictate to the voters to elect any other. A man who would attempt this would be apt to be insulted, and I have known illustrious examples of some of the most popular men; aye, Sir, in the zenith of their popularity, who could not control an election in favour of another. Do you ever hear in this State of a man being called, as in some of the States the partizan of some great name? A Livingston man, or a Clinton man for example? Ask one of our freeholders whose man he is, he will tell you he is his own man. These men know that their land is their own, that they are the lords of the soil; that according to the principles of the common law, their house is their castle, and that no man dare invade either, with impunity. Do you believe, Mr. Chairman, that there is any property which attaches a man so much to the country as the land? There is none. His attachment to his home, is connected with the best sympathies of the human heart. It is the place of his boyish sports, the birth place of his children; and contains the bones of his ancestors. He will love his country which contains a home so dear to him, and defend that country at the hazard of his life.

There is one consideration which shows the propriety of making land the basis of political power. It is, that the land, has always been, and will continue to be, the principal source from which all your taxes are derived. The freeholders, if they are an aristocracy, are the most lenient aristocrats who ever existed. From the foundation of our Republic, and long before, land-holders, who are the largest slave-holders too, have paid your principal taxes. We have parted with the customs to the General Government, and the only other sources of revenue of any great extent, are your lands and negroes. The freeholders too, pay a large share of the other taxes, such as taxes on licenses, horses and carriages. You can never expect to see a capitation tax, nor an income tax. They both are odious in their character; the first is very unjust, and the second must be attended with such inquisitorial powers to your officers, and be so easily eluded by fraud, that it will not be attempted. They tried it in England, and it was the cause of overturning the ministry which introduced it. But the great advantage of the freehold system is, that it keeps the Government in the hands of the middling classes. So far from being aristocratic, it is the best safeguard against aristocracy. It places the power in the hands of those who are interested to guard both property and persons against oppression. The idea of aristocracy is absurd. Did you ever hear of an aristocracy of fifty dollars, or twenty-five dollar freeholders? In the hands of these freeholders, personal rights are just as secure as the rights of property. Many of the non-freeholders are the sons of freeholders. Would they support measures which would oppress their own sons? Besides, have not the great body of the freeholders such perfect identity of condition with the non-freeholders, that they could pass no law for the regulation of personal rights which would not equally affect them as well as the non-freeholders. To those who take a superficial view of things, it might appear that placing the power in the hands of men, without regard to their condition, would advance the cause of liberty. Many will tell you, Sir, that they would do this to counteract the influence of wealth in society.

But these men, many of whom are ardent friends of liberty, are unconsciously laboring to undermine the cause of which they mean to be the strenuous advocates. As long as political power is placed as it now is in Virginia, in the hands of the middling classes, who, though not rich, are yet sufficiently so, to secure their independence, you have nothing to fear from wealth. But place power in the hands of those who have none, or a very trivial stake in the community, and you expose the poor and dependent to the influence and seductions of wealth. The extreme rich, and the extreme poor, if not natural allies, will become so in fact. The rich will relieve the necessities of the poor, and the latter will become subservient to the ambition of the rich. You hear nothing of the bribery and corruption of freeholders. No man is hardy enough to attempt it. But extend the Right of Suffrage to every man dependent, as well as independent, and you immediately open the flood-gates of corruption. You will undermine the public and private virtue of your people, and this your boasted Republic, established by the wisdom of your ancestors, and defended at the hazard of their lives, will share the fate of all those which have preceded it, whose gradual decline, and final extinction, it has been the melancholy task of history to record. . . .

28. The Reformers' Rebuttal

After Benjamin Watkins Leigh made a lengthy defense of the freehold suffrage on November 20, 1829, he was answered by Lucas P. Thompson of Amherst, in the same district as Albemarle. He avowed his belief in universal suffrage, castigated the conservatives for knocking Jefferson from the pedestal of Virginia Republicanism and setting Burke in his place, and threw back at them the epithets "visionary" and "theoretical." Thompson, a young man, was one of the staunchest friends of reform east of the Blue Ridge. He was later, and for many years, a respected circuit-court judge.

Two brief excerpts follow: one from Philip Doddridge's speech on the suffrage, in which he expresses his contempt for pretentious and irrelevant historical analogies; the other from the western delegate Charles S. Morgan, in which the defense of slavery and the South is offered as a reason for democratization of the suffrage.

Mr. Chairman, I scruple not *in limine*[22] to avow that I am one of those *visionary* politicians who advocate General Suffrage,

---

From *Proceedings*, pp. 410–419, 425, 382.

[22] On the threshold [Ed.].

what gentleman are pleased to term *Universal* Suffrage. And, in this avowal, I believe I speak the sentiments of a large majority of my constituents. What I mean by General Suffrage, is the extension of that inestimable right of voting in the election of all public functionaries, made eligible by the people to all white freemen of the age of twenty-one years and upwards, who are citizens by birth or residence for a certain time, and who have discharged all the burthens personal, including militia duties, and pecuniary, such as taxes, imposed upon them by the laws of the land, and excluding such as are rendered infamous by the commission of crime. In other words, I wish to establish a qualification that is personal, and respects age and residence, and to abolish forever the freehold qualification, which to me has always appeared an invidious and anti-republican test. Like the gentleman from Charlotte, (Mr. Randolph,) I did not come here to vote for the disfranchisement of one human being qualified to vote under the old Constitution, but to aid in the enfranchisement of all who come within the foregoing description. I came here to contribute my feeble aid in the great cause of *non-freehold* emancipation, but not to imitate an example set us elsewhere, of disfranchising the forty shilling freeholders. I am, therefore, diametrically opposed to the amendment proposed by the gentleman from Chesterfield, as I am to all amendments that go to restrict the Right of Suffrage; and upon this question, I will meet and take issue with the friends of freehold qualification, amongst the most strenuous of whom, the gentleman from Chesterfield, has proved himself, by the argument which he yesterday addressed to this Committee. I am willing to rest this argument upon the authority of reason and common sense, the Bill of Rights, upon the doctrine of expediency, or upon experience, which, *visionary as I am*, I consider more valuable than volumes of speculation and theory. It is with me perfectly indifferent, whether this right be regarded as a natural, a social, a civil, or a political one; the conclusion at which I arrive, satisfactorily at least to myself, is the same.

Before I proceed with my argument, I must trouble the Committee with a few general observations suggested by the course of this debate. I cannot forbear to express my surprise and regret at some of the principles avowed by gentlemen on this floor, and the change which public sentiment seems to have undergone in this ancient Commonwealth. In the opinion of some gentlemen, Government has no principles. The idea of patriotism and virtue even are exploded, and self-love and self-interest are the only springs of human action. The rights of men are a mere chimera of distempered imaginations, and in this debate have been made the theme of ridicule and derision, rather than eulogy. Against this, I solemnly protest. There was a time when this would not have been endured, when such language would have been offensive to republican ears. In the whole progress of this debate, the name of Thomas Jefferson, the great Apostle of liberty, has never once been invoked, nor has one appeal been made to the author of the Rights of Man, whose immortal work, in the darkest days of our revolution, served as a political decalogue and operated as a talisman to lead our armies to victory. There was a time when it was honorable to profess the faith of these great fathers of the church, when it was perilous to be a sceptic, when the name of Fox was venerated, and the principles of Burke abhorred—but the sentiment of the Latin poet quoted in this debate are but too true, *"tempora mutantur,"* &c. rendered into English.

> *"Men change with manners, manners change with climes,*
> *"Tenets with books and principles with times."*

Then, the authority of the sage of Monticello would have stood against the world; now, there are "none so poor as to do him reverence." Then, was Burke regarded as the enemy of human rights and the firmest defender of aristocracy and monarchy—but now, Burke, Filmer,[23] and Hobbes, judging from their arguments, have become the text books of our statesmen.

Mr. Chairman, I have spoken of political faith and political church—it recalls to my mind an observation I have often made, and no doubt has often occurred to the mind of every member of this Committee—and that is the great similarity in the conduct of the votaries of religion and politics. In these days, you find no atheist and few professed deists, but how many practical ones? men who, whilst they yield a sort of historical belief or assent to divine truths, live in the open and daily disregard of them, and utterly refuse all practical obedience. They cannot impose upon themselves that forbearance, self-denial, and humility enjoined by the author of that religion—their pride and their manhood revolt at that text, which informs them that they must emulate the simplicity of infant innocence ere they can enter the kingdom of Heaven. So, Mr. Chairman, with a large class of our politicians, who, whilst they have not the bold daring to deny the great principles of our political faith, whilst they profess to keep that faith, they refuse all practical obedience. They say the theory is very good—but the pride of intellect and of wealth, that inherent love of distinction in man, that overwhelming self-love, and that pharasaical spirit which induces frail man to plume himself on his own supposed perfections, and to congratulate himself on the infirmities of his fellow-man—revolt at that political equality taught us by the precepts and practice of our forefathers. I like not their theoretical republicanism. I care not for professions unless the precept and the practice correspond —as I will judge the tree by its fruit, as I will judge the

---

[23] Sir Robert Filmer (d. 1653), divine-right theorist, author of *Patriarcha or the Natural Power of Kings* (1680), which was refuted by Locke and Sidney [Ed.].

christian by his works, so I will judge the professor of republicanism by his practice.

Let us now, Mr. Chairman, return to the subject immediately under consideration—the Right of Suffrage—I shall bestow but little time upon the consideration of the question, whether it is a natural, social, civil, or political right—for the inquiry is rather curious than useful. What boots it, if it be a valuable right, whether it be the one or the other? Nor shall I, like other gentlemen have done, resort to any laborious inquiry into the question, whether a state of nature ever in fact existed? I leave this task where those gentlemen have left it, who have endeavoured by most metaphysical arguments to prove it a creature of abstraction. This, however, I will say, that whether it ever did or could exist or not, it is as fair and necessary to suppose its existence, and to assume it as a postulate on which to bottom a political deduction, as for the mathematician to suppose the existence of a straight line on a point, as a postulate on which to found his demonstrations; nor are maxims in politics less useful in practical results to the statesman, than are the axiomata and postulata to the practical geometrician.

What, then, is the Right of Suffrage? Not what gentlemen seem to understand it, in its technical and confined sense, the right to vote for public functionaries only, in a regular organized Government: in its enlarged sense, it is the right by which man first signifies his will to become a member of Government of the social compact—the means by which that same man gives expression to his will in the formation of that compact, his consent to, or his veto upon, measures of the Government in legislation in a pure democracy, as at Athens, and in others of the ancient republics, and some of the modern, or the right of voting for public functionaries as above mentioned, in a Representative Democracy such as ours, where the people do by their agents what they could not conveniently or even possibly do in person. This being its definition then, is it a natural right?

I understand natural rights to mean such as appertain to man in a state of nature; this appertained to him in a state of nature, for it was by its exercise in that state that he agreed to relinquish the natural state and enter into society—But, say the gentlemen, such a state never existed—the consequence is that man has no natural rights, if my definition of natural rights be correct—but the gentlemen admit he has natural rights, life, liberty, the pursuit of happiness, and the means of acquiring and enjoying property. Suffrage is the substratum, the paramount right upon which all these rest for protection, preservation, and safety. This right, as has been very properly said, has its origin in every human being, when he arrives at the age of discretion: it is inherent, and appertains to him in right of his existence; his person is the title deed, unless it be those on whom the same natural law has pronounced judgment of disability, or those who have forfeited it by crime or profligacy; and one other class in this country who must be the victims of necessity, that can never be urged as an example for disfranchising the white man. It is said; that it is forfeitable, and that our exceptions include more than our rule. Life, liberty, &c. are curtailed, restricted, and forfeitable, and subjected to exceptions, yet they are admitted to be natural rights. Natural rights may be transplanted into the social, civil, and political state, yet they are still natural rights. A distinguished statesman has informed us that most of our civil rights have natural rights to rest upon—nor do I think I should be far wrong, were I to assert that all our important rights, whether civil, social, or political, are, properly speaking, natural rights. The exceptions, we all admit to the universality of the right, by which the gentlemen endeavour to overthrow the rule itself, I shall notice a little farther on. But suppose it be not a natural right, it must be one of the other three, and I care not which— why should a majority of freeholders have it in exclusion of a minority of non-freeholders? If the non-freeholders were consulted, and upon the score of expediency voluntarily made the surrender, there would be no cause of complaint on their part— but it is claimed of them as a right. Have they ever been consulted? No. Do you purpose to consult them? No. Then it comes to this, that a minority of one class have taken possession to the exclusion of a majority, not by the consent of that majority, but by consent among themselves, or by accident, or by *jure divino*[24] I suppose, and now claim to hold the possession against the right. Have not the majority as much right to exclude the minority as the minority the majority? Yea, more. But we claim for the poor no right to exclude the rich, for the many no right to exclude the few; we claim only equality (which is equity,) for all, and deny the right of any arbitrarily to exclude the rest. These claims and these denials, I stated in the beginning, to be founded upon reason and common sense, upon our declaration of rights, which is a plain and simple deduction of principles from that paramount source, *right reason*, upon experience, and expediency, the gentlemen's own grounds. . . .

. . . Mr. Chairman, it has been said by the gentleman from Chesterfield, and by other gentlemen, that we derive a rule from the law of nature and the Bill of Rights, in relation to Suffrage, that is in its terms universal, and that we ourselves abandon it, and thereby prove its fallacy: the females, including one half of the population, are disfranchised at one fell swoop; minors, convicts, paupers, slaves, &c., which together, compose a large majority of every community: and hence they argue, that as our rule, if carried out to its extreme results, will not work well, it must be erroneous. For this argument, I have a short answer; it will not do to test any rule by extreme cases. I presume it cannot be necessary for me to assign a reason for the exceptions. In this the gentleman and myself would doubtless agree. He has himself very happily assigned the reason for excluding females; and could assign reasons as

---

[24] (By) divine right [Ed.].

satisfactory for the other exceptions. In the foregoing exceptions we are all agreed. I do not understand any of those excepted classes, as now complaining, nor that any member of the Committee wishes to include them. Why then lug their claims into this debate? . . . But, other discrepancies exist in the arguments which could not have escaped the attention of this Committee. They complain, that by extending Suffrage, you augment the power of the rich; a singular complaint coming from the friends of restricted Suffrage, and most generally, if not always, used by the rich themselves. They say that tenants are not to be trusted, because they will vote for their landlords, or as they direct; the poor will vote for the rich, or as they direct; yet these very same gentlemen claim power in Representation, for the protection of the property of the rich. They disguise the effect of the claim by telling us, they claim it not for individuals, nor counties, but for sections of country; and that the effect of it is, to ascribe power to the poor, in right of their vicinity to wealth, for its protection; in other words, to give them all equal portions of this surplus power reserved on the score of wealth, in trust for the benefit of their rich neighbours. If this be so, why should the gentleman from Chesterfield and his associates, fear the subserviency of the tenant to the landlord, or of the poor to the rich? If they hold power for the benefit of the landlord and the rich, they must either yield to the views of those persons, or set up for themselves; if they set up for themselves and disregard the wishes of the property-holders, they would prove unfaithful trustees, and the object of property Representation would be defeated; if, on the contrary, they should prove subservient, then only could the object of protection be accomplished by the means of property Representation; and the gentleman should, therefore, not complain, of this effect of universal or extended Suffrage. But again: the gentleman, on yesterday, objected to tenants being voters, because, said he, the landlord held them by their very heart-strings; could distrain upon them, sell their last cow, and even the cradle on which their infants reposed. If the gentleman's argument be a good one, I think it will prove too much. I think it will prove that his favourite freehold test, is not quite so good a one as he seems to think, unless there be something in the ownership of land, that by enchantment or magic converts frail erring man, into an infallible and impeccable being. I think all the tests, except those of age and residence, will be found too imperfect to act upon. . . .

. . . Mr. Chairman, will not the reasons assigned by the gentleman from Chesterfield, for the exclusion of tenants, operate in equal degree to exclude his own favorite freeholders? will it not furnish a good reason for excluding every man that is indebted, and for putting the Government in the hands of the creditor class of the community? And if this be the rule of exclusion, how many of the freeholders, think you, will be excluded? I venture to affirm at least one half or three-fourths: is there not that proportion indebted to their neighbours, their merchants, to the Banks, &c., by account, by bond, and by trust deed, or otherwise; and will not a debt have the same influence upon a freeholder, as upon a tenant or other non-freeholders? Indebtedness is, in substance, the reason assigned for excluding the tenant; and can it be a matter of any importance what sort of debt it be, whether it be for rent or any other consideration; whether it be collectable by distress-warrant, or by *fieri facias,* whether the cow or the cradle be sold by the constable, the sheriff, or a trustee or marshal, or whether the person indebted be turned out of possession by notice, to quit if a tenant, or by a *habere facias possessionem,*[25] or *sesinam* [*seisinam*][26] if a mortgaged freeholder? I, therefore, conclude, the gentleman's own rule, tried by his own argu-

---

[25] A writ used to recover the possession of property [Ed.].

[26] Elliptical for *habere facias seisinam,* a writ used to recover the possession of a freehold estate in land by the title holder [Ed.].

ments, would include as much too many voters as it would exclude, improperly, tried by our arguments. The gentleman's argument has evidently on several occasions varied with itself. This has not been the fault of the gentleman's ingenuity or ability, but the fault of the principles he advocates; his premises are wrong; "he has laboured under a cause too light to carry him, and too heavy to be borne by him." . . .

. . . But we are told, if the Right of Suffrage be extended, the rights of property will be invaded: we shall have an agrarian law, tumults, confusion, civil discord, and finally despotism. The only answer I have to make to arguments so derogatory to the dignity of human nature in these United States, is, that twenty-two out of twenty-four sister Republics, many of them situated precisely as we are in relation to slave population, have this Free Suffrage, called by the gentleman Universal, and none of these results have happened, or are likely to happen there, so far as we are informed. Virginia and North Carolina are the only States that adhere to the freehold test, and the latter only in one branch of the Legislature. What length of time the gentleman requires for the fulfilment of his lugubrious prophecies, he has not informed us. Believe me, Sir, it is all speculation and theory, against the rights of man, and we have this advantage, if we are theorists and speculators, we speculate and theorise in favour of equal rights, and our theories and vagaries have been reduced to succesful operation. They have been called on, and cannot shew one case in point: on the contrary, we can triumphantly point to the example of twenty-two Republics, our sisters in this great confederacy of States. . . .

And is Virginia less fit for free Government than her sister States? Would the same causes produce different effects here? In my poor judgment, we are better situated to adopt the principle of extended Suffrage than the free States, according to the gentlemen's own theories. The presence of upwards of four hundred thousand slaves entitled to no political power, and excluding perhaps as many of that class denominated by the gentleman from Chesterfield as peasantry, at once diminishes the number of dangerous voters by that amount, dangerous in the estimation of others, not in mine. In addition to this, we have no overgrown cities—no overgrown manufactory establishments. With a population proverbial for their attachment to law, order, and public tranquillity, I boldly say, if any State in this Union can adopt Free Suffrage with safety, Virginia is that State. The extension of the right does not endanger the tranquillity of election—as the experience of the Eastern States has conclusively proven—and if we adopt it, and pursue the policy now in progress, of establishing precinct or separate elections, we disarm these primary assemblies of any dangerous tendencies to excess, which they may be supposed to have. . . .

. . . Mr. Chairman, the non-freeholders are told they are contending for a shadow—a right, if extended to them, would be of no great importance—that under the old state of things, every thing has gone on well—we have lived happily, and that their complaints are unfounded, and their grievances imaginary. We are told, the owners of the country should govern the country: that the freeholders are the safest depositories of power; that they hold it in their trust for the whole community, and that through them all are virtually represented. My reply to this is, that a man who has no voice in the Government, holds his rights by the sufferance of him who has; and he that thus holds his liberty at the will of another, is already half a slave. Because the non-freeholders have not been hung up without a Judge or Jury—because they have been allowed their civil rights, the gentlemen say they have not been injured. Free negroes are allowed all their civil rights; the non-freeholders no more: and here I would recall to mind a very proper distinction heretofore taken by the gentleman from Orange, (Mr. Barbour,) between civil and political rights. Civil rights may be, often are, and have been, respected and secure under the veriest despotism: and he very properly illustrated his remark by a reference to the reign of Augustus, and many of his successors. I consider the denial to any man of any portion of his political rights, or giving to his neighbour more than his own, an injury of the gravest character. If the right be ideal, existing only in the fancy of men, equally so are many of the possessions men hold dearest—liberty itself, reputation, fair fame, all dearer than life, and the invasion of which inflicts the deepest wound on the peace and happiness of their possessors. But I have shewn sufficient injury done to the non-freeholders, by simply announcing, that a Convention has been called and members delegated to it, without consulting them any more than if they were slaves or free negroes—an example, so far as I am informed, never before set in these United States. . . .

. . . We are told there is a great crisis in our affairs, big with danger to the peace, safety and integrity of the State. I doubt not the sincerity nor the moral courage of those gentlemen, who have admonished us of these dangers; but, Mr. Chairman, I have no faith in these predictions—I am not perturbed by the alarms that have been sounded: the dangers so much dreaded by gentlemen, are the creatures of their own imaginations: that bloody sword which has been brandished over our heads by the gentleman from Hanover (Mr. Morris), reeking with the best blood of the land, has inspired no terror, in my mind; because I trust that his sword, and that of every true Virginian, like the noble Roman's sword, "for their friends have only leaden points,"[27] and that they will never be formidable except to the enemies of the Commonwealth. I trust that ere the time shall arrive to unsheathe a sword to shed each other's blood, "consideration will, like an angel, come to save us from the obloquy."[28] Is it possible that Virginia, of all the

---

[27] Shakespeare's Brutus: "to you our swords have leaden points, Mark Antony" (*Julius Caesar*, Act III, Scene 1, Line 173) [Ed.].

[28] Shakespeare's Archbishop of Canterbury: "Consideration like an angel came" (*King Henry V*, Act I, Scene 1, Line 28) [Ed.].

States in this Union, the birth-place of sons whose sires were foremost in the revolutionary struggle, has not the wisdom and the patriotism to reform her fundamental law without violent revolution and blood-shed—to perform quietly, and without tumult, an act of sovereignty, which even the Cherokee Indians can perform without violence; for, they lately established for themselves a Constitution for their government? For one moment to suppose separation, disunion, or dismemberment possible, is to pronounce a libel upon the wisdom and the patriotism of our constituents. Believe me, Sir, it would be beyond our power to produce such a result, were each of us to return to our constituents, and exert our utmost powers to bring about so calamitous a consummation. In vain would be all our puny efforts to agitate into a tempest the great body of the people. They would remain, in despite of all our efforts, as tranquil as the great ocean, when it is unruffled by the storm—that ocean, whose awful sublimity, the people in their sovereign power and grandeur, so much resemble. . . .

. . . MR. DODDRIDGE—The effort we are making is one, the object of which, is to reform our Constitution, on our own principles, and to give practical effect to those declared in the Bill of Rights. What we contemplate is not a revolution. The Government is an elective Republic, and we mean to leave it so. Yet we are warned of the dangers and horrors of revolution. Revolutions, it is said, never stop at the objects first had in view, but the ball once set in motion, goes downward on the road to anarchy or despotism, and never stops. One false step can never be recalled; the descent to ruin is easy, but to return, difficult, if not impossible: *hoc opus, hic labor est.*[29] Could we forget where we are, and listen to the speeches of gentlemen in opposition, we should forget the business we are engaged in; we should imagine we were listening to Burke on the French Revolution. All the horrors of that volcano are set be-

---

[29] This work is hard work [Ed.].

fore us, as if in our madness, we were ready to plunge into it.
We are likened to the impious priests of France in the last age;
we are called fanatics, dreamers, and even drivellers, by a
gentleman of this city: the history of the ancient Republics is
invoked to alarm us: at one time it is said, that each of these
perished when Suffrage was made general, and Governments
established on the rights of numbers. With much more truth
we are again told, that these Republics with all their temporary Governments, have fallen, without leaving in their
histories any thing for our instruction: the truth is, that neither
in antiquity, nor in the ages succeeding the fall of Rome, were
there any Governments formed on our model; not one. Before
ours, there never existed one Government in the world in which
the whole power was vested in the people, and exercised by
them through their Representatives; in which, powers were
divided between separate and distinct bodies of magistracy,
and in which no nobility or privileged order existed. It is in
vain, therefore, that we are incessantly lectured like school-
boys about the Republics of Greece, Sparta, Lacedaemon,
Rome, and Carthage. In our sense of the term, in the Virginia
sense of it, neither of these was a Republic; they have perished
indeed, as all others of the same age have done; some by war
and conquest, some by one cause, and some by another. Perhaps, among the inscrutable decrees of Providence, there is
one by which all Governments like the men composing them,
are to have a beginning, a maturity, and an end.

. . . Mr. Morgan—There is one other argument which ought
to have some influence on this question. It is one of delicacy,
and I will say but little upon the subject of this argument;
however, I will say something. We find that all the slave-
holding States south of us, deemed it of the utmost importance
to make all the free white men as free and independent, as
Government could make them: and why? Sir, it is known that
all the slave-holding States are fast approaching a crisis truly
alarming: a time when freemen will be needed—when every

man must be at his post. Do we not see the peculiar condition of society? Yes, all see, all feel, and all lament the approach of the crisis before us. It must be in the contemplation of gentlemen, who presume to look upon the progress of events, that the time is not far distant, when not only Virginia, but all the Southern States, must be essentially military; and will have military Governments! It will be so! We are going to such a state of things as fast as time can move. The youth will not only be taught in the arts and sciences, but they will be trained to arms—they must be found at every moment in arms —they must be ready to serve their country in the hour of peril and of danger. Is it not wise now, to call together at least every free white human being, and unite them in the same common interest and Government? Surely it is. Let us give no reason for any to stand back, or refuse their service in the common cause of their country. These considerations had their influence on the Southern States, when forming their Constitutions, I doubt not; and ought to have great influence with us.

Structure and Change

29. The Executive

The debate on the executive branch, November 26, centered on Philip Doddridge's resolution for a governor elected by the people. Philip N. Nicholas stated the conservative position. He was answered by Richard H. Henderson of Loudoun, an ardent reformer who, with John R. Cooke, finally supported the Gordon compromise and cast his vote for the revised constitution. The speeches contrast, rather too neatly perhaps, the old republican fear of a "splendid executive" and the new democratic commitment to an executive authority armed by the will of the people and held responsible to it.

From *Proceedings*, pp. 468–469, 470–473.

MR. NICHOLAS— . . . I take it for granted, that every gentleman would think it proper, to construct the Executive Department on principles suited to republican institutions. The Government from which we were separated by the Revolution, was one which concentrated inordinate authority in the hands of a single Executive Magistrate. The monarch had the powers of war and peace, was the fountain of honour and office, and could increase the House of Peers, who are a body of hereditary nobles, to an unlimited extent. Look at the preamble to your Constitution, which enumerates the causes which induced our ancestors to separate from Great Britain, and you will see, that our revolution was to great extent, founded on the tyrannical and oppressive exercise of the vast powers and prerogatives of the British King. Smarting as our ancestors did, under what they declared to be "a detestable and insupportable tyranny," it was natural as well as proper, that in the Government they were about to establish, they should endeavour to conform the structure of the Executive Department to the genius of a Republic. But, now, we are about, it would seem, to depart from these principles. We are to have a splendid Executive. It is contemplated to vest this authority in a single magistrate; and the appointment to all offices in the gift of this Department, is to be given to him, as some contend, without controul, and as others maintain, with no other check, save the power of rejecting his nominations by the Senate. I am not prepared for this. The gentleman from Monongalia, (Mr. Morgan,) says he is for a feeble Executive. This is not precisely the phrase I would adopt. I wish the Executive to have power enough to execute the laws and no more. I would not invest it with splendor, or extensive patronage, or make it the mark, or instrument of inordinate ambition. Our Executive as at present constituted, is simple and unostentatious. Your Governor is nothing more than a citizen called upon, temporarily, to execute the laws; this done, he returns to the level of the great body of the people. Whilst in office, he has with the advice of the Council all the power which is necessary to give efficacy to your Government. What more can be desired? If you invest all power and extensive patronage in a single magistrate, you create a petty monarchy. The gentlemen who are on the other side of this question, admit the propriety of interposing checks to prevent the abuse of power in the other Departments of Government; but the framers of our Constitution felt that these checks were equally, indeed, more necessary in the Executive. The check they interposed, was the Executive Council. This is a constitutional body, not dependent on the Governor.

The President of the United States has enormous powers and patronage, and he has no constitutional Council. The Constitution authorises him to call for the opinion of the principal officer, in each of the Executive Departments, upon any subject relating to the duties of his office; and usage has erected these officers into what is called the Cabinet. But there is all the difference in the world between such a body, and a Council organized as ours. These Executive officers hold at the will of the President, and he can act without, or contrary to their advice. The Governor can do no important act, without the advice of Council. They not only know his acts, but they understand the motives and secret springs which set these acts in motion. If you entrust power to one man to act in the dark, and without the possibility of determining his motives, you give facilities and temptations to do wrong, you enable him to indulge a spirit of favouritism, and to confer offices, in promotion of objects of personal ambition.

By a constitutional Council, you superadd to the responsibility of the Governor, the means, if not of preventing the formation of improper schemes, yet of their being carried into effect.

But, it is proposed to give the election of Governor to the people. It seems to me, that the power is essentially exercised by the people, when carried into effect by their immediate representatives. Both the Governor and the members of the

Legislature are elected for short periods, which constitutes a sufficient security for the proper exercise of this power of appointment, by those to whom the present Constitution has entrusted it. This is one of those selections for office, which can be best exercised by intermediate agents. It is impossible that the candidates for Governor, can be known but in a very few counties of the State. But, to the members of the Legislature, who are on the scene of action, all the public men of the State, who would be fit for the station, would be known, and they could make the best choice. If the Governor is to be elected by the people at large, they must depend upon the representations made to them of the characters of the candidates. The persons who may make these representations, will, in effect, control the election. In the one case, then, the elections would be made by the representatives of the people, acting under a sense of duty and official responsibility; in the other, by the influence of heated and interested partizans.

But it is said, that the creation of a single Executive magistrate, and vesting his choice in the people, will increase responsibility. Strange, that a large increase of power, and the investiture in a single hand, should have that effect. It is further said, that the existence of the Council destroys all responsibility in the Governor. This is not so. The Governor cannot act without the advice of Council, and that advice is to be spread on their journal, signed by each member, and laid before the Legislature when required; besides, any member may enter his protest. The Governor and Council then, are both responsible; the former for following, or not following their advice, and the latter for that which they give. I beg gentlemen before they adopt a system which gives all power and patronage to one man, and the election of him to the people, to turn their eyes to the operation of this system in our sister States. Look at New York, Pennsylvania and Kentucky. It appears from the debates of the Convention in New York, that before the recent change in her Constitution, about eight thousand offices,

were in the gift of the Executive, including militia appointments, prothonotaries and a multitude of smaller offices. Whenever the election comes round, in some of these States, the
community is convulsed to the centre. Every man is made an
office-hunter and dabbler in elections. As soon as a new Governor is elected, all the incumbents in office go by the board.
And then begins a new struggle, so that the State is kept in
continual ferment and agitation. The inevitable effect of these
systems is, not only to destroy the peace and happiness of the
people, but to undermine their political morality. Under our
plan, the machine of Government works so smoothly, that
whilst our Executive possesses power all-sufficient to execute
the laws, no sensation is felt on the change of the Chief Magistrate, and it is not unlikely that many citizens of the State are
frequently ignorant who the Governor is, unless he happens to
be a man who has acquired distinction in other political
stations.

But it is objected by the gentleman from Brooke, (Mr. Doddridge,) that in giving the election of the Governor to the
Legislature, you violate that valuable political maxim, which
requires the different departments to be kept separate and
distinct. If the gentleman will advert to the forty-seventh Number of the Federalist, in which this subject is discussed, he
will find that the true meaning of the maxim laid down by
Montesquieu, is "that where *the whole power* of one department is exercised by the same hands which possess *the whole
power* of another department, the fundamental principles of a
free Constitution are subverted." And that he did not mean,
"that these departments ought to have no *partial agency in,* or
no controul over, the acts of each other." And this Number
also demonstrates by reference to the British Government, and
the Governments of the different States (to which may be now
added, that of the United States,) that it is extremely difficult,
if not impossible, to prevent the powers of one department
from running into those of another. Besides, how does the

power of appointment of Governor, confer on the Legislature, Executive power in the sense in which the maxim before quoted, can alone apply? As well might it be contended, that the appointment of the Judges, confers on the Legislature, Judicial powers. . . .

. . . MR. HENDERSON—The gentleman from this city, who has just taken his seat, has amused us with something like a declamation upon the topic of a splendid Executive. In this, the gentleman has leaped before he reached the stile. He has invested the Governor with an imaginary splendor; and, having done this, he has very gravely proceeded to prove that this gorgeous pageant ought not to be elected by the people. Now, Sir, this is varying the question in a manner singular enough. We contend that the Governor should be elected by the people; and to prove this political position untrue, we are told that he ought not to be so elected, because he is to be armed with great powers, and arrayed in great magnificence. The presumption is, that this body, in its wisdom, will give to this department of the Government, such powers as are consistent with the interest and honor of the Commonwealth. Thus presuming, we are called upon to decide on the mode of his election. My opinion is, that he ought to be elected by the people, and for the space of three years. I voted for striking out the term of years, conceiving it more regular to test the principle first, and fill the blank afterwards.

Let us then, Mr. Chairman, without heeding nicknames, by which principles are too often prejudiced, proceed with the enquiry. And here, Sir, I venture to assume a ground, the soundness of which may defy criticism, that, *as an individual ought, in no important concern, to do by another what he can as well do by himself, so a people ought not to execute by agency that to which it is competent in its proper original character.* If this be true, then, we have to ascertain whether the citizens at large can perform this duty, as well as their

Legislature, or not. I maintain the affirmative, not only of this proposition, but of the other one; that they can perform it better; and that strong, very strong objections to the action of the Legislature upon the subject, exist. . . .

. . . He who will study the European Governments, and especially that of England, will be struck with the idea, that they are built upon the ground of making the principles of *monarchy, aristocracy,* and *democracy,* conflict with each other in such proportions, as to preserve the energy of the whole. Such is the theory of the British Government. I will not examine it now, in the abstract, or in its supposed aptitude or inaptitude, to the circumstances or character of that or any other people. Suffice it to say, that no American politician ought to resist the declaration, that the theory of our Governments is the *sovereignty of the people,* and the *responsibility of their agents.* And, to maintain this responsibility in its full vigor, the wise men who framed our institutions, have so ordered, that the Legislative and Executive Departments, should emanate *directly from the people themselves.* Thus, each looking to its source, will feel that jealousy of the other, which inspires mutual vigilance, perpetuates liberty, and establishes public security. This is the broad, the vital, the beautiful principle, which stands substitute for the European plan of checks and balances. This it is, that gives to the Governments composing our happy political fraternity, the spirit which assures us, they will not prove disloyal to the societies over which they preside. Remove this responsibility, destroy this laudable and manly jealousy; and, although circumstances may prostrate the existence of free institutions, they are the sport of casualty. It is no answer to this argument, to say, that all the powers of the Government are vested, not in *one man,* but in *many. Many tyrants are not more tolerable than one.* It is against the *principle* of tyranny, that I struggle with, in its *details.* Sir, said Mr. H., I am advancing no novelties. I am the humble echo of the voice of the fathers of the Revolution; the

Statesmen whom Virginia has delighted to honor. Few of those to whom I allude, are gathered to their fathers; another graces, by his venerable presence, the deliberations of this body.

Here Mr. H. read from Jefferson's Notes on Virginia, as follows: "All the powers, Legislative, Executive, and Judiciary, result to the Legislative body. *The concentration of these, in the same hands, is precisely the definition of despotic Government.* It will be no alleviation, that these powers will be exercised by a plurality of hands, and not by a single one. *One hundred and seventy-three Despots, would surely be as oppressive as one.*"

Again: Mr. H. read, "They, [meaning the Legislature] have, accordingly, in many instances, decided rights, which should have been left to Judiciary controversy; and *the direction of the Executive, during the whole time of their session, is becoming habitual and familiar.*"

He then referred to the 47th No. of the Federalist, written by Mr. Madison, and read as follows: "No political truth is of greater intrinsic value, or is stamped with the authority of more enlightened patrons of liberty, than that on which the objection is founded. The accumulation of all powers, Legislative, Executive and Judiciary, in the same hands whether of one, a few, or many, and whether hereditary, self-appointed, or *elective,* may justly be pronounced the very definition of tyranny." Mr. H. here called the attention of the Committee to the 40th No. of the same work, written by the same gentleman, and read as follows: "It is agreed on all sides, that the powers properly belonging to one of the Departments ought not to be directly and completely administered by either of the other Departments. It is equally evident, that in reference to each other, neither of them ought to possess, directly or indirectly, *an overruling influence* in the administration of their respective powers." Mr. H. then referred to the 51st No. of the Federalist, written by General Hamilton, and read as follows: "In order to lay a due foundation for that separate and distinct exercise of the different powers of Government, which, to a certain extent, is admitted to be essential to the preservation of liberty, it is evident that each Department should have *a will of its own;* and, consequently, should be so constituted, that the members of each should have *as little agency as possible in the appointment of the members of the others.*"

. . . I ask, Sir, if my doctrine is not fully borne out by the writings of those great men, who, however they may have differed on other subjects, all unite in proclaiming the principles of the *sovereignty of the people,* the separation of the different Departments of Government, and their *independence of each other,* the folly and danger *of permitting the one Department to appoint the other,* and that to allow one an undue influence *indirectly,* is equivalent to a *direct* control. These, Sir, are the springs of republican Government, its vital elements, the pledges of its durability, the rock of its safety.

Mr. Chairman: Gentlemen in the face of one of the greatest men in America, the political patriarch of Virginia, over the ashes of his illustrious compatriots, persist in denying these great political truths. They pronounce our Governors wise and good, and challenge us, to specify acts of official abuse or turpitude. Surrounded as we are by gentlemen who have acted in the affairs of the Executive; mingling as many of these respectable gentlemen do in our deliberations, shall we perform the invidious and painful office to which we are invited? And for what? We are not scanning the official conduct of any body. We came here on no such errand. Their acts are embodied in the history of the Commonwealth: the citizens know them well. In the year 1781, Thomas Jefferson prepared his Notes. He had recently filled the Chair of Governor, and knew better than any man in the State, the action of the Legislature on the Executive. What does he say? That the direction of the Executive by the Legislature was *habitual* and *familiar.* He had felt it. This is history, not speculation. It proves that your *Governor has no will of his own;* that he is the creature of the Legislature; a very man of straw.

The gentleman to whose remarks I have heretofore alluded, gave us a fine picture of Executive excellence; and finished it by informing us, that so harmless an Executive had we, that *a great portion of the people actually did not know who the Governor was.* Is this desirable? A free people, professing to be intelligent, and to take an interest in their *own affairs,* not to know who their Governor is! and to be felicitated upon it in this assemblage. Truly, the gentleman has placed the sovereign people in a most dreamy and beatified state! Sir, I wish to arouse them from their unmanly torpor. I wish, Sir, that the people *may* know their Governor, and that the Governor may *know the people.* Mr. Jefferson in his Notes, states, "in December, 1776, our circumstances being much distressed, it was proposed in the House of Delegates to create a *Dictator,* invested with every power, Legislative, Executive, and Judiciary, civil and military, of life and death, over our own persons and over our own properties; and in June, 1781, again under calamity, the same proposition was repeated, *and wanted a few votes only of being passed.*" Is there a living man who will doubt the wisdom and patriotism of the Legislatures of 1776, and 1781? Surely the gentleman from Chesterfield [Mr. Leigh], who seems so confident that we can give no good reasons for the course we recommend, is not that man. The cause, then, of this most extraordinary and appalling project of clothing one man with absolute despotism, *in order that the Republic might receive no harm,* is to be found in the utter imbecility of the Executive Department of the Government. Any other supposition, imputes treason against the freedom of the people, to the fathers of the Revolution. Are we, in the teeth of reason, against the advice of the wise, the warnings of history, to continue an Executive utterly incompetent? An Executive for the "piping times of peace," that will tremble to its centre when war blows its blast? A fair-weather Government, that may be wrecked on the first billow of the tempest? I trust not, Sir. No, let us embark our fortunes in a vessel that will ride proudly amidst the roarings of the storm, and bear unshaken, that broad pendant of freedom under the lightening's flash.

Mr. Chairman,—I am not a gloomy politician; on the contrary, I hope the best of men and things; but I cannot shut my ears to what passes around me. An able gentleman told us, we ought to prepare for a state of affairs within the scope of possibility, and to which all good men look with mournful apprehension. The day may come, when Virginia may be compelled to take her rank amongst the nations of the earth. Suppose a scene of turmoil, of peril, is there a man of sense in the Commonwealth, who would rest securely, at such a crisis, on an Executive constructed like ours? Let us, for Heaven's sake, frame such a Government as will bring out and wield the energies of the whole people, when the fortune of war imperiously demands it. Again, Sir; the very term *Legislature* indicates the appropriate functions of the body. It is no part of that duty to elect the Executive. How many, how various, how difficult the subjects of legislation! What labour, reflection, devotion, and sober-minded men are necessary to do justice to them? Surely, our law-givers have ample employment, if confined within their legitimate sphere. We all know how the passions, intrigues, combinations, incident to these elections, agitate any body of men, and unfit them for that cool though accurate analysis, and profound research, so indispensable to public usefulness in this great department. I appeal to the people of Virginia, if the past is not a lucid commentary upon this doctrine. Some gentlemen are so very tender of the public repose, that they would not expose the people to the agitations arising from the election of their Governor. Sir, I maintain that a moderate exercise of the public mind, has a most salutary effect in instructing the people, in habituating them to think of their rights and interests, and in preserving that vigilance and self-respect, which are the strength and glory of a Republic. The people will not thank gentlemen for consulting their *case* by curtailing their *rights*. I am not one of those zealous and minute politicians, who would continually teaze the citizens of the country with the election of constables and all the little machinery of place. I despise it; I will not

> "*Ocean into tempest work,*
> *To waft a feather, or to drown a fly.*"[30]

But the great Legislative and Executive Departments of Government ought to be elected, not by each other, but by the people themselves.

The gentleman from this city told us, that the citizens elected the Legislature, and the Legislature the Governor; and that, therefore, the citizens elected the Governor. Sir, this is very good doctrine at that forum where the gentleman plays an eminent part; but he will not be able to satisfy the common sense of his fellow-citizens by this political special pleading. And he will permit me to express my surprise, that he should so far play upon their credulity, as to present them a law-adage in lieu of their political privileges. We are informed, that our Councillors are endued with great wisdom and efficiency. It may be so. But I remain to learn that they are the superiors, or the peers of the Attorney General and Auditor of Public Accounts. At any rate, we certainly can provide an inexpensive and dignified advisory Council. It is objected, that we are about to confide the interesting prerogative of mercy to a single man. Why so? May we not provide, that advice shall be taken under our plan as well as under that the abolition of which we seek?

---

[30] Edward Young "Night," *Night Thoughts*, Part I, Lines 153–154.
    Ocean into Tempest Wrought
    To waft a feather or to drown a fly.
[Ed.].

30. The County Courts

In the debate on the county courts, December 1, the Reverend Alexander Campbell made the principal plea for their reform. From the same northwestern county as Philip Doddridge, Campbell is well-known to history as the founder and leader of the Disciples of Christ, a great new Protestant denomination born of the American frontier. John Randolph had the habit of answering his opponents' arguments with sneers, invective, and anecdote; in the present instance he entertained the delegates with a piece of apocrypha about Thomas Jefferson. In the miseries of his old age Randolph constantly reflected on the degeneracy of Virginia, and he thought Jefferson, with his "visionary" ideas, the principal culprit. Viewing the county court system and the freehold suffrage as the two remaining pillars of the political edifice, he was determined to maintain them.

Mr. Campbell—. . .Without hazarding any thing, I think, Sir, I may say, more of the happiness of this Commonwealth, depends upon the County Government under which we live, than upon the State or United States' Government. The more we circumscribe the supervision of any tribunal, the more interest we feel in it, and the more happiness or misery it bestows upon us. The more you enlarge it, the less interest. And, therefore, I venture to affirm, that no question which has been discussed in this Committee, is more intimately allied to our interests, or more conducive to our political happiness or misery, than the very question now before us. What Government is that, Sir, which has the greatest power to afflict us, or make us happy? It is that, Sir, which has the most limited jurisdiction; it is the tribunal of our own conscience. . . . Self-government, the government of our own passions, appetites, and propensities, more than any other Government, contributes

From *Proceedings*, pp. 526–530, 532–533.

to our individual happiness. Next to this, *family* government. We derive much of our social happiness from domestic government; because we are always under its influence. For the same reasons we are more interested in the County Government than in the State, or United States' Government, and more of our happiness depends upon it, than upon any other. Not merely, because it is nigher home, but because we have more to do with it, or under its jurisdiction. All the laws of the Commonwealth, reach us through the County Government. No matter whence the laws are promulged, they first reach us through the county tribunals.

Now, Sir, the citizens of any county in this Commonwealth, have no more control over these tribunals, than they have over the Government of France or England. They never created the officers who preside on the benches of the County Courts, nor the ministers who execute their decisions. We live under a Government not amenable to us, not *responsible* to us; because not created by us. The objections to these tribunals, arise from the *manner* in which they are created, from their incompetency to discharge those duties assigned them, and the consequent evil influence which they may exercise over the destinies of a county.

I heard, with much regret, the gentleman from Frederick, (Mr. Powell,) rise to sustain them: I say regret, because I have heard him with pleasure support the most Republican principles on this floor. But, how to reconcile these tribunals with Republican Government, I know not. At best, they are [an] elective, and most generally terminate in a *hereditary* aristocracy. How a republican can advocate a system, which, forever, puts a county under the control of a few individuals, without a perfect abandonment of his creed, I am unable to perceive. And is not, Mr. Chairman, every county in this Commonwealth, by the system, necessarily subjected to the government of a few individuals by a legal investment?

Let us, for example, place before us, the erection of a new

county. A new county and a new court are by the same authority at once erected. Some four or five justices are assigned to the bench of this new county, and the county assigned to them. These justices are to nominate their *successors forever*. Thus the county is by an act of incorporation, or a charter, or by whatever instrument you may please to call it, signed, sealed, and delivered over to the four or five magistrates first appointed and their successors, as far as all the offices of trust, honor, and profit, as far as the public concerns and interests, as far as the public levies and their appropriations are concerned, or assignable; they are all given over by one general deed of gift to these justices, and their successors forever. . . .

. . . Next to the manner of creating these tribunals, the variety of powers and functions which are lodged in the same hands, and their incompatibility with each other, have been for a long time an object of serious and just complaint. These are fully exposed in the very learned dissertations of a highly respectable authority, (Judge St. Geo. Tucker). I do not quote his words, but I think I give the substance: Justices of the bench, says he, as such, may be elected to either branch of the Legislature, and are very frequently elected to the House of Delegates. While the character of the justice is merged in that of the Legislator, he is under the present system, Constitutionally authorised to legislate for himself. He may enact the law under which he chooses to officiate at home, and thus, make his own office, what he wishes it to be. He can also in part create the Governor, who, is afterwards to appoint and commission such of his friends as he may nominate to fill vacancies on the bench. He may also assist, in creating the Judges of the Supreme Courts, who, are to judge of his official proceedings. As Legislator, he may create Major and Brigadier Generals from amongst his friends upon the bench, if he pleases. Under the present system, he may, and in part does, create, and govern all the State officers, from the Treasurer down to the State Attorney in his own county.

When on the bench at home, they are judges in all cases of life and death, when a slave is to be tried, and of all offences under the grade of felony. They constitute an Examining Court, when any free person is brought before them accused of any crime amounting to felony at common law, and may remand him for a trial to the District Court, or discharge him as they think proper. They are also judges in all other civil causes arising within the county, whatever may be the amount, both at common law and equity, and without appeal when the sum is not over ten dollars.

As police officers, they open roads, build bridges, erect prisons, and court houses; and levy the expenses thereof upon the county; and last of all, recommend to the Executive, whom they are willing to admit into their own body.

At one and the same time, they may be the Judges of the County Courts, military officers of any rank whatever, State Legislators and members of Congress. They, in short, unite in their own persons all sorts of powers, Legislative, Executive, Judicial, military; and if all these can be safely lodged in the same hands, and at the same time, then it must follow, and undeniably too, that all the doctrines on which our political system is founded are erroneous and fallacious.

May I not ask, Sir, what are the fundamental doctrines of our Government? Is not the following one of them? "All power is vested in and consequently derived from the people. Magistrates are their trustees and servants, and at all times *amenable* to them." When did the justices of the peace derive their power from the people; and how, or in what sense are they responsible or *amenable* to them? Why then hold this doctrine to be true, and deny it in practice? I must always recur to fundamental principles, for one good reason, because I cannot reason without them. If I mistake not, it is written in the sixth article of our Bill of Rights, that no persons in this Commonwealth, "ought to be taxed, or deprived of their property for public uses, without their own consent or that of their Representative elected by them." This is deemed essential to the liberty and happiness of our community. Now, I ask, do not the magistrates composing the County Courts tax us, and deprive us of our property for public uses without our consent, or that of our Representatives? When did we authorise them, by any act of ours, to levy taxes upon us? They have no more right to tax us, by any act of ours, nor according to the doctrine just now *quoted*, than we have in this Convention to tax the citizens of Ohio. It is, in my humble opinion, as real a grievance of which we complain, resulting to us from this system, as was the complaint of this Commonwealth when a Colony, against the right usurped by the English Government, to tax us without our own consent, or that of our Representatives.

Does not another of our political maxims teach—"that no man, or set of men, are entitled to *exclusive*, or separate emoluments or privileges from the community, but in consideration of public services, which, not being descendible, neither ought the offices of magistrate, Legislator, or Judge, to be *hereditary?*" Does not the County Court system virtually repudiate this maxim? Does not the system confer *exclusive* privileges, without, and anterior to any public services? And does it not tend to make the magistracy *hereditary* in certain families?

But again, does not the third article of the Constitution, the existing Constitution of this Commonwealth, declare, that "the Legislative, Executive, and Judiciary Departments of Government, shall be separate and distinct, so that neither exercise the powers properly belonging to the other; nor shall ever any person exercise the powers of more than one of them." This is clear and express. But mark what follows—"Except that the justices of the County Courts shall be eligible to either House of Assembly." This arbitrary exception shews, that it is not compatible with the doctrine of the framers of the old Constitution. They saw it was incompatible with the truth which they had propounded, and declared it an *exception*. Why was the exception made? Tradition informs us, that most of the influential men, in what is now called Virginia, at the time of the Revolution, were magistrates on the bench; and if proscribed from the Legislative Hall, it would have endangered the great cause of liberty and the rights of man; and as Virginia wished to rally all her forces and to concentrate all her energies, she was willing to make an exception in favour of the magistrates of that day. But they declared it an *inconsistency,* and so it is. Attached to such a declaration, it is as incongruous, as if to a series of laws prohibiting murder, it were added, "but killing a man is not murder." But time has consecrated the *exception,* and the error equally with the principle; and many are as tenacious now of the exception as they are, yes, more than they are of *the principle* from which it is an exception. However well it may have operated at that time, during the struggle for independence, it has not operated so well since.

The Constitution gave the magistrates no reward whatever for their services. But in making them eligible to the General Assembly, it put it in their power to provide for themselves, which they have since done. It is known, I presume, to every member of this Committee, that generally a quorum, and often a majority of the House of Delegates, is composed of magistrates, sheriffs, and their deputies. Tradition informs us, that such a Legislative body found it easy to seize the sheriffalty and to attach it to their own office, or to secure it by way of an indirect compensation for their services, so indirect as not to disqualify them from being eligible to the office of Legislators. In this way they dispense justice for nothing! In this way they compensate themselves! Thus, too, the sheriffs are irresponsible to the people, and this has been a grievance at least from the days of Patrick Henry, who gives them the following admirable character in one of his speeches in the Convention which ratified the Federal Constitution. "Our State sheriffs," says he, "those unfeeling blood-suckers, have under the watchful eye of the Legislature, committed the most horrid and barbarous ravages upon our people. It has required the constant vigilance of the Legislature, to keep them from totally ruining the people. A repeated succession of laws has been made to suppress their iniquitous speculations and cruel extortions, and as often has their nefarious ingenuity devised methods of evading these laws." Such was the character of the sheriffs in those days, in the opinion of one of Virginia's most distinguished men. It must often be so, when public functionaries are not responsible to the people.

But we love a cheap magistracy, and the justices serve for nothing! It is true, they only divide among them, between 50 and 60,000 dollars per annum, in the way of sheriffs' fees. Valuing the one hundred and five sheriffalties in this Commonwealth at 500 dollars per annum, we can easily estimate what serving for *nothing* means, when applied to our present system. They are paid in the most exceptionable way, and it is all one and the same, whether they receive the amount of the sheriffalty in succession, or divide it annually amongst them according to their services; it is still *in principle* a compensation, and the office of justice is so far *lucrative*. . . .

. . . Time was, when Montesquieu was considered as high authority in matters of this sort; and what does Montesquieu say of the principle on which our County Courts are founded? His words are, "In a Republic, if any body of magistracy, have the power of *filling vacancies* occurring in their own body, or of appointing their own successors; if they once become corrupt, which in all probability will be the case, the evil will become *incurable*, because corrupt men will appoint *corrupt successors*." Is this true or is it false? Is it entitled to no weight; to no consideration on this question? I think it is. If, let me ask, one body of Judges may appoint their own successors, why may not another body? Why not then permit the Judges of the Inferior Courts, of the Court of Appeals, to appoint their own successors? Certainly they are as competent as the judges of the County Courts! I might here appeal to; nay, I might ask the venerable gentleman from Richmond, the Chief Justice of these United States, would he, with all his wisdom and experience, undertake to appoint his successor? and if not, would he sanction and consecrate this principle and this practice, in any other body of Judges?

But some gentlemen eulogize these tribunals and the whole system as the wisest in the world. One thing only is wanting to give them the highest dignity, and to entitle them to the unqualified approbation of some, and that would seem to be, to invest them with the power of filling all vacancies in the Legislative Assemblies; to give them the right to elect all our Representatives. This they virtually do in some instances already, by the *exclusive* privileges which they now possess. But to invest them with this exclusive privilege, would prevent those tumults and cabals attendant on elections, and thus give perfect peace to the Commonwealth!

But, I have yet to learn, why the corporate towns in this Commonwealth, Richmond, Petersburg, Norfolk, &c. can elect their magistrates, who are at least as well qualified judges as any in the Commonwealth, and why the counties of Ohio, and Brooke, and other counties in the State cannot do the same? The only relevant reasons which I have as yet heard assigned, why the Legislature should elect the Judges of the supreme tribunals, is, because the people do not always, cannot always, know the claims of the aspirants or candidates. If this be good logic or good sense, it will prove that the counties ought to elect their own magistrates, because they can know them better than any persons living out of the counties; and the recommendation of a whole ward of qualified voters, is better evidence to the chief Executive of their competency, than is the recommendation of a few, *perhaps* interested magistrates. I am for reposing the greatest confidence in the people. The power is safely lodged in their hands; more safely, I am sure, than in a few privileged ones, whom they never appointed their *trustees. . . .*

. . . Mr. Randolph— . . . In the course of my life I have repeatedly been called upon by various eminent men, to explain to them the system of Government in this Commonwealth; and I never knew a single individual of the number, who was not struck with admiration at the structure of our County Court system. I have been asked, whether it was the effect of design, or of one of those fortunate combinations of circumstances, which enabled its framers to "snatch a grace beyond the reach of art."[31] Whether it was design or chance, one thing is certain, that the plan has proved in practice, to be one of the very best which the wit of man could have devised for this Commonwealth; preserving in the happiest manner, a just administration of our affairs, between the instability attendant upon popular elections, and the corruption or oppression of Executive patronage. It insures to us, that the power of the Commonwealth will always be in the hands of good and lawful men. I never met an individual who cursed the appointment of Jackson, or a Federalist, when Federalism was uppermost, or a Republican, when it was downmost, who did not express envy at this feature of our polity. Virginia stands between Scylla and Charybdis. We must have magistrates appointed by the people or by the Executive, (unless the present mode be continued). Suppose by the people. Then, in a cause between a man of great influence, popularity, and power —and a poor man,—he that is poor will have no chance of justice. If they are appointed by the Executive, it must be by recommendation:—but of what sort? Such as prevails at Washington? (thank God no man ever dared to approach me, for my name to one of them,) recommendations obtained by cabal and intrigue?—and after all—you must be doomed to instability—yes, to utter instability. At present the Government of each county, is in, hands best fitted for it. The gentleman from Chesterfield [Mr. Leigh], in enumerating so ably and clearly

---

[31] Alexander Pope, *Essay on Criticism*, Line 153 [Ed.].

the Herculean labours of their office, has truly said, that they step in between the accused and the Commonwealth in all cases, where the crime is not so great as to be sent on to the higher courts. Their mode of appointment may be an anomaly —but I consider it the most valuable feature of the system.

If we abandon this, we must resort to infamous jobbers and trading justices; who will foment instead of allaying village quarrels. If you will strike the pettifogger out of existence, you shall have my vote most heartily. It can be done thus alone. But there are some (I speak, of course, of those *out* of this House,) who delight to excite clamour—who long to suck blood—and raise popular commotion;—who want to be Judges and justices, because the people refuse them a livelihood as lawyers. I was pained and surprised at the description given, by the gentleman from Loudoun,[32] of drunken justices. I had thought there were none of such a description; but the testimony is given by a respectable gentleman—and in his county, the fact must be so. I bless God it is so no where else. Our justices are not so ignorant as he imagines—my confidence is infinitely greater in County Courts than in the Superior Courts. The bench of the latter is filled too often by lawyers—who can't get a livelihood at the bar. I speak not of Judges in general. But the gentleman says, that when he wants a pair of boots, he goes to a skilful boot-maker: but, Sir, when I want either boots or a Constitution, I will go to capable workmen, and not to cobblers.

---

[32] Richard H. Henderson, who, in answer to the praise of the courts as "admirable machines for the diffusion of political information," said: "In my humble opinion, they are better calculated, much better, for the diffusion of intemperance amongst the people. A Court-house or a tavern is a poor political lecture-room. . . . Establish good schools. Educate your people, and they will become politicians fast enough, without giving you the trouble to make courts to render them so. The true interest of individuals, as well as of the community, is to interrupt the people as little as possible in their pursuits of industry, and their domestic quiet and purity. Frequent assemblages, in large numbers, with little business, lead to drunkenness and vice." [Ed.].

Great stress has been laid on the opinion of Mr. Jefferson, by a gentleman not now in his place. Sir, the opinion of Mr. Jefferson comes strangely from him. He has gone beyond the Ganges into the uttermost East. But I have no hesitation to say, that on a subject like this, I have not much deference for the opinion of Mr. Jefferson. We all know he was very confident in his theories—but I am a practical man and have no confidence *a priori* in the theories of Mr. Jefferson, or of any other man under the sun.

Not an argument has been advanced against County Courts, but would be equally good *a priori* against jury-trial. What could have taught us its value, but experience? *A priori*, it seems absurd to trust a dozen ploughmen—good and lawful of the vicinage I grant, but still ploughmen—with a point of law in criminal cases, without appeal—and in civil cases under circumstances almost equivalent. We can hardly conceive any thing more ridiculous in theory—yet we find none half so valuable in practice:—So vain is it to argue against fact. I once witnessed a contest of argument against fact; and if it will relieve the oppression and ennui of this debate, I will relate it: I saw one of the best and worthiest men on a visit at some distance from home, urging his lady to make preparation to ride, for "the Sun was down"—His lady said, "the Sun was not down." Her lord gravely replied, "the Sun sets at half past six: it is now past that time." (Every man's watch is right and his was in his hand.) The company looked out of the window and saw the Sun in all his blaze of glory—but the Sun ought to have been down, as fleas ought to have been lobsters. The Sun, however, was not down, and fleas are not lobsters: whether it be because they have not souls, I leave to St. Jerome and the Bishops to settle.

We are not to be struck down by the authority of Mr. Jefferson. Sir, if there be any point in which the authority of Mr. Jefferson might be considered as valid, it is in the mechanism of a plough. He once mathematically and geometrically demonstrated the form of a mould-board which should present the least resistance: his mould-board was sent to Paris, to the *Savants*—it was exhibited to all the visitors at the Garden of Plants. The *Savants* all declared *una voce*[33] that this was the best mould-board that had ever been devised. They did not decree to Mr. Jefferson the honors of Hermes Trismegistus, but they cast his mould-board in plaister; and there it remains an eternal proof, that this form of mould-board presents less resistance than any other on the face of the earth. Some time after, an adversary brought into Virginia the Carey plough; but it was such an awkward ill-looking thing, that it would not sell: at length some one tried it, and though its mould-board was not that of least resistance, it beat Mr. Jefferson's plough as much as common sense will always beat theory and reveries. Now there is not in Virginia, I believe, one plough with the *mould-board of least resistance*. I have had some experience in its use, and find it the handsomest plough to draw I ever saw. So much for authority!

Sir, when we shall have given up County Courts, and jury-trial, and Freehold Suffrage, there will be nothing in the Commonwealth worth attention to any one of practical sense. The County Courts hold the just balance between popular mutability, (the opprobrium and danger of all popular systems) on the one hand, and Executive patronage, on the other. I said before that there must be recommendation of some sort. Quaere then, which is better? that it shall be made openly by the justices when assembled, on notice, or by a private letter? Sir, I am for a strict adherence to the anchorage ground of the Constitution: it has hitherto kept the Commonwealth from swinging from its moorings: when it shall drag its anchors, or slip its cable, God knows what will become of the vessel of State. But my hand may not be wanting at the plough. If gentlemen succeed in introducing the newest, theoretical, pure, defecated

---

[33] With one voice, i.e., unanimously [Ed.].

Jacobinism into this Commonwealth, I do upon my soul believe, they will have inflicted a deeper wound on Republican Government, than it ever experienced before.

31. The Amendment Article

The reform program called for the addition of an amendment article to the constitution. Near the close of the convention a resolution from the bill of rights committee, which also had jurisdiction over miscellaneous matters, finally came to the floor. John Randolph at once rose to speak against it. Without further ado, the delegates voted 25 to 68 to kill the resolution. The precipitancy of the decision and the size of the majority were surprising. It might have been expected that western delegates would place great weight on an article permitting future amendments. But either they were intimidated by the gentleman from Charlotte or they saw little value in the amendment process.

Mr. President—I shall vote against this resolution: and I will state as succinctly as I can, my reasons for doing so. I believe that they will, in substance, be found in a very old book, and conveyed in these words "sufficient unto the day, is the evil thereof."[34] Sir, I have remarked since the commencement of our deliberations—and with no small surprise—a very great anxiety to provide for *futurity*. Gentlemen, for example, are not content with any present discussion of the Constitution, unless

---

From *Proceedings,* pp. 789–791.

[34] The full quotation is "Take therefore no thought for the morrow; for the morrow shall take thought for the things of itself. Sufficient unto the day is the evil thereof" (Matthew 6:34) [Ed.].

we will consent to prescribe for all time hereafter. I had always thought him the most skilful physician, who, when called to a patient, relieved him of the existing malady, without undertaking to prescribe for such as he might by possibility endure thereafter.

Sir, said Mr. R. what is the amount of this provision? It is either mischievous, or it is nugatory. I do not know a greater calamity that can happen to any nation, than having the foundations of its Government unsettled.

Dr. Franklin, who, in shrewdness, especially in all that related to domestic life, was never excelled, used to say, that two movings were equal to one fire. So to any people, two Constitutions are worse than a fire. And gentlemen, as if they were afraid that this besetting sin of Republican Governments, this *rerum novarum lubido*,[35] (to use a very homely phrase, but one that comes pat to the purpose,) this *maggot* of innovation, would cease to bite, are here gravely making provision, that this Constitution, which we should consider as a remedy for all the ills of the body politic, may itself be amended or modified at any future time. Sir, I am against any such provision. I should as soon think of introducing into a marriage contract a provision for divorce; and thus poisoning the greatest blessing of mankind at its very source—at its fountain head. He has seen little, and has reflected less, who does not know that "necessity" is the great, powerful, governing principle of affairs here. Sir, I am not going into that question which puzzled Pandoemonium, the question of liberty and necessity.

"Free will, fix'd fate, foreknowledge, absolute;"[36]

---

[35] Desire for new things [Ed.].

[36] Milton, *Paradise Lost*, Book II, Line 557. The full quotation is:
> Others apart sat on a hill retir'd,
> In thoughts more elevate, and reason'd high
> Of providence, foreknowledge, will and fate.
> Fix'd fate, free-will, foreknowledge absolute;
> And found no end, in wand'ring mazes lost.

[Ed.]

but, I do contend, that necessity is one principal instrument of all the good that man enjoys.

The happiness of the connubial union itself depends greatly on necessity; and when you touch this, you touch the arch, the key-stone of the arch, on which the happiness and well-being of society is founded.

Look at the relation of master and slave; (that opprobrium, in the opinion of some gentlemen, to all civilized society and all free Government). Sir, there are few situations in life where friendships so strong and so lasting are formed, as in that very relation. The slave knows that he is bound, indissolubly, to his master, and must from necessity, remain always under his controul. The master knows that he is bound to maintain and provide for his slave so long as he retains him in his possession. And each party accommodates himself to his situation. I have seen the dissolution of many friendships, such, at least, as were so called; but I have seen that of master and slave endure so long as there remained a drop of the blood of the master to which the slave could cleave. Where is the necessity of this provision in the Constitution? Where is the use of it? Sir, what are we about? Have we not been undoing what the wiser heads —I must be permitted to say so—yes, Sir, what the wiser heads of our ancestors did more than half a century ago? Can any one believe that we, by any amendments of ours—by any of our scribbling on that parchment—by any amulet—any leger-demain—charm—abracadabra—of ours, can prevent our sons from doing the same thing? that is, from doing as they please, just as we are doing as we please? It is impossible. Who can bind posterity? When I hear gentlemen talk of making a Constitution "for all time"—and introducing provisions into it, "for all time"—and yet see men here, that are older than the Constitution we are about to destroy—(I am older myself than the present Constitution—it was established when I was a boy)—it reminds me of the truces and the peaces in Europe. They always begin, "In the name of the most holy and undivided

Trinity," and go on to declare, "there shall be perfect and perpetual peace and unity between the subjects of such and such potentates, for all time to come"—and, in less than seven years, they are at war again.

Sir, I am not a prophet or a seer; but I will venture to predict, that your new Constitution, if it shall be adopted—does not last twenty years. And so confident am I in this opinion, that if it were a proper subject for betting, and I was a sporting character, I believe I would *take ten* against it.[37]

It would seem as if we were endeavouring—(God forbid that I should insinuate, that such was the intention of any here)—as if we were endeavouring to corrupt the people at the fountain head. Sir, the great opprobrium of popular Government, is its *instability*. It was this which made the people of our Anglo-Saxon stock cling with such pertinacity to an independent Judiciary, as the only means they could find to resist this vice of popular Governments. By such a provision as this, we are now inviting, and in a manner prompting the people, to be dissatisfied with their Government. Sir, there is no need of this. Dissatisfaction will come, soon enough. I foretell now, and with a confidence surpassed by none I ever felt on any occasion, that those who have been the most anxious to destroy the Constitution of Virginia, and to substitute in its place this *thing* will not be more dissatisfied now with the result of our labours, than this new Constitution will very shortly be opposed by all the people of the State. I speak not at random. I have high authority for what I say now in my eye. Though it was said that the people called for a new state of things, yet the gentleman from Brooke himself (Mr. Doddridge) who came into the Legislative Committee armed with an axe to lay at the root of the tree, told the Convention that he would sooner go home and live under the old Constitution than adopt some of the provisions which have received the sanction of this body. But I am wandering from the point.

---

[37] Give 10–1 odds [Ed.].

Sir, I see no wisdom in making this provision for future changes. You must give Governments time to operate on the people, and give the people time to become gradually assimilated to their institutions. Almost any thing is better than this state of perpetual uncertainty. A people may have the best form of Government that the wit of man ever devised; and yet, from its uncertainty alone, may, in effect, live under the worst Government in the world. Sir, how often must I repeat, that *change* is not *reform*. I am willing that this new Constitution shall stand as long as it is possible for it to stand, and that, believe me, is a very short time. Sir, it is vain to deny it. They may say what they please about the old Constitution—the defect is not there. It is not in the form of the old edifice, neither in the design nor the elevation: it is in the *material*— it is in the people of Virginia. To my knowledge that people are changed from what they have been. The four hundred men who went out to David were in *debt*. The partizans of Caesar were in *debt*. The fellow-labourers of Cataline were in *debt*. And I defy you to shew me a desperately indebted people any where, who can bear a regular sober Government. I throw the challenge to all who hear me. I say that the character of the good old Virginia planter—the man who owned from five to twenty slaves, or less, who lived by hard work, and who paid his debts, is passed away. A new order of things is come. The period has arrived of living by one's wits—of living by contracting debts that one cannot pay—and above all, of living by office-hunting. Sir, what do we see? Bankrupts— branded bankrupts—giving great dinners—sending their children to the most expensive schools—giving grand parties—and just as well received as any body in society. I say, that in such a state of things, the old Constitution was too good for them, they could not bear it. No, Sir, they could not bear a freehold suffrage and a property representation. I have always endeavoured to do the people justice—but I will not flatter them—I will not pander to their appetite for change. I will do nothing to provide for change. I will not agree to any rule of future apportionment, or to any provision for future changes called amendments to the Constitution. They who love change—who delight in public confusion—who wish to feed the cauldron and make it bubble—may vote if they please for future changes. But by what spell—by what formula are you going to bind the people to all future time? *Quis custodiet custodes?*[38] The days of Lycurgus are gone by, when he could swear the people not to alter the Constitution until he should return —*animo non revertendi* [*sic*].[39] You may make what entries upon parchment you please. Give me a Constitution that will last for half a century—that is all I wish for. No Constitution that you can make will last the one-half a century. Sir, I will stake any thing short of my salvation, that those who are malcontent now will be more malcontent three years hence than they are at this day. I have no favour for this Constitution. I shall vote against its adoption, and I shall advise all the people of my district to set their faces—aye—and their shoulders against it. But if we are to have it—let us not have it with its death warrant in its very face: with the *facies hypocratica*[40]— the Sardonic grin of death upon its countenance.

32. The Question of Ratification

John Randolph's speech may be read as the final testament of conservatism in the convention. Still later, on the last day, he attempted to persuade the delegates to provide for ratification of the revised constitution by the existing electorate. In this, he failed. Leaving

---

38 Who would guard the guardians? [Ed.].

39 His mind not to be changed [Ed.].

40 Hippocratic face, the face named by Hippocrates; the face as it appears after death, long sickness, excessive hunger, etc. [Ed.].

aside the technical aspects of the question, it involved the determination of whether the power to establish a constitution belongs to the electorate in being or to the potential electorate. The latter, of course, was the more democratic position, though it did not follow the doctrine of popular sovereignty to its logical conclusion—the admission of all the people to the exercise of constituent power. Lucas P. Thompson answered Randolph. A portion of his speech suggests the feelings of the reform party as the convention drew to a close.

MR. THOMPSON said he was constrained by an imperious sense of duty, to trespass (he hoped for the last time) upon the patience and attention of this Convention, for the purpose of expressing his most decided disapprobation of, and his objections to, the passage of the resolution just offered by the gentleman from Charlotte, (Mr. Randolph). He regretted, that the gentleman had felt it his duty at this late hour to urge its consideration, because its adoption could not possibly accomplish any valuable purpose, but on the contrary might, and he verily believed, would produce excitement, heart-burnings, and dissatisfaction, with that part of the community, the non-freeholders, whom your new Constitution invests with the elective franchise—*Cui bono?*[41] will you do this. Can those who are friendly to the new Constitution, and really desire its ratification by the people, expect to accomplish their wishes by the adoption of this resolution, the necessary effect of which will be, gratuitously to insult and exasperate that portion of your fellow-citizens. Reject this resolution, and permit them to have a voice in the decision of this question, and they will be the fast friends of this new charter. Adopt it and you make them its enemies and create an excitement in the country to be deprecated by all; an excitement that will not be confined to

---

From *Proceedings*, pp. 885–888.
[41] For whose good? [Ed.].

them, but which will prevail with the freeholder, in common with the non-freeholder. For, permit me to tell gentlemen, who deem the freeholders indifferent on this subject, that they do them the most flagrant injustice. It should be recollected that this Convention was called by the freeholders, and an object not the least prominent, was that of enfranchising their disfranchised brethren.

Mr. T. said, this new Constitution was no very great favourite with him. He had voted for it, it was true, but with the most unfeigned reluctance—he had done so in the spirit of conciliation and compromise. It had been his misfortune to represent on this floor a divided people, a people entertaining conflicting views and opinions on the great and delicate questions involved in our recent deliberations—and he had felt it his duty thus circumstanced, to consult in some measure, the wishes, the hopes, and the fears of both sides—to yield somewhat to the unforeseen circumstances of the occasion, and to offer up some of his own individual convictions of political right and political justice, upon the altar of the public peace: for these reasons only, had he recorded his vote in favour of the passage of the Constitution: that he did so with *extreme reluctance*, was not because he considered the new devoid of all recommendation; far from it; (he would frankly confess, that he considered it a valuable improvement upon the old, containing many valuable features of reform;) but because representation had not been based at the present and in all future time upon free white population, the only true basis; because the election of Governor was not referred to the people; because an Executive Council was retained, the Right of Suffrage not sufficiently extended, and the County Court system in its organization and powers left unreformed. A hard necessity, however, had compelled him to give his assent to this new charter, notwithstanding these great objections; and whenever as one of the people he should be brought to choose between the new and the old, he should not hesitate to give to the new his decided preference and support. When he voted for it, he had done so in good faith: he should vote for it at the polls, and should recommend it to the adoption of his constitutents. But, said Mr. T., notwithstanding this avowal, and as anxious as he was that this day should terminate our labours in peace, harmony, and mutual good feeling, *he would say*, that should that resolution be adopted, he should esteem it his duty to move a re-consideration of the vote adopting the amended Constitution—and would, if sustained in this motion, vote against its adoption, preferring to submit no Constitution at all, to submitting any, in a manner as he believed, so violative of the natural, inherent, and original rights of man, as that proposed by the resolution under consideration. He contended, that according to the theory and principles of free government and the equal rights of man, the question of ratification or rejection should be submitted to the whole community—freeholder and non-freeholder, whether entitled or not to the Right of Suffrage under the Constitution submitted, or the existing one. This, he said, had been the invariable practice of every State in the Union, that had submitted an original or amended Constitution. It was the only way in which a government could regularly and rightfully be called into existence. It is then the act of a majority, all having been consulted—and if a majority exclude a part from Suffrage, they have the unquestionable right to do so. From their decision there is no appeal. Then, and then only is decided rightfully the question, whether it is expedient to surrender this great natural right. Then is there less cause of complaint against its abridgment. Then might the plea of expediency be urged with plausibility and effect to sustain the decree of the majority, in which resides the rightful sovereignty in all free governments. All the gentlemen who have advocated a restricted Suffrage on this floor, have founded the right to exclude upon the ground of expediency, and not that one man by nature has more right than another; but the difference between us is, that they make the minority the judges of the expediency of retaining power in their own hands. I claim for the majority the right to decide this question. The same principle that would sanction the right of less than a majority to decide this question of expediency, would justify monarchy, oligarchy, aristocracy, despotism. If the freeholders, without consulting the non-freeholders, arrogate to themselves the exclusive right to govern this land, whether they be a majority or not, why may not a part of them with equal propriety assume that right in exclusion of the rest? why may not the large landed proprietors deposing the petty freeholders, say, that they alone are the rightful sovereigns?

. . . No one ever supposed, that the acts to take *the sense of the people* and *to organize a Convention,* were acts of ordinary legislation, or properly speaking, acts of legislation at all, as little so as an election by that body of any officer. No one ever supposed, that the old Constitution either expressly or impliedly gave such a power—for it must be recollected, the old Constitution contained no provision for its own amendment, and to expect that it could, strictly speaking, be changed *according to law,* would be to suppose an absurdity. The acts spoken of, were called for by their constituents, resulted from the *necessity* of the case, and were justified by that supreme and paramount law, the *salus populi.*[42] In short, they supplied the only mode, by which the original right of the people to meet in full and free Convention to reform, alter, or abolish their form of government, could be exercised, without jeopardizing the peace, tranquillity, and harmony of the State. The gentleman has himself stated over and over again, that the people could not exercise this right *in propria persona,*[43] and independently of the existing government—and that an attempt to call a Convention, without Legislative facilities, would be flagitious. The gentleman's various arguments taken together,

---

[42] Welfare of the people [Ed.].

[43] In their own right [Ed.].

prove too much: that is—that although the right of the people to call a Convention is conceded by all, yet the practical exercise of this right is usurpation or crime, for that is the sum and substance of his arguments. In one breath with the gentleman, the Legislature is very trust-worthy—and their acts are to be deemed the acts of their constituents—but when those acts incur his dispprobation [*sic*], and are not entirely to his taste, they are acts of usurpation.

The truth is, the action of the ordinary Legislature on this subject, as before remarked, is not of the character of ordinary legislation. It is, in the nature of a resolve or ordinance, adopted by the agents of the people, not in their Legislative character, for the purpose of collecting and ascertaining the public will, both as to the call and organization of a Convention, and upon the ratification or rejection of the work of that Convention. If the substance of the thing, to wit: the ascertainment of the public will, is accomplished, it is needless to stickle about forms. For this purpose only is the aid of the old government, its officers, and instruments, invoked, to perform the office of a scaffolding on which to stand, whilst you are erecting the new. Thus has this matter been viewed in other States similarly circumstanced as ourselves; and in their Legislative action on the subject of a Convention, they have adopted the language of resolve, recommendation, and advice, instead of the technical and imperative language of enactment: I allude particularly to the example of Pennsylvania. Mr. T. concluded by saying, he should extremely regret the passage of the resolution. Let us not add another to the many causes of excitement already produced by our proceedings. Having agreed with so much difficulty upon a Constitution, let us, *at least*, submit it to those, who are declared by it, worthy of the Right of Suffrage.

TABLE 3·1

Population and Representation in Virginia by Districts, 1820–1830, and the Vote on Ratification of the Constitution of 1830

| | No. of Counties 1829 | Population in 1820 | | | Ratio of Increase, 1810–1820 | | Estimated White Population 1829 | Revenue Taxes Assessed 1828† |
		White	Slave	Total°	White	Slave		
Trans-Allegheny	26	133,112	13,366	147,540	27.5	46.	181,000	$39,099
Shenandoah Valley	14	121,096	29,785	154,162	11.8	25.5	138,000	$62,537
Piedmont	29	187,186	205,501	402,336	.8	10.8	197,000	$164,171
Tidewater	40‡	161,687	176,496	361,314	5.5	1.3	165,000	$157,756
Totals	109	603,081	425,153	1,065,352	11.4§	10.9§	681,000	$423,563

° Including Free Negroes
† Excluding licenses
‡ Counting the cities of Richmond and Williamsburg, the Borough of Norfolk, and the Town of Petersburg
§ Averages

TABLE 3.1
(*continued*)

| | Representation in the House | | | | Representation in Senate | | Vote on Ratification | |
| | In 1829 | Projected on | | | In 1829 | By Constitution | Yea | Nay |
		White Basis	Federal Numbers	Gordon Plan	By Constitution				
Trans-Allegheny	52	34	26	29	31	9	13	2,123	11,289
Shenandoah Valley	28	26	23	24	25			3,842	2,097
Piedmont	58	37	42	40	42	15	19	12,417	1,086
Tidewater	76	31	35	34	36			7,673	1,091
Totals	214	128	126	127	134	24	32	26,055	15,563

TABLE 3.2

The Sectional Division on Selected Questions in the Virginia Convention

Vote in committee of the whole on Leigh's resolution to base representation in the house on federal numbers, November 16, 1829

	Aye	Nay
East	47	13
West	0	36
	47	49

Vote in convention on Gordon's "mixed basis" plan of representation, December 18, 1829

	Aye	Nay
East	50	10
West	0	36
	50	46

Vote in convention on Wilson's motion to extend the suffrage to all taxpayers, December 17, 1829

	Aye	Nay
East	15	43
West	32	4
	47	47

Vote in convention on Bayly's motion to abolish the county courts as constituted judicial bodies, December 23, 1829

	Aye	Nay
East	8	52
West	19	16
	27	68

TABLE 3.2

(*continued*)

Vote in convention on Gordon's motion to make the governor elective of the general assembly, reversing the earlier decision for popular election, January 7, 1830

	Aye	Nay
East	49	11
West	1	35
	50	46

Vote in convention on Cooke's motion to provide for decennial reapportionment without change in the total representation from any of the four great districts or two great divisions of the state, January 8, 1830

	Aye	Nay
East	52	8
West	4	31
	56	39

Vote in convention on the passage of the engrossed constitution, January 14, 1830

	Aye	Nay
East	54	6
West	1	34
	55	40

INDEX

Adams, John, 3, 5-6, 12, 68, 75-77, 94

Agricultural interest, 136, 192-194, 201-203, 208-209, 381-383, 390-395

Amendment
Massachusetts, 15, 16, 119
New York, 141
Virginia, 284, 433-438

Appointive power (New York), 127-129, 133-135, 141, 172-187

Austin, James T., 6, 19, 29-31, 59, 66-67

Bacon, Ezekial, 131, 141
Baldwin, Thomas, 53-54
Baptists, 36, 54
Barbour, Philip P., 271, 274
Bayly, Thomas M., 283
Blake, George, 59, 60, 63
Blasphemy, 233
Buel, David, Jr., 187, 197-206, 249, 258-264
Burke, Edmund, 397-398, 407

Campbell, Alexander, 283, 421
Carpenter, Matthew, 140, 249
Childs, Henry H., 6, 10, 16, 32, 37-40
Clarke, Robert, 214-215, 219-225, 249, 254-255
Clinton, DeWitt, 127, 129
Clinton, George, 127, 168-172
Congregational church, 7-11, 34, 36, 40-41, 44-49, 49-52, 54-59
Connecticut, 129, 130, 133, 138, 155, 160, 170-171, 189, 216, 225
Constituent sovereignty, xiv, 439-443

Constitutional convention, xiii-xiv
western states, xiv
Cooke, John R., 276, 278-279, 284, 287-306, 409
Council of Appointment, 127-128, 134, 141, 172-175
Council of Revision, 126-127, 129, 132-133, 141, 144-163, 185
Cramer, John, 163, 164-166

Dearborn, Henry, 6, 11, 13, 68-69
Declaration of Independence, xiii, 157, 224
Declaration of rights
of Massachusetts, 7-8, 31-49, 54, 75-76, 110-112, 121
of Virginia, 274-275, 288-302, 332-333, 345-348, 355-356, 379-381, 388-389
Democracy, xiv-xvii
Doddridge, Philip, 273, 276, 279-280, 282, 331-337, 395, 407-408, 409
Duer, John, 135, 173
Dutton, Warren, 55-57, 59, 61-63

Edwards, Ogden, 136, 163, 168-172, 173, 249, 250-254
Emerson, Ralph Waldo, 92
Executive
Massachusetts, 14, 15, 93-94
New York, 126-129, 132-135, 141, 144-187
Virginia, 281-282, 284, 409-420, 440

Fay, Samuel P. P., 49, 53
Federalist Party, 3, 4, 6, 9, 127-130, 131-132
Foster, Edmund, 59, 60-61

449